GACE Chemistry

028
029

Teacher Certification Exam

By: Sharon Wynne, M.S
Southern Connecticut State University

"And, while there's no reason yet to panic, I think it's only prudent that we make preparations to panic."

XAMonline, INC.
Boston

To obtain permission(s) to use the material from this work for any purpose including workshops or seminars, please submit a written request to:

XAMonline, Inc.
21 Orient Ave.
Melrose, MA 02176
Toll Free 1-800-509-4128
Email: info@xamonline.com
Web www.xamonline.com
Fax: 1-781-662-9268

Library of Congress Cataloging-in-Publication Data

Wynne, Sharon A.
    Chemistry 028, 029: Teacher Certification / Sharon A. Wynne. -2nd ed.
    ISBN: 978-41-58197-540-6
    1. Chemistry 028, 029.   2. Study Guides.   3. GACE
    4. Teachers' Certification & Licensure.   5. Careers

Disclaimer:
The opinions expressed in this publication are the sole works of XAMonline and were created independently from the National Education Association, Educational Testing Service, or any State Department of Education, National Evaluation Systems or other testing affiliates.

Between the time of publication and printing, state specific standards as well as testing formats and website information may change that is not included in part or in whole within this product. Sample test questions are developed by XAMonline and reflect similar content as on real tests; however, they are not former tests. XAMonline assembles content that aligns with state standards but makes no claims nor guarantees teacher candidates a passing score. Numerical scores are determined by testing companies such as NES or ETS and then are compared with individual state standards. A passing score varies from state to state.

Printed in the United States of America   œ-1

GACE: Chemistry 028, 029
ISBN: 978-1-58197-540-6

Massachusetts Tests for Educator Licensure®

Test Date: March 4, 2006

See reverse side for an explanation of how to read your score report.

MARC SHELIKOFF has met the qualifying score on the
following test(s) as of March 4, 2006:
12 Chemistry

MARC SHELIKOFF
26 WEBSTER AVE #3
CAMBRIDGE MA 02141

Your scores have been reported to the Massachusetts
Department of Education.

---

12 Chemistry

Your Score: 94   **Minimum Qualifying Score: 70**   **Status: Met the Qualifying Score**

Number of Questions	Subarea Name	Graphic Display
1 to 10	The Nature of Chemical Inquiry	
11 to 20	Matter and Atomic Structure	
11 to 20	Energy/Chemical Bonds/Molecular Struct	
11 to 20	Chemical Reactions	
1 to 10	Quantitative Relationships	
11 to 20	Chemistry, Society, and the Environment	
2	Open-Response Items	

Table of Contents

SUBAREA III.   CHEMICAL REACTIONS

SUBAREA IV.   CHARACTERISTICS OF SCIENCE

Great Study and Testing Tips!

What to study in order to prepare for the subject assessments is the focus of this study guide but equally important is *how* you study.

You can increase your chances of truly mastering the information by taking some simple, but effective steps.

Study Tips:

1. Some foods aid the learning process. Foods such as milk, nuts, seeds, rice, and oats help your study efforts by releasing natural memory enhancers called CCKs (*cholecystokinin*) composed of *tryptopha*n, *choline*, and *phenylalanine*. All of these chemicals enhance the neurotransmitters associated with memory. Before studying, try a light, protein-rich meal of eggs, turkey, and fish. All of these foods release the memory enhancing chemicals. The better the connections, the more you comprehend.

Likewise, before you take a test, stick to a light snack of energy boosting and relaxing foods. A glass of milk, a piece of fruit, or some peanuts all release various memory-boosting chemicals and help you to relax and focus on the subject at hand.

2. Learn to take great notes. A by-product of our modern culture is that we have grown accustomed to getting our information in short doses (i.e. TV news sound bites or USA Today style newspaper articles.)

Consequently, we've subconsciously trained ourselves to assimilate information better in neat little packages. If your notes are scrawled all over the paper, it fragments the flow of the information. Strive for clarity. Newspapers use a standard format to achieve clarity. Your notes can be much clearer through use of proper formatting. A very effective format is called the *"Cornell Method."*

> Take a sheet of loose-leaf lined notebook paper and draw a line all the way down the paper about 1-2" from the left-hand edge.

> Draw another line across the width of the paper about 1-2" up from the bottom. Repeat this process on the reverse side of the page.

Look at the highly effective result. You have ample room for notes, a left hand margin for special emphasis items or inserting supplementary data from the textbook, a large area at the bottom for a brief summary, and a little rectangular space for just about anything you want.

3. Get the concept then the details. Too often we focus on the details and don't gather an understanding of the concept. However, if you simply memorize only dates, places, or names, you may well miss the whole point of the subject.

A key way to understand things is to put them in your own words. If you are working from a textbook, automatically summarize each paragraph in your mind. If you are outlining text, don't simply copy the author's words.

Rephrase them in your own words. You remember your own thoughts and words much better than someone else's, and subconsciously tend to associate the important details to the core concepts.

4. Ask Why? Pull apart written material paragraph by paragraph and don't forget the captions under the illustrations.

Example: If the heading is "Stream Erosion", flip it around to read "Why do streams erode?" Then answer the questions.

If you train your mind to think in a series of questions and answers, not only will you learn more, but it also helps to lessen the test anxiety because you are used to answering questions.

5. Read for reinforcement and future needs. Even if you only have 10 minutes, put your notes or a book in your hand. Your mind is similar to a computer; you have to input data in order to have it processed. *By reading, you are creating the neural connections for future retrieval.* The more times you read something, the more you reinforce the learning of ideas.

Even if you don't fully understand something on the first pass, *your mind stores much of the material for later recall.*

6. Relax to learn so go into exile. Our bodies respond to an inner clock called biorhythms. Burning the midnight oil works well for some people, but not everyone.

If possible, set aside a particular place to study that is free of distractions. Shut off the television, cell phone, pager and exile your friends and family during your study period.

If you really are bothered by silence, try background music. Light classical music at a low volume has been shown to aid in concentration over other types. Music that evokes pleasant emotions without lyrics is highly suggested. Try just about anything by Mozart. It relaxes you.

7. Use arrows not highlighters. At best, it's difficult to read a page full of yellow, pink, blue, and green streaks. Try staring at a neon sign for a while and you'll soon see that the horde of colors obscure the message.

A quick note, a brief dash of color, an underline, and an arrow pointing to a particular passage is much clearer than a horde of highlighted words.

8. Budget your study time. Although you shouldn't ignore any of the material, *allocate your available study time in the same ratio that topics may appear on the test.*

Testing Tips:

1. <u>Get smart, play dumb</u>. Don't read anything into the question. Don't make an assumption that the test writer is looking for something else than what is asked. Stick to the question as written and don't read extra things into it.

2. <u>Read the question and all the choices *twice* before answering the question</u>. You may miss something by not carefully reading, and then re-reading both the question and the answers.

If you really don't have a clue as to the right answer, leave it blank on the first time through. Go on to the other questions, as they may provide a clue as to how to answer the skipped questions.

If later on, you still can't answer the skipped ones . . . *Guess.* The only penalty for guessing is that you *might* get it wrong. Only one thing is certain; if you don't put anything down, you will get it wrong!

3. <u>Turn the question into a statement</u>. Look at the way the questions are worded. The syntax of the question usually provides a clue. Does it seem more familiar as a statement rather than as a question? Does it sound strange?

By turning a question into a statement, you may be able to spot if an answer sounds right, and it may also trigger memories of material you have read.

4. <u>Look for hidden clues</u>. It's actually very difficult to compose multiple-foil (choice) questions without giving away part of the answer in the options presented.

In most multiple-choice questions you can often readily eliminate one or two of the potential answers. This leaves you with only two real possibilities and automatically your odds go to Fifty-Fifty for very little work.

5. <u>Trust your instincts</u>. For every fact that you have read, you subconsciously retain something of that knowledge. On questions that you aren't really certain about, go with your basic instincts. **Your first impression on how to answer a question is usually correct.**

6. <u>Mark your answers directly on the test booklet</u>. Don't bother trying to fill in the optical scan sheet on the first pass through the test.

7. <u>Watch the clock</u>! You have a set amount of time to answer the questions. Don't get bogged down trying to answer a single question at the expense of 10 questions you can more readily answer.

SUBAREA I.   ATOMIC STRUCTURE AND THE PROPERTIES OF MATTER

COMPETENCY 1.0 UNDERSTAND THE VARIOUS MODELS OF ATOMIC
                STRUCTURE, THE PRINCIPLES OF QUANTUM
                THEORY, AND THE PROPERTIES AND INTERACTIONS
                OF SUBATOMIC PARTICLES.

Skill 1.1   Identifying major features of models of atomic structure (e.g.,
             Bohr, Rutherford, Heisenberg, Schrödinger) and the
             supporting evidence for these models (e.g., gold foil
             experiment, emission spectra)

Our current understanding of atomic structure and the nuclear atom took over
two thousand of years and the work of many individuals, often thinking outside of
the box.

The concept of the atom can be traced back to the ancient Greek philosophers
but may have actually originated with the founder of Buddhism, Gutama who
said, "Death is actually the disaggreation of atoms" on his deathbed.

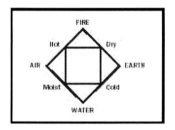

Atoms created quite a controversy
in the Greek forum. Two opinions
existed; those who believed that
matter was continuous followed
Aristotle and Plato and those who
believed that matter was not
continuous followed Leucippetius.

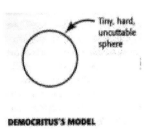

DEMOCRITUS'S MODEL

Leucippitus believed that a fragment of matter existed
that could not be divided and still retain properties of that matter. A student of
Leucippetius, Democritus, named the smallest piece of matter atomos, Greek for
indivisible.

> "sweet or sour, hot or cold by convention, existing are only atoms and
> void"

Aristotle and Plato had reputations of being very wise and knowledgeable men
and so most people believed them. Aristotle did not like the randomness of
Democritus' ideas. He preferred a more ordered matter. Therefore, the idea of
atoms and those who believed in their existence had to go underground.

Epicuious created a school and society for those who believed in atoms. Titus Leucritius wrote *de Rurum Natura* in 55 B.C. This poem described the nature of atoms. In the poem there is reference to some phrases of Parmenidis which bear a striking resemblance to what is now known as the law of mass conservation.

> "*the content of the universe was never before more or less condensed than it is today*"

Dalton

The existence of fundamental units of matter called atoms of different types called elements was proposed by ancient philosophers without any evidence to support the belief. Modern atomic theory is credited to the work of **John Dalton** published in 1803-1807. Observations made by him and others about the composition, properties, and reactions of many compounds led him to develop the following postulates:

1) Each element is composed of small particles called atoms.
2) All atoms of a given element are identical in mass and other properties.
3) Atoms of different elements have different masses and differ in other properties.
4) Atoms of an element are not created, destroyed, or changed into a different type of atom by chemical reactions.
5) Compounds form when atoms of more than one element combine.
6) In a given compound, the relative number and kind of atoms are constant.

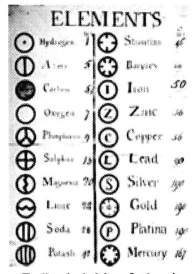

Dalton's table of atomic symbols and masses

Dalton determined and published the known relative masses of a number of different atoms. He also formulated the law of partial pressures. Dalton's work focused on the ability of atoms to arrange themselves into molecules and to rearrange themselves via chemical reactions, but he did not investigate the composition of atoms themselves. **Dalton's model of the atom** was a tiny, indivisible, indestructible **particle** of a certain mass, size, and chemical behavior, but Dalton did not deny the possibility that atoms might have a substructure.

Prior to the late 1800s, atoms, following Dalton's ideas, were thought to be small, spherical and indivisible particles that made up matter. However, with the discovery of electricity and the investigations that followed, this view of the atom changed.

Thomson

Joseph John Thomson, often known as **J. J. Thomson**, was the first to examine this substructure. In the mid-1800s, scientists had studied a form of radiation called "cathode rays" or "electrons" that originated from the negative electrode (cathode) when electrical current was forced through an evacuated tube. Thomson determined in 1897 that **electrons have mass**, and because many different cathode materials release electrons, Thomson proposed that the **electron is a subatomic particle. Thomson's model of the atom** was a uniformly positive particle with electrons contained in the interior. This has been called the "plum-pudding" model of the atom where the pudding represents the uniform sphere of positive electricity and the bits of plum represent electrons. For more on Thomson, see http://www.aip.org/history/electron/jjhome.htm.

Planck

Max Planck determined in 1900 that **energy is transferred by radiation in exact multiples of a discrete unit of energy called a quantum**. Quanta of energy are extremely small, and may be found from the frequency of the radiation, v, using the equation:

$$\Delta E = hv$$

where h is Planck's constant and hv is a quantum of energy.

Rutherford

Ernest Rutherford studied atomic structure in 1910-1911 by firing a beam of alpha particles at thin layers of gold leaf. According to Thomson's model, the path of an alpha particle should be deflected only slightly if it struck an atom, but Rutherford observed some alpha particles bouncing almost backwards, suggesting that **nearly all the mass of an atom is contained in a small positively charged nucleus. Rutherford's model of the atom** was an analogy to the sun and the planets. A small positively charged nucleus is surrounded by circling electrons and mostly by empty space. Rutherford's experiment is explained in greater detail in this flash animation: http://www.mhhe.com/physsci/chemistry/essentialchemistry/flash/ruther14.swf.

Bohr

Niels Bohr incorporated Planck's quantum concept into Rutherford's model of the atom in 1913 to explain the **discrete frequencies of radiation emitted and absorbed by atoms with one electron** (H, He^+, and Li^{2+}). This electron is attracted to the positive nucleus and is closest to the nucleus at the **ground state** of the atom. When the electron absorbs energy, it moves into an orbit further from the nucleus and the atom is said to be in an electronically **excited state**. If sufficient energy is absorbed, the electron separates from the nucleus entirely, and the atom is ionized:

$$H \rightarrow H^+ + e^-$$

The energy required for ionization from the ground state is called the atom's **ionization energy**. The discrete frequencies of radiation emitted and absorbed by the atom correspond (using Planck's constant) to discrete energies and in turn to discrete distances from the nucleus. **Bohr's model of the atom** was a small positively charged nucleus surrounded mostly by empty space and by electrons orbiting at certain discrete distances ("shells") corresponding to discrete energy levels. Animations utilizing the Bohr model may be found at the following two URLs: http://artsci–ccwin.concordia.ca/facstaff/a–c/bird/c241/D1.html and http://www.mhhe.com/physsci/chemistry/essentialchemistry/flash/linesp16.swf.

Bohr's model of the atom didn't quite fit experimental observations for atoms other than hydrogen. He was, however, on the right track. DeBroglie was the first to suggest that possibly matter behaved like a wave. Until then, waves were understood as having properties such as wavelength, frequency and amplitude while matter had properties such as mass and volume. DeBroglie's suggestion was quite unique and interesting to scientists.

De Broglie
Depending on the experiment, radiation appears to have wave-like or particle-like traits. In 1923-1924, Louis de Broglie applied this **wave/particle duality to all matter with momentum**. The discrete distances from the nucleus described by Bohr corresponded to permissible distances where standing waves could exist. **De Broglie's model of the atom** described electrons as **matter waves in standing wave orbits** around the nucleus. The first three standing waves corresponding to the first three discrete distances are shown in the figure. De Broglie's model may be found here: http://artsci-ccwin.concordia.ca/facstaff/a-c/bird/c241/D1-part2.html.

Heisenberg
The realization that both matter and radiation interact as waves led Werner Heisenberg to the conclusion in 1927 that the act of observation and measurement requires the interaction of one wave with another, resulting in an **inherent uncertainty** in the location and momentum of particles. This inability to measure phenomena at the subatomic level is known as the **Heisenberg uncertainty principle**, and it applies to the location and momentum of electrons in an atom. A discussion of the principle and Heisenberg's other contributions to quantum theory is located here: http://www.aip.org/history/heisenberg/.

Schrödinger

When Erwin Schrödinger studied the atom in 1925, he replaced the idea of precise orbits with regions in space called **orbitals** where electrons were likely to be found. **The Schrödinger equation** describes the **probability** that an electron will be in a given region of space, a quantity known as **electron density** or Ψ^2. The diagrams below are surfaces of constant Ψ^2 found by solving the Schrödinger equation for the hydrogen atom $1s$, $2p_z$ and $3d_0$ orbitals. Additional representations of solutions may be found here: http://library.wolfram.com/webMathematica/Physics/Hydrogen.jsp.

Schrödinger's model of the atom is a mathematical formulation of quantum mechanics that describes the electron density of orbitals. It is the atomic model that has been in use from shortly after it was introduced up to the present.

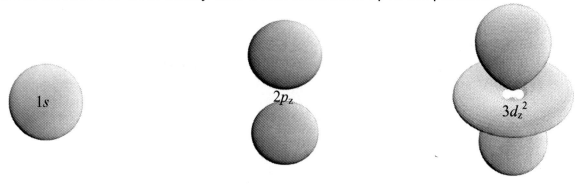

This model explains the movement of electrons to higher energy levels when exposed to energy. It also explains the movement of electrons to lower energy levels when the source of energy has disappeared. Accompanying this drop in energy level is the emission of electromagnetic radiation (light as one possibility).

Using Plank's equation, the frequency of that electromagnetic radiation, EMR, can be determined, radiation caused by the movement of matter.

The union of deBroglie's, Planck, Heisenberg, Schrodinger and Bohr's ideas lead to the development of the wave-mechanical view of the atom. The solution to Schrodinger's equation provides for 3 quantum numbers. This added to Pauli's idea that no two electrons could have the same solution set for Schrodinger's equation (known as Pauli exclusion principle) provides four quantum numbers that describe the most probable orbital for an electron of a given energy or the quantum mechanical model of the atom.

Skill 1.2   Identifying the characteristics of protons, neutrons, and electrons and the contribution each makes to atomic number, mass number, and the formation of ions

Atomic theory basically states that atoms are the smallest unit of matter that retains the properties of a substance.   While they were considered for some time to be the smallest, indivisible type of matter, they are in fact composed of subatomic particles, including protons, neutrons, and electrons. The nucleus of the atom is very small in relationship to the atom and much of the atom is actually empty space. Within the nucleus are positively charge protons and uncharged neutrons. Thus, the nucleus has a net positive charge. Electrons circle the nucleus and carry a negative charge.

Atoms differ depending upon the element. The simplest atom is hydrogen, which has one proton and one electron that are attracted to each other due to an electrical charge. The spinning force of the electron keeps the electron from crashing into the proton and keeps the electron always moving.

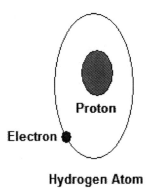

Hydrogen Atom

This is the hydrogen atom, abbreviated H. It has a single neutron and single rotating electron.

The **nucleus** is the center of the atom. The positive particles inside the nucleus are called **protons.** The mass of a proton is about 2,000 times that of an electron. The number of protons in the nucleus of an atom is called the **atomic number**. All atoms of the same element have the same atomic number.

Neutrons are another type of particle in the nucleus. Neutrons and protons have about the same mass, but neutrons have no charge. Neutrons were discovered because scientists observed that not all atoms in neon gas have the same mass. They had identified isotopes. **Isotopes** of an element have the same number of protons, but have different masses. Neutrons explain the difference in mass. They have mass but no charge.

The mass of matter is measured against a standard mass such as the gram. Scientists measure the mass of an atom by comparing it to that of a standard atom. The result is relative mass. The **relative mass** of an atom is its mass expressed in terms of the mass of the standard atom. The isotope of the element carbon is the standard atom. It has six (6) neutrons and is called carbon-12. It is assigned a mass of 12 atomic mass units (amu). Therefore, the **atomic mass unit (amu)** is the standard unit for measuring the mass of an atom.

The **mass number** of an atom is the sum of its protons and neutrons. For any element, there are various isotopes, distinguished by their varying number of neutrons. The **atomic mass** of an element is a weighted (by natural abundance- see Skill 1.3) average of the mass numbers of its isotopes.

The following table summarizes the terms used to describe atomic nuclei:

Term	Example	Meaning	Characteristic
Atomic Number	# protons (p)	same for all atoms of a given element	Carbon (C) atomic number = 6 (6p)
Mass number	# protons + # neutrons (p + n)	changes for different isotopes of an element	C-12 (6p + 6n) C-13 (6p + 7n)
Atomic mass	average mass of the isotopes (weighted by abundance)	usually not a whole number	atomic mass of carbon equals 12.011

Skill 1.3 Analyzing the relationship between atomic mass and the relative abundance of different isotopes of a particular element

The atomic mass of an element is the mass of an atom of the element at rest. Relative atomic mass, also called atomic weight and average atomic mass, is the average of the atomic masses of all isotopes of a given element, adjusted for isotopic abundance. Thus, the atomic weight given for each element on the periodic table is not a round number because it is an average value that takes the relative abundance of isotopes into consideration.

Isotopes of an element vary in the number of neutrons in the nucleus. For example, nitrogen exists in two isotopes, N-14 and N-15. In other words, some nitrogen atoms have a mass of 14 while others have a mass of 15. The atomic weight of nitrogen is 14.007 (as listed in the periodic table). Thus, we can determine the approximate relative abundance of the two nitrogen isotopes as follows.

$$14 (x) + 15 (1 - x) = 14.007$$
$$14x + 15 - 15x = 14.007$$
$$15 - x = 14.007$$
$$x = 15 - 14.007$$
$$x = 0.993$$

The relative abundance of the N-14 isotope is x, 99.3%. The relative abundance of the N-15 isotope is $1 - x$, 0.7%.

Skill 1.4 Analyzing an atom's electron configuration

Quantum numbers
The quantum-mechanical solutions from the Schrödinger Equation utilize three quantum numbers (n, l, and m_l) to describe an orbital and a fourth (m_s) to describe an electron in an orbital. This model is useful for understanding the frequencies of radiation emitted and absorbed by atoms and chemical properties of atoms.

The **principal quantum number n** may have positive integer values (1, 2, 3, ...). n is a measure of the **distance** of an orbital from the nucleus, and orbitals with the same value of n are said to be in the same **shell**. This is analogous to the Bohr model of the atom.

The **azimuthal quantum number** may have integer values from 0 to n-1. It describes the angular momentum of an orbital. This determines the orbital's **shape**. Orbitals with the same value of n and l are in the same **subshell**. Subshells are usually referred to by the principle quantum number followed by a letter corresponding to l as shown in the following table:

Azimuthal quantum number l	0	1	2	3	4
Subshell designation	s	p	d	f	g

The **magnetic quantum number** m_l **or** m may have integer values from $-l$ to l. m_l is a measure of how an individual orbital responds to an external magnetic field, and it often describes an orbital's **orientation**. A subscript—either the value of m_l or a function of the x-, y-, and z-axes—is used to designate a specific orbital. Each orbital may hold up to two electrons.

The **spin quantum number** m_s **or** s has one of two possible values: $-1/2$ or $+1/2$. m_s differentiates between the two possible electrons occupying an orbital. Electrons moving through a magnet behave as if they were tiny magnets themselves spinning on their axis in either a clockwise or counterclockwise direction. These two spins may be described as $m_s = -1/2$ and $+1/2$ or as down and up.

The **Pauli exclusion principle** states that **no two electrons in an atom may have the same set of four quantum numbers** and provides this forth quantum number, m_s.

The following table summarizes the relationship among n, l, and m_l through $n=3$:

n	l	Subshell	m_l	Orbitals in subshell	Maximum number of electrons in subshell
1	0	1s	0	1	2
2	0	2s	0	1	2
	1	2p	−1, 0, 1	3	6
3	0	3s	0	1	2
	1	3p	−1, 0, 1	3	6
	2	3d	−2, −1, 0, 1, 2	5	10

Subshell energy levels
In single-electron atoms (H, He^+, and Li^{2+}) above the ground state, subshells within a shell are all at the same energy level, and an orbital's energy level is only determined by n. However, in all other atoms, multiple electrons repel each other. Electrons in orbitals closer to the nucleus create a screening or **shielding effect** on electrons further away from the nucleus, preventing them from receiving the full attractive force of the nucleus. **In multi-electron atoms, both** n **and** l **determine the energy level of an orbital.** In the absence of a magnetic field, **orbitals in the same subshell with different** m_l **all have the same energy** and are said to be **degenerate orbitals**.

The following list orders subshells by increasing energy level:
$1s < 2s < 2p < 3s < 3p < 4s < 3d < 4p < 5s < 4d < 5p < 6s < 4f < 5d < 6p < 7s < 5f < \ldots$

This list may be constructed by arranging the subshells according to *n* and *l* and drawing diagonal arrows as shown below:

1s

2s 2p

3s 3p 3d

4s 4p 4d 4f

5s 5p 5d 5f 5g

6s 6p 6d 6f 6g

7s 7p 7d 7f 7g

8s 8p 8d 8f 8g

Skill 1.5 **Demonstrating knowledge of how atomic spectra relate to the quantum properties of atoms, including how spectra are used for identifying elements and determining their electron configuration**

Atomic spectra are the patterns of light emitted by a particular element resulting from the energy released when excited electrons fall to lower energy levels. When we heat a sample of gas made up of atoms of a single element, the electrons become excited and jump to higher energy levels within their atoms. Over time, these electrons fall back to their original energy levels, releasing photons of light in the process. When the emitted light passes through a spectrum, it separates into distinct wavelengths. We can identify and record the wavelengths in the visible spectrum by noting their different colors. Thus, each element has a characteristic banding pattern consisting of a different number of emissions and different color emissions.

The arrangement of electrons in distinct orbitals or energy levels within an atom allows for the identification of elements by atomic spectra. Because each element has a different number and pattern of electrons, each element has a different atomic spectrum.

**COMPETENCY 2.0   UNDERSTAND THE ORGANIZATION OF THE
                    PERIODIC TABLE.**

**Skill 2.1   Analyzing the organization of the Periodic Table in terms of
               atomic numbers and properties of the elements**

The **periodic table of elements** is an arrangement of the elements in rows and
columns so that it is easy to locate elements with similar properties. The
elements of the modern periodic table are arranged in numerical order by atomic
number.

The **periods** are the rows down the left side of the table. They are called first
period, second period, etc. The columns of the periodic table are called **groups**,
or **families.** Elements in a family have similar properties.

There are three types of elements that are grouped by color: metals, nonmetals,
and metalloids.

Element Key
Atomic
Number

↓

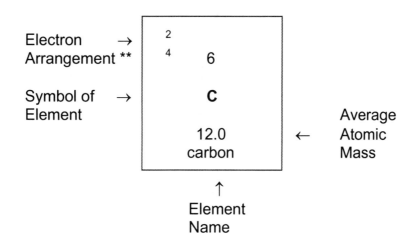

** Number of electrons on each level. Top number represents the innermost
level.

The first periodic table was developed in 1869 by Dmitri Mendeleev several decades before the nature of electron energy states in the atom was known. Mendeleev arranged the elements in order of increasing atomic mass into **columns of similar physical and chemical properties.** He then boldly **predicted the existence and the properties of undiscovered elements** to fill the gaps in his table. These interpolations were initially treated with skepticism until three of Mendeleev's theoretical elements were discovered and were found to have the properties he predicted. It is the correlation with properties—not with electron arrangements—that have placed the periodic table at the beginning of most chemistry texts.

Skill 2.2 Predicting periodic trends within periods and groups of the Periodic Table

The elements in a column are known as a group, and groups are numbered from 1 to 18. Older numbering styles used roman numerals and letters. **A row of the periodic table is known as a period**, and periods of the known elements are numbered from 1 to 7. For instance, the lanthanoids are all in period 6, and the actinoids are all in period 7.

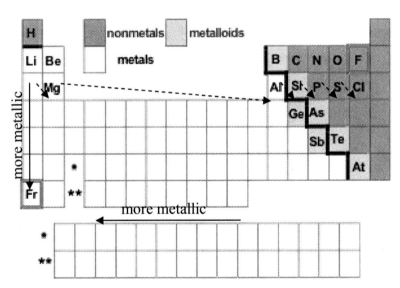

Metals, nonmetals, and atomic radius

Elements in the periodic table are divided into the two broad categories of **metals** and **nonmetals** with a jagged line separating the two as shown in the figure.

Seven elements near the line dividing metals from nonmetals exhibit some properties of each and are called **metalloids** or **semimetals**. These elements are boron, silicon, germanium, arsenic, antimony, tellurium and astatine.

The most metallic element is francium at the bottom left of the table. The most nonmetallic element is fluorine. The metallic character of elements within a group increases with period number. This means that **within a column, the more metallic elements are at the bottom**. The metallic character of elements within a period decreases with group number. This means that **within a row, the more metallic elements are on the left**. Among the main group atoms, **elements diagonal to each other** as indicated by the dashed arrows **have similar properties** because they have a similar metallic character. The noble gases are nonmetals, but they are an exception to the diagonal rule.

Physical properties relating to metallic character are summarized in the following table:

Element	Electrical/thermal conductivity	Malleable/ductile as solids?	Lustrous?	Melting point of oxides, hydrides, and halides
Metals	High	Yes	Yes	High
Metalloids	Intermediate. Altered by dopants (semiconductors)	No (brittle)	Varies	Varies (oxides). Low (hydrides, halides)
Nonmetals	Low (insulators)	No	No	Low

Malleable materials can **be beaten into sheets**. **Ductile** materials can **be pulled into wires**. **Lustrous** materials **have a shine**. Oxides, hydrides, and halides are compounds with O, H, and halogens respectively. Measures of intermolecular attractions other than melting point are also higher for metal oxides, hydrides, and halides than for the nonmetal compounds. A dopant is a small quantity of an intentionally added impurity. The controlled movement of electrons in doped silicon semiconductors carries digital information in computer circuitry.

The **size of an atom** is not an exact distance due to of the probabilistic nature of electron density, but we may compare radii among different atoms using some standard. As seen to the right, the sizes of neutral atoms increase with period number and decrease with group number. This trend is similar to the trend described above for metallic character. The smallest atom is helium.

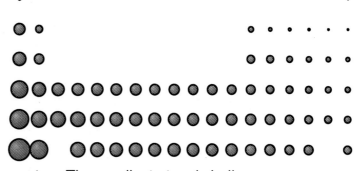

Group names, melting point, density, and properties of compounds

Groups 1, 2, 17, 18 are often identified with a **group name**. These names are shown in the table the right. Several elements are found as **diatomic molecules: (H_2, O_2, and the halogens: F_2, Br_2, and I_2).** Mnemonic devices to remember the diatomic elements

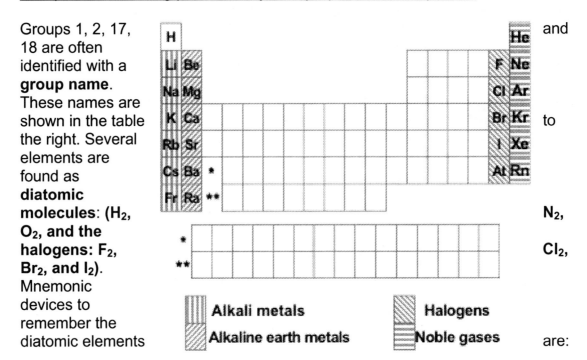

and

to

N_2,

Cl_2,

are:

"$Br_2I_2N_2Cl_2H_2O_2F_2$" (pronounced "Brinklehof") and "**H**ave **N**o **F**ear **O**f **I**ce **C**old **B**eer." These molecules are attracted to one another using **weak London dispersion forces**.

Note that **hydrogen** is <u>not</u> an alkali metal. Hydrogen is a colorless gas and is the most abundant element in the universe, but H_2 is very rare in the atmosphere because it is light enough to escape gravity and reach outer space. Hydrogen atoms form more compounds than any other element.

Alkali metals are shiny, soft, metallic solids. They have **low melting points and low densities** compared with other metals (see squares in figures on the following page) because they have a weaker metallic bond. Measures of intermolecular attractions including their **melting points decrease further down the periodic table due to weaker metallic bonds** as the size of atoms increases.

Alkaline earth metals (group 2 elements) are grey, metallic solids. They are harder, denser, and have a higher melting point than the alkali metals (see asterisks in figures on the following page), but values for these properties are still low compared to most of the transition metals. Measures of metallic bond strength like melting points for alkaline earths do not follow a simple trend down the periodic table.

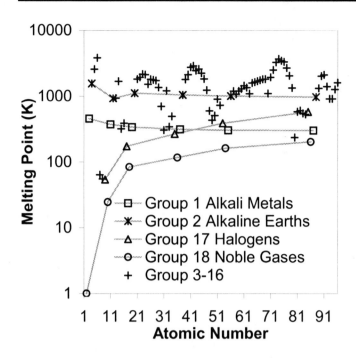

Halogens (group 17 elements) have an irritating odor. Unlike the metallic bonds between alkali metals, **London forces between halogen molecules increase in strength further down the periodic table**. Their melting points increase as shown by the triangles to the left. London forces make Br_2 a liquid and I_2 a solid at 25 °C. The lighter halogens are gases.

Noble gases (group 18 elements) have no color or odor and exist as **individual gas atoms** that experience London forces. These attractions also increase with period number as shown by the circles to the left

The known **densities** of liquid and solid elements at room temperature are shown to the right. **Intermolecular forces contribute to density** by bringing nuclei closer to each other, so the periodicity is similar to trends for melting point. These group-to-group differences are superimposed on a general trend for **density** to **increase with period number** because heavier nuclei make the material denser.

Trends among properties of **compounds** may often be deduced from **trends among their atoms**, but caution must be used. For example, the densities of three potassium halides are:

2.0 g/cm^3 for KCl
2.7 g/cm^3 for KBr
3.1 g/cm^3 for KI.

We would expect this trend for increasing atomic mass within a group. We might also expect the density of KF to be less than 2.0 g/cm^3, but it is actually 2.5 g/cm^3 due to a change in crystal lattice structure.

Skill 2.3   Inferring physical and chemical properties of the elements based on their position in the Periodic Table

The periodic table arranges metals into families with similar properties. The periodic table has its columns marked IA - VIIIA. These are the traditional group numbers. Arabic numbers 1 - 18 are also used, as suggested by the Union of Physicists and Chemists. The Arabic numerals will be used in this text.

Metals:

With the exception of hydrogen, all elements in Group 1 are **alkali metals**. These metals are shiny, softer, and less dense, and the most chemically active.

Group 2 metals are the **alkaline earth metals.** They are harder, denser, have higher melting points, and are chemically active.

The **transition elements** can be found by finding the periods (rows) from 4 to 7 under the groups (columns) 3 - 12. They are metals that do not show a range of properties as you move across the chart. They are hard and have high melting points. Compounds of these elements are colorful, such as silver, gold, and mercury.

Elements can be combined to make metallic objects. An **alloy** is a mixture of two or more elements having properties of metals. The elements do not have to be all metals. For instance, steel is made up of the metal iron and the non-metal carbon.

Nonmetals:

Nonmetals are not as easy to recognize as metals because they do not always share physical properties. However, in general the properties of nonmetals are the opposite of metals. They are not shiny, are brittle, and are not good conductors of heat and electricity.

Nonmetals are solids, gases, and one liquid (bromine).

Nonmetals have four to eight electrons in their outermost energy levels and tend to attract electrons to their outer energy levels. As a result, the outer levels usually are filled with eight electrons. This difference in the number of electrons is what caused the differences between metals and nonmetals. The outstanding chemical property of nonmetals is that react with metals.

The **halogens** can be found in Group 17. Halogens combine readily with metals to form salts. Table salt, fluoride toothpaste, and bleach all have an element from the halogen family.

The **Noble Gases** got their name from the fact that they did not react chemically with other elements, much like the nobility did not mix with the masses. These gases (found in Group 18) will only combine with other elements under very specific conditions. They are **inert** (inactive).

In recent years, scientists have found this to be only generally true, since chemists have been able to prepare compounds of krypton and xenon.

Metalloids:

Metalloids have properties in between metals and nonmetals. They can be found in Groups 13 - 16, but do not occupy the entire group. They are arranged in stair steps across the groups.

Physical Properties:
1. All are solids having the appearance of metals.
2. All are white or gray, but not shiny.
3. They will conduct electricity, but not as well as a metal.

Chemical Properties:
1. Have some characteristics of metals and nonmetals.
2. Properties do not follow patterns like metals and nonmetals. Each must be studied individually.

Boron is the first element in Group 13. It is a poor conductor of electricity at low temperatures. However, increase its temperature and it becomes a good conductor. By comparison, metals, which are good conductors, lose their ability as they are heated. It is because of this property that boron is so useful. Boron is a semiconductor. **Semiconductors** are used in electrical devices that have to function at temperatures too high for metals.

Silicon is the second element in Group 14. It is also a semiconductor and is found in great abundance in the earth's crust. Sand is made of a silicon compound, silicon dioxide. Silicon is also used in the manufacture of glass and cement.

Skill 2.4   Demonstrating knowledge of how the chemical properties of elements are related to their electron configurations

Physics of electrons and stability of electron configurations

For an isolated atom, the **most stable arrangement of valence electrons is a filled set of orbitals**. For the main group elements, this corresponds to group 18 (ns^2np^6 and $1s^2$ for helium), and, to a lesser extent, group 2 (ns^2). The next most stable state is a set of degenerate half-filled orbitals. These occur in group 15 (ns^2np^3). The least stable valence electron configuration is a single electron with no other electrons in similar orbitals. This occurs in group 1 (ns^1) and to a lesser extent in group 13 (ns^2np^1).

An atom's first **ionization energy** is the energy required to remove one electron by the reaction $M(g) \rightarrow M^+(g) + e^-$. Periodicity is in the opposite direction from the trend for atomic radius. The most metallic atoms have electrons further from the nucleus, and these are easier to remove.

An atom's **electron affinity** is the energy released when one electron is added by the reaction $M(g) + e^- \rightarrow M^-(g)$. A large negative number for the exothermic reaction indicates a high electron affinity. Halogens have the highest electron affinities.

Trends in **ionization energy and electron affinity** within a period reflect the **stability of valence electron configurations**. A stable system requires more energy to change and releases less when changed. Note the peaks in stability for groups 2, 13, and 16 to the right.

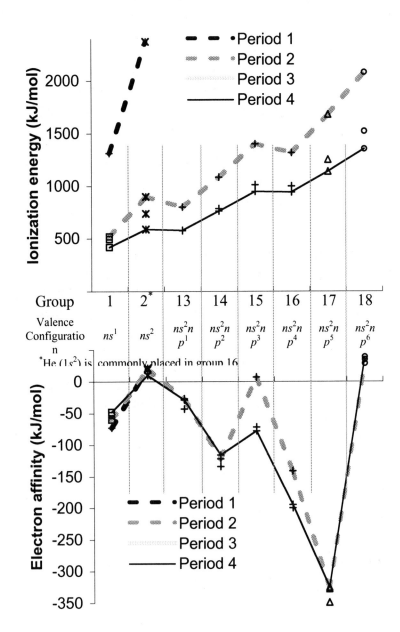

Much of chemistry consists of atoms **bonding** to achieve stable valence electron configurations. **Nonmetals gain electrons or share electrons** to achieve these configurations and **metals lose electrons** to achieve them.

Qualitative group trends

When cut by a knife, the exposed surface of an **alkali metal or alkaline earth metal** quickly turns into an oxide. These elements **do not occur in nature as free metals**. Instead, they react with many other elements to form white or grey water-soluble salts. With some exceptions, the oxides of group 1 elements have the formula M_2O, their hydrides are MH, and their halides are MX (for example, NaCl). The oxides of group 2 elements have the formula MO, their hydrides are MH_2, and their halides are MX_2, for example, $CaCl_2$.

Halogens form a wide variety of oxides and also combine with other halogens. They combine with hydrogen to form HX gases, and these compounds are also commonly used as acids (hydrofluoric, hydrochloric, etc.) in aqueous solution. Halogens form salts with metals by gaining electrons to become X^- ions. Astatine is an exception to many of these properties because it is an artificial metalloid.

Noble gases are **nearly chemically inert**. The heavier noble gases form a number of compounds with oxygen and fluorine such as KrF_2 and XeO_4

Electronegativity and reactivity series

Electronegativity measures the ability of an atom to attract electrons in a chemical bond. The most metallic elements have the lowest electronegativity. The most nonmetallic have the highest electronegativity.

In a reaction with a metal, the most reactive chemicals are the **most electronegative elements** or compounds containing those elements. In a reaction with a nonmetal, the most reactive chemicals are the **least electronegative elements** or compounds containing them. The reactivity of elements may be described by a **reactivity series**: an ordered list with chemicals that react strongly at one end and nonreactive chemicals at the other. The following reactivity series is for metals reacting with oxygen:

Metal	K	Na	Ca	Mg	Al	Zn	Fe	Pb	Cu	Hg	Ag	Au
Reaction with O_2	Burns violently		Burns rapidly					Oxidizes slowly			No reaction	

Copper, silver, and gold (group 11) are known as the **noble metals** or **coinage metals** because they rarely react.

Valence and oxidation numbers

The term **valence** is often used to describe the number of atoms that may react to form a compound with a given atom by sharing, removing, or losing **valence electrons**. A more useful term is **oxidation number**. The **oxidation number of an ion is its charge**. The oxidation number of an atom sharing its electrons is **the charge it would have if the bonding were ionic**. There are four rules for determining oxidation number:

1) The oxidation number of an element (i.e., a Cl atom in Cl_2) is zero because the electrons in the bond are shared equally.
2) In a compound, the more electronegative atoms are assigned negative oxidation numbers and the less electronegative atoms are assigned positive oxidation numbers equal to the number of shared electron-pair bonds. For example, hydrogen may only have an oxidation number of –1 when bonded to a less electronegative element or +1 when bonded to a more electronegative element. Oxygen almost always has an oxidation number of –2. Fluorine always has an oxidation number of –1 (except in F_2).
3) The oxidation numbers in a compound must add up to zero, and the sum of oxidation numbers in a polyatomic ion must equal the overall charge of the ion.
4) The charge on a polyatomic ion is equal to the sum of the oxidation numbers for the species present in the ion. For example, the sulfate ion, SO_4^{2-}, has a total charge of -2. This comes from adding the -2 oxidation number for 4 oxygen (total -8) and the +6 oxidation number for sulfur.

Example: What is the oxidation number of nitrogen in the nitrate ion, NO_3^-?
Oxygen has the oxidation number of –2 (rule 2), and the sum of the oxidation numbers must be –1 (rule 3). The oxidation number for N may be found by solving for x in the equation $x + 3 \times (-2) = -1$. The oxidation number of N in NO_3^- is +5.

There is a **periodicity in oxidation numbers** as shown in the table below for examples of oxides with the maximum oxidation number. Remember that an element may occur in different compounds in several different oxidation states.

Group	1	2	13	14	15	16	17	18
Oxide with maximum oxidation number	Li_2O	BeO	B_2O_3	CO_2	N_2O_5		Cl_2O_7	XeO_4
	Na_2O	MgO	Al_2O_3	SiO_2	P_2O_5	SO_3	Br_2O_7	
Oxidation number	+1	+2	+3	+4	+5	+6	+7	+8

They are called "oxidation numbers" because oxygen was the element of choice for reacting with materials when modern chemistry began, and the result was Mendeleev arranging his first table to look similar to this one.

Acidity/alkalinity of oxides

Metal oxides form basic solutions in water because the ionic bonds break apart and the O^{2-} ion reacts to form hydroxide ions:

metal oxide $\rightarrow$ metal cation(aq) $+O^{2-}(aq)$ and $O^{2-}(aq)+H_2O(l) \rightarrow 2\,OH^-(aq)$

Ionic oxides containing a large cation with a low charge (Rb_2O, for example) are most soluble and form the strongest bases.

Covalent oxides form acidic solutions in water by reacting with water. For example:

$$SO_3(l)+H_2O(l) \rightarrow H_2SO_4(aq) \rightarrow H^+(aq)+HSO_4^-(aq)$$

$$Cl_2O_7(l)+H_2O(l) \rightarrow 2HClO_4(aq) \rightarrow 2H^+(aq)+2ClO_4^-(aq)$$

Covalent oxides at high oxidation states and high electronegativities form the strongest acids. For this skill, note that the periodic trends for acid and base strength of the oxide of an element follows the same pattern we've seen before.

A summary of periodic trends is shown to the right. The properties tend to decrease or increase as shown depending on a given element's proximity to fluorine in the table.

http://jcrystal.com/ steffenweber/JAVA /jpt/jpt.html contains an applet of the periodic table and trends.

http://www.webele ments.com is an on-line reference for information on the elements.

Metallic character ⇓   Ionization energy ⇑
Ionic character of halides ⇓   Covalent character of halides ⇑
Atomic radius   ⇓   Electroneativity   ⇑
Alkalinity of oxides   ⇓   Acidity of oxides   ⇑

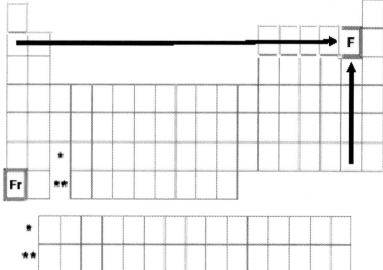

http://www.uky.edu/Projects/Chemcomics/ has comic book pages for each element.

An **electron configuration** is a **list of subshells** with superscripts representing the **number of electrons** in each subshell.

Electrons are found outside the nucleus in a fuzzy area called the electron cloud. We don't know exactly where the electron is but we do know the most probable place to find an electron with a certain energy. This is an orbital or an energy level.

When an electron is in its unexcited or ground state, there are seven energy levels. These seven energy levels match the seven periods (rows)of the Periodic Table. The valence, or outermost, electrons are found in the energy level that corresponds to the period number.

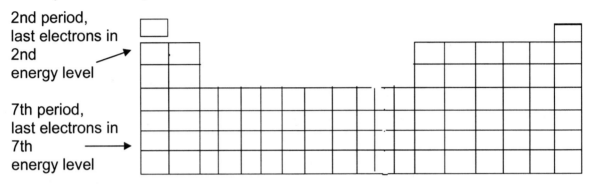

2nd period, last electrons in 2nd energy level

7th period, last electrons in 7th energy level

Each energy level varies in the number of electrons it can hold.

Within each energy level, the electrons are arranged into various sublevels called orbitals. The orbitals of the unexcited state atom include s, p, d, and f orbitals. The electrons fill these orbitals in a pre-determined pattern; filling the lowest energy orbitals first. "S" orbitals are the lowest energy so they fill with a maximum of two electrons first, followed by the "p" orbitals. There are three different "p" orbitals, each holding up to two electrons on each energy level. There are five different "d"

Energy level	Maximum Number of Electrons
1	2
2	8
3	18
4	32
5	50, theoretical, not filled
6	72, theoretical, not filled
7	98, theoretical, not filled

orbitals followed by seven different "f" orbitals. Filling of the "d" and "f" orbitals are very complicated. The 3 d orbitals are of higher energy than the 4s but less energy than the 4 p so they fill between the 4 s and 4 p orbitals, completing the third energy level. The same holds true for the s, p, and d orbitals on the 4th, 5th and 6th energy levels. The 4f orbital has more energy than the 6s but less energy than the 6p or 5d orbitals so it fills between the 6s and the 5d orbitals.

This pattern really does make sense.

According to the Pauli Exclusion Principle, and Hund's Rule for filling electron orbitals, each orbital of the same type must fill with two electrons, spinning in opposite directions, before a new type of orbital is occupied. However, before electrons can double up in an orbital, all orbitals on the same energy level of the same type must have one electron in it, all spinning in the same direction.

An electron of an atom can be identified using a shorthand notation called electron configuration. This gives the energy level, orbital type and number of electrons present.

For example, carbon has six electrons and they are located as follows:
    1st energy level, s orbital: 2 electrons,
    2nd energy level, 4 electrons; 2 in the s orbital and 2 in the p orbital.

For an electron configuration of: $1s^2, 2s^2, 2p^4$.

Chlorine has 17 electrons:
    1st energy level: 2 in the s orbital,
    2nd energy level: 2 in the s orbital, 6 in the p orbital
    3rd energy level: 2 in the s orbital, 5 in the p orbital.

For an electron configuration of: $1s^2, 2s^2, 2p^6, 3s^2, 3p^5$

Let's try a hard one: lead has 82 electrons.
    1st energy level: 2 in the s orbital,
    2nd energy level: 2 in the s orbital, 6 in the p orbital
    3rd energy level: 2 in the s orbital, 6 in the p orbital.

Then the 4s orbital fills with 2 electrons followed by the 3d orbital with 10 electrons then the 4p orbital with 6 electrons.

Now the 5s fills with 2 electrons, followed by the 4d orbital with 10 electrons, and then the 5p orbital with 6 electrons.

The sixth energy starts to fill next with 2 electrons in the 6s orbital, followed by 14 in the 4f and 10 electrons in the 5d and two electrons in the 6p orbital.

For an electron configuration of: $1s^2, 2s^2, 2p^6, 3s^2, 3p^6 4s^2 3d^{10} 4p^6 5s^2 4d^{10} 5p^6 6s^2 4f^{14} 5d^{10} 6p^2$

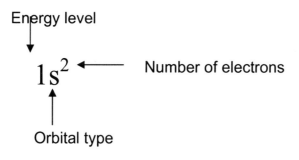

Energy level

$1s^2$ ← Number of electrons

Orbital type

There is an electron configuration pattern that coincides with the Periodic Table. The last electrons in the electron cloud of all alkali and alkali earth metals are found in the "s" orbitals.

Element	Last electron to fill	Element	Last electron to fill
Li	$2s^1$	Be	$2s^2$
Na	$3s^1$	Mg	$3s^2$
K	$4s^1$	Ca	$4s^2$

Groups 13-18 have their last electrons in the "P" orbitals. Transition metals, groups 3-12, have their last electrons in the "d" orbitals. The lanthanide and actinide series have their last electrons in the "f" orbital.

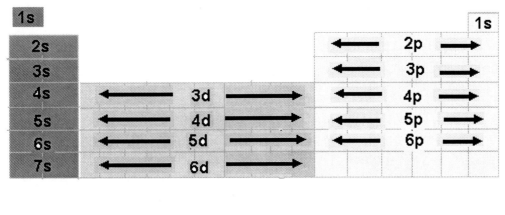

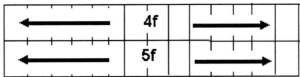

Nonmetals gain electrons or share electrons to achieve stable configurations and **metals lose electrons** to achieve them.

Valence electrons are the electron involved in chemical reactions so let's take a look at the relationship between the valence electron configuration and chemical activity. Remember the octet rule, it seems logical that when there are less than four valence electrons, the atom would want to lose electrons to go back to the previous energy level that was full. And that when the outer energy level is more than half full (more than 4 valence electrons) that the atom would want to gain electrons to complete the valence energy level.

For example: aluminum has 13 electrons with a configuration of $1s^2, 2s^2, 2p^6, 3s^2, 3p^1$.

There are only three electrons in the 3rd energy level and the octet rule says there should be eight. Aluminum can try and find 5 more electrons to fill the 3 p orbital or lose the $3s^2$, and $3p^1$ electrons. It takes less energy to lose the three electrons (circled), when these electrons are lost an aluminum +3 ion forms with an electron configuration of $1s^2$, $2s^2$, $2p^6$ which has a complete octet in the outer shell.

Keeping this in mind, along with the electron configuration chart above, it seems that the families with valence configurations s^1, s^2 or s^2, p^1 would tend to lose electrons to form ionic compounds. Families with valence configurations s^2, p^2; s^2, p^3; s^2, p^4; s^2, p^5 would tend to gain electrons to form ionic compounds or share electrons to form molecular substances. The noble gas family with a s^2, p^6 configuration has a complete octet in its valence shell so this configuration tends to be unreactive. However, the heavier noble gases form a number of compounds with oxygen and fluorine such as KrF_2 and XeO_4. Don't forget that atoms with electrons in the "d" or "f" orbitals, have s^1 or s^2 as their valence configuration of electrons.

This information helps us to understand some other characteristics.
For example, the elements in the alkali metal family, for example, are not found as free elements in nature. This is due to their high chemical activity. The one valence electron in the outermost energy level is high unstable, and it tends to be easily lost, forming many different ionic compounds in the process. The halogen family consists of molecules instead of free elements. The almost complete valence energy level is easily completed by two halogen atoms sharing electrons to form a covalent molecule.

In a reaction with a metal, the most reactive chemicals are the **most electronegative elements** or compounds containing those elements. In a reaction with a nonmetal, the most reactive chemicals are the **least electronegative elements** or compounds containing them. The reactivity of elements may be described by a **reactivity series**: an ordered list with chemicals that react strongly at one end and nonreactive chemicals at the other. The following reactivity series is for metals reacting with oxygen:

Metal	K	Na	Ca	Mg	Al	Zn	Fe	Pb	Cu	Hg	Ag	Au
Reaction with O_2	Burns violently		Burns rapidly					Oxidizes slowly			No reaction	

COMPETENCY 3.0   UNDERSTAND THE PHYSICAL AND CHEMICAL PROPERTIES AND CHANGES OF MATTER.

Skill 3.1   Distinguishing between physical and chemical properties and changes of matter

A **physical property** of matter is a property that can be determined without inducing a chemical change. All matter has mass and takes up space with an associated size. Matter experiencing gravity has a weight. Most matter we encounter exists in one of three phases. Some other examples of physical properties of matter include.

Melting point refers to the temperature at which a solid becomes a liquid. **Boiling point** refers to the temperature at which a liquid becomes a gas. Melting takes place when there is sufficient energy available to break the intermolecular forces that hold molecules together in a solid. Boiling occurs when there is enough energy available to break the intermolecular forces holding molecules together as a liquid.

Hardness describes how difficult it is to scratch or indent a substance. The hardest natural substance is diamond.

Density measures the mass of a unit volume of material. Units of g/cm^3 are commonly used. SI base units of kg/m^3 are also used. One g/cm^3 is equal to one thousand kg/m^3. Density (ρ) is calculated from mass (m) and volume (V) using the formula:

$$\rho = \frac{m}{V}.$$

The above expression is often manipulated to determine the mass of a substance if its volume and density are known ($m = \rho V$) or the volume of a substance if its mass and density are known ($V = m / \rho$).

Electrical conductivity measures a material's ability to conduct an electric current. The high conductivity of metals is due to the presence of metallic bonds. The high conductivity of electrolyte solutions is due to the presence of ions in solution.

Chemical characteristics or behavior are the ways substances interact with each other or the substance's ability to form different substances. Chemical properties are observable only during a chemical reaction.

Some common chemical properties are:

Flammability: some substances have the property to react with oxygen under elevated temperature

Acidity: some substances have the property to produce hydrogen ions when in an aqueous solution.

Oxidation-reduction: some substances have the ability to gain or lose electrons. Some examples are tarnishing, rusting, patination.

Precipitation: some substances have the ability to combine with others, changing their solubility.

A **physical change** does not create a new substance. **Atoms are not rearranged into different compounds**. The material has the same chemical composition as it had before the change. Changes of state as described in the previous section are physical changes. Frozen water or gaseous water is still H_2O. Taking a piece of paper and tearing it up is a physical change. You simply have smaller pieces of paper.

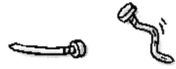

Compare these two nails....They are still iron nails, made of iron atoms. The difference is that one is bent while the other is straight. This is a physical change.

A **chemical change** is a chemical reaction. It **converts one substance into another** because atoms are rearranged to form a different compound. Paper undergoes a chemical change when you burn it. You no longer have paper. A chemical change to a pure substance alters its properties.

An iron nail rusts to form a rusty nail. The rusty nail, however, is not made up of the same iron atoms. It is now composed of iron (III) oxide molecules that form when the iron atoms combine with oxygen molecules during oxidation (rusting).

Skill 3.2   Identifying methods for determining physical and chemical properties of substances

Examples of these methods are contained in Skill 3.3.

Skill 3.3   Identifying unknown substances based on physical and chemical properties

To identify an unknown substance based on its physical properties, one would start by using the five senses and noting color, hardness, luster, odor, and its state at room temperature. Using a thermometer, one would determine temperatures for state changes such as melting point, boiling point and freezing point. If it is a mixture, one would want to determine if the various parts could be separated using tweezers or by filtering through filter paper, or by evaporating various parts at various temperatures. One would also want to see what the mass and volume of the sample are and then calculate the density (D = m/V). Using a hammer, one could test the malleability. Running an electrical current through the substance would help determine its electrical and thermal conductivity. The results of these tests can be compared to tables of known values for various elements and compounds to determine the identity of the unknown.

To identify an unknown substance based on its chemical properties would necessitate having a large enough sample to test a variety of things, knowing that many of those tests could change the substance into something else. One would test its reactivity with a spark, oxygen, water, a weak acid, a strong acid, a weak base, and a strong base. Passing an electrical current through it would show if it could be decomposed in that way. One would watch for (and measure) how much heat, light, smoke, electricity, or other forms of energy are needed or are released with each reaction. The results of these tests can be compared to tables of known values for various elements and compounds to determine the identity of the unknown.

Skill 3.4   Selecting appropriate techniques to achieve a desired separation of a mixture

A mixture consists of two or more substances that when put together retain their individual physical and chemical properties. That is, no new substances are formed. Differences in physical and chemical properties of the components of the mixture can be used to separate the mixture. For example, salt and pepper have different colors and can be separated by physically moving the white crystals away from the dark particles. Or salt dissolves in water while pepper does not and the two can be separated by adding water to the mixture. The salt will dissolve while the pepper will float on top of the water. Skim off the pepper and then evaporate the water. The salt and pepper are now separated.

Common methods for separating mixtures include filtration, chromatography, distillation and extraction.

Filtering relies on one of the substances being soluble in the solvent, and the other being insoluble. The soluble substance ends up in the **filtrate** (the liquid that passes through the filter paper). The insoluble substance ends up in the filter paper as the **residue**.

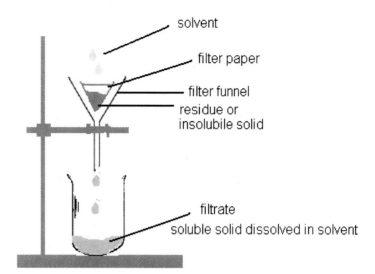

solvent

filter paper

filter funnel

residue or insolubile solid

filtrate
soluble solid dissolved in solvent

Distillation and **fractional distillation** rely on the fact that the liquids in the mixture are different. Each liquid has its own unique **boiling point**. As the temperature rises, it reaches the lowest boiling point liquid and so this liquid boils. The temperature remains at that temperature until all of the liquid has boiled away. The vapor passes into a condenser and is cooled and so turns back into a liquid. The pure liquid is now in a different part of the

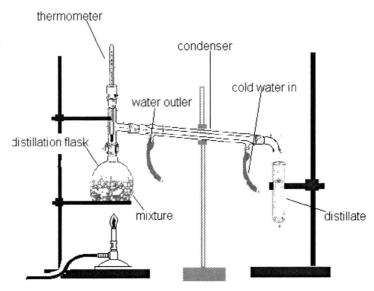

apparatus and rolls down into a test tube. This liquid has been separated from the mixture.

Chromatography is a technique, which is used to separate mixtures based on differential migration. Differential migration uses differences in physical properties such as solubility, molecular size and polarity to separate the substance. The mixture is placed in a solution, which becomes the mobile phase. This solution then passes over a stationary phase. Different components of the mixture travel at different rates. After the separation, the time that component took to emerge from the instrument (or its location within the stationary phase) is found with a detector. These chromatographic separations have many different types of stationary phases including paper, silica on glass or plastic plates (thin-layer chromatography), volatile gases (gas chromatography) and liquids, (liquid chromatography including column and high-performance liquid chromatography or HPLC) as well as gels (electrophoresis).

The result is a **chromatogram** like the one shown below. The **identity of an unknown** peak is found by comparing its location on the chromatogram to standards. The **concentration** of a component is found from signal strength or peak area by comparison to calibration curves of known concentrations.

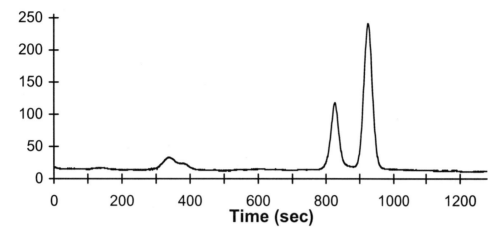

In **paper chromatography** and **thin layer chromatography (TLC)**, the sample rises up by capillary action through a solid phase.

In **gas chromatography (GC)**, the sample is vaporized and forced through a column filled with a packing material. GC is often used to separate and determine the concentration of **low molecular weight volatile organic** compounds.

In **liquid chromatography (LC)**, the sample is a liquid. It is either allowed to seep through an open column using the force of gravity or it is forced through a closed column under pressure. The variations of liquid chromatography depend on the identity of the packing material. For example, an ion-exchange liquid chromatograph contains a material with a charged surface. The mixture components with the opposite charge interact with this packing material and spend more time in the column. LC is often used to separate **large organic polymers** like proteins.

Each component in the mixture can be identified by its retention factor or retention time once it has been separated. Both retention factor, R_f, and retention time are quantitative indications of how far a particular compound travels in a particular solvent or how long the component is retained on the column before eluting with the mobile phase (for gas chromatography and liquid chromatography). By comparing the R_f of the components in the mixture to known values for substances, identification of the components in the mixture can be achieved.

R_f = distance the component color traveled from the point of application
distance the solvent front traveled from the point of application

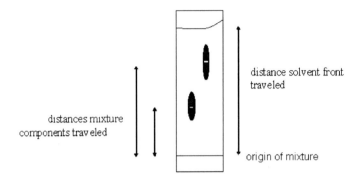

distances mixture
components traveled

distance solvent front
traveled

origin of mixture

In an ideal chemical world, reactions would produce products in exactly the right amount and in exactly the right way; no product loss, no competing side reactions. But then things would be very simple for the chemist. In the real chemical world, things are not so simple for the chemist. Most chemical reactions produce product intermingled

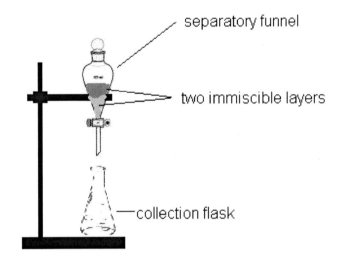

separatory funnel

two immiscible layers

collection flask

with by-products or impurities. **Extraction** is a method used to separate the desired product from impurities. This process is used in product purification and results from an unequal distribution of solute between two immiscible solvents. This process, then, makes use of differences is solubilities to separate components in what is called a work-up. The work-up is a planned sequence of extracting and washing.

The planning involves determining the two solvents. One is usually water, the aqueous layer, while the other is an organic solvent, the organic layer. The important feature here is that the two solvents are immiscible and the mixture is the partition between the two solvents. The mixture is then separated as its components are attracted to the solvents differently. Most charged particles and inorganic salts will move towards the aqueous layer and dissolve in it, while the neutral organic molecules will move towards the organic layer

COMPETENCY 4.0 **UNDERSTAND THE FACTORS THAT AFFECT THE SOLUBILITY OF A SUBSTANCE AND THE PROPERTIES OF SOLUTIONS.**

Skill 4.1 **Demonstrating knowledge of the dissolution process at the atomic and molecular levels**

Solutions form when the intermolecular attractive forces between solute and solvent molecules are about as strong as those that exist in the solute alone or in the solvent alone. For example, NaCl dissolves in water because:

1) The water molecules interact with the Na^+ and Cl^- ions with sufficient strength to overcome the attraction between them in the crystalline form.

2) Na^+ and Cl^- ions interact with the water molecules with sufficient strength to overcome the attraction water molecules have for each other in the liquid.

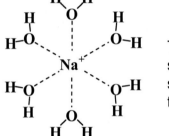

The intermolecular attraction between solute and solvent molecules is known as **solvation**. When the solvent is water, it is known as **hydration**. The figure to the left shows a hydrated Na^+ ion.

Skill 4.2 **Analyzing factors that affect the solubility of a substance (e.g., temperature, pressure) and the rate of the dissolving process**

<u>Polar and nonpolar solutes and solvents</u>

A nonpolar liquid like heptane (C_7H_{16}) has intermolecular bonds with relatively weak London dispersion forces. Heptane is immiscible in water because the attraction that water molecules have for each other via hydrogen bonding is too strong.

Unlike Na^+ and Cl^- ions, heptane molecules cannot break these bonds. Because bonds of similar strength must be broken and formed for solvation to occur, nonpolar substances tend to be soluble in nonpolar solvents, while ionic and polar substances are soluble in polar solvents like water. Polar molecules are often called **hydrophilic** and non-polar molecules are called **hydrophobic**. This observation is often stated as "**like dissolves like**." Network solids (e.g., diamond) are soluble in neither polar nor nonpolar solvents because the covalent bonds within the solid are too strong for these solvents to break.

<u>Temperature and solubility</u>: When attempting to dissolve a solid like NaCl into a liquid, the higher temperature facilitates the solubility of the ionic solution and more of the NaCl will enter into the solution. If the solution is highly saturated at a high temperature, the NaCl will fall out of solution and recrystallize as a solid as the solution cools.

<u>Vapor pressure lowering, boiling point elevation, freezing point lowering</u>

After a nonvolatile solute is added to a liquid solvent, only a fraction of the molecules at a liquid-gas interface are now volatile and capable of escaping into the gas phase. The vapor consists of essentially pure solvent that is able to condense freely. This imbalance drives equilibrium away from the vapor phase and into the liquid phase and **lowers the vapor pressure** by an amount proportional to the solute particles present.

It follows that from a lowered vapor pressure, a higher temperature is required for a vapor pressure equal to the external pressure over the liquid. Thus **the boiling point is raised** by an amount proportional to the solute particles present.

Solute particles in a liquid solvent are not normally soluble in the solid phase of that solvent. When solvent crystals freeze, they typically align themselves with each other at first and keep the solute out. This means that only a fraction of the molecules in the liquid at the liquid-solid interface are capable of freezing while the solid phase consists of essentially pure solvent that is able to melt freely. This imbalance drives equilibrium away from the solid phase and into the liquid phase and **lowers the freezing point** by an amount proportional to the solute particles present. Boiling point elevation and freezing point depression are both caused by a lower fraction of solvent molecules in the liquid phase than in the other phase.

Skill 4.3   Interpreting solubility curves

To have a clear understanding of solubility curves, we need to take a close look at basic terms like solubility, solubility curve, saturated solution, etc.

The **solubility** is typically measured as the mass of salt that would saturate 100 grams of water at a particular temperature.
The **solubility curve** shows how the solubility of a salt varies with temperature. A solution is **saturated** if no more salt can be dissolved by that solution at that particular temperature.

Interpreting solubility curves:

A solubility curve tells us the solubility of a substance at a particular temperature. One way to look at it is to see what happens if the temperature is decreased at a given concentration. For example, take a near boiling solution of potassium nitrate in water. This solution has 100g of potassium nitrate and 100g of water. Let the solution cool. From examining a curve (the data), we conclude that at 57 degrees C, all the potassium nitrate dissolves in water. The solution at this point is saturated. Even if we slightly lower the temperature, some potassium nitrate will be insoluble. The lower the temperature, the less solubility of potassium nitrate in water, since water will not be able to dissolve the salt. We find crystals of potassium nitrate. At this point, there are two phases, a solution and some solid potassium nitrate. At 57 degrees C and above, there is only one phase, a solution of potassium nitrate. The solubility curve represents the boundary between these two different conditions.

Finally, a solubility curves indicates the different phases of a solution due to the change in temperature.

1. At one particular temperature, a solution is said to be saturated, because all the solute is dissolved completed. Above that temperature, we can see a homogeneous solution.

2. Below that particular temperature, there are two phase evident - one is the solution phase, the other is the solid phase due to the undissolved solute.

3. A solubility curve is the indicator of a solution due to the change in temperature.

Skill 4.4   Solving problems involving solution concentrations (e.g., molarity, molality, percent by mass, mole fraction)

The **molarity** (abbreviated M) of a solute in solution is defined as the number of moles of solute in a liter of solution.

$$Molarity = \frac{\text{moles solute}}{\text{volume of solution in liters}}$$

Molarity is the most frequently used concentration unit in chemical reactions because it reflects the number of moles available for chemical reactions.

Molarity is useful for dilutions because the moles of solute remain unchanged even if more solvent is added to the solution. Thus we can perform the following dilution conversion:

$$(\text{Initial molarity})(\text{Initial volume}) = (\text{molarity after dilution})(\text{final volume})$$

or

$$M_{initial}V_{initial} = M_{final}V_{final}$$

Molality, m, compares the moles of solute present in the solution to the mass of the solvent in kilograms.

$$m = \frac{\text{moles of solute}}{\text{kg of solvent}}$$

Problem: What is the molality of a solution composed of 2.55 g of acetone [$(CH_3)_2CO$; MW = 58.0 g/mol], dissolved in 200g of water?

Solution: mol acetone = 2.55 g x 1 mol/ 58 g = 0.0440 mol

m= mol solute/ kg solvent

0.0440 mol/ .200 kg water = 0.220 m

Mass percentage is frequently used to represent every component of a solution (possibly including the solvent) as a portion of the whole in terms of mass.

$$\text{Mass percentage of a component} = \frac{\text{mass of component in solution}}{\text{total mass of solution}} \times 100\%.$$

Parts per million (or ppm) in solution usually refers to a dilute component of a solution as a portion of the whole in terms of mass. A solute present in one part per million would amount to one gram solute in one million grams of solution.

$$\text{Parts per million of a component} = \frac{\text{mass of solute}}{\text{total mass of solution}} \times 10^6$$
$$= \frac{\text{number of mg of solute}}{\text{number of kg of solution}}$$

Strictly speaking, the expression above is a **"ppm by mass."** Parts per million is also sometimes used for ratios of moles or volumes.

The **normality** (abbreviated N) of a solution is defined as the number of **equivalents** of a solute per liter of solution.

$$\text{Normality} = \frac{\text{equivalents solute}}{\text{volume of solution in liters}}$$

An equivalent is defined according to the type of reaction being examined, but the number of equivalents of solute is always a whole number multiple of the number of moles of solute, and so the normality of a solute is always a whole-number multiple of its molarity. An equivalent is defined so that one equivalent of one reagent will react with one equivalent of another reagent. For acid-base reactions, an equivalent of an acid is the quantity that supplies 1 mol of H^+ and an equivalent of a base is the quantity reacting with 1 mol of H^+. For example, one mole of H_2SO_4 in an acid-base reaction supplies two moles of H+. The mass of one equivalent of H_2SO_4 is half of the mass of one mole of H_2SO_4, and its normality is twice its molarity. In a redox reaction, an equivalent is the quantity of substance that gains or loses 1 mol of electrons.

A **mole fraction** is used to represent a component in a solution as a portion of the entire number of moles present. If you were able to pick out a molecule at random from a solution, the mole fraction of a component represents the probability that the molecule you picked would be that particular component. Mole fractions for all components must sum to one, and mole fractions are just numbers with no units.

Skill 4.5 Demonstrating knowledge of how to prepare solutions of desired concentration and properties

Buffers are usually composed of weak acids and their salts, or weak bases and their salts. An appropriate acid or base/ salt combination will buffer a solution only when it is at sufficient concentration and has a pK_a close to the desired pH of the solution. Thus, a buffered solution can be created as follows:

1. Select a compound with a pK_a close the desired pH.

2. Determine what the buffer concentration must be; typical concentrations are between 1mM and 200 mM.

3. Using the pK_a, calculate the number of moles of acid/salt or base/salt that must be present at the desired pH.

4. Covert moles to grams and weigh out the components

   a. If both salt and acid (or base) are available, use the appropriate amount of each.

   b. If only the acid is available, add the entire needed compound is in acid form, then use enough base (NaOH) to convert the proper portion to salt.

5. Dissolve all components in slightly less water than is needed to reach the final volume.

Check the pH and adjust if necessary. Add water to reach the final volume.

Skill 4.6 **Analyzing the colligative properties of solutions (e.g., freezing point, boiling point, osmotic pressure, vapor pressure)**

A **colligative** property is a physical property of a solution that **depends on the number of solute particles present in solution** and usually not on the identity of the solutes involved. Colligative properties may be predicted by imagining ourselves shrinking down to the size of molecules in a solution and visualizing the impact of an increasing number of generic solute particles around us.

Vapor pressure lowering, boiling point elevation, freezing point lowering
After a nonvolatile solute is added to a liquid solvent, only a fraction of the molecules at a liquid-gas interface are now volatile and capable of escaping into the gas phase. The vapor consists of essentially pure solvent that is able to condense freely. This imbalance drives equilibrium away from the vapor phase and into the liquid phase and **lowers the vapor pressure** by an amount proportional to the solute particles present.

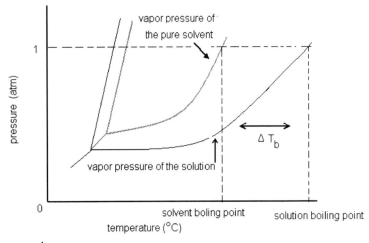

It follows from a lowered vapor pressure that a higher temperature is required for a vapor pressure equal to the external pressure over the liquid. Thus **the boiling point is raised** by an amount proportional to the solute particles present.

Solute particles in a liquid solvent are not normally soluble in the solid phase of that solvent. When solvent crystals freeze, they typically align themselves with each other at first and keep the solute out. This means that only a fraction of the molecules in the liquid at the liquid-solid interface are capable of freezing while the solid phase consists of essentially pure solvent that is able to melt freely. This imbalance drives equilibrium away from the solid phase and into the liquid phase and **lowers the freezing point** by an amount proportional to the solute particles present.

Boiling point elevation and freezing point depression are both caused by a lower fraction of solvent molecules in the liquid phase than in the other phase. For pure water at 1 atm there is equilibrium at the normal boiling and freezing points:

At 100 °C, $H_2O(l) \underset{\text{condensation}}{\overset{\text{vaporization}}{\rightleftharpoons}} H_2O(g)$.

At 0 °C, $H_2O(l) \underset{\text{melting}}{\overset{\text{freezing}}{\rightleftharpoons}} H_2O(s)$.

For water with a high solute concentration, equilibrium is not present:

At 100 °C, less interfacial $H_2O(l) \underset{\text{condensation}}{\overset{\text{vaporization}}{\rightleftharpoons}} H_2O(g)$.

At 0 °C, less interfacial $H_2O(l) \underset{\text{melting}}{\overset{\text{freezing}}{\rightleftharpoons}} H_2O(s)$.

Osmotic pressure

A **semipermeable membrane** is a material that permits some particles to pass through it but not others. The diagram shows a membrane that permits solvent but not solute to pass through it. When a semipermeable membrane separates a dilute solution from a concentrated solution, the solvent flows from the dilute to the concentrated solution (i.e., from higher solvent to lower solvent concentration) in a process called **osmosis** until equilibrium is achieved.

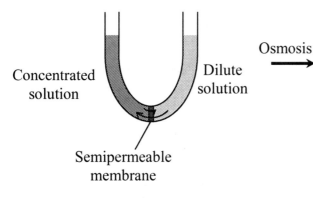

The pressure required to prevent osmosis from a pure solvent into a solution is called **osmotic pressure**. Osmotic pressure is proportional to the molarity of the solution and thus it is a colligative property of solutions, and the osmotic pressure of a pure solvent is zero.

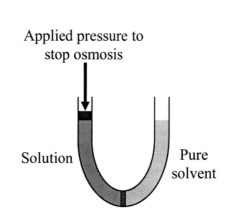

A simulation of solutes and solvent molecules interacting and an animation of osmotic flow between two flexible compartments are located here: http://physioweb.med.uvm.edu/bodyfluids/osmosis.htm. A simulation of the osmotic pressure experiment above for NaCl, sucrose, and albumin (a protein) is found here: http://arbl.cvmbs.colostate.edu/hbooks/cmb/cells/pmemb/hydrosim.html. Typical changes in a pressure/temperature phase diagram after adding a non-volatile solute are found here: http://chemmovies.unl.edu/ChemAnime/SOLND/SOLND.html.

Quantitative colligative property problems typically involve a change related to a solute concentration by a direct proportionality.

Raoult's law states that the vapor pressure of a solution with nonvolatile solutes is the mole fraction of solvent multiplied by the pure solvent vapor pressure:

$$P^{vapor}_{solution} = P^{vapor}_{pure\ solvent} \left(\text{mole fraction}\right)_{solvent}$$

Raoult's law is often used to describe the vapor pressure change from pure solvent using the solute concentration:

$$\Delta P^{vapor} = P^{vapor}_{solution} - P^{vapor}_{pure\ solvent} = P^{vapor}_{pure\ solvent}\left(\text{mole fraction}\right)_{solvent} - P^{vapor}_{pure\ solvent}$$

$$= -P^{vapor}_{pure\ solvent}\left(1 - \left(\text{mole fraction}\right)_{solvent}\right)$$

$$= -P^{vapor}_{pure\ solvent}\left(\text{mole fraction}\right)_{solute}$$

Different concentration units are used for other colligative properties to express a **change from pure solvent**. The following table summarizes these expressions for nonelectrolytes:

Colligative property	Equation for property X $\Delta X = X_{solution} - X_{pure\ solvent}$	Proportionality constant
Vapor pressure lowering	$\Delta P^{vapor} = -P^{vapor}_{pure\ solvent}\left(\textbf{mole fraction}\right)_{solute}$	Pure solvent vapor pressure
Boiling point elevation	$\Delta T_b = K_b\left(\textbf{molality}\right)$	Solvent-dependant constant K_b
Freezing point lowering	$\Delta T_f = -K_f\left(\textbf{molality}\right)$	Solvent-dependant constant K_f
Osmotic pressure	$P_{osmotic} = RT\left(\textbf{molarity}\right)$	(Gas constant) □ (Temperature)

For solutions that contain electrolytes, the change from the pure solvent to solution is different from what is predicted by the above equations. Due to the dissolving process, these substances will dissociate to put many more ions in solution than their molal concentration would predict. And their numbers will change the colligative properties even more.

The van't Hoff factor is an important factor in the extent of the change in boiling point or freezing point of a solution after solute has been added. For substances that do not dissociate in water, such as sugar ($C_{12}H_{22}O_{11}$), has an *i* value of 1. Substances that dissociate in water to give two ion particles, such as salt (NaCl), have an *i* value of 2. This pattern continues for any number of particles into which a solute can dissociate.

The van 't Hoff factor is symbolized by the lower-case letter i. It is a unitless constant directly associated with the degree of dissociation of the solute in the solvent.

Substances which do not ionize in solution, like sugar, have i = 1.
Substances which ionize into two ions, like NaCl, have i = 2.
Substances which ionize into three ions, like $MgCl_2$, have i = 3.

What this implies is exactly what van 't Hoff observed as he was compiling and examining boiling point and freezing point data. At the time, he did not understand what i meant. His use of i was strictly to try and make the data fit together. He took a 1.0 molal aqueous solution of sugar, NaCl, and $MgCl_2$ and checked the boiling point temperature of each solution. He found that the NaCl had a boiling point elevation twice as high as that of the sugar and the $MgCl_2$ elevated the boiling point temperature three times higher than the sugar. Upon testing other substances, he found groups but he had no idea why until Svante Arrhenius' theory of electrolytic dissociation was published. The explanation seemed clear then.

Many colligative property problems compare one solution to another and may be solved without the use of the above expressions. All that is required for these comparison problems is knowledge of what the colligative properties are, how they are altered, and which solution contains the greater concentration of dissolved particles.

Problem: One mole of each of the following compounds is added to water in separate flasks to make 1.0 L of solution.

Potassium phosphate
Silver chloride
Sodium chloride
Sugar (sucrose)

A. Which solution will provide the greatest change in the freezing point temperature?
B. Which solution will provide the least change in the boiling point temperature?
Be sure to explain you choices.

Solution:
Analyze the choices for solubility and dissociation:

Potassium phosphate   soluble in water → 4 ions
Silver chloride   soluble in water → 2 ions
Sodium chloride   soluble in water → 2 ions
Sugar (sucrose)   soluble in water →1 molecule (nonelectrolyte)

A. Of the choices, potassium phosphate forms the most ions so given the concentration of all of the choices is the same, K_3PO_4 will effect the boiling point temperature and the freezing point temperature the most. For every 1 mole of K_3PO_4 that dissolve, 4 moles of ions will be present in solution.

B. Sugar, a nonelectrolye, will have the least effect on the freezing point and boiling point temperatures due to the fact that it is a molecular substance and does not dissociate into ions. For every 1 mole of sugar in solution, only 1 mole of molecules will be present.

Changes to boiling point temperature and freezing point temperature may be determined by looking at the molal concentration of the solute in the pure substance.

Remember that a colligative property is one that depends only on the number of particles present, not their nature.

For boiling point temperature changes, $\Delta T_b = mk_b i$ where m is the molal concentration of the solute, K_b is a constant specific for each solvent and i is the number of particles or ions in solution. For water, $K_b = 0.52$ °C/m

$\Delta T_f = mk_f i$ is the equation to use to determine changes in freezing point temperature. K_f is a constant specific for each solvent. For water, $K_f = -1.86$ °C/m

Example: How much of an increase in boiling point temperature will 31.5 grams of potassium chloride make when added to 225 g of water?

Solution: KCl is an electrolyte so $i = 2$
Mass of water = 225 g=0.225 kg
Mass KCl = 31.5 g, moles KCl = 0.423 mole
m = 0.423/0.225 kg =1.88 m
$K_b = 0.52$ °C/m
$\Delta T_b = mk_b i$
  = 1.88 m (0.56 °C/m) 2 = 1.96 °C

Example: How many grams of benzoic acid, $C_7H_6O_2$, a nonelectrolyte must be added to 178 g of water to increase the boiling point temperature 4°C?

Solution:
MM benzoic acid = 122 g/mol
Benzoic acid is a nonelectrolyte so $i = 1$,
 Mass of water = 178 g =0.178 kg
$\Delta T = 4$ °C
$K_b = 0.52$ °C/m

$\Delta T_b = mk_b i$

m= $\Delta T_b / K_b i$ = 4/0.52 °C/m (1) = 7.69 m

7.69 m= moles benzoic acid/0.178 kg water =1.37 mole benzoic acid

1.37 moles benzoic acid = grams benzoic acid / 122 g/mol =167 g benzoic acid are needed.

Example: The custard used to make ice cream does not "freeze" until the temperature reaches –15 to –18 °C. With ice, it will only go down to 0 °C. In order to reach the lower temperature needed to freeze the custard, sodium chloride, NaCl, is added to the ice. How much salt is needed to freeze the ice cream?

Solution:

Each sodium chloride particle dissociates into a Na^+ ion and a Cl^- ion, making two solvated ions present for every one NaCl particle present. So, NaCl has an i value of 2.

The temperature change needed is -15°C and the K_f value for water is −1.86 °C/m.

Using the freezing point depression expression we can determine the *molality* of the salt-ice solution that will reach −15°C.

$$\Delta T = K_f\, m\, i \text{ and rearranging it to solve for } m = \frac{\Delta T}{m\, i} = \frac{-15°C}{-1.86°C/m} = 4.0 \quad (2)$$

Remember that $m = \dfrac{\text{\# moles solute}}{\text{kg solvent}}$ so the moles of NaCl can be determined if we know the kilograms of ice used. In this case, 1 bag of ice is about 2.3 kg. So the number of moles of NaCl needed would be:

\# moles solute = m (kg solute) = 4.0 *mol/kg* (2.3 kg) = 9.3 mol of NaCl.

Now, the mass of NaCl needed can be found by using the relationship between moles and molar mass: \# mol = mass/ Molar Mass

In this case, mass = \# mol (Molar Mass) = 9.3 mol (58.5 g/mol) or about 540 g of NaCl is needed for every bag of ice used.

The most common errors in solving all types of colligative property problems arise from considering some value other than **the number of particles in solution**. Remember that one mole of glucose(*aq*) forms one mole of hydrated particles, but one mole of NaCl(*aq*) forms two moles of hydrated particles, and one mole of $Al_2(SO_4)_3(aq)$ forms five moles of them. We would expect a 0.5 M solution of glucose to have roughly the same colligative properties as a 0.25 M solution of sodium hydroxide and a 0.1 M solution of aluminum sulfate. Also remember that undissolved solids do not contribute anything to colligative properties.

Skill 4.7   Distinguishing among colloids, solutions, and suspensions

Colloids, solutions, and suspensions are types of mixtures consisting of two or more components. Solutions are homogenous mixtures because they are uniform throughout. In other words, the individual components are evenly distributed throughout the mixture. Colloids and suspensions are heterogeneous mixtures. Heterogeneous mixtures are not uniform. Rather, they consist of clumps or pockets of the individual components.

Solutions are homogenous mixtures of two or more components. The components of solutions are atoms and molecules, thus the particles are 1 nm or less in diameter. Solutions are transparent and do not usually absorb visible light. An example of a solution is sugar and water.

Suspensions are heterogeneous mixtures consisting of particles larger than those found in solutions. The diameter of particles found in suspensions is greater than 1000 nm. Thus, these particles are visible to the naked eye. Suspensions are murky or opaque. Machine shaking can evenly distribute suspensions, but the components will settle out in time. Examples of suspensions include blood and mixtures of oil and water.

Colloids are heterogeneous mixtures consisting of particles intermediate in size between those found in solutions and suspensions. The diameter of particles found in colloids is between 1 and 1000 nm. Colloids appear homogenous to the naked eye, and do not settle out into components. Colloids scatter light and are opaque. Milk is an example of a colloid.

COMPETENCY 5.0 UNDERSTAND CHEMICAL FORMULAS AND THE NOMENCLATURE OF IONIC AND COVALENT COMPOUNDS.

Skill 5.1 Predicting the formulas of stable ionic compounds based on the charges of the ions that compose them

The following rules have been established for the naming of ionic compounds.

Naming Binary Ionic Compounds in which the cation has only one valence (such as 1A, 2A, and aluminum):

1. The cation is named first, the anion second.
2. A monatomic cation takes its name from the name of the element.
3. A monatomic anion is named by taking the first part of the element name and adding –ide.
4. Examples: sodium chloride is NaCl, lithium nitride is Li_3N

Naming Binary Ionic Compounds in which the cation has more than one <u>valence</u> (such as transition ions):

1. The charge on the metal ion must be specified, such as iron(II) and iron(III) denoting Fe^{+2} and Fe^{+3} respectively. In an older method, the ion with the lower charge has a name ending in –ous (Ferrous = Fe^{+2}) and the ion with the higher charge has a name ending in –ic (Ferric = Fe^{+3}).
2. The cation is named first, the anion second.
3. A monatomic anion is named by taking the first part of the element name and adding –ide.
4. Examples: iron(III) oxide (ferric oxide) is Fe_2O_3, tin(IV) chloride is $SnCl_4$

Naming Acids Created from Ions:

1. Normally the cation in acids is H^+ and the compounds are dissolved in water or give water as a product. Most of these compounds can be named two ways.
2. When the anion ends in –ide, the acid name begins with the prefix *hydro-* such that HCl is hydrogen chloride or hydrochloric acid and H_2S is hydrogen sulfide or hydrosulfuric acid.
3. Polyatomic ions ending in –ate become –ic acids such that $HClO_3$ is hydrogen chlorate or chloric acid and $HClO_4$ is hydrogen perchlorate or perchloric acid.
4. Polyatomic ions ending in –ite become –ous acids such that $HClO_2$ is hydrogen chlorite or chlorous acid and HClO is hydrogen hypochlorite or hypochlorous acid.

Skill 5.2   Applying knowledge of IUPAC and common nomenclature in the analysis of the names and formulas of ionic and covalent compounds

The IUPAC is the **International Union of Pure and Applied Chemistry**, an organization that formulates naming rules. **Organic compounds contain carbon**, and they have a separate system of nomenclature but some of the simplest molecules containing carbon also fall within the scope of inorganic chemistry.

Naming rules depend on whether the chemical is an ionic compound or a molecular compound containing only covalent bonds. There are special rules for naming acids. The rules below describe a group of traditional "semi-systematic" names accepted by IUPAC.

Ionic compounds: Cation

Ionic compounds are named with the **cation (positive ion) first**. Nearly all cations in inorganic chemistry are **monatomic**, meaning they just consist of one atom (like Ca^{2+}, the calcium ion.) This atom will be a **metal ion**. For common ionic compounds, the **alkali metals always have a 1+ charge** and the **alkali earth metals always have a 2+ charge.**

Many metals may form cations of more than one charge. In this case, a Roman numeral in parenthesis after the name of the element is used to indicate the ion's charge in a particular compound. This Roman numeral method is known as the **Stock system**. An older nomenclature used the suffix –*ous* for the lower charge and –*ic* for the higher charge and is still used occasionally.

Example: Fe^{2+} is the iron(II) ion and Fe^{3+} is the iron(III) ion.

The only common inorganic **polyatomic cation** is **ammonium: NH_4^+.**

Ionic compounds: Anion

The **anion** (negative ion) is named and written last. Monatomic anions are formed from nonmetallic elements and are named by **replacing the end of the element's name with the suffix –*ide.***

Examples: Cl^- is the chloride ion, S^{2-} is the sulfide ion, and N^{3-} is the nitride ion.

These anions also end with *–ide*:

C_2^{2-}	N_3^-	O_2^{2-}	O_3^-	S_2^{2-}	CN^-	OH^-
carbide or acetylide	azide	peroxide	ozonide	disulfide	cyanide	hydroxide

Oxoanions (also called oxyanions) **contain one element in combination with oxygen.** Many common polyatomic anions are oxoanions that **end with the suffix –ate.** If an element has two possible oxoanions, the one with the element at a lower oxidation state **ends with –ite.** This anion will also usually have **less oxygen per atom.** Additional oxoanions are named with the prefix *hypo-* if they have a lower oxidation number than the *–ite* form and the prefix *per–* if they have a higher oxidation number than the *–ate* form.

Common examples:

			CO_3^{2-}	carbonate		
	SO_3^{2-}	sulfite	SO_4^{2-}	sulfate		
	PO_3^{3-}	phosphite	PO_4^{3-}	phosphate		
$N_2O_2^{2-}$	hyponitrite	NO_2^-	nitrite	NO_3^-	nitrate	
ClO^-	hypochlorite	ClO_2^-	chlorite	ClO_3^-	chlorate	ClO_4^-	perchlorate
BrO^-	hypobromite	BrO_2^-	bromite	BrO_3^-	bromate	BrO_4^-	perbromate
			MnO_4^{2-}	manganate	MnO_4^-	permanganate
			CrO_4^{2-}	chromate	CrO_8^{3-}	perchromate

Note that manganate/permanganate and chromate/perchromate are exceptions to the general rules because there are *–ate* ions but no *–ite* ions and because the charge changes.

Other polyatomic anions that end with *–ate* are:

$C_2O_4^{2-}$	$Cr_2O_7^{2-}$	SCN^-	HCO_2^-	$CH_3CO_2^-$
oxalate	dichromate	thiocyanate	formate	acetate

HCO_2^- and $CH_3CO_2^-$ are condensed **structural formulas** because they show how the atoms are linked together. Their molecular formulas would be CHO_2^- and $C_2H_3O_2^-$

If an H atom is added to a polyatomic anion with a negative charge greater than one, the word *hydrogen* or the prefix *bi-* are used for the resulting anion. If two H atoms are added, *dihydrogen* is used.

Examples: bicarbonate or hydrogen carbonate ion: HCO_3^-
dihydrogen phosphate ion: $H_2PO_4^-$

Ionic compounds: Hydrates

Water molecules often occupy positions within the lattice of an ionic crystal. These compounds are called **hydrates**, and the water molecules are known as **water of hydration**. The water of hydration is added after a centered dot in a formula. In a name, a number-prefix (listed below for molecular compounds) indicating the number of water molecules is followed by the root –*hydrate*.

Ionic compounds: Putting it all together

We now have the tools to name most common salts given a formula and to write a formula for them given a name. To determine a formula given a name, the number of anions and cations that are needed to achieve a neutral charge must be found.

Example: Determine the formula of cobalt(II) phosphite octahydrate.

Solution: For the cation, find the symbol for cobalt (Co) and recognize that it is present as Co^{2+} ions from the Roman numerals. For the anion, remember the phosphite ion is PO_3^{3-}. A neutral charge is achieved with 3 Co^{2+} ions for every 2 PO_3^{3-} ions. Add eight H_2O for water of hydration for the answer:

$$Co_3 (PO_3)_2 \bullet 8H_2O.$$

Molecular compounds

Molecular compounds (compounds making up molecules with a neutral charge) are usually composed entirely of nonmetals and are named by placing the **less electronegative atom first**.

The suffix –*ide* is added to the second, more electronegative atom, and prefixes indicating numbers are added to one or both names if needed.

Prefix	mono-	di-	tri-	tetra-	penta-	hexa-	hepta-	octa-	nona-	deca-
Meaning	1	2	3	4	5	6	7	8	9	10

The final "o" or "a" may be left off these prefixes for oxides.

The electronegativity requirement is the reason the compound with two oxygen atoms and one nitrogen atom is called nitrogen dioxide, NO_2 and <u>not</u> dioxygen nitride O_2N. The hydride of sodium is NaH, sodium hydride, but the hydride of bromine is HBr, hydrogen bromide (or hydrobromic acid if it's in aqueous solution). Oxygen is only named first in compounds with fluorine such as oxygen difluoride, OF_2, and fluorine is never placed first because it is the most electronegative element.

Examples: N_2O_4, dinitrogen tetroxide (or tetraoxide)
Cl_2O_7, dichlorine heptoxide (or heptaoxide)
ClF_5 chlorine pentafluoride

<u>Acids</u>

There are special naming rules for acids that correspond with the **suffix of their corresponding anion** if hydrogen were removed from the acid. Anions ending with *–ide* correspond to acids with the prefix *hydro–* and the suffix *–ic*. Anions ending with *–ate* correspond to acids with no prefix that end with *–ic*. Oxoanions ending with *–ite* have associated acids with no prefix and the suffix *–ous*. The *hypo–* and *per–* prefixes are maintained. Some examples are shown in the following table:

anion	anion name	acid	acid name
Cl^-	chloride	HCl(*aq*)	hydrochloric acid
CN^-	cyanide	HCN(*aq*)	hydrocyanic acid
CO_3^{2-}	carbonate	H_2CO_3(*aq*)	carbonic acid
SO_3^{2-}	sulfite	H_2SO_3(*aq*)	sulfurous acid
SO_4^{2-}	sulfate	H_2SO_4(*aq*)	sulfuric acid
ClO^-	hypochlorite	HClO(*aq*)	hypochlorous acid
ClO_2^-	chlorite	$HClO_2$(*aq*)	chlorous acid
ClO_3^-	chlorate	$HClO_3$(*aq*)	chloric acid
ClO_4^-	perchlorate	$HClO_4$(*aq*)	perchloric acid

Example: What is the molecular formula of phosphorous acid?

Solution: If we remember that the *–ous* acid corresponds to the *–ite* anion, and that the *–ite* anion has one less oxygen than (or has an oxidation number 2 less than) the *–ate* form, we only need to remember that phosphate is PO_4^{3-}. Then we know that phosphite is PO_3^{3-} and phosphorous acid is H_3PO_3.

For additional resources, see:

http://chemistry.alanearhart.org/Tutorials/Nomen/nomen-part7.html has <u>thousands</u> of sample questions. Don't do them all in one sitting.

http://www.iupac.org/reports/provisional/abstract04/connelly_310804.html - IUPAC's latest report on inorganic nomenclature

Properly written and named formulas

Proper formulas will follow the rules of the previous skill. Here are some ways to identify _improper_ formulas that are emphasized below by underlining them.

In all common names for **ionic compounds, number prefixes are not used** to describe the number of anions and cations.
Examples: $CaBr_2$ is calcium bromide, not calcium dibromide.
Ba(OH)$_2$ is barium hydroxide, not barium dihydroxide.
Cu_2SO_4 is copper(I) sulfate, not dicopper sulfate or copper(II) sulfate or

dicopper sulfur tetroxide.

All ionic compounds must have a **neutral charge in their formula** representations.

Example: MgBr is an improperly written formula because Mg ion always exists as 2+ and Br ion is always a 1− ion. $MgBr_2$, magnesium bromide, is correct.

Proper oxoanions and acids use the correct prefixes and suffixes.

Example: HNO_3 is nitric acid because NO_3^- is the nitrate ion.

In both ionic and molecular compounds, the **less electronegative element comes first**.

Example: CSi is an improperly written formula because Si is below C on the periodic table and therefore less electronegative. SiC, silicon carbide, is correct.

Skill 5.3   Analyzing the basic composition and chemical structure of organic compounds (e.g., alkanes, alkenes, alkynes)

The IUPAC is the **International Union of Pure and Applied Chemistry**. **Organic compounds contain carbon,** and have their own branch of chemistry because of the huge number of carbon compounds in nature, including nearly all the molecules in living things. The 1979 IUPAC organic nomenclature is used and taught most often today, and it is the nomenclature described here.

The simplest organic compounds are called **hydrocarbons** because they **contain only carbon and hydrogen.** Hydrocarbon molecules may be divided into the classes of **cyclic** and **open-chain** depending on whether they contain a ring of carbon atoms. Open-chain molecules may be divided into **branched** or **straight-chain** categories.

Hydrocarbons are also divided into classes called **aliphatic** and **aromatic**. Aromatic hydrocarbons are related to benzene and are always cyclic. Aliphatic hydrocarbons may be open-chain or cyclic. Aliphatic cyclic hydrocarbons are called **alicyclic**. Aliphatic hydrocarbons are one of three types: alkanes, alkenes, and alkynes.

Alkanes
Alkanes contain only single bonds. Alkanes have the maximum number of hydrogen atoms possible for their carbon backbone, so they are called **saturated**. Alkenes, alkynes, and aromatics are **unsaturated** because they have fewer hydrogens.

Straight-chain alkanes are also called **normal alkanes**. These are the simplest hydrocarbons. They consist of a linear chain of carbon atoms. The names of these molecules contain the suffix –*ane* and a **root based on the number of carbons in the chain** according to the table on the following page. The first four roots, *meth–*, *eth–*, *prop–*, and *but–* have historical origins in chemistry, and the remaining alkanes contain common Greek number prefixes. Alkanes have the general formula C_nH_{2n+2}.

A single molecule may be represented in multiple ways. Methane and ethane in the table are shown as three-dimensional structures with dashed wedge shapes attaching atoms behind the page and thick wedge shapes attaching atoms in front of the page.

Number of carbons	Name	Formula	Structure
1	Methane	CH_4	
2	Ethane	C_2H_6	
3	Propane	C_3H_8	
4	Butane	C_4H_{10}	
5	Pentane	C_5H_{12}	
6	Hexane	C_6H_{14}	
7	Heptane	C_7H_{16}	
8	Octane	C_8H_{18}	

Additional ways that pentane might be represented are:

n-pentane (the *n* represents a *normal* alkane)
$CH_3CH_2CH_2CH_2CH_3$
$CH_3(CH_2)_3CH_3$

If one hydrogen is removed from an alkane, the residue is called an **alkyl** group. The *–ane* suffix is replaced by an *–yl–* infix when this residue is used as **functional group**. Functional groups are used to systematically build up the names of organic molecules.

Branched alkanes are named using a four-step process:

1) Find the longest continuous carbon chain. This is the parent hydrocarbon.
2) Number the atoms on this chain beginning at the end near the first branch point, so the lowest locant numbers are used. Number functional groups from the attachment point.
3) Determine the numbered locations and names of the substituted alkyl groups. Use *di–*, *tri–*, and similar prefixes for alkyl groups represented more than once. Separate numbers by commas and groups by dashes.
4) List the locations and names of alkyl groups in alphabetical order by their name (ignoring the *di–*, *tri–* prefixes) and end the name with the parent hydrocarbon.

Example—Name the following hydrocarbon:

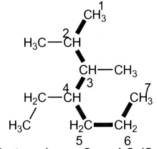

Solution—
1) The longest chain is seven carbons in length, as shown by the bold lines below. This molecule is a heptane.
2) The atoms are numbered from the end nearest the first branch as shown:

3) Methyl groups are located at carbons 2 and 3 (2,3-dimethyl), and an ethyl group is located at carbon 4.
4) "Ethyl" precedes "methyl" alphabetically. The hydrocarbon name is: 4-ethyl-2,3-dimethylheptane.

The following branched alkanes have IUPAC-accepted common names:

Structure	Systematic name	Common name
H₃C – CH – CH₃ / H₃C	2-methylpropane	isobutane
CH₃ / H₃C – CH₂ – CH – CH₃	2-methylbutane	isopentane
CH₃ / H₃C – C(CH₃) – CH₃ / CH₃	2,2-dimethylpropane	neopentane

The following alkyl groups have IUPAC-accepted common names. The systematic names assign a locant number of 1 to the attachment point:

Structure	Systematic name	Common name
H₃C – CH – CH₃	1-methylethyl	isopropyl
H₃C – CH – CH₂ / H₃C	2-methylpropyl	isobutyl
H₃C – CH₂ – CH – CH₃	1-methylpropyl	*sec*-butyl
CH₃ / H₃C – C – CH₃ / CH₃	1,1-dimethylethyl	*tert*-butyl

Alkenes

Alkenes contain one or more double bonds. Alkenes are also called olefins. The suffix used in the naming of alkenes is –*ene*, and the number roots are those used for alkanes of the same length.

A number preceding the name shows the location of the double bond for alkenes of length four and above. Alkenes with one double bond have the general formula C_nH_{2n}. Multiple double bonds are named using –*diene*, –*triene*, etc. The suffix –*enyl*–is used for functional groups after a hydrogen is removed from an alkene. Ethene and propene have the common names **ethylene** and **propylene**. The ethenyl group has the common name **vinyl** and the 2-propenyl group has the common name **allyl**.

Examples:

$H_2C{=}CH_2$ is ethylene or ethene. $H_2C{=}CH$ is a vinyl or ethenyl group.

is propylene or propene. is an allyl or 2-propenyl group.

is 2-hexene.

is 2-methyl-1,3-butadiene (common name: isoprene).

Cis-trans isomerism is often part of the complete name for an alkene. Note that isoprene contains two adjacent double bonds, so it is a **conjugated** molecule.

Alkynes and alkenynes

Alkynes contain one or more triple bonds. They are named in a similar way to alkenes. The suffix used for alkynes is –yne. Ethyne is often called **acetylene**. Alkynes with one triple bond have the general formula C_nH_{2n-2}. Multiple triple bonds are named using –diyne, –triyne, etc. The infix –ynyl–is used for functional groups composed of alkynes after the removal of a hydrogen atom.

Hydrocarbons with **both double and triple bonds are known as alkenynes**. The locant number for the double bond precedes the name, and the locant for the triple bond follows the suffix –en– and precedes the suffix –yne.

Examples: $HC{\equiv}CH$ is acetylene or ethyne.

$HC{\equiv}C{-}CH_2{-}CH_3$ is 1-butyne.

$HC{\equiv}C{-}C{\equiv}C{-}CH_3$ is 1,3-pentadiyne.

is a 4-hexynyl group.

is 1-buten-3-yne. This compound has the common name of vinylacetylene

Cycloalkanes, –enes, and –ynes

Alicyclic hydrocarbons use the prefix cyclo– before the number root for the molecule. The structures for these molecules are often written as if the molecule lay entirely within the plane of the paper even though in reality, these rings dip above and below a single plane. When there is more than one substitution on the ring, numbering begins with the first substitution listed in alphabetical order.

Examples:

H_2C—CH_2

H_2C C H_2 CH_2 is cyclopropane

is methylcyclohexane.

is 1,3-cyclohexadiene.

is 1-ethyl-3-propylcyclobutane.

Cis-trans isomerism is often part of the complete name for a cycloalkane.

Aromatic hydrocarbons
Aromatic hydrocarbons are structurally related to benzene or made up of benzene molecules fused together. These molecules are called **arenes** to distinguish them from alkanes, alkenes, and alkynes. All atoms in arenes lie in the same plane. In other words, aromatic hydrocarbons are flat. Aromatic molecules have electrons in delocalized π orbitals that are free to migrate throughout the molecule.

Substitutions onto the benzene ring are named in alphabetical order using the lowest possible locant numbers. The prefix *phenyl–* be used for C_6H_5- (benzene less a hydrogen) attached as a functional group to a larger hydrocarbon residue. Arenes in general form aryl functional groups. A phenyl group may be represented in a structure by the symbol Ø. The prefix *benzyl–*used for $C_6H_5CH_2-$ (methylbenzene with a hydrogen removed from the methyl group) attached as a functional group.

Examples: (structure) or (structure) is benzene.

(structure) is 2-isopropyl-1,4-dimethylbenzene.

(structure) is 3-phenyloctane or (1-ethylhexyl)benzene.

CHEMISTRY 59

The most often used common names for aromatic hydrocarbons are listed in the following table. Naphthalene is the simplest molecule formed by fused benzene rings.

Structure	Systematic name	Common name
	methylbenzene	toluene
	1,2-dimethylbenzene	*ortho*-xylene or o-xylene
	1,3-dimethylbenzene	*meta*-xylene or *m*-xylene
	1,4-dimethylbenzene	*para*-xylene or *p*-xylene
	ethenylbenzene	styrene
		naphthalene

Skill 5.4 **Distinguishing among the common functional groups of organic compounds (e.g., alcohols, ketones, aldehydes, esters, ethers, carboxylic acids, amines, alkylhalides)**

Many organic molecules contain functional groups that are groups of atoms of a particular arrangement that gives the entire molecule certain characteristics. Function groups are named according to the composition of the group. The carboxyl group is the arrangement of -COOH atoms to make a molecule exhibit acidic properties.

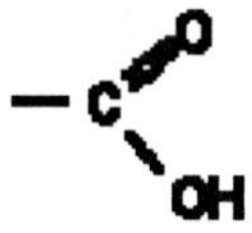

Some functional groups are polar and can ionize. For example, the hydrogen atom in the –COOH group can be removed (providing H^+ ions in solution). When this occurs, the oxygen retains both the electrons it shared with the hydrogen and will give the molecule a negative charge.

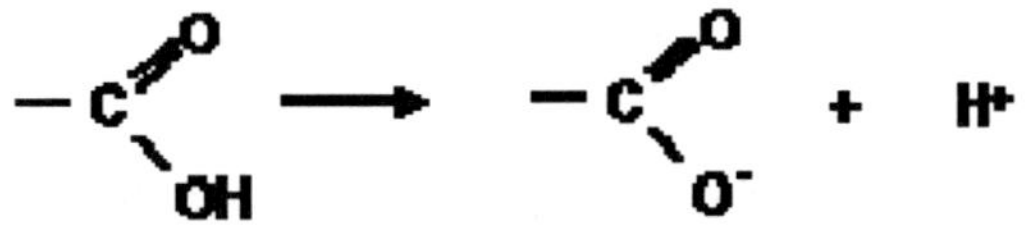

If polar or ionizing functional groups are attached to hydrophobic molecules, the molecule may become hydrophilic due to the functional group. Some ionizing functional groups are: -COOH, -OH, -CO, and $-NH_2$.

Some common functional groups include:

Hydroxyl group:

The hydroxyl group, -OH, is the functional group identifying alcohols. The hydroxyl group makes the molecule polar which increase the solubility of the compound.

Carbonyl group:

The carbonyl group is a -C=O attached to either a carbon chain or a hydrogen atom. It is found in aldehydes and ketones. If the carbon is bonded to a hydrogen, the molecule is an aldehyde.

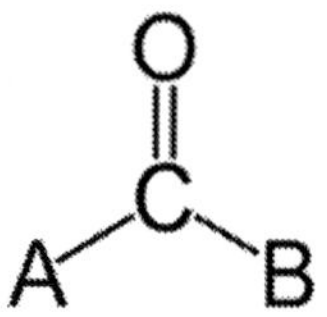

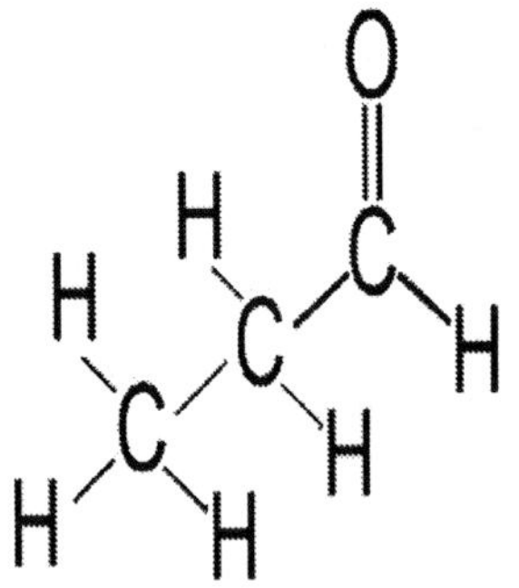

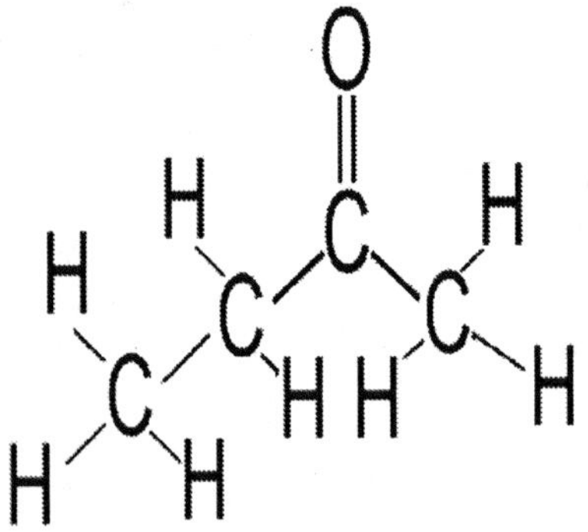

Aldehyde   ketone

If the carbon is attached to two carbon chains, the molecule is a ketone.

The double bonded oxygen atom is highly electronegative so it creates a polar molecule and will exhibit properties of polar molecules.

Carboxyl group:

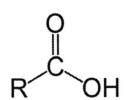

The –COOH group has the ability to donate a proton or H^+ ion giving the molecule acidic properties.

Amino group:

An amino group contains an ammonia-like functional group composed of a nitrogen and two hydrogen atoms covalently bonded. The nitrogen atom has unshared electrons and can add H^+ ions (proton). This gives the molecule basic properties. An organic compound that contains an amino group is called an amine. the amines are weak bases because the unshared electron pair of the nitrogen atom can form a coordinate bond with a proton. Another molecule that contains an amino group is an amino acid. It consists of the –NH_2 group of an amine and the –COOH group of an acid.

This is the amino acid glycine.

H—CH—COOH
    |
    NH_2

Sulfhydryl group:
R—S—H

A **thiol** is a compound that contains the functional group composed of a sulfur atom and a hydrogen atom (-SH). This functional group is referred to either as a *thiol group* or a *sulfhydryl group*. More traditionally, thiols have been referred to as *mercaptans*.

The small difference in electronegativity between the sulfur and the hydrogen atom produces a non-polar covalent bond. This in turn provides for no hydrogen bonding giving thiols lower boiling points and less solubility in water than alcohols of a similar molecular mass.

Phosphate group:

$$-O-\overset{\overset{\displaystyle O}{\|}}{\underset{\underset{\displaystyle O}{|}}{P}}-O$$

The phosphate ion is contained in a hydrocarbon chain making a phosphate group present in the molecule. This molecule is ideal for energy transfer reactions (ATP) because of its symmetry and rotating double bond.

In biological systems, phosphates are most commonly found in the form of adenosine phosphates, (AMP, ADP and ATP) and in DNA and RNA and can be released by the hydrolysis of ATP or ADP.

COMPETENCY 6.0 UNDERSTAND THE PROCESSES OF NUCLEAR TRANSFORMATIONS.

Skill 6.1 Differentiating between nuclear and chemical reactions

Chemical reactions are the interactions of substances resulting in chemical change and change in energy. Chemical reactions involve changes in electron motion and the breaking and forming of chemical bonds. Reactants are the original substances that interact to form distinct products. Endothermic chemical reactions consume energy while exothermic chemical reactions release energy with product formation. Chemical reactions occur continually in nature and are also induced by man for many purposes.

Nuclear reactions, or **atomic reactions**, are reactions that change the composition, energy, or structure of atomic nuclei. Nuclear reactions change the number of protons and neutrons in the nucleus. The two main types of nuclear reactions are fission (splitting of nuclei) and fusion (joining of nuclei). Fusion reactions are exothermic, releasing heat energy. Fission reactions are endothermic, absorbing heat energy. Fission of large nuclei (e.g. uranium) releases energy because the products of fission undergo further fusion reactions. Fission and fusion reactions can occur naturally, but are most recognized as man-made events. Particle acceleration and bombardment with neutrons are two methods of inducing nuclear reactions.

Skill 6.2 Comparing the characteristics (e.g., mass, charge, penetrating power) of different types of emanations from the decay of radioactive elements

Nuclear equations are balanced by equating the sum of mass numbers on both sides of a reaction equation and the sum of atomic numbers on both sides of a reaction equation.

The electron is assigned an atomic number of −1 to account for the conversion during radioactive decay of a neutron to a proton and an emitted electron called a **beta particle**:

$$_0^1 n \rightarrow \, _1^1 p + \, _{-1}^0 e \, .$$

Sulfur-35 is an isotope that decays by beta emission:

$$_{16}^{35} S \rightarrow \, _{17}^{35} Cl + \, _{-1}^0 e \, .$$

In most cases nuclear reactions result in a **nuclear transmutation** from one element to another. Transmutation was originally connected to the mythical "philosopher's stone" of alchemy that could turn cheaper elements into gold. When Frederick Soddy and Ernest Rutherford first recognized that radioactive decay was changing one element into another, Soddy remembered saying, "Rutherford, this is transmutation!" Rutherford replied, "Soddy, don't call it transmutation. They'll have our heads off as alchemists."

Isotopes may also decay by **electron capture** from an orbital outside the nucleus:

$$^{196}_{79}\text{Au} + ^{0}_{-1}e \rightarrow ^{196}_{78}\text{Pt} .$$

A **positron** is a particle with the small mass of an electron but with a positive charge. A positron emission converts a proton into a neutron. Carbon-11 decays by positron emission:

$$^{11}_{6}\text{C} \rightarrow ^{11}_{5}\text{B} + ^{0}_{1}e .$$

Large isotopes often decay by **alpha particle** emission:

$$^{238}_{92}\text{U} \rightarrow ^{234}_{90}\text{Th} + ^{4}_{2}\text{He} .$$

Gamma rays are high-energy electromagnetic radiation, and gamma radiation is almost always emitted when other radioactive decay occurs. Gamma rays usually aren't written into equations because neither the mass number nor the atomic number is altered. One exception is the annihilation of an electron by a positron, an event that only produces gamma radiation:

$$^{0}_{-1}e + ^{0}_{1}e \rightarrow 2^{0}_{0}\gamma .$$

Skill 6.3 Analyzing the processes of natural radioactivity and artificial transmutation

Some nuclei are unstable and emit particles and electromagnetic radiation. These emissions from the nucleus are known as **radioactivity**; the unstable isotopes are known as **radioisotopes**; and the nuclear reactions that spontaneously alter them are known as **radioactive decay**. Particles commonly involved in nuclear reactions are listed in the following table:

Particle	Neutron	Proton	Electron	Positron	Alpha particle	Beta particle	Gamma rays
Symbol	$^{1}_{0}n$	$^{1}_{1}p$ or $^{1}_{1}H$	$^{0}_{-1}e$	$^{0}_{1}e$	$^{4}_{2}\alpha$ or $^{4}_{2}He$	$^{0}_{-1}\beta$ or $^{0}_{-1}e$	$^{0}_{0}\gamma$

The **half-life** of a reaction is the **time required to consume half the reactant**. The rate of radioactive decay for an isotope is usually expressed as a half-life. Solving these problems is straightforward if the given amount of time is an exact multiple of the half-life. For example, the half-life of ^{233}Pa is 27.0 days. This means that of 200 grams of ^{233}Pa will decay according to the following table:

Day	Number of half-lives	^{233}Pa remaining	^{233}Pa decayed since day 0
0	0	200 g	0 g
27.0	1	100 g	100 g
54.0	2	50.0 g	150.0 g
81.0	3	25.0 g	175.0 g
108.0	4	12.5 g	187.5 g

Regardless of whether the given amount of time is an exact multiple of the half-life, the following equation may be used:

$$A_{remaining} = A_{initially}\left(\frac{1}{2}\right)^{\frac{t}{t_{halflife}}}$$

where: $A_{remaining} \Rightarrow$ amount remaining

$A_{initially} \Rightarrow$ amount initially

$t \Rightarrow$ time

$t_{halflife} \Rightarrow$ half-life

Skill 6.4   Solving problems involving half-life of radioactive particles

Every radioisotope has its own characteristic rate of decay. The half-life of an isotope is the time it takes for half the atoms of the radioactive material in a given sample to decay.

For example, the half-life of carbon-14 is 5730 years. If there are 25 grams of carbon-14 in a petrified log, then 5730 years later it will contain 12.5 grams of carbon-14. Another 5730 years later it will contain 6.25 grams of C-14.

Example: The half-life of barium-139 is 86 minutes. If you have a 20-gram sample of barium-139, how much would be left after 4 hours and 18 minutes?

Solution: At 0 minutes, the beginning, you have 20 grams
At 86 minutes (1 hr 26 min), you have half of 20 grams (20/2) or 10 g
At 2 x 86 minutes, or 172 minutes (2 hr 52 min), you have (10/2) or 5 g
At 3 x 86 min, or 258 min (4 hr 18 min), you have (5/2) or 2.5 g

Skill 6.5   Calculating the energies associated with various nuclear reactions

Isotopes are called radioisotopes when they have unstable nuclei that are radioactive. **Alpha particles** (α) are positively charged particles ($^+2$) emitted from a radioactive nucleus. They consist of two protons and two neutrons and are identical to the nucleus of a helium atom (^4_2He).

Example: $^{226}_{88}Ra \rightarrow {}^4_2He + {}^{222}_{86}Rn + 4.87$ MeV

When an atom loses an alpha particle, the Z number (atomic number) is lower by two, so you would move back two spaces on the periodic table to find what the new element is. The new element has an A number (atomic mass number) that is four less than the original element. The energy released by radioactive decay is typically reported in electronvolts (eV), a tiny quantity of energy equal to 1.602×10^{-19} J. Using Einsten's mass-energy equivalence ($E=mc^2$), we can calculate the energy released by alpha decay by determining the difference in mass between the products and reactants of decay.   In this example, the difference between the mass of the radium (226.02536 u) and the sum of the masses of the radon (222.01753 u) and the helium (4.00260 u) is 0.00523 u, or 4.87 MeV.

One electron mass = 0.0005486 u = 0.511 MeV / (number of particles)^2

Because alpha particles are large and heavy, paper or clothing or even dead skin cells shield people from their effects.

Beta rays (β) are negatively charged (-1) and fast moving because they are actually electrons. They are written as an electron $^0_{-1}e$ (along with a proton), which is emitted from the nucleus as a neutron decays. A well known is example is beta decay is exploited for carbon dating; carbon-14 decays by emitting a beta particle.

Example: $^{14}_6C \rightarrow {}^{14}_7N + {}^0_{-1}e$

The Z number (atomic number) actually adds one since its total must be the same on both the left and the right of the arrow and the electron on the right adds a negative one. The A (atomic mass) number is unchanged. The Z determines what the element is, so look for it on the periodic table to determine the product. The electrons are at various energies ranging from 0 to 1.2 MeV. Beta particles from the various radioactive species each have specific energies. Metal foil or wood is needed to shield from its effects.

Gamma rays (γ) are high energy electromagnetic waves. They are the same kind of radiation as visible light but of much shorter wavelength and higher frequency. Gamma rays have no mass or charge, so the Z (atomic) and A (atomic mass) numbers are not affected. Radioactive atoms often emit gamma rays along with either alpha or beta particles. Gamma rays from a specific radioactive species have their own specific energies. Protection from gamma radiation requires lead or concrete.

Example 1 (with an alpha): $\quad {}^{226}_{88}\text{Ra} \rightarrow {}^{222}_{86}\text{Rn} + {}^{4}_{2}\text{He} + \gamma$

Example 2 (with a beta): $\quad {}^{234}_{90}\text{Th} \rightarrow {}^{234}_{91}\text{Pa} + {}^{0}_{-1}e + \gamma$

A **positron** is a particle with the mass of an electron but a positive charge ($ {}^{0}_{+1}e$). It may be emitted as a proton changes to a neutron.

Transmutation is the conversion of an atom of one element to an atom of another element such as occurs in alpha and beta radiation. It also occurs when high-energy particles (such as protons, neutrons, or alpha particles) bombard the nucleus of an atom. All the elements in the periodic table with atomic numbers above 92, called the transuranium elements, are radioactive elements that have been synthesized in nuclear reactors and nuclear accelerators.

Example: ${}^{238}_{92}\text{U} + {}^{1}_{0}n \rightarrow {}^{239}_{92}\text{U} \rightarrow {}^{0}_{-1}e + {}^{239}_{93}\text{Np} \rightarrow {}^{239}_{94}\text{Pu} + {}^{0}_{-1}e$

Nuclear fission is the splitting of a nucleus into smaller fragments by bombardment with neutrons. Fission releases enormous amounts of energy. Controlled fission is the source of the energy in nuclear power plants.

Example: ${}^{235}_{92}\text{U} + {}^{1}_{0}n \rightarrow {}^{145}_{56}\text{Ba} + {}^{88}_{36}\text{Kr} + 3\,{}^{1}_{0}n + 200 \text{ MeV}$

In nuclear fusion hydrogen nuclei fuse together to make helium nuclei. Fusion releases even more energy than fission.

Example: ${}^{2}_{1}\text{H} + {}^{3}_{1}\text{H} \rightarrow {}^{4}_{2}\text{He} + {}^{1}_{0}n + 17.6 \text{ MeV energy}$

The energy released in a nuclear reaction such as this is calculated by subtracting the mass of the reaction products from the mass of the interacting particles. The hydrogen bomb is an example of a fusion device.

Skill 6.6   Demonstrating knowledge of nuclear fission and its applications

A heavy nucleus may split apart into smaller nuclei by **nuclear fission.** **Nuclear power** currently provides 17% of the world's electricity. Heat is generated by **nuclear fission of uranium-235 or plutonium-239.** This heat is then converted to electricity by boiling water and forcing the steam through a turbine. Fission of ^{235}U and ^{239}Pu occurs when **a neutron strikes the nucleus and breaks it apart into smaller nuclei and additional neutrons.** One possible fission reaction is:

$$_{0}^{1}n + _{92}^{235}U \rightarrow _{56}^{141}Ba + _{36}^{92}Kr + 3\,_{0}^{1}n$$

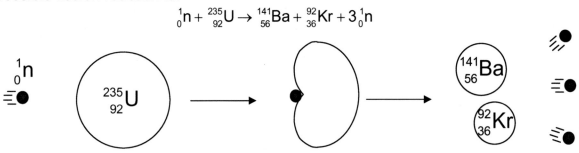

Gamma radiation, kinetic energy from the neutrons themselves, and the decay of the fission products (^{141}Ba and ^{92}Kr in the example above) all produce heat. The neutrons produced by the reaction strike other uranium atoms and produce more neutrons and more energy in a **chain reaction.** If enough neutrons are lost, the chain reaction stops and the process is called **subcritical.** If the mass of uranium is large enough so that one neutron on average from each fission event triggers another fission, the reaction is said to be **critical.** If the mass is larger than this so that few neutrons escape, the reaction is called **supercritical.** The chain reaction then multiplies the number of fissions that occur and the violent explosion of an atomic bomb will take place if the process is not stopped. The concentration of **fissile material** in nuclear power plants is sufficient for a critical reaction to occur but too low for a supercritical reaction to take place.

The alpha decay of **Plutonium-238 is used as a heat source for localized power generation** in space probes and in heart pacemakers from the 1970s.

Skill 6.7   Recognizing the role of nuclear fusion in the production of elements more massive than hydrogen

When two nuclei collide, they sometimes stick to each other and synthesize a new nucleus. This **nuclear fusion** was first demonstrated by the synthesis of oxygen from nitrogen and alpha particles:

$$_{7}^{14}N + _{2}^{4}He \rightarrow _{8}^{17}O + _{1}^{1}H.$$

Fusion is also used to create new heavy elements, causing periodic tables to grow out of date every few years. In 2004, IUPAC approved the name roentgenium (in honor of Wilhelm Roentgen, the discoverer of X-rays) for the element first synthesized in 1994 by the following reaction:

$$_{83}^{209}\text{Bi} + _{28}^{64}\text{Ni} \rightarrow _{111}^{272}\text{Rg} + _{0}^{1}\text{n}.$$

The most promising nuclear reaction for producing power by nuclear fusion is:

$$_{1}^{2}\text{H} + _{1}^{3}\text{H} \rightarrow _{2}^{4}\text{He} + _{0}^{1}\text{n}$$

Hydrogen-2 is called **deuterium** and is often represented by the symbol D. Hydrogen-3 is known as **tritium** and is often represented by the symbol T. Nuclear reactions between very light atoms similar to the reaction above are the energy source behind the sun and the hydrogen bomb.

SUBAREA II.   **CHEMICAL BONDING AND ENERGY**

COMPETENCY 7.0   UNDERSTAND THE DIFFERENT TYPES OF CHEMICAL
                  BONDS, THE FORMATION OF THESE BONDS, AND
                  THE EFFECT BOND TYPE HAS ON THE PROPERTIES
                  OF SUBSTANCES.

Skill 7.1   **Comparing the characteristics of the different types of bonds
              between particles (e.g., bond strength, polarity, hybridization)**

Chemical compounds form when two or more atoms join together. A stable
compound occurs when the total energy of the combination of the atoms together
is lower than the atoms separately. The combined state suggests an attractive
force exists between the atoms. This attractive force is called a chemical bond.

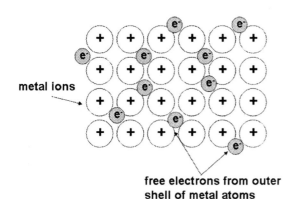

metal ions →

free electrons from outer
shell of metal atoms

Metallic bonds occur when the bonding
is between two metals. Metallic
properties, such as low ionization
energies, conductivity, and malleability,
suggest that metals possess strong forces
of attraction between atoms, but still have
electrons that are able to move freely in
all directions throughout the metal. This
creates a "sea of electrons" model where
electrons are quickly and easily
transferred between metal atoms. In this
model, the outer shell electrons are free to
move. The metallic bond is the force of attraction that results from the moving
electrons and the positive nuclei left behind. The strength of metal bonds usually
results in regular structures and high melting and boiling points.

Ionic Bonds
An **ionic bond** describes
the electrostatic forces
that exist between
**particles of opposite
charge.** An ionic bond
is the result of an
atom(s) losing electrons
to form a positive ion
being attracted to an
atom(s) that has gained
electrons to form a
negative ion.

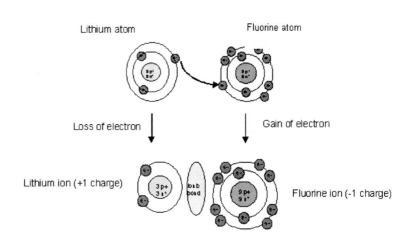

Lithium atom   Fluorine atom

Loss of electron   Gain of electron

Lithium ion (+1 charge)   Fluorine ion (-1 charge)

Due to low ionization energies, metals have a tendency to lose valence electrons relatively easily, whereas non-metals, which have high ionization energies and high electronegativites, gain electrons easily. This produces cations (positively charged) and anions (negatively charged). Coulomb's Law says that opposites attract, and so do the oppositely charged ions. This *electrostatic interaction* between the anion and the cation results in an ionic bond. Ionic bonds will only occur when a metal is bonding to a non-metal, and is the result of the periodic trends (ionization energy and electronegativity). Elements that form an ionic bond with each other have a large difference in their electronegativity. Anions and cations pack together into a crystal **lattice** as shown to the right for NaCl. Ionic compounds are also known as **salts**.

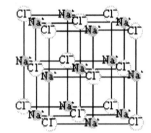

Single and multiple covalent bonds

A **covalent bond** forms when at least one pair of electrons is shared by two atoms. The shared electrons are found in the valence energy level and lead to a lower energy if they are shared in a way that creates a noble gas configuration (a full octet). Covalent, or molecular, bonds occur when a non-metal is bonding to a non-metal. This is due primarily to the fact that non-metals have high ionization energies and high electronegativities. Neither atom wants to give up electrons; both want to gain them. In order to satisfy both octets, the electrons can be shared between the two atoms.

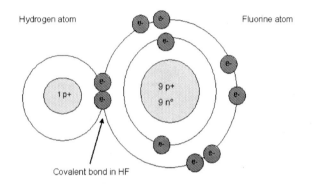

Sharing of electrons can be equal or unequal, resulting in a separation of charge (polar) or an even distribution of charge (non-polar). The polarity of a bond can be determined through an examination of the electronegativities of the atoms involved in the bond. The more electronegative atom will have a stronger attraction to the electrons, thus possessing the electrons more of the time. This results in a partial negative charge (δ^-) on the more electronegative atom and a partial positive charge (δ^+) on the less electronegative atom.

The simplest covalent bond is between the two single electrons of hydrogen atoms. Covalent bonds may be represented by an electron pair (a pair of dots) or a line as shown below. The shared pair of electrons provides each H atom with two electrons in its valence shell (the 1s orbital), so both have the stable electron configuration of helium.

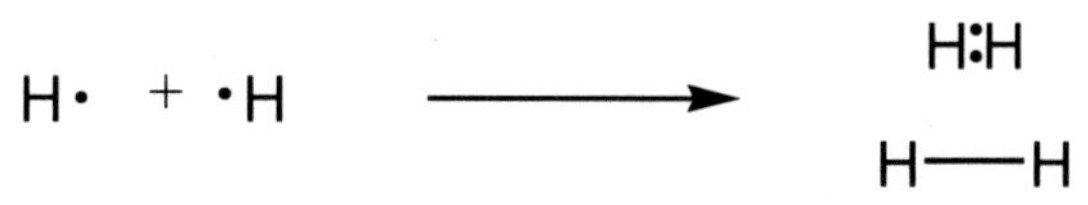

H· + ·H $\longrightarrow$ H:H
H——H

Chlorine molecules have 7 electrons in their valence shell and share a pair of electrons so both have the stable electron configuration of argon.

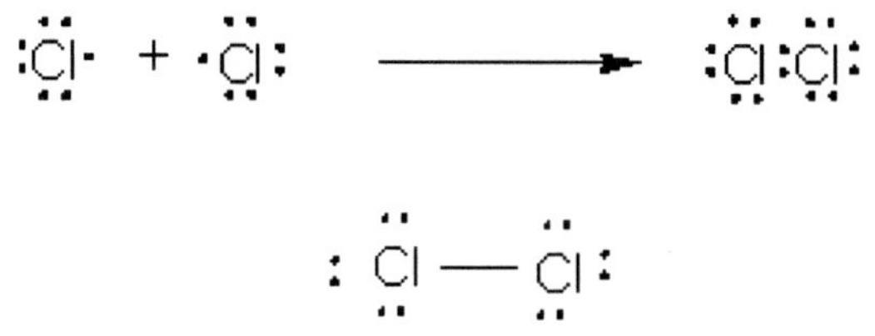

:Cl· + ·Cl: $\longrightarrow$:Cl:Cl:

: Cl — Cl :

In the previous two examples, a single pair of electrons was shared, and the resulting bond is referred to as a **single bond**. When two electron pairs are shared, two lines are drawn, representing a **double bond**, and three shared pairs of electrons represents a **triple bond** as shown below for CO_2 and N_2. The remaining electrons are in **unshared pairs**.

O :: C :: O
O = C = O

: N : : N :
: N ≡ N :

Polar/nonpolar covalent bonds

Electron pairs shared between **two atoms of the same element are shared equally**. At the other extreme, **for ionic bonding there is no electron sharing** because the electron is transferred completely from one atom to the other. Most bonds fall somewhere between these two extremes, and the electrons are **shared unequally**. This will increase the probability that the shared electrons will be located on one of the two atoms, giving that atom a **partial negative charge**, and the other atom a **partial positive charge** as shown below for gaseous HCl. Such bonds are referred to as **polar bonds**. A particle with a positive and a negative region is called a **dipole**. A lower-case delta (δ) is used to indicate partial charge or an arrow is draw from the partial positive to the partial negative atom.

$$\overset{\delta+}{\text{H}}\text{---}\overset{\delta-}{\text{Cl}} \qquad \overset{\longrightarrow}{\text{H---Cl}}$$

Electronegativity is a measure of **the ability of an atom to attract electrons** in a chemical bond. Metallic elements have low electronegativities and nonmetallic elements have high electronegativities.

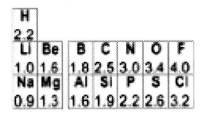

Linus Pauling developed the concept of electronegativity and its relationship to different types of bonds in the 1930s.

A **large electronegativity difference** (greater than 1.7) results in an **ionic bond**. Any bond composed of two different atoms will be slightly polar, but for a **small electronegativity difference** (less than 0.4), the distribution of charge in the bond is so nearly equal that the result is called a **nonpolar covalent bond**. An **intermediate electronegativity difference** (from 0.4 to 1.7) results in a **polar covalent bond**. HCl is polar covalent because Cl has a very high electronegativity (it is near F in the periodic table) and H is a nonmetal (and so it will form a covalent bond with Cl), but H is near the dividing line between metals and nonmetals, so there is still a significant electronegativity difference between H and Cl. Using the numbers in the table above, the electronegativity for Cl is 3.2 and it is 2.2 for H. The difference of 3.2 – 2.2 = 1.0 places this bond in the middle of the range for polar covalent bonds.

Bond type is actually a continuum as shown in the following chart for common bonds. Note that the **C-H bond** is considered **nonpolar**.

Type of bonding	Electronegativity difference	Bond
Very ionic		$Fr^+\!-\!F^-$
		$Na^+\!-\!F^-$
	3.0	
Ionic		$Na^+\!-\!Cl^-$
	2.0	$Na^+\!-\!Br^-$
Mostly ionic		$Na^+\!-\!I^-$
Mostly polar covalent	1.5	$C^{\square+}\!-\!F^{\square-}$
		$H^{\square+}\!-\!O^{\square-}$
Polar covalent	1.0	$H^{\square+}\!-\!Cl^{\square-}$
		$C^{\delta+}\!=\!O^{\delta\check{s}}$
		$H^{\square+}\!-\!N^{\square-}$
		$C^{\square+}\!-\!Cl^{\square-}$
	0.5	$C^{\delta+}\!\equiv\!N^{\delta\check{s}}$
Mostly nonpolar covalent		$C\!-\!H$
Fully nonpolar covalent	0	$H_2, N_2, O_2,$ $F_2, Cl_2, Br_2, I_2,$ $C\!-\!C, S\!-\!S$

Increasing ionic character ⇑

A **polar molecule** has positive and negative regions as shown above for HCl. **Bond polarity is necessary but not sufficient for molecular polarity.** A molecule containing polar bonds will still be nonpolar if the most negative and most positive location occurs at the same point. In other words, **in a polar molecule, bond polarities must not cancel**.

To determine if a molecule is polar perform the following steps.

1) Draw the molecular structure.
2) Assign a polarity to each bond with an arrow (remember C-H is nonpolar). If none of the bonds are polar, the molecule is nonpolar.
3) Determine if the polarities cancel each other in space. If they do, the molecule is nonpolar. Otherwise the molecule is polar.

Examples: Which of the following are polar molecules: CO_2, CH_2Cl_2, CCl_4?

Solution: 1)

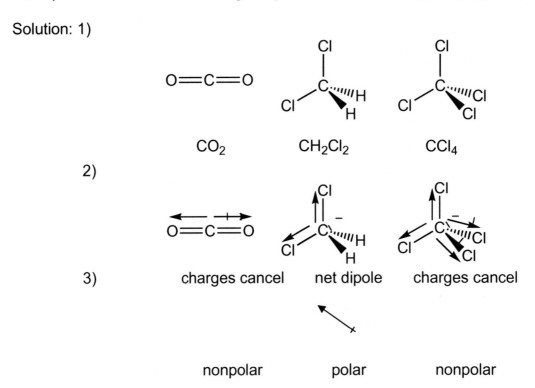

The polarity of molecules is critical for determining a good solvent for a given solute. Additional practice on the topic of polar bonds and molecules is available at http://cowtownproductions.com/cowtown/genchem/09_17M.htm.

Skill 7.2   Predicting the properties of a substance (e.g., ductility, electrical and thermal conductivity) based on the type of bonds

Covalent bonds in a network solid
A covalent network solid may be considered **one large molecule connected by covalent bonds**. These materials are **very hard, strong, and have a high melting point**. Diamond, C_n or C_∞, and quartz, $(SiO_2)_n$ or $(SiO_2)_\infty$, are two examples.

Ionic bonds
All common salts (compounds with **ionic bonds**) are solids at room temperature. **Salts are brittle, have a high melting point**, and do not conduct electricity because their ions are not free to move in the crystal lattice. Salts do conduct electricity in molten form. The formation of a salt is a highly exothermic reaction between a metal and a nonmetal.

Salts in solid form are generally stable compounds, but in molten form or in solution, their component ions often react to form a more stable salt.

Some salts decompose to form more stable salts, as in the decomposition of molten potassium chlorate to form potassium chloride and oxygen:
$$2KClO_3(l) \rightarrow 2KCl(s) + 3O_2(g).$$

Metallic bonds
The physical properties of metals are attributed to the **electron sea model of metallic bonds** shown on the right.   Metals **conduct heat and electricity** because electrons are not associated with the bonding between two specific atoms and they are able to flow through the material. They are called **delocalized** electrons. Metals are **lustrous** because electrons at their surface reflect light at many different wavelengths. Metals are **malleable** and **ductile** because the electrons are 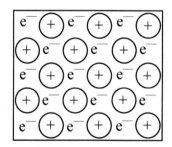 able to rearrange their positions to maintain the integrity of the solid when the metallic lattice is deformed, acting like glue between the cations. The strengths of different metallic bonds can be related to the relative amounts and positions of electrons in this glue.

Alkali metals contain only one valence electron ("less glue"), and that electron is a considerable distance away from the nucleus ("weaker glue") because it is shielded from nuclear attraction by the noble gas configuration of the remaining electrons. The result is a weak metallic bond and a low melting point. Heavier alkali metals contain a valence electron even further from the nucleus, resulting in a very weak metallic bond and a lowering of the melting point. With two valence electrons and smaller atoms, alkaline earth metals have stronger metallic bonds than the alkali metals. This explains some of the periodic trends.

The metal with the weakest metallic bonds is mercury. Hg is a liquid at room temperature because Hg atoms hold on tightly to a stable valence configuration of full *s*, *f*, and *d* subshells. Fewer electrons are shared to create bonds than in other metals.

The reactivity of metals increases with lower electronegativity in reactions with nonmetals to form ionic bonds.

Skill 7.3   Predicting molecular geometry based on Lewis structures

Lewis dot structures are a method for keeping track of each atom's valence electrons in a molecule. Drawing Lewis structures is a three-step process:

1) Add the number of valence shell electrons for each atom. If the compound is an anion, add the charge of the ion to the total electron count because anions have "extra" electrons. If the compound is a cation, subtract the charge of the ion.
2) Write the symbols for each atom showing how the atoms connect to each other.
3) Draw a single bond (one pair of electron dots or a line) between each pair of connected atoms. Place the remaining electrons around the atoms as unshared pairs. If every atom has an octet of electrons except H atoms with two electrons, the Lewis structure is complete. Shared electrons count towards both atoms. If there are too few electron pairs to do this, draw multiple bonds (two or three pairs of electron dots between the atoms) until an octet is around each atom (except H atoms with two). If there are two many electron pairs to complete the octets with single bonds then the octet rule Is broken for this compound.

Example: Draw the Lewis structure of HCN.
Solution:
1) From their locations in the main group of the periodic table, we know that each atom contributes the following number of electrons: H—1, C—4, N—5. Because it is a neutral compound, the molecule will have a total of 10 valence electrons.
2) The atoms are connected with C at the center and will be drawn as: H   C   N.

Having H as the central atom is impossible because H has one valence electron and will always only have a single bond to one other atom. If N were the central atom then the formula would probably be written as HNC.

3) Connecting the atoms with 10 electrons in single bonds gives the structure to the right. H has two electrons to fill its valence subshells, but C and N only have six each. A triple bond between these atoms fulfills the octet rule for C and N and is the correct Lewis structure.

$$H : C \vdots\vdots\vdots N \vdots$$

To select the most probable Lewis dot structure for a compound or molecule that follows the octet rule, review the structures and compare to the method for constructing Lewis dot structures from the previous page.

Example: Which of the electron-dot structures given below for nitrous oxide (laughing gas), N_2O, is/are acceptable?

$$\text{I. } \quad \overset{..}{:}N::\overset{..}{N}:\overset{..}{O}:$$

$$\text{II. } \quad \overset{..}{:}N:\overset{..}{N}::\overset{..}{O}:$$

$$\text{III. } \quad :N:::N::\overset{..}{O}:$$

Solution: Both nitrogen and oxygen follow the octect rule so the Lewis structure should show each atom in the molecule with 8 electrons, either unshared or shared. Upon examination, only choice I provides each atom in the molecule with 8 electrons. Choice II has only 6 electrons around each of the nitrogen atoms and choice III has 10 electrons around the center nitrogen atom.

Molecular geometry is predicted using the valence-shell electron-pair repulsion or **VSEPR** model. VSEPR uses the fact that **electron pairs around the central atom of a molecule repel each other**. Imagine you are one of two pairs of electrons in bonds around a central atom (like a bonds in BeH_2 in the table below). You want to be as far away from the other electron pair as possible, so you will be on one side of the atom and the other pair will be on the other side. There is a straight line (or a 180° angle) between you to the other electron pair on the other side of the nucleus. In general, electron pairs lie at the **largest possible angles** from each other.

Electron pairs	Geometrical arrangement		Predicted bond angles	Example
2		Linear	180°	
3		Trigonal planar	120°	
4		Tetrahedral	109.5°	
5		Trigonal bipyramidal	120° and 90°	
6		Octahedral	90°	

X represents a generic central atom. Lone pair electrons on F are not shown in the example molecules.

<u>Unshared Electron Pairs</u>
The **shape of a molecule is given by the location of its atoms**. These are connected to central atoms by shared electrons, but unshared electrons also have an important impact on molecular shape. Unshared electrons may determine the angles between atoms. Molecular shapes in the following table take into account total and unshared electron pairs.

Electron pairs	Molecular shape				
	All shared pairs	1 unshared pair	2 unshared pairs	3 unshared pairs	4 unshared pairs
2	A — X — A Linear				
3	Trigonal planar	Bent			
4	Tetrahedral	Trigonal pyramidal	Bent		
5	Trigonal bipyramidal	Seesaw or sawhorse	T-shaped	Linear	
6	Octahedral	Square pyramidal	Square planar	T-shaped	Linear

X represents a generic central atom bonded to atoms labeled A.

Altered Bond Angles

Unpaired electrons also have a less dramatic impact on molecular shape. Imagine you are an unshared electron pair around a molecule's central atom. The shared electron pairs are each attracted partially to the central atom and partially to the other atom in the bond, but you are different. You are attracted to the central atom, but there's nothing on your other side, so you are free to expand in that direction. That expansion means that you take up more room than the other electron pairs, and they are all squeezed a little closer together because of you. Multiple bonds have a similar effect because more space is required for more electrons. In general, **unshared electron pairs and multiple bonds decrease the angles between the remaining bonds**. A few examples are shown in the following tables.

Compound	CH_4	NH_3	H_2O
Unshared electrons	0	1	2
Shape	Tetrahedral	Trigonal pyramidal	Bent

Compound	BF_3	C_2H_4 (ethylene)
Multiple bonds	0	1
Shape	Trigonal planar	Trigonal planar

Summary

In order to use VSEPR to predict molecular geometry, perform the following steps:

1) Write out Lewis dot structures.
2) Use the Lewis structure to determine the number of unshared electron pairs and bonds around each central atom counting multiple bonds as one (for now).
3) The second table of this skill gives the arrangement of total and unshared electron pairs to account for electron repulsions around each central atom.
4) For multiple bonds or unshared electron pairs, decrease the angles slightly between the remaining bonds around the central atom.
5) Combine the results from the previous two steps to determine the shape of the entire molecule.

http://www.shef.ac.uk/chemistry/vsepr/ is a good site for explaining and visualizing molecular geometries using VSEPR.

http://cowtownproductions.com/cowtown/genchem/09_16T.htm provides some practice for determining molecular shape

Hybridized atomic orbitals

Electron shell structures are built up by considering different energy levels for different subshells to explain spectroscopic data about individual atoms. However, when Lewis dot structures are drawn or molecular geometries are determined (later in this skill), all valence electrons are treated identically to explain the bonding between atoms regardless of whether the electrons once belonged to the s or the p subshell of their atom. Reconciling these views of the individual and the bonded atom requires a theory known as hybridization.

Hybridization describes the pre-bonding **promotion of one or more electrons** from a lower energy subshell to a higher energy subshell followed by a **combination** of the orbitals into degenerate **hybrid orbitals**.

Example: A boron atom has the valence electron configuration $2s^2 2p^1$ as shown to the right. Before bonding to three other atoms, the capability to form three equivalent bonds is achieved by hybridization. First a $2s$ electron is promoted to an empty p orbital. Next the occupied orbitals combine into three hybrid $2sp^2$ orbitals. Now three electrons in degenerate orbitals are available to create covalent bonds with three atoms.

Hybridization occurs for atoms with a valence electron configuration of ns^2, $ns^2 np^1$, or $ns^2 p^2$. For period 2, this corresponds with Be, B, C, and N in the NH_3^+ ion.

An atom joined to its neighbor by **multiple covalent bonds** is prepared for bonding by hybridization with incomplete combination. Electrons that remain in p orbitals can contribute additional bonds between the same two atoms.

Example: An isolated carbon atom has the valence electron configuration $2s^2 2p^2$. Hybridization to four $2sp^3$ orbitals occurs before bonding to four atoms. Three hybrid sp^2 orbitals form if there is a double bond so the C atom is bonded to three atoms and one electron remains in the p orbital. Two hybrid sp orbitals occur if there is a triple bond or two double bonds. In this case, C is bonded to two atoms with two electrons remaining in p orbitals.

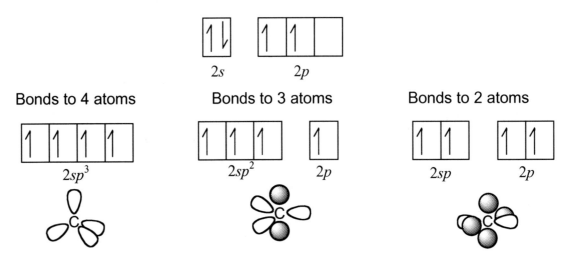

Note: p orbitals are shaded in the diagrams. These models are meant to illustrate the **locations** and **angles** of hybrid and p orbitals relative to the central atom. A mathematical solution would also show that each type of hybrid orbital (sp^3, sp^2, and sp) has a slightly different shape from the other two.

See
http://www.mhhe.com/physsci/chemistry/essentialchemistry/flash/hybrv18.swf
for a flash animation tutorial of hybridization.

COMPETENCY 8.0 UNDERSTAND THE DIFFERENT TYPES OF INTERMOLECULAR FORCES AND THE EFFECTS THEY HAVE ON THE PROPERTIES OF SUBSTANCES.

Skill 8.1 Identifying and comparing the characteristics of the different types of intermolecular forces

Ion-dipole interactions
Salts tend to dissolve in several polar solvents. An ion with a full charge in a polar solvent will **orient nearby solvent molecules** so that their opposite partial charges are pointing towards the ion. In aqueous solution, certain salts react to form solid **precipitates** if a combination of their ions is insoluble.

Hydrogen bonds
Hydrogen bonds are particularly **strong dipole-dipole interactions** that form between the H-atom of one molecule and an **F, O, or N** atom of an adjacent molecule. The partial positive charge on the hydrogen atom is attracted to the partial negative charge on the electron pair of the other atom. The hydrogen bond between two water molecules is shown as the dashed line below:

Dipole-dipole interactions
The intermolecular forces between polar molecules are known as dipole-dipole interactions. The partial positive charge of one molecule is attracted to the partial negative charge of its neighbor.

Ion-induced dipole
When a nonpolar molecule (or a noble gas atom) encounters an ion, its **electron density is temporarily distorted** resulting in an **induced dipole** that will be attracted to the ion. Intermolecular attractions due to induced dipoles in a non-polar molecule are known as **London forces or Van der Waals interactions**. These are very weak intermolecular forces.

For example, carbon tetrachloride, CCl_4, has polar bonds but is a nonpolar molecule due to the symmetry of those bonds. An aluminum cation will draw the unbonded electrons of the chlorine atom towards it, distorting the molecule (this distortion has been exaggerated in the figure) and creating an attractive force as shown by the dashed line below.

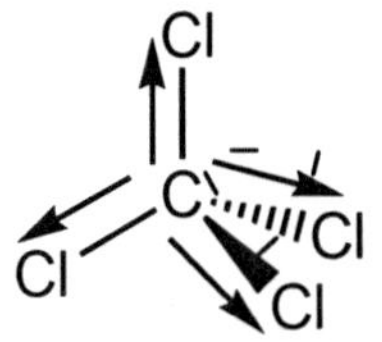

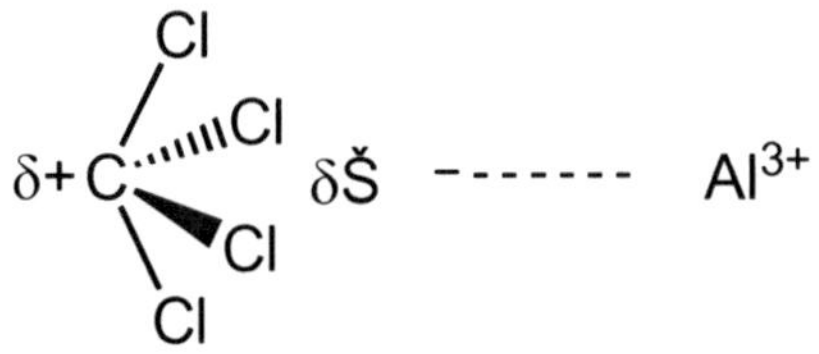

Dipole-induced dipole

The partial charge of **a permanent dipole may also induce a dipole in a nonpolar molecule** resulting in an attraction similar to-but weaker than-that created by an ion.

London dispersion force: induced dipole-induced dipole

The above two examples required a permanent charge to induce a dipole in a nonpolar molecule. A nonpolar molecule may also induce a temporary dipole on its identical neighbor in a pure substance. These forces occur because at any given moment, electrons are located within a certain region of the molecule, and **the instantaneous location of electrons will induce a temporary dipole** on neighboring molecules. For example, an isolated helium atom consists of a nucleus with a 2+ charge and two electrons in a spherical electron density cloud. An attraction of He atoms due to London dispersion forces (shown below by the dashed line) occurs because when the electrons happen to be distributed unevenly on one atom, a dipole is induced on its neighbor. This dipole is due to intermolecular repulsion of electrons and the attraction of electrons to neighboring nuclei.

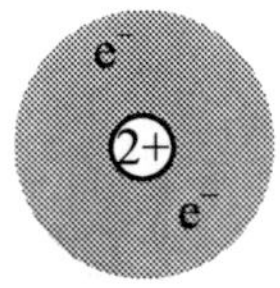

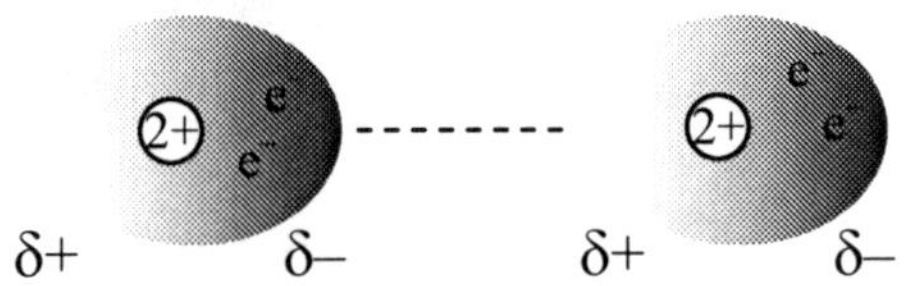

The strength of London dispersion forces **increases for larger molecules** because a larger electron cloud is more easily polarized. The strength of London dispersion forces also **increases for molecules with a larger surface area** because there is greater opportunity for electrons to influence neighboring molecules if there is more potential contact between the molecules. Paraffin in candles is an example of a solid held together by weak London forces between large molecules. These materials are soft.

Skill 8.2   Determining the type of intermolecular force present between the particles of a given substance

Intermolecular forces are a class of attractions between molecules of a substance that are weaker than covalent bonds. The strength of intermolecular forces determines the physical properties of a substance such as melting point and boiling point. The types of intermolecular forces are hydrogen bonding, dipole-dipole forces, ion-dipole forces, and London dispersion forces.

Hydrogen bonding is the strongest type of intermolecular attraction. Hydrogen atoms of polar bonds (e.g., H-F, H-O, and H-N) experience an attractive force toward electronegative atoms that have an unshared pair of electrons, usually an F, O, or N atom. Because hydrogen atoms have no inner core of electrons, when bonded with a strongly electronegative atom, the side of the atom facing away from the bond is a virtually naked nucleus with a positive charge. Thus, the positive charge interacts strongly with electronegative atoms of nearby molecules.

$$^-N - H^+ \,-----\, ^-F - H^+$$

Hydrogen Bond

Hydrogen bonding is responsible for many of the unique properties of water. Because each water molecule contains an electronegative oxygen atom bonded with two hydrogen atoms, the potential for intermolecular hydrogen bonding is great (each water molecule can participate in four hydrogen bonds). Extensive hydrogen bonding creates the highly structured nature of water. For example, frozen water (ice) is less dense than liquid water and water has a high heat capacity and specific heat.

Ion-dipole forces involve the interaction between a charged ion and a polar molecule (i.e. a dipole). Positively charged cations interact with the negative end of a dipole. Negatively charged anions interact with the positive end of a dipole. Ion-dipole forces are important interactions in solutions of ionic substances in polar solvents.

Dipole-dipole forces exist between neutral, polar molecules. Partial positive ends of polar molecules interact with partial negative ends of other polar molecules. Dipole-dipole forces are weaker than ion-dipole forces and polar molecules must be close together for such forces to have a significant effect.

London dispersion forces exist between neutral, non-polar molecules. As electrons orbit around atomic nuclei, the distribution of electrons may not be symmetrical at any given instance. Thus, even the atoms of non-polar molecules experience transient positive and negative dipoles. Because of electron repulsion, these transient dipoles can induce similar dipoles in neighboring molecules. When atoms are close together, London dispersion forces are a significant factor.

Scientists use the term '**van der Waals forces**' to describe dipole and dispersion forces as a group.

Skill 8.3   **Demonstrating knowledge of the relationship between the physical properties of substances (e.g., boiling point, solubility, vapor pressure) and their intermolecular forces**

Intermolecular forces are electromagnetic forces that act between molecules or between widely separated regions of a macromolecule. All types of intermolecular forces are based on the attraction of a positive charge to a negative charge. The magnitude of this force (U) is determined by the distance between charges (d) and the strengths of the two charges (Q1 and Q2). This relationship is expressed by Coulomb's Law, where k is a proportionality constant:

$$U = k(Q1Q2 / d)$$

Intermolecular forces can be electrostatic or electrodynamic interactions. These forces differ in terms of charge strength. Listed in order of decreasing strength, these interactions include: Ion-ion interactions, hydrogen bonding, dipole-dipole interactions and London dispersion (Van der Waals) forces.

The strongest intermolecular force is ion-ion attraction, the intermolecular force found in ionic compounds (salts). These bonds form when the difference in electronegativity between two atoms is large enough that one atom is able to steal an electron from the other molecule. The two molecules are then oppositely charged and attracted to one another. Table salt (NaCl) is a common example of an ionic compound.

The second strongest type of intermolecular forces is hydrogen bonding. Hydrogen bonds occur between an electronegative atom and a hydrogen atom bonded to another electronegative atom. Hydrogen bonding can be seen in the compound ethanol (C_2H_6O).

Dipole-dipole interactions are weaker than ionic and hydrogen bonds. This type of interaction takes place between two molecules with permanent dipoles, which are spatially oriented areas of positive or negative charge within the molecule. Dipole-dipole interactions are similar to ionic interactions, but weaker because only partial charges are involved. This type of interaction is seen in the compound hydrochloric acid (HCl).

London dispersion forces are the weakest intermolecular forces, and involve the attraction between temporarily induced dipoles. Such polarization is usually induced by the presence of a polar molecule. These are the weakest intermolecular forces because they occur spontaneously and are easily broken. London dispersion forces are seen between molecules of the halogens, such as chlorine gas (Cl_2).

The **boiling point** of a substance is the temperature at which the majority of the substance can change from liquid to gas form at a given pressure. Boiling is a bulk process, meaning that at the boiling point of a substance, molecules anywhere in the liquid may be vaporized, resulting in the formation of vapor bubbles. Vaporization requires the input of heat, which enables the molecules of a substance to obtain enough energy to overcome intermolecular forces and change from the liquid to gaseous state. The stronger the forces of intermolecular attraction between molecules of a substance, the higher its boiling point. Ionic compounds, therefore, demonstrate extremely high boiling points because of the large amount of heat required to break the intermolecular forces of attraction between the charged ions. On the opposite end of the spectrum are substances demonstrating London dispersion forces. These substances, such as O_2, have very low boiling points, and will commonly be found in gas form.

Vapor pressure is the pressure of a vapor in equilibrium with its non-vapor phases. This equilibrium results from the tendency of all solids and liquids to evaporate to a gaseous form, and the tendency of all gases to condense back. The vapor pressure of a particular substance at a given temperature is the partial pressure at which the gas of that substance is in dynamic equilibrium with its liquid or solid forms. When comparing two substances at any given temperature, the substance with the stronger intermolecular forces will have the lowest vapor pressure. As explained above, the stronger the intermolecular forces of a substance, the more energy required to convert this substance from liquid to gas form. Substances with ionic or hydrogen bonding will therefore have lower vapor pressures than substances with dipole-dipole interactions or Van der Waals forces.

Solubility refers to the ability for a given substance, the solute, to dissolve in a solvent. It is measured in terms of the maximum amount of solute dissolved in a solvent at equilibrium. The resulting solution is called a saturated solution of miscible components. The general rule of solubility is "like dissolves like." This means that polar solutes will dissolve in polar solvents, and non-polar solutes will dissolve in non-polar solvents. For this reason, ionic solutes such as sodium chloride (NaCl) will generally dissolve in polar solvents but not in non-polar solvents. Using NaCL dissolved in water as an example, the positive ion Na+ is attracted the partially negatively charged atom in the water molecule OH-, and the negative ion of the solute Cl- is attracted to the partially positively charged atom on the solvent molecule H+. Many ionic compounds are easily dissolved in water because of the ease at which hydrogen bonds are formed between ionic molecules and water molecules.

In respect to substances demonstrating dipole-dipole and London dispersion forces, the higher the polarity of these substances (be it permanent or induced), the higher their solubility in polar solvents, and the lower their solubility in non-polar solvents.

Skill 8.4   Interpreting phase diagrams

A **phase diagram** is a graphical way to summarize the conditions under which the different states of a substance are stable. The diagram is divided into three areas representing each state of the substance.
The curves separating each area represent the boundaries of phase changes Below is a typical phase diagram. It consists of three curves that divide the diagram into regions labeled "solid, liquid, and gas".

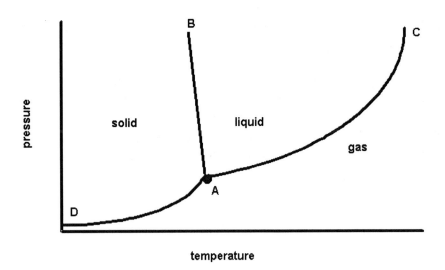

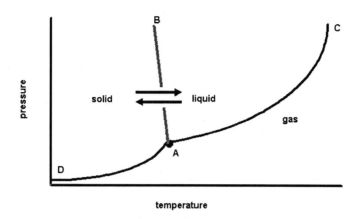

Curve **AB**, dividing the solid region from the liquid region, represents the conditions under which the solid and liquid are in equilibrium.

Usually, the melting point is only slightly affected by pressure. For this reason, the melting point curve, AB, is nearly vertical

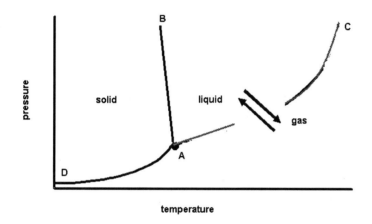

Curve **AC**, which divides the liquid region from the gaseous region, represents the boiling points of the liquid for various pressures.

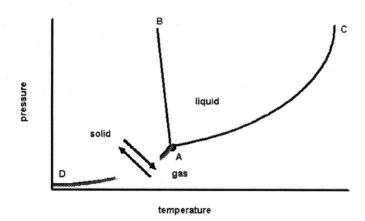

Curve **AD**, which divides the solid region from the gaseous region, represents the vapor pressures of the solid at various temperatures

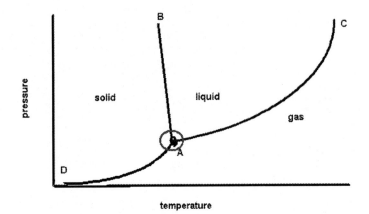

The curves intersect at **A**, the **triple point**, which is the temperature and pressure where three phases of a substance exist in equilibrium.

The temperature above which the liquid state of a substance no longer exists regardless of pressure is called the **critical temperature**.

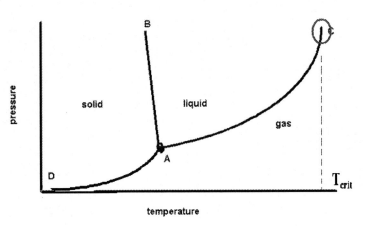

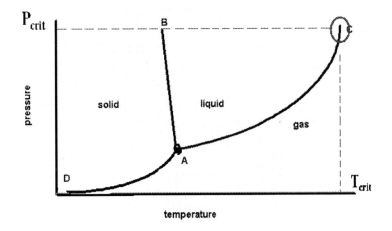

The vapor pressure at the critical temperature is called the **critical pressure**. Note that curve AC ends at the **critical point, C.**

The phase diagram for water (shown below) is unusual. The solid/liquid phase boundary slopes to the left with increasing pressure because the melting point of water decreases with increasing pressure. Note that the normal melting point of water is lower than its triple point. The diagram is not drawn to a uniform scale. Many anomalous properties of water are discussed here: http://www.lsbu.ac.uk/water/anmlies.html.

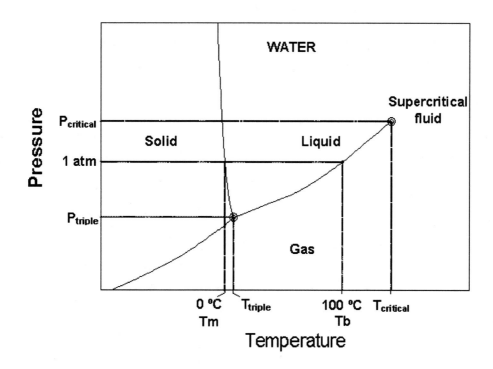

Normal melting point (T_m) and **normal boiling point** (T_b) are defined at 1 atm. Note that freezing point and melting point refer to an identical temperature approached from different directions, but they represent the same concept.

This is the phase diagram for carbon dioxide, CO_2. It shows the same features, only at different temperatures and pressures.

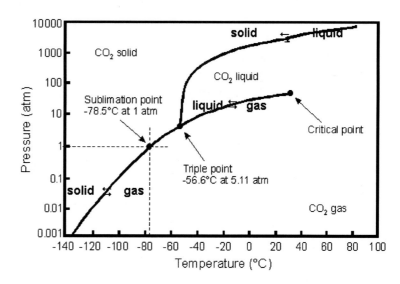

COMPETENCY 9.0   UNDERSTAND THE KINETIC MOLECULAR THEORY AND THE GAS LAWS.

Skill 9.1   Comparing the arrangement and movement of particles in the solid, liquid, gas, and plasma phases of matter

There are three common states of matter: solid, liquid and gas. Recently, a fourth state of matter, known as plasma, has been identified. It exists only under high energy and high temperature conditions. The conversion of matter from one state to another is a physical change during which the particles of a substance remain the same, but their relative positions change.

The Kinetic Molecular Theory states that all molecules are in constant motion. The greater the temperature of these molecules, the greater their kinetic energy and speed. Acting in opposition to the movement of particles are intermolecular forces of attraction. These electromagnetic forces draw molecules together, while kinetic energy forces them apart. Energy and temperature conditions determine which force is stronger, and thus determine the state of matter of the molecules.

Solids:

Solids have definite shape and volume at a given temperature. The particles of a material in solid form are touching and fixed in place, often forming a regular, crystalline arrangement. The kinetic energy of the molecules of a material in solid form is much lower than the attraction forces acting between the molecules. For this reason, movement of the particles of a solid are restricted to vibration or rotation in place. Because there is little free space between the particles of a solid, these particles cannot easily slide past one another. Solids, therefore, do not easily flow and are not easily compressed.

Liquids:

Liquids have definite volumes, but assume the shape of their container. The particles in a liquid are less tightly packed, and spaces can be seen between some particles. However, because of minimal free space between particles, liquids are not easily compressible. The particles of liquids do not exist in a regular arrangement, and flow easily by sliding past each other. The amount and speed of the movement of particles in liquid form are greater than those of particles in solid form because of the existence of higher kinetic energy.

Gases:

The volume and shape of a quantity of gas are dependent on surrounding temperature and pressure. If affected by gravity, the gas will expand to fill empty space, taking the volume and shape of its container. The particles of a gas may have great distances between them, and move about freely at high speeds. Because of the large amount of space between particles, gases are easily compressible, and do not exist in a regular arrangement due to very high kinetic energy.

Plasma:

At extreme temperatures, such as those that exist on the Sun, matter may become ionized through the loss of all electrons. This matter, in combination with turbulence caused by heat, is known as plasma. Particles that make up plasma include free-floating ions, electrons and neutral atoms. These particles move at extremely high speeds with no regular arrangement.

Skill 9.2   Demonstrating knowledge of basic principles of kinetic molecular theory

These relationships were found by experimental observation and may be explained by the kinetic molecular theory.

Gas **pressure** results from molecular collisions with container walls. The **number of molecules** striking an **area** on the walls and the **average kinetic energy** per molecule are the only factors that contribute to pressure. A higher **temperature** increases speed and kinetic energy. There are more collisions at higher temperatures, but the average distance between molecules does not change, and thus density does not change in a sealed container.

Kinetic molecular theory explains how the pressure and temperature influences behavior of gases by making a few assumptions, namely:

1) The energies of intermolecular attractive and repulsive forces may be neglected.
2) The average kinetic energy of the molecules is proportional to absolute temperature.
3) Energy can be transferred between molecules during collisions and the collisions are elastic, so the average kinetic energy of the molecules doesn't change due to collisions.
4) The volume of all molecules in a gas is negligible compared to the total volume of the container.

Strictly speaking, molecules also contain some kinetic energy by rotating or experiencing other motions. The motion of a molecule from one place to another is called **translation**. Translational kinetic energy is the form that is transferred by collisions, and kinetic molecular theory ignores other forms of kinetic energy because they are not proportional to temperature.

The following table summarizes the application of kinetic molecular theory to an increase in container volume, number of molecules, and temperature:

Effect of an **increase** in one variable with other two constant	Impact on gas: − = decrease, **0** = no change, **+** = increase						
	Average distance between molecules	Density in a sealed container	Average speed of molecules	Average translational kinetic energy of molecules	Collisions with container walls per second	Collisions per unit area of wall per second	Pressure (P)
Volume of container (V)	+	−	0	0	−	−	−
Number of molecules	−	+	0	0	+	+	+
Temperature (T)	0	0	+	+	+	+	+

Additional details on the kinetic molecular theory may be found at http://hyperphysics.phy-astr.gsu.edu/hbase/kinetic/ktcon.html. An animation of gas particles colliding is located at http://comp.uark.edu/~jgeabana/mol_dyn/

Skill 9.3 Explain the properties of solids, liquids, and gases and changes of state in terms of the kinetic molecular theory and intermolecular forces.

Molecules have **kinetic energy** (they move around), and they also have **intermolecular attractive forces** (they stick to each other). The relationship between these two determines whether a collection of molecules will be a gas, liquid, or solid.

A **gas** has an indefinite shape and an indefinite volume. The kinetic model for a gas is a collection of widely separated molecules, each moving in a random and free fashion, with negligible attractive or repulsive forces between them. Gases will expand to occupy a larger container so there is more space between the molecules. Gases can also be compressed to fit into a small container so the molecules are less separated. **Diffusion** occurs 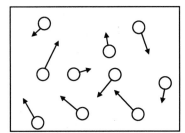 when one material spreads into or through another. Gases diffuse rapidly and move from one place to another.

A **liquid** assumes the shape of the portion of any container that it occupies and has a specific volume. The kinetic model for a liquid is a collection of molecules attracted to each other with sufficient strength to keep them close to each other but with insufficient strength to prevent them from moving around randomly. Liquids have a higher density and are much less compressible than gases because the 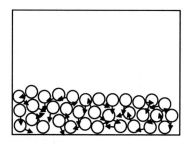 molecules in a liquid are closer together. Diffusion occurs more slowly in liquids than in gases because the molecules in a liquid stick to each other and are not completely free to move.

A **solid** has a definite volume and definite shape. The kinetic model for a solid is a collection of molecules attracted to each other with sufficient strength to essentially lock them in place. Each molecule may vibrate, but it has an average position relative to its neighbors. If these positions form an ordered pattern, the solid is called **crystalline**. Otherwise, it is called **amorphous**. Solids have a high density and are almost incompressible because the molecules are close together. Diffusion occurs extremely slowly because the molecules almost never alter their position.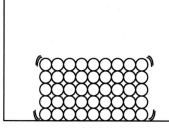

In a solid, the energy of intermolecular attractive forces is much stronger than the kinetic energy of the molecules, so kinetic energy and kinetic molecular theory are not very important. As temperature increases in a solid, the vibrations of individual molecules grow more intense and the molecules spread slightly further apart, decreasing the density of the solid.

In a liquid, the energy of intermolecular attractive forces is about as strong as the kinetic energy of the molecules and both play a role in the properties of liquids.

In a gas, the energy of intermolecular forces is much weaker than the kinetic energy of the molecules. Kinetic molecular theory is usually applied for gases and is best applied by imagining ourselves shrinking down to become a molecule and picturing what happens when we bump into other molecules and into container walls.

Skill 9.4   Analyzing the effects of intermolecular forces on real gases

Intermolecular forces are electrical forces that exist between molecules and cause one molecule to influence another. Such forces will make gases behave in a way that is different from that of ideal gases. These forces are stronger in solids and liquids.

The ideal gas law states that a gas sample is composed of molecules that are totally independent of each other and hence behave ideally. In reality, the ideal gas law is an equation:

$PV = nRT$

Where R = universal gas constant
P = Pressure
V = Volume
n = number of moles
T = Temperature

If a gas behaves exactly as the ideal gas laws would predict, then it is an ideal gas. A 'real gas' is a gas that deviates from ideal gas behavior.
Now, with this background, let us examine the effects of intermolecular forces on real gases:

1. Effect of pressure: Lowering of pressure allows gas molecules to spread out farther from one another. Because the molecules are far apart, there will be fewer intermolecular forces acting on them to the extent that the intermolecular forces are almost zero. As pressure decreases, intermolecular forces become weaker and the gas approaches ideal behavior.

2. Effect of temperature: Raising the temperature of gas increases the average kinetic energy of the gas molecules and increases the speed at which they travel. This increased speed will overcome intermolecular forces acting between the molecules and the gas would behave almost as an ideal gas.

Skill 9.5   **Solving problems involving relationships among temperature, pressure, volume, and moles of a gas (e.g., ideal and combined gas laws)**

The kinetic molecular theory describes how an ideal gas behaves when conditions such as temperature, pressure, volume or quantity of gas are varied within a system. An **ideal gas** is an imaginary gas that obeys all of the assumptions of the kinetic molecular theory. While an ideal gas does not exist, most gases will behave like an ideal gas except when at very low temperatures or very high pressures. Under these conditions, gases vary from ideal behavior.

Charles's law states that the volume of a fixed amount of gas at constant pressure is directly proportional to absolute temperature, or:

$$V \propto T.$$

Or V=kT where k is a constant. This gives a mathematical equation $\dfrac{V_1}{T_1} = \dfrac{V_2}{T_2}$.

Changes in temperature or volume can be found using Charles's law.

Problem: What is the new volume of gas if 0.50 L of gas at 25°C is allowed to heat up to 35°C at constant pressure?

Solution: This is a volume-temperature change so use Charles's law. Temperature must be on the Kelvin scale. K= °C + 273.

T_1= 298K
V_1= 0.50 L
T_2= 308K
V_2 = ?

Use the equation: $\dfrac{V_1}{T_1} = \dfrac{V_2}{T_2}$ and rearrange for $V_2 = \dfrac{T_2 V_1}{T_1}$. Substitute and solve

V_2=0.52L.

Boyle's law states that the volume of a fixed amount of gas at constant temperature is inversely proportional to the gas pressure, or:

$$V \propto \frac{1}{P}.$$

Or V=k/P where k is a constant. This gives a mathematical equation $P_1V_1=P_2V_2$. Pressure-volume changes can be determined using Boyle's law.

Problem: A 1.5 L gas has a pressure of 0.56 atm. What will be the volume of the gas if the pressure doubles to 1.12 atm at constant temperature?

Solution: This is a pressure-volume relationship at constant temperature so usse Boyle's law.

P_1= 0.56 atm
V_1= 1.5 L
P_2= 1.12 atm
V_2=?

Use the equation $P_1V_1=P_2V_2$, rearrange to solve for $V_2 = \dfrac{P_1V_1}{P_2}$.

Substitute and solve. V_2=0.75 L

Gay-Lussac's law states that the pressure of a fixed amount of gas in a fixed volume is proportional to absolute temperature, or:
$$P \propto T.$$

Or P=kT where k is a constant. This gives a mathematical equation $\dfrac{P_1}{T_1} = \dfrac{P_2}{T_2}$.

Changes in temperature or pressure can be found using Gay-Lussac's law.

Problem: A 2.25 L container of gas at 25°C and 1.0 atm pressure is cooled to 15°C. How does the pressure change if the volume of gas remains constant?
Solution: This is a pressure-volume change so use Gay-Lussac's law.

P_1= 1.0 atm
T_1= 25 °C
T_2= 15 °C
Change the temperatures to the Kelvin scale. K=°C+ 273.

Use the equation $\dfrac{P_1}{T_1} = \dfrac{P_2}{T_2}$ to solve. Rearrange the equation to solve for P_2, substitute and solve.

$$P_2 = \dfrac{P_1 T_2}{T_1} = 0.97 \text{ atm}$$

The **combined gas law** uses the above laws to determine a proportionality expression that is used for a constant quantity of gas:

$$V \propto \frac{T}{P}.$$

The combined gas law is often expressed as an equality between identical amounts of an ideal gas at two different states ($n_1 = n_2$):

$$\frac{P_1 V_1}{T_1} = \frac{P_2 V_2}{T_2}.$$

Problem: 1.5 L of a gas at STP is is allowed to expand to 2.0 L at a pressure of 2.5 atm. What is the temperature of the expanded gas?

Since pressure, temperature and volume are changing use the combined gas gas law to determine the new temperature of the gas.

P_1= 1.0 atm
T_1= 273K
V_1= 1.5 L
V_2= 2.0L
P_2= 2.5 atm
T_2=?

Using this equation, $\dfrac{P_1 V_1}{T_1} = \dfrac{P_2 V_2}{T_2}$, rearrange to solve for T_2.

$$T_2 = \frac{P_2 V_2 T_1}{P_1 V_1}$$

Substitute and solve T_2=910 K or 637 °C

Avogadro's hypothesis states that equal volumes of different gases at the same temperature and pressure contain equal numbers of molecules.
Avogadro's law states that the volume of a gas at constant temperature and pressure is directly proportional to the quantity of gas, or:

$$V \propto n \text{ where } n \text{ is the number of moles of gas.}$$

Avogadro's law and the combined gas law yield $V \propto \dfrac{nT}{P}$. The proportionality constant R--the **ideal gas constant**--is used to express this proportionality as the **ideal gas law**:

$$PV = nRT.$$

The ideal gas law ($PV = nRT$) is useful because it contains all the information of Charles's, Avogadro's, Boyle's, and the combined gas laws in a single expression.

If pressure is given in atmospheres and volume is given in liters, a value for R of **0.08206 L-atm/(mol-K)** is used. If pressure is given in Pascal (newtons/m^2) and volume in cubic meters, then the SI value for R of **8.314 J/(mol-K)** may be used because a joule is defined as a Newton-meter. A value for R of **8.314 m^3-Pa/(mol-K)** is identical to the ideal gas constant using joules.

Many problems are given at "**standard temperature and pressure**" or "**STP.**" Standard conditions are *exactly* **1 atm** (101.325 kPa) and **0 °C (273.15 K)**. At STP, one mole of an ideal gas has a volume of:

$$V = \frac{nRT}{P}$$

$$= \frac{(1 \text{ mole})\left(0.08206 \ \frac{\text{L-atm}}{\text{mol-K}}\right)(273 \text{ K})}{1 \text{ atm}} = 22.4 \text{ L.}$$

The value of 22.4 L is known as the **standard molar volume of any gas at STP**.

Solving gas law problems using these formulas is a straightforward process of algebraic manipulation. **Errors commonly arise from using improper units**, particularly for the ideal gas constant R. An absolute temperature scale must be used (never °C) and is usually reported using the Kelvin scale, but volume and pressure units often vary from problem to problem. Temperature in Kelvin is found from:

$$T \text{ (in K)} = T(\text{in } °C) + 273.15$$

Tutorials for gas laws may be found online at:
http://www.chemistrycoach.com/tutorials-6.htm. A flash animation tutorial for problems involving a piston may be found at
http://www.mhhe.com/physsci/chemistry/essentialchemistry/flash/gasesv6.swf.

Problem: What volume will 0.50 mole an ideal gas occupy at 20.0 °C and 1.5 atm?

Solution: Since the problem deals with moles of gas with temperature and pressure, use the ideal gas law to find volume.

$Pv = nRT$ $V = nRT/ P$

$P = 1.5$ atm $= 0.50$ mol (0.0821 atm L/mol K) 293 K/

$V= ?$ 1.5 atm

$n= 0.50$ mol $= 8.0$ L

$T=20.0$ °C$= 293$ K

$R = 0.0821$ atm L/mol K

Problem: At STP, 0.250 L of an unknown gas has a mass of 0.491 g. Is the gas SO_2, NO_2, C_3H_8, or Ar? Support your answer.

Solution: Identify what is given and what is asked to determine.

Given: $T_1= 273K$
$P_1=1.0$ atm
$V_1= 0.250$ L
Mass$= 0.419$ g

Determine: Identity of the gas. In order to do this, must find molar mass of the gas. $n = \dfrac{mass}{MM}$. Find the number of moles of gas present using $PV=nRT$ and then determine the MM to compare to choices given in the problem.

Solve for $n=\dfrac{PV}{RT}$ $= 0.011$ moles

$MM= \dfrac{mass}{n} = 38.1$ g/mol

Compare to MM of SO_2 (96 g/mol), NO_2 (46 g/mol), C_3H_8 (44 g/mol and Ar (39.9 g/mol). It is closest to Ar, so the gas is probably Argon.

For mixtures of gases in a container, each gas exerts a **partial pressure** that it would have if it were present in the container alone. **Dalton's law** of partial pressures states that the total pressure of a gas mixture is simply the sum of these partial pressures:

$$P_{total} = P_1 + P_2 + P_3 + \ldots$$

Dalton's law may be applied to the ideal gas law:

$$P_{total}V = (P_1 + P_2 + P_3 + \ldots)V = (n_1 + n_2 + n_3 + \ldots)RT.$$

Effusion occurs when gas escapes through a tiny opening into a vacuum or into a region at lower pressure. **Graham's law** states that the rate of effusion (r) for a gas is inversely proportional to the square root of its molecular weight (M):

$$r \propto \frac{1}{\sqrt{M}}.$$

Graham's law may be used to compare the ratios of effusion rates and molecular weights for two different gases:

$$\frac{r_1}{r_2} = \sqrt{\frac{M_2}{M_1}}.$$

Graham's law uses the same two expressions above to describe the dependence of the **diffusion** rate on molecular weight.

COMPETENCY 10.0   UNDERSTAND THE LAWS OF THERMODYNAMICS AND THE FLOW OF HEAT IN PHYSICAL AND CHEMICAL PROCESSES.

Skill 10.1   Distinguishing between heat and temperature

Heat and temperature are different physical quantities. **Heat** is a measure of energy. **Temperature** is the measure of how hot (or cold) a body is with respect to a standard object.

Two concepts are important in the discussion of temperature changes. Objects are in thermal contact if they can affect each other's temperatures. Imagine, for instance, a hot cup of coffee on a desktop. The coffee, the cup, and the desktop are all in thermal contact. The coffee will become cooler as thermal energy is transferred to the cup and the desktop. Eventually, all three objects will be same temperature. When this happens, they are in **thermal equilibrium.**

We cannot rely on our sense of touch to determine temperature because certain material are better conductors so they may "feel" hotter or colder. **Thermometers** are used to measure temperature. A small amount of mercury in a capillary tube will expand when heated. The thermometer and the object whose temperature it is measuring are put in contact long enough for them to reach thermal equilibrium. Then the temperature can be read from the thermometer scale.

Three temperature scales are used:

Celsius: The freezing point of water is set at 0 and the boiling point is 100. The interval between the two is divided into 100 equal parts called degrees Celsius.

Fahrenheit: The freezing point of water is 32 degrees and the boiling point is 212. The interval between is divided into 180 equal parts called degrees Fahrenheit.

Temperature readings can be converted from one to the other as follows.

Fahrenheit to Celsius	Celsius to Fahrenheit
$C = 5/9 \ (F - 32)$	$F = (9/5) \ C + 32$

Kelvin Scale has the degrees the same size as the Celsius scale, but the zero point is moved to absolute zero. Because the degrees are the same size in the two scales, temperature changes are the same in Celsius and Kelvin. Temperature readings can be converted from Celsius to Kelvin:

Celsius to Kelvin	Kelvin to Celsius
$K = C + 273.15$	$C = K - 273.15$

Heat is a measure of energy. If two objects that have different temperatures come into contact with each other, heat flows from the hotter object to the cooler.

Skill 10.2   Analyzing heating and cooling curves both qualitatively and quantitatively

In order to analyze heating and cooling curves, we need to understand what a system is and its relationship to the heating and cooling of any substance.

A system is an imaginary closed container isolated from its environment. In reality, or course, no system (except the universe itself) can be entirely closed. For the sake of practicality, a system is anything from a container to any closed /confined area, whether it is big or small. A system is isolated and under a controlled atmosphere, so that we will be able to observe any changes that take place inside it due to a transfer of mass and energy from or into it.

Let's first analyze a system when energy is added to it. As a response to this addition of energy, the system adjusts and this response can be measured by the increase in temperature. The important thing here is the quantitative measurement of the change in this system. Qualitatively, we are able to see the system warming up after the addition of heat energy and quantitatively we can measure it and plot a curve of temperature versus time. This is known as a heating curve and a sample is presented on the next page.

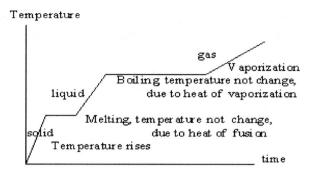

When a system contains only one phase, the temperature will increase when it receives energy. The rate of temperature increase will be dependent on the heat capacity of the phase in the system. When the heat capacity is large, the temperature increases slowly, because much energy is required to increase the substance's temperature by one degree. When a phase change occurs, however, the temperature will remain the same. This is because the energy being put into the system is being used to melt or vaporize the substance.

For example, the temperature of a system containing ice below its melting point will increase when heated. However, at 273.15 K, the temperature stops rising. At this temperature, the ice will start to melt, and the heat is used to melt the ice. The melting of ice is called a phase transition. When energy supplied is used for a phase transition, the temperature stays constant. After the phase transition is complete, the temperature rise will follow a different rate than that of the solid due to different heat capacity, as shown in the heating curve.

For one mole of water (18 g), we have the following data:
- Heat capacity of ice = 37.6 J $(K\ mol)^{-1}$.
- Heat capacity of water = 75.3 J $(K\ mol)^{-1}$.
- Heat capacity of steam = 35.8 J $(K\ mol)^{-1}$ (at constant pressure of 1 atm).
- Melting point = 273.15 K
- Heat of fusion of ice = 6.01 kJ mol^{-1}.
- Boiling point = 373.15 K.
- Heat of vaporization = 40.67 kJ mol^{-1}.
- Heat of sublimation = 46.7 kJ mol^{-1}.

The heating curve given above is drawn according to the above data. In a real experiment, the heat transferred into the system is hardly at a constant rate unless the heat source is at a very high temperature. However, for the sake of simplicity, let us assume the heat flow into the system to be at a constant rate.

Water is a common substance. Ice is the stable phase below 273.15 K. Both solids and liquids coexist at 273.15 K. When heat is put into the system, more solid will melt. Thus, the temperature does not change. The normal boiling point is 373.15 K. As heat is absorbed, some water will boil off but the temperature is kept at 373.15 K.

A **cooling curve** is a line graph that represents the temperature and phase changes as a substance is cooled. Typically, this will mean a transition from gas to a solid or a liquid to a solid. Time is plotted on the x-axis while temperature is on the y-axis.

Cooling curves are useful as they clearly show us the phenomenon of phase changes of matter. To explain this, we can again use water as our example. This time, however, we will begin with steam at a temperature of 150° C. As we measure the temperature of the rapidly cooling gas, we see that it falls at a rate governed by the specific heat capacity of steam until it reaches 100° C, then the temperature levels off. After an amount of liquid water has collected the temperature continues to drop, again proportional to the specific heat capacity of water (different to that of steam), until the temperature remains constant, this time at 0° C. Later, the temperature again begins to fall.

The explanation is that different phases of matter are associated with different energy levels. Steam at 100° C is the same temperature, but contains much more thermal energy than liquid water at 100° C. The same goes for water and ice at 0° C. This is because molecules of water are much more free to move around in a gas (as the bonds between molecules are broken by thermal energy) than in a liquid, and that freedom of movement means there is much more kinetic energy associated with each molecule, and that energy is transferred as the substance changes from one phase to the other. The kinetic energy decreases and the potential energy stays the same, except at the plateaus (phase changes) where the kinetic energy stays the same and the potential energy decreases.

Skill 10.3   Solving problems involving calorimetry

Heat Capacity of an object is the amount of heat energy that it takes to raise the temperature of the object by one degree.

Heat capacity (C) per unit mass (m) is called **specific heat** (c):

$$c \;=\; \frac{C}{m} \;=\; \frac{Q/\Delta}{m}$$

Specific heats for many materials have been calculated and can be found in tables.

There are a number of ways that heat is measured. In each case, the measurement is dependent upon raising the temperature of a specific amount of water by a specific amount. These conversions of heat energy and work are called the **mechanical equivalent of heat**.

A **calorimeter** uses the transfer of heat from one substance to another to determine the specific heat of the substance.

The **calorie** is the amount of energy that it takes to raise one gram of water one degree.

The **kilocalorie** is the amount of energy that it takes to raise one kilogram of water by one degree Celsius. Food calories are kilocalories.

In the International System of Units **(SI),** the calorie is equal to 4.184 **joules**.

British thermal units (BTU) - (BTU = 252 calories = 1.054 kJ)

Skill 10.4   Interpreting the laws of thermodynamics and their applications to chemical systems

The three laws of thermodynamics are as follows:

1. The total amount of energy in the universe is constant, energy cannot be created or destroyed, but can merely change form.

> Equation:
> $\Delta E = Q + W$
> Change in energy = (Heat energy entering or leaving) + (work done)

This is really a statement of the law of conservation of energy, which states that energy is neither created nor destroyed. Thus, energy changes form when energy transactions occur in nature. Because the total energy in the universe is constant, energy continually transitions between forms. For example, an engine burns gasoline converting the chemical energy of the gasoline into mechanical energy, a plant converts radiant energy of the sun into chemical energy found in glucose, or a battery converts chemical energy into electrical energy.

2. In energy transformations, entropy (disorder) increases and useful energy is lost (as heat).

> Equation:
> $\Delta S = \Delta Q / T$
> Change in entropy = (Heat transfer) / (Temperature)

3. As the temperature of a system approaches absolute zero, entropy (disorder) approaches a constant.

Sample Problems:
1. A car engine burns gasoline to power the car. An amount of gasoline containing 2000J of stored chemical energy produced 1500J of mechanical energy to power the engine. How much heat energy did the engine release?

Solution:

$\Delta E = Q + W$	the first law of thermodynamics
00J = Q + 1500J	apply the first law
Q (work) = 500J	

2. 18200J of heat leaks out of a hot oven. The temperature of the room is 25°C (298K). What is the increase in entropy resulting from this heat transfer?

Solution:

$\Delta S = \Delta Q/T$ the second law of thermodynamics
$\Delta S = 18200J / 298K$ apply the second law
$= 61.1$ J/K   solve

Skill 10.5   **Predicting the spontaneity of chemical reactions based on enthalpy changes, entropy changes, and the temperature of the system**

Enthalpy, ΔH, is the internal energy of the molecules within a system.

Entropy, ΔS, may be thought of as **the disorder in a system** or as a measure of the **number of states a system may occupy**. Changes due to entropy occur in one direction with no driving force. For example, a small volume of gas released into a large container will expand to fill it, but the gas in a large container never spontaneously collects itself into a small volume. This occurs because a large volume of gas has more disorder and has more places for gas molecules to be. This change occurs because **processes increase in entropy** when given the opportunity to do so.

Gibbs Free Energy, ΔG, is the free energy within the system that is, energy available to do work. It is determined by $\Delta G = \Delta H - T\Delta S$. When $\Delta G = 0$ the system is at equilibrium. If $\Delta G > 0$ the reaction is nonspontaneous. When $\Delta G < 0$, the reaction is spontaneous.

Spontaneity
A reaction with a negative $\square H$ and a positive $\square S$ causes a decrease in energy and an increase in entropy. **These reactions will always occur spontaneously**. A reaction with a positive $\square H$ and a negative $\square S$ causes an increase in energy and a decrease in entropy. These reactions never occur to an appreciable extent because the reverse reaction takes place spontaneously.

Whether reactions with the remaining two possible combinations ($\square H$ and $\square S$ are both positive or both negative) occur depends on the temperature. If $\square H - T\square S$ (known as the **Gibbs Free Energy** is negative, the reaction will take place. If it is positive, the reaction will not occur to an appreciable extent. If $\square H - T\square S = 0$ exactly, then at equilibrium there will be 50% reactants and 50% products. This chart will help identify four possible scenarios for the values of ΔH, ΔS and ΔG to predict spontaneity of the reaction.

This chart will help identify four possible scenarios for the values of ΔH, ΔS and

ΔH	ΔS	ΔG
-	+	-, spontaneous
-	-	-, spontaneous
+	+	- if |TΔS|< |ΔH|, spontaneous
+	-	- if TΔS > ΔH

ΔG to predict spontaneity of the reaction.

A spontaneous reaction is called *exergonic*. A non-spontaneous reaction is known as *endergonic*. These terms are used much less often than *exothermic* and *endothermic*.

Skill 10.6   Analyzing energy changes in terms of the breaking and formation of chemical bonds

The Arrhenius equation is a formula that **relates temperature to the rate constant of a chemical reaction**. Developed in 1884 by JH van't Hoff and physically verified by Svante Arrhenius, this important equation is both simple and accurate for many reactions. It is:

$$k = Ae^{\frac{-E_a}{RT}}$$

where
k = the reaction rate constant
E_a = activation energy
T = absolute temperature
R = the gas constant
A = the frequency factor (a constant specific to a given reaction)

The implication of this equation is that **the rate of a reaction can be increased by increasing the temperature or by decreasing the activation energy** (as is done by a catalyst).

The Arrhenius equation is also very important in experimental chemical kinetics. To see why, we must take the natural log of the equation:

$$\ln(k) = \frac{-E_a}{R}\frac{1}{T} + \ln(A)$$

This means that a plot of ln(k) versus 1/T will yield a straight line and its slope and intercept allow the calculation of E_a and A. This **allows chemists to determine the activation energy of any chemical reaction** that obeys the Arrhenius equation.

In order for one species to be converted to another during a chemical reaction, the reactants must collide. The collisions between the reactants determine how fast the reaction takes place. However, during a chemical reaction, only a fraction of the collisions between the appropriate reactant molecules convert them into product molecules. This occurs for two reasons:

1) Not all collisions occur with a **sufficiently high energy** for the reaction to occur.
2) Not all collisions **orient the molecules properly** for the reaction to occur.

The **activation energy**, E_a, of a reaction is the **minimum energy to overcome the barrier to the formation of products**. This is the minimum energy needed for the reaction to occur.

At the scale of individual molecules, a reaction typically involves a very small period of time when old bonds are broken and new bonds are formed. During this time, the molecules involved are in a **transition state** between reactants and products. A threshold of maximum energy is crossed when the arrangement of molecules is in an unfavorable intermediate between reactants and products known as the **activated complex**. Formulas and diagrams of activated complexes are often written within brackets to indicate they are transition states that are present for extremely small periods of time.

Skill 10.7 **Solving problems involving energy changes during chemical reactions using standard heats of formations**

Heat of formation of each element is the heat that is absorbed or released when one mole of the element forms a compound. An endothermic reaction requires heat to occur. This is a positive change in heat ($+\Delta H$), so the products have more heat content than the reactants. Exothermic reactions give off heat as they occur, so have a negative change in heat ($-\Delta H$). The products have less heat content than the reactants.

Enthalpy (ΔH) is a measure of the tendency of a reaction toward a more stable compound since it measures the amount of heat a substance has at a given temperature and pressure. If it is negative, the reaction is exothermic and is very likely to occur spontaneously.

The enthalpy of the reaction is equal to the enthalpies of the products minus the enthalpies of the reactants.

$$\Delta H = \Delta H \text{ (products)} - \Delta H \text{ (reactants)}$$

To calculate the change in enthalpy (ΔH) for:

$$3\,CO(g) + Fe_2O_3(s) \rightarrow 2\,Fe(s) + 3\,CO_2(g)$$

Use the standard heats of formation (either given in the problem or taken from a chart): $CO(g)$ = -110.5 kJ/mol; $Fe_2O_3(s)$ = -822.1 kJ/mol; $Fe(s)$ = 0.0 kJ/mol; $CO_2(g)$ = -393.5 kJ/mol

ΔH = ΔH (products) - ΔH (reactants)
ΔH = [(2 mol)(0.0 kJ/mol) + (3 mol)(-393.5 kJ/mol)] –
   [(3 mol)(-110.5 kJ/mol) + (1 mol)(-822.1 kJ/mol)]
ΔH = -1180.5 kJ - -1153.6 kJ
ΔH = -26.9 kJ

Skill 10.8   Interpreting potential energy diagrams for chemical reactions

The activation energy, E_a, is the difference between the energy of reactants and the energy of the activated complex.   The energy change during the reaction, ΔE, is the difference between the energy of the products and the energy of the reactants. The activation energy of the reverse reaction is $E_a - \Delta E$. These energy levels are represented in an **energy diagram** such as the one shown below for $NO_2 + CO \rightleftharpoons NO + CO_2$. This is an exothermic reaction because products are lower in energy than reactants.

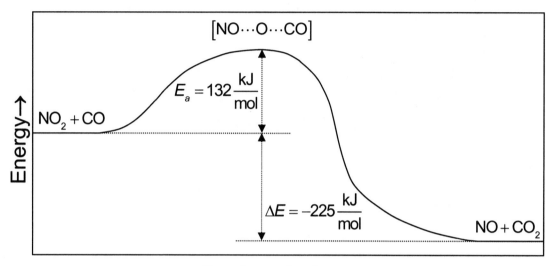

Reaction pathway

An energy diagram is a conceptual tool, so there is some variability in how its axes are labeled. The y-axis of the diagram is usually labeled energy (E), but it is sometimes labeled "enthalpy (H)" or (rarely) "free energy (G)." There is an even greater variability in how the x-axis is labeled. The terms "reaction pathway," "reaction coordinate," "course of reaction," or "reaction progress" may be used on the x-axis, or the x-axis may remain without a label.

The energy diagrams of an endothermic and exothermic reaction are compared below.

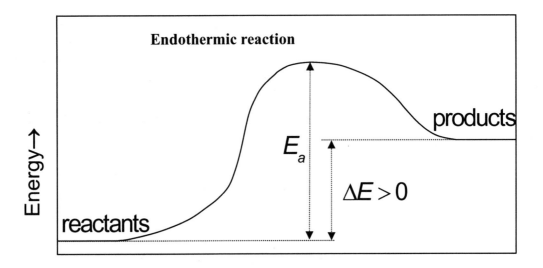

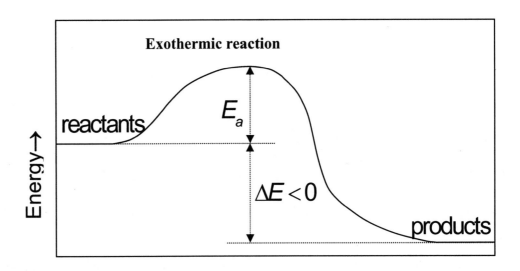

COMPETENCY 11.0   UNDERSTAND THE BASIC TYPES AND CHARACTERISTICS OF CHEMICAL REACTIONS.

Skill 11.1   Identifying the basic types of chemical reactions (i.e., synthesis, decomposition, single replacement, double replacement, and combustion)

There are chemical reactions occurring all around us everyday. Millions of them, in fact. So many different chemical reactions would be very difficult to understand. However, the millions of chemical reactions that take place each and everyday fall into only a few basic categories. Using these categories can help predict products of reactions that are unfamiliar or new.

Once we have an idea of the **reaction type**, we can make a good prediction about the products of chemical equations, and also balance the reactions. **General reaction types** are listed in the following table. Some reaction types have multiple names.

Reaction type	General equation	Example
Combination / Synthesis	$A + B \rightarrow C$	$2H_2 + O_2 \rightarrow 2H_2O$
Decomposition	$A \rightarrow B + C$	$2KClO_3 \rightarrow 2KCl + 3O_2$
Single substitution / Single displacement / Single replacement	$A + BC \rightarrow AB + B$	$Mg + 2HCl \rightarrow MgCl_2 + H_2$
Double substitution / Double displacement / Double replacement / Ion exchange / Metathesis	$AC + BD \rightarrow AD + BC$	$HCl + NaOH \rightarrow NaCl + H_2O$
Isomerization	$A \rightarrow A'$	

C_3H_6 cyclopropane $\rightarrow$ C_3H_6 propene

Example: Determine the products of a reaction between Cl_2 and a solution of NaBr.

Solution: The first step is to write "$Cl_2 + NaBr(aq) \rightarrow$?" Now examine the possible choices from the table. Decomposition and isomerization reactions require only one reactant. It also can't be a double substitution reaction because one of the reactants is an element. A synthesis reaction to form some NaBrCl compound would require very unusual valences! The most likely reaction is the remaining one: Cl replaces Br in aqueous solution with Na:
$Cl_2 + NaBr(aq) \rightarrow NaCl(aq) + Br_2$. After balancing, the equation is:
$$Cl_2 + 2NaBr(aq) \rightarrow 2NaCl(aq) + Br_2.$$

Chemical equations not only show the reactants and products, but they also must follow the Law of Conservation of Mass, which says that matter can not be created nor destroyed, merely rearranged in ordinary chemical reactions. Equations, then, must be *balanced*, to follow this law.

A properly written chemical equation must contain properly written formulas and must be **balanced**. Chemical equations are written to describe a certain number of moles of reactants becoming a certain number of moles of reaction products. The number of moles of each compound is indicated by its **stoichiometric coefficient**.

Example: In the reaction
$$2H_2(g) + O_2(g) \rightarrow 2H_2O(l),$$
hydrogen has a stoichiometric coefficient of two, oxygen has a coefficient of one, and water has a coefficient of two because 2 moles of hydrogen react with 1 mole of oxygen to form two moles of water.

In a balanced equation, the stoichiometric coefficients are chosen such that the equation contains an **equal number of each type of atom on each side**. In our example, there are four H atoms and two O atoms on both sides. Therefore, the equation is properly written.

Balancing equations is a four-step process.

1) Write an **unbalanced equation**. This requires writing the chemical formulas for the species involved in the reaction.
2) Determine the **number of each type of atom on each side** of the equation to find if the equation is balanced.
3) Assume that **the molecule with the most atoms** has a stoichiometric coefficient of one, and determine the other stoichiometric coefficients required to create the **same number of atoms on each side** of the equation.
4) Multiply all the stoichiometric coefficients by a whole number if necessary to eliminate fractional coefficients.

Example: Balance the chemical equation describing the combustion of methanol in oxygen to produce only carbon dioxide and water.

Solution:
1) The structural formula of methanol is CH_3OH, so its molecular formula is CH_4O. The formula for carbon dioxide is CO_2. Therefore the unbalanced equation is:

$$CH_4O + O_2 \rightarrow CO_2 + H_2O.$$

2) On the left there are 1C, 4H, and 3O. On the right, there are 1C, 2H, and 3O. It seems close to being balanced, but there's work to do.

3) Assuming that CH_4O has a stoichiometric coefficient of one means that the left side has 1C and 4H that also must be present on the right. Therefore the stoichiometric coefficient of CO_2 will be 1 to balance C and the stoichiometric coefficient of H_2O will be 2 to balance H. Now we have:

$$CH_4O + ?O_2 \rightarrow CO_2 + 2H_2O.$$

and only oxygen remains unbalanced. There are 4O on the right and one of these is accounted for by methanol leaving 3O to be accounted for by O_2. This gives a stoichiometric coefficient of 3/2 and a balanced equation:

$$CH_4O + \frac{3}{2}O_2 \rightarrow CO_2 + 2H_2O.$$

4) Whole-number coefficients are achieved by multiplying by two:

$$2CH_4O + 3O_2 \rightarrow 2CO_2 + 4H_2O.$$

Reactions among ions in aqueous solution may often be represented in three ways. When solutions of hydrochloric acid and sodium hydroxide are mixed, a reaction occurs and heat is produced. The **molecular equation** for this reaction is:

$$HCl(aq) + NaOH(aq) \rightarrow H_2O(l) + NaCl(aq).$$

It is called a molecular equation because the **complete chemical formulas** of reactants and products are shown. But in reality, both HCl and NaOH are strong electrolytes and exist in solution as ions. This is represented by a **complete ionic equation** that shows all the dissolved ions:

$$H^+(aq) + Cl^-(aq) + Na^+(aq) + OH^-(aq) \rightarrow H_2O(l) + Na^+(aq) + Cl^-(aq).$$

Because $Na^+(aq)$ and $Cl^-(aq)$ appear as both reactants and products, they play no role in the reaction. Ions that appear in identical chemical forms on both sides of an ionic equation are called **spectator ions** because they aren't part of the action. When spectator ions are removed from a complete ionic equation, the result is a **net ionic equation** that shows the actual changes that occur to the chemicals when these two solutions are mixed together:

$$H^+(aq) + OH^-(aq) \rightarrow H_2O(l)$$

An additional requirement for **redox** reactions is that the equation contains an **equal charge on each side**. Redox reactions may be divided into half-reactions which either gain or lose electrons.

Many **specific reaction types** also exist. Always determine the complete ionic equation for reactions in solution. This will help you determine the reaction type. The most common specific reaction types are summarized in the following table:

Reaction type	General equation	Example
Precipitation	Molecular: $AC(aq) + BD(aq) \rightarrow AD(s \text{ or } g) + BC(aq)$	Molecular: $NiCl_2(aq) + Na_2S(aq) \rightarrow NiS(s) + 2NaCl(aq)$
	Net ionic: $A^+(aq) + D^-(aq) \rightarrow AD(s \text{ or } g)$	Net ionic: $Ni^{2+}(aq) + S^{2-}(aq) \rightarrow NiS(s)$
Acid-base neutralization	Arrhenius: $H^+ + OH^- \rightarrow H_2O$	Arrhenius: $HNO_3 + NaOH \rightarrow NaNO_3 + H_2O$ $H^+ + OH^- \rightarrow H_2O$ (net ionic)
	Brønsted-Lowry: $HA + B \rightarrow HB + A$	Brønsted-Lowry: $HNO_3 + KCN \rightarrow HCN + KNO_3$ $H^+ + CN^- \rightarrow HCN$ (net ionic)
	Lewis: $A + {:}B \rightarrow A{:}B$	Lewis:
Redox	Full reaction: $A + B \rightarrow C + D$	$Ni + CuSO_4 \rightarrow NiSO_4 + Cu$ $Ni + Cu^{2+} \rightarrow Ni^{2+} + Cu$ (net ionic)
	Half reactions: $A \rightarrow C + e^-$ and $e^- + B \rightarrow D$	$Ni \rightarrow Ni^{2+} + 2e^-$ $2e^- + Cu^{2+} \rightarrow Cu$
Combustion	organic molecule $+ O_2 \rightarrow CO_2 + H_2O + $ heat	$2C_2H_6 + 7O_2 \rightarrow 4CO_2 + 6H_2O$

Whether precipitation occurs among a group of ions—and which compound will form the precipitate—may be determined by the solubility rules.

Ion	Solubility	Exception
All compounds containing alkali metals	All are soluble	
All compounds containing ammonium, NH_4^+	All are soluble	
All compounds containing nitrates, NO_3^-	All are soluble	
All compounds containing chlorates, ClO_3^- and perchlorates, ClO_4^-	All are soluble	
All compounds containing acetates, $C_2H_3O_2^-$	All are soluble	
Compounds containing Cl^-, Br^-, and I^-	Are soluble	Except halides of Ag^+, Hg_2^{2+}, and Pb^{2+}
Compounds containing F^-	Are soluble	Except fluorides of Mg^{2+}, Ca^{2+}, Sr^{2+}, Ba^{2+}, and Pb^2
Compounds containing sulfates, SO_4^{2-}	Are soluble	Except sulfates of Mg^{2+}, Ca^{2+}, Sr^{2+}, Ba^{2+}, and Pb^2
All compounds containing carbonates, CO_3^{2-}	Are insoluble	Except those containing alkali metals or NH_4^+
All compounds containing phosphates, PO_4^{3-}	Are insoluble	Except those containing alkali metals or NH_4^+
All compounds containing oxalates, $C_2O_4^{2-}$	Are insoluble	Except those containing alkali metals or NH_4^+
All compounds containing chromates, CrO_4^{2-}	Are insoluble	Except those containing alkali metals or NH_4^+
All compounds containing oxides, O^{2-}	Are insoluble	Except those containing alkali metals or NH_4^+
All compounds containing sulfides, S^{2-}	Are insoluble	Except those containing alkali metals or NH_4^+
All compounds containing sulfites, SO_3^{2-}	Are insoluble	Except those containing alkali metals or NH_4^+
All compounds containing silicates, SiO_4^{2-}	Are insoluble	Except those containing alkali metals or NH_4^+
All compounds containing hydroxides	Are insoluble	Except those containing alkali metals or NH_4^+, or Ba^{2+}

If protons are available for combination or substitution then it's likely they are being transferred from an acid to a base. An unshared electron pair on one of the reactants may form a bond in a Lewis acid-base reaction.

The possibility that oxidation numbers may change among the reactants indicates an electron transfer and a redox reaction. Combustion reactants consist of an organic molecule and oxygen.

Example: Determine the products and write a balanced equation for the reaction between sodium iodide and lead (II) nitrate in aqueous solution.

Solution: We know that sodium iodide is NaI and lead (II) nitrate is $Pb(NO_3)_2$.

The reactants of the complete ionic equation are:

$$Na^+(aq) + Pb^{2+}(aq) + I^-(aq) + NO_3^-(aq) \rightarrow ?$$

The solubility rules indicate that lead iodide is insoluble and will form as a precipitate. The unbalanced net ionic equation is then:

$$Pb^{2+}(aq) + I^-(aq) \rightarrow PbI_2(s)$$

and the unbalanced molecular equation is:

$$NaI(aq) + Pb(NO_3)_2(aq) \rightarrow PbI_2(s) + NaNO_3(aq).$$

Balancing yields:

$$2NaI(aq) + Pb(NO_3)_2(aq) \rightarrow PbI_2(s) + 2NaNO_3(aq).$$

Skill 11.2   Recognizing possible indications of a chemical reaction (e.g., precipitation, gas evolution, color change)

A chemical reaction is an interaction in which atoms exchange or share electrons, forming new chemicals. The substance or substances initially involved in this process are called reactants. Such reactions are characterized by a chemical change and yield one or more products that are different from the reactants.

There are several possible distinct indications that a chemical reaction has occurred. Which ones are observed depends on the type of reaction that takes place and the reactants involved.

1. Formation of a precipitate is one indicator of a chemical reaction. Precipitation is the term used to describe the formation of a solid out of solution during a chemical reaction. In most cases, the precipitate falls out of solution, and then sinks or floats in solution depending on its density. The formation of a precipitate can occur when solutions containing ionic compounds are mixed and an insoluble product is formed. Precipitates may also be seen in single displacement reactions when one metal ion in solution is replaced by another metal ion. A common experiment used to demonstrate precipitation is the mixing of silver nitrate and sodium chloride. This reaction is:

$$AgNO_3 + NaCl \rightarrow AgCl + NaNO_3$$

In this case, the precipitate is AgCl, which is insoluble in water.

2. A change in the color of a solution may also indicate that a chemical reaction has taken place. When two solutions are mixed, a color change indicates a chemical reaction has occurred if the change does not simply result from the dilution of one reactant in another. The Briggs-Rauscher reaction, also known as 'the oscillating clock', is one of the most common demonstrations of a color change reaction. In this experiment, three colorless solutions are mixed together, and the resulting mixture oscillates between clear, amber and deep blue, and over time becomes stable in color as a blue-black mixture. This reaction is:

$$IO_3- + 2\ H_2O_2 + CH_2(CO_2H)_2 + H+ \rightarrow$$
$$ICH(CO_2H)_2 + 2\ O_2 + 3\ H_2O$$

The amber color results from the formation of I_2, which is then consumed to produce the deep blue color as it binds to the starch present in solution.

3. The formation of a gas is the third sign that a reaction may have occurred, and is seen when bubbles form after two solutions have been mixed, or a solid is added to a solution. For example, in the reaction

$$Zn + 2HCl \rightarrow ZnCl_2 + H_2$$

hydrogen gas is released after zinc is added to hydrochloric acid.

4. An increase or decrease in temperature also indicates that a chemical reaction (exothermic or endothermic reaction respectively) has taken place. For example, when solutions of barium hydroxide and ammonium nitrate are mixed, the following endothermic reaction occurs, producing temperatures as low as -20 degrees Celsius.

$$Ba(OH)_2 \cdot 8H2O_{(s)} + 2NH_4NO_{3(s)} \rightarrow Ba(NO_3)_{2(s)} + 2NH_{3\ (aq)} + 10H_2O_{(li)}$$

Skill 11.3   Determining net ionic equations for chemical reactions

Oxidation numbers are used for tracking electrons in a chemical equation. Some ions always have the same oxidation number, but many can change oxidation numbers depending on what other ions are in the compound. The sum of the oxidation numbers (times the subscripts for those ions) of a compound must equal zero.

1. To determine oxidation numbers, start by placing the oxidation number above those ions whose oxidation number does not change – any ion from Group 1A is +1, from 2A is +2, from 6A is -2, and from 7A is -1.
2. Any uncombined element (listed by itself) is 0.
3. Hydrogen is always +1 except in a metal hydride (NaH) when it is -1.
4. Oxygen is always -2 except in hydrogen peroxide, H_2O_2, when it is -1.
5. In polyatomic ions, the sum of the oxidation numbers must equal the charge on the polyatomic ion.

<u>Example 1</u>: In SO_2, each oxygen is -2, so the net negative charge is -4, giving a net positive charge of +4. Each sulfur is +4.

<u>Example 2</u>: For $Na_2Cr_2O_7$ the oxygens are -2 each for a total of $(7)(-2) = -14$ and the sodiums are each +1 for a total of $(2)(+1) = +2$. That is a difference of -12. There are 2 chromiums, so $(-12)/(2) = -6$ for each chromium.

The total number of electrons on the left of the equation must equal the total number of electrons on the right. A *decrease* in an element's oxidation number from the left of the arrow (reactants) to the right of the arrow (products) signifies **reduction**. An *increase* in an element's oxidation number left to right signifies **oxidation**. The element undergoing the reduction is reduced and serves as the oxidizing agent (electron acceptor). The element undergoing the oxidation is oxidized and serves as the reducing agent (electron donor). Reduction and oxidation (known as redox) go hand-in-hand in an equation, one cannot happen without the other also happening.

<u>Example 1</u>: $Cl_2 + 2\,HBr \rightarrow 2\,HCl + Br_2$

Both Cl_2 and Br_2 will be zero since they are elements. H will be +1, which makes Br^{-1} and Cl^{-1}. That means that chlorine goes from 0 to -1, so it is reduced, and bromine goes from -1 to 0 so it is oxidized.

If the electrons are balanced, the coefficients are easier to balance. Once oxidation numbers have been assigned to all the elements on both sides of the equation and the atoms that are oxidized and reduced have been identified, use coefficients to make the total increase in oxidation number (loss of electrons) equal to the total decrease in oxidation number (gain of electrons). Then balance the equation as normal.

CHEMISTRY   125

Example: $Ca + 2 H_2O \rightarrow Ca(OH)_2 + H_2$
            0   +1 -2   +2 -2 +1   0

Ca: $0 \rightarrow +2$, so add electrons (e-) to right side to make it equal 0
    Ca: $0 \rightarrow +2 + 2$ e-
    H: $+1 \rightarrow 0$, so add electrons to left side to make it equal 0
    H: $+1 + 1$ e- $\rightarrow 0$ multiply this half-reaction by 2 so the
    numbers of electrons are equal, then put that 2 in front of the H_2O

Net ionic reaction: $Ca^0 + 2 H_2^{+1} + 1$ e- $\rightarrow Ca^{+2} + H_2^0 + 1$ e-
Spectator ions are those ions that are unchanged. In this case, O^{-2}.

Now see how close to balanced the equation is:
    Ca = 1   Ca = 1
    H = 4   H = 2 + 2 = 4
    O = 2   O = 2

Skill 11.4 Applying knowledge of the principle of conservation of mass as it applies to chemical reactions and balancing chemical equations

The principle of conservation states that certain measurable properties of an isolated system remain constant despite changes in the system. Two important principles of conservation are the conservation of mass and charge.

The principle of conservation of mass states that the total mass of a system is constant. Examples of conservation in mass in nature include the burning of wood, rusting of iron, and phase changes of matter. When wood burns, the total mass of the products, such as soot, ash, and gases, equals the mass of the wood and the oxygen that reacts with it. When iron reacts with oxygen, rust forms. The total mass of the iron-rust complex does not change. Finally, when matter changes phase, mass remains constant. Thus, when a glacier melts due to atmospheric warming, the mass of liquid water formed is equal to the mass of the glacier.

The principle of conservation of charge states that the total electrical charge of a closed system is constant. Thus, in chemical reactions and interactions of charged objects, the total charge does not change. Chemical reactions and the interaction of charged molecules are essential and common processes in living organisms and systems.

No matter is ever gained or lost during a chemical reaction; therefore the chemical equation must be *balanced.* This means that there must be the same number of molecules on both sides of the equation. Many chemical reactions give off energy. Like matter, energy can change form but it can neither be created nor destroyed during a chemical reaction. This is the **law of conservation of energy.**

Skill 11.5   Analyzing redox reactions in terms of oxidation and reduction half-reactions

Redox reactions may always be written as **two half-reactions**, a **reduction half-reaction** with **electrons as a reactant** and an **oxidation half-reaction** with **electrons as a product**.

For example, the redox reactions considered in the previous skill:
$$Zn(s) + Cu^{2+}(aq) \rightarrow Zn^{2+}(aq) + Cu(s) \quad \text{and} \quad H_2 + F_2 \rightarrow 2HF$$
may be written in terms of the half-reactions:
$$2e^- + Cu^{2+}(aq) \rightarrow Cu(s) \qquad \qquad 2e^- + F_2 \rightarrow 2F^-$$
$$\text{and}$$
$$Zn(s) \rightarrow Zn^{2+}(aq) + 2e^-. \qquad H_2 \rightarrow 2H^+ + 2e^-.$$
An additional (non-redox) reaction, $2F^- + 2H^+ \rightarrow 2HF$, achieves the final products for the second reaction.

Determining whether a chemical equation is balanced requires an additional step for redox reactions because there must be a **charge balance.** For example, the equation:
$$Sn^{2+} + Fe^{3+} \rightarrow Sn^{4+} + Fe^{2+}$$
contains one Sn and one Fe on each side but it is not balanced because the sum of charges on the left side of the equation is +5 and the sum on the right side is +6. One electron is gained in the reduction half-reaction ($Fe^{3+} + e^- \rightarrow Fe^{2+}$), but two are lost in the oxidation half-reaction ($Sn^{2+} \rightarrow Sn^{4+} + 2e^-$).

The equation:
$$Sn^{2+} + 2Fe^{3+} \rightarrow Sn^{4+} + 2Fe^{2+}$$
is properly balanced because both sides contain the same sum of charges (+8) and electrons cancel from the half-reactions:
$$2Fe^{3+} + 2e^- \rightarrow 2Fe^{2+}$$
$$Sn^{2+} \rightarrow Sn^{4+} + 2e^-.$$

Oxidation Number Method:

Redox reactions must be balanced to observe the Law of Conservation of Mass. This process is a little more complicated than balancing other reactions because the number of electrons lost must equal the number of electrons gained. Balancing redox reactions, then, conserves not only mass but also charge or electrons. It can be accomplished by slightly varying our balancing process.

$$Cr_2O_3(s) + Al(s) \longrightarrow Cr(s) + Al_2O_{3(s)}$$

Assign oxidation numbers to identify which atoms are losing and gaining electrons.

$$Cr_2O_3(s) + Al(s) \longrightarrow Cr(s) + Al_2O_{3(s)}$$
$$3+ \ 2- \quad\quad 0 \quad\quad\quad 0 \quad\quad 3+ \ 2-$$

Identify those atoms gaining and losing electrons:

$Cr^{3+} \longrightarrow Cr^0$ gained 3 electrons : reduction
$Al^0 \longrightarrow Al^{3+}$ lost 3 electrons: oxidation

Balance the atoms and electrons:

$$Cr_2O_3(s) \longrightarrow 2Cr(s) + 6 \text{ electrons}$$
$$2Al(s) + 6 \text{ electrons} \longrightarrow Al_2O_3(s)$$

Balance the half reactions by adding missing elements. Ignore elements whose oxidation number does not change. Add H_2O for oxygen and H^+ for hydrogen.

$$Cr_2O_3(s) \longrightarrow 2Cr(s) + 6 \text{ electrons} + \mathbf{3\ H_2O}$$

Need 3 oxygen atoms on product side. This requires $6H^+$ on the reactant side.

$$Cr_2O_3(s) + \mathbf{6\ H^+} \longrightarrow 2Cr(s) + 6 \text{ electrons} + \mathbf{3\ H_2O}$$

AND

$$2Al(s) + 6 \text{ electrons} + \mathbf{3\ H_2O} \longrightarrow Al_2O_{3(s)} + \mathbf{6\ H^+}$$

Need 3 oxygen atoms on reactant side. This requires $6H^+$ on the product side.

Put the two half reactions together and add the species. Cancel out the species that occur in both the reactants and products.

$$Cr_2O_3(s) + 6\ H^+ + 2Al(s) + 6 \text{ electrons} + 3\ H_2O \longrightarrow 2Cr(s) + 6 \text{ electrons} + 3\ H_2O + Al_2O_{3(s)} + 6\ H^+$$

The balanced equation is:

$$Cr_2O_3(s) + 2Al(s) \longrightarrow 2Cr(s) + Al_2O_{3(s)}$$

Try another: $AgNO_3 + Cu \longrightarrow CuNO_3 + Ag$

Assign oxidation numbers to identify which atoms are losing and gaining electrons.

$$AgNO_3 + Cu \longrightarrow Cu(NO_3)_2 + Ag$$
$$1+\ 5+\ 2-\quad 0\qquad 2+\ 5+\ 2-\quad 0$$

Identify those atoms gaining and losing electrons:

$Ag^{1+} + 1\ e^- \longrightarrow Ag^0$ 1 electron gained: reduction
$Cu^0 \longrightarrow Cu^{2+} + 2\ e^-$ 2 electrons lost: oxidation

Balance the atoms and electrons:

$AgNO_3 + 1\ e^- \longrightarrow Ag^0$
$Cu^0 \longrightarrow Cu(NO_3)_2 + 2\ e^-$
$Cu^0 \longrightarrow Cu^{2+} + 2\ e^-$

Balance the electrons:

$AgNO_3 + 1\ e^- \longrightarrow Ag^0$
$Cu^0 \longrightarrow Cu(NO_3)_2 + 2\ e^-$

1 electron gained and 2 electrons lost. Needs to be equal so 2 electrons need to be gained.

$$2\ [Ag + 1\ e^- \longrightarrow Ag^0] = \mathbf{2\ AgNO_3 + 2\ e^- \longrightarrow 2\ Ag^{0+}}$$

Reduction: $2\ AgNO_3 + 2\ e^- \longrightarrow 2\ Ag^{0+}$
Oxidation: $Cu^0 \longrightarrow Cu(NO_3)_2 + 2\ e^-$

Balance the half reactions by adding missing elements. Ignore elements whose oxidation number does not change. Add H_2O for oxygen and H^+ for hydrogen

$$2\ AgNO_3 + 2\ e^- \longrightarrow 2\ Ag^{0+} \mathbf{+ 2\ NO_3}$$
$$\mathbf{2NO_3 +}\ Cu^0 \longrightarrow Cu(NO_3)_2 + 2\ e^-$$

Put the two half reactions together and add the species. Cancel out the species that occur in both the reactants and products.

Reduction: $2\ AgNO_3 + 2\ e^- \longrightarrow 2\ Ag^{0+} + 2\ NO_3$
Oxidation: $2NO_3 +\ Cu^0 \longrightarrow Cu(NO_3)_2 + 2\ e^-$

The balanced reaction is:
$2\ AgNO_3 + Cu \longrightarrow Cu(NO_3)_2 + 2\ Ag$

Try this one: $Ag_2S + HNO_3 \longrightarrow AgNO_3 + NO + S + H_2O$

Assign oxidation numbers:
$$Ag_2S + HNO_3 \longrightarrow AgNO_3 + NO + S + H_2O$$
$$1+\ 2-\quad 1+\ 5+\ 2-\qquad 1+\ 5+\ 2-\quad 2+\ 2-\quad 0\qquad 1+\ 2-$$

Identify those atoms gaining and losing electrons:
oxidation: $S^{2-} \longrightarrow S^0 + 2\ e^-$
reduction: $N^{5+} + 3\ e^{-+} \longrightarrow N^{2+}$

3. Balance the atoms:
Oxidation: $2\ NO_3 + Ag_2S \longrightarrow S + 2\ e^- + 2\ AgNO_3$
Reduction: $3\ H^+ + HNO_3 + 3\ e^- \longrightarrow NO + 2\ H_2O$

Balance electrons lost and gained:
2 electrons lost and 3 electron gained. Need to be equal so find multiple: 6

Oxidation: $3[\ 2\ NO_3 + Ag_2S \longrightarrow S + 2\ e^- + 2\ AgNO_3]$
$6\ NO_3 + 3\ Ag_2S \longrightarrow 3\ S + 6\ e^- + 6\ AgNO_3$

Reduction: $2[\ 3\ H^+ + HNO_3 + 3\ e^- \longrightarrow NO + 2\ H_2O]$
$6\ H^+ + 2\ HNO_3 + 6\ e^- \longrightarrow 2\ NO + 4\ H_2O$

5. Put the two half reactions together and add the species. Cancel out the species that occur in both the reactants and products.

$6\ NO_3 + 3\ Ag_2S + 6\ H^+ + 2\ HNO_3 + 6\ e^- \longrightarrow 3\ S + 6\ e^- + 6\ AgNO_3 + 2\ NO + 4\ H_2O$

The balanced equation is:
$$3\ Ag_2S + 8\ HNO_3 \longrightarrow 6\ AgNO_3 + 2\ NO + 3\ S + 4\ H_2O$$

To balance a redox reaction which occurs in basic solution is a very similar to balancing a redox reaction which occurs in acidic conditions. First, balance the reaction as you would for an acidic solution and then adjust for the basic solution. Here is an example using the half-reaction method:

Solid chromium(III) hydroxide, $Cr(OH)_3$, reacts with aqueous chlorate ions, ClO_3^-, in basic conditions to form chromate ions, CrO_4^{2-}, and chloride ions, Cl^-.

$Cr(OH)_3(s) + ClO_3^-(aq) \rightarrow CrO_4^{2-}(aq) + Cl^-(aq)$ (basic)

1. Write the half-reactions:
$Cr(OH)_3(s) \rightarrow CrO_4^{2-}(aq)$ and
$ClO_3^-(aq) \rightarrow Cl^-(aq)$

2. Balance the atoms in each half-reaction. Use H_2O to add oxygen atoms and H^+ to add hydrogen atoms.

$$H_2O \ (l) + Cr(OH)_3(s) \rightarrow CrO_4^{2-}(aq) + 5\ H^+ \ (aq)$$

$$6H^+ \ (aq) + ClO_3^-(aq) \rightarrow Cl^-(aq) + 3\ H_2O \ (l)$$

3. Balance the charges of both half-reactions by adding electrons.

$$H_2O \ (l) + Cr(OH)_3(s) \rightarrow CrO_4^{2-}(aq) + 5\ H^+ \ (aq)$$

has a charge of +3 on the right and 0 on the left. Adding 3 electrons to the right side will give that side a 0 charge as well.

$$H_2O \ (l) + Cr(OH)_3(s) \rightarrow CrO_4^{2-}(aq) + 5\ H^+ \ (aq) + 3e^-$$

$$6H^+ \ (aq) + ClO_3^-(aq) \rightarrow Cl^-(aq) + 3\ H_2O \ (l)$$

has a charge of -1 on the right side and a +5 on the left. Six electrons need to be added to the left side to equal the -1 charge on the right side.

$$6\ e^- + 6H^+ \ (aq) + ClO_3^-(aq) \rightarrow Cl^-(aq) + 3\ H_2O \ (l)$$

4. The number of electrons lost must equal the number of electrons gained so multiply each half-reactions by a number that will give equal numbers of electrons lost and gained.

$$H_2O \ (l) + Cr(OH)_3(s) \rightarrow CrO_4^{2-}(aq) + 5\ H^+ \ (aq) + 3e^-$$
$$6\ e^- + 6H^+ \ (aq) + ClO_3^-(aq) \rightarrow Cl^-(aq) + 3\ H_2O \ (l)$$

The first half reaction needs to be multiplied by 2 to equal the 6 electrons gained in the second half-reaction.

$$2[H_2O \ (l) + Cr(OH)_3(s) \rightarrow CrO_4^{2-}(aq) + 5\ H^+ \ (aq) + 3e^-\ ] =$$
$$2H_2O \ (l) + 2\ Cr(OH)_3(s) \rightarrow 2\ CrO_4^{2-}(aq) + 10\ H^+ \ (aq) + 6e^-$$

5. Add the two half-reactions together; canceling out species that appear on both sides of the reaction.

$$2H_2O + 2\ Cr(OH)_3(s) + 6e^- + 6H^+ \ (aq) + ClO_3^-(aq) \rightarrow 2\ CrO_4^{2-}(aq) + 10\ H^+ \ (aq) + 6e^- + Cl^-(aq) + 3H_2O$$

$$4\ H^+ \ (aq) \qquad\qquad 1\ H_2O \ (l)$$

6. Since the reaction occurs in basic solution and there are 4 H^+ ions on the right side, 4 OH^- need to be added to both sides. Combine the H^+ and OH^- where appropriate to make water molecules.

4 OH^- (aq)+ 2 $Cr(OH)_3$(s) +ClO_3^-(aq) → 2 CrO_4^{2-}(aq) + 4 H^+ (aq) + Cl^-(aq) + 1H_2O (l) + 4 OH^- (aq)

4 H_2O (l)

7. Write final balanced equation:

4 OH^- (aq)+ 2 $Cr(OH)_3$(s) +ClO_3^-(aq)→ 2 CrO_4^{2-}(aq) + Cl^-(aq) + 5 H_2O (l)

57 videos of redox experiments are presented here: http://chemmovies.unl.edu/chemistry/redoxlp/redox000.html.

Skill 11.6   Identifying oxidizing and reducing agents in a chemical reaction

Redox is shorthand for *reduction* and *oxidation*. **Reduction** is the **gain of an electron** by a molecule, atom, or ion. **Oxidation** is the **loss of an electron** by a molecule, atom, or ion. These two processes always occur together. Electrons are lost by one substance are gained by another. In a redox process, the **oxidation numbers** of atoms are altered. Reduction decreases the oxidation number of an atom. Oxidation increases the oxidation number.

The easiest redox processes to identify are those involving monatomic ions with altered charges. For example, the reaction

$$Zn(s) + Cu^{2+}(aq) \rightarrow Zn^{2+}(aq) + Cu(s)$$

is a redox process because electrons are transferred from Zn to Cu.

However, many redox reactions involve the transfer of electrons from one molecular compound to another. In these cases, **oxidation numbers must be determined** as follows:

Oxidation numbers, sometimes called oxidation states, are signed numbers assigned to atoms in molecules and ions. They allow us to keep track of the electrons associated with each atom. Oxidation numbers are frequently used to write chemical formulas, to help us predict properties of compounds, and to help balance equations in which electrons are transferred. Knowledge of the oxidative state of an atom gives us an idea about its positive or negative character. In themselves, oxidation numbers have no physical meaning; they are used to simplify tasks that are more difficult to accomplish without them.

The Rules:

1. Free elements are assigned an oxidation state of 0.

e.g. Al, Na, Fe, H_2, O_2, N_2, Cl_2 etc have zero oxidation states.

2. The oxidation state for any simple one-atom ion is equal to its charge.

e.g. the oxidation state of Na^+ is +1, Be^{2+}, +2, and of F^-, -1.

3. The alkali metals (Li, Na, K, Rb, Cs and Fr) in compounds are always assigned an oxidation state of +1.

e.g. in LiOH (Li, +1), in Na_2SO_4(Na, +1).

4. Fluorine in compounds is always assigned an oxidation state of -1.

e.g. in HF_2^-, BF_2^-.

5. The alkaline earth metals (Be, Mg, Ca, Sr, Ba, and Ra) and also Zn and Cd in compounds are always assigned an oxidation state of +2. Similarly, Al & Ga are always +3.

e.g. in $CaSO_4$(Ca, +2), $AlCl_3$ (Al, +3).

6. Hydrogen in compounds is assigned an oxidation state of +1. Exception - Hydrides, e.g. LiH (H=-1).

e.g. in H_2SO_4 (H, +1).

7. Oxygen in compounds is assigned an oxidation state of -2. Exception - Peroxide, e.g. H_2O_2 (O = -1).

e.g. in H_3PO_4 (O, -2).

8. The sum of the oxidation states of all the atoms in a species must be equal to net charge on the species.

e.g. Net Charge of $HClO_4$ = 0, i.e. [+1(H)+7(Cl)-2*4(O)] = 0

Net Charge of CrO_4^{2-}=-2,

To solve Cr's oxidation state: x - 4*2(O) = -2, x = +6, so the oxidation state of Cr is +6.

For example, the reaction

$$H_2 + F_2 \rightarrow 2HF$$

is a redox process because the oxidation numbers of atoms are altered. The oxidation numbers of elements are always zero, and oxidation numbers in a compound are never zero. Fluorine is the more electronegative element, so in HF it has an oxidation number of –1 and hydrogen has an oxidation number of +1. This is a redox process where electrons are transferred from H_2 to F_2 to create HF.

In the reaction

$$HCl + NaOH \rightarrow NaCl + H_2O,$$

the H-atoms on both sides of the reaction have an oxidation number of +1, the atom of Cl has an oxidation number of –1, the Na-atom has an oxidation number of +1, and the atom of O has an oxidation number of –2. **This is not a redox process because oxidation numbers remain unchanged** by the reaction.

When electrons are being transferred, there is a flow of electrons from the anode to the cathode. This flow of electrons is electricity. When electrons are flowing spontaneously, the cell potential is positive. This cell potential is calculated from the standard reduction potentials of each half reaction occurring in the electrochemical cell.

A **standard cell potential, E°_{cell}**, is the voltage generated by an electrochemical cell at **100 kPa and 25 °C** when all components of the reaction are pure materials or solutes at a **concentration of 1 M**. Older textbooks may use 1 atm instead of 100 kPa. Standard solute concentrations may differ from 1 M for solutions that behave in a non-ideal way, but this difference is beyond the scope of general high school chemistry.

Standard cell potentials are calculated from the **sum of the two half-reaction potentials** for the reduction and oxidation reactions occurring in the cell:

$$E^\circ_{cell} = E^\circ_{red}(\text{cathode}) + E^\circ_{ox}(\text{anode}$$

All half-reaction potentials are relative to the reduction of H^+ to form H_2. This potential is assigned a value of zero:

$$\text{For } 2H^+(aq \text{ at } 1 \text{ M}) + 2e^- \rightarrow H_2(g \text{ at } 100 \text{ kPa}), \quad E^\circ_{red} = 0 \text{ V.}$$

The standard potential of an oxidation half-reaction E°_{ox} **is equal in magnitude but has the opposite sign to the potential of the reverse reduction reaction**. Standard half-cell potentials are **tabulated as reduction potentials**. These are sometimes referred to as **standard electrode potentials $E°$**. Therefore,

$$E^\circ_{cell} = E^\circ(\text{cathode}) - E^\circ(\text{anode}.$$

Example: Given $E°=0.34$ V for $Cu^{2+}(aq)+2e^-\square Cu(s)$ and
$E°= -0.76$ V for $Zn^{2+}(aq)+2e^-\square Zn(s)$, what is the standard cell potential
of the $Zn(s)+Cu^{2+}(aq) \rightarrow Zn^{2+}(aq)+Cu(s)$ system?

Solution:
$$E^°_{cell} = E^°(\text{cathode}) - E^°(\text{anode})$$
$$= E^°\left(Cu^{2+}(aq)+2e^- \rightarrow Cu(s)\right) - E^°\left(Zn^{2+}(aq)+2e^- \rightarrow Zn(s)\right)$$
$$= 0.34 \text{ V} - (-0.76 \text{ V}) = 1.10 \text{ V}.$$

Spontaneity

When the value of E° is positive, the reaction is spontaneous. If the E° value is negative, an outside energy source is necessary for the reaction to occur. In the above example, the E° is a positive 1.10 V, therefore this reaction is spontaneous.

An **oxidizing agent** (also called an oxidant or oxidizer) has the ability to oxidize other substances by removing electrons from them. The **oxidizing agent is reduced** in the process. A **reducing agent** (also called a reductive agent, reductant or reducer) is a substance that has the ability to reduce other substances by transferring electrons to them. The **reducing agent is oxidized** in the process.

Skill 11.7   Analyzing the components (e.g., anode, cathode, salt bridge) and operating principles of electrochemical cells

Electrolytic cells use electricity to force non-spontaneous redox reactions to occur while **electrochemical cells generate electricity** by permitting spontaneous redox reactions to occur. The two types of cells have some components in common.

Both systems contain two **electrodes**. An electrode is a piece of conducting metal that is used to make contact with a nonmetallic material. One electrode is an **anode**. An **oxidation reaction occurs at the anode**, so electrons are removed from a substance there. The other electrode is a **cathode.** A **reduction reaction occurs at the cathode**, so electrons are added to a substance there. Electrons flow from anode to cathode outside either device.

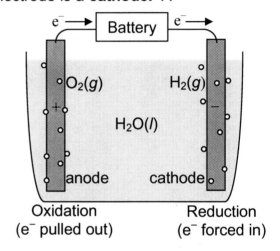

Oxidation   Reduction
(e⁻ pulled out)   (e⁻ forced in)

Electrolytic systems
Electrolysis is a chemical process **driven by a battery** or another source of electromotive force. This source pulls electrons out of the chemical process at the anode and forces electrons in the cathode. The result is a **negatively charged cathode and a positively charged anode**.

Electrolysis of pure water forms O_2 bubbles at the anode by the oxidation half-reaction:

$$2H_2O(l) \rightarrow 4H^+(aq) + O_2(g) + 4e^-$$

and forms H_2 bubbles at the cathode by the reduction half-reaction:

$$2H_2O(l) + 2e^- \rightarrow H_2(g) + 2OH^-(aq).$$

The net redox reaction is:

$$2H_2O(l) \rightarrow 2H_2(g) + O_2(g).$$

Neither electrode took part in the reaction described above. An electrode that is only used to contact the reaction and deliver or remove electrons is called an **inert electrode**. An electrode that takes part in the reaction is called an **active electrode**.

Electroplating is the process of **depositing dissolved metal cations** in a smooth even coat onto an object used as an active electrode. Electroplating is used to protect metal surfaces or for decoration. For example, to electroplate a copper surface with nickel, a nickel rod is used for the anode and the copper object is used for the cathode. $NiCl_2(aq)$ or another substance with free nickel ions is used in the electrolytic cell. $Ni(s) \rightarrow Ni^{2+}(aq) + 2e^-$ occurs at the anode and $Ni^{2+}(aq) + 2e^- \xrightarrow{\text{onto Cu}} Ni(s)$ occurs at the cathode.

An **electrochemical cell** separates the half-reactions of a redox process into two compartments or half-cells. Electrochemical cells are also called *galvanic cells* or *voltaic cells*.

A **battery** consists of one or more electrochemical cells connected together. Electron transfer from the oxidation to the reduction reaction may only take place through an external circuit.

Electrochemical systems provide a **source of electromotive force**. This force is also called or *voltage* or *cell potential* and is measured in **volts**. Electrons are allowed to leave the chemical process at the anode and permitted to enter at the cathode. The result is a **negatively charged anode and a positively charged cathode**.

Electrical neutrality is maintained in the half-cells by **ions migrating** through a **salt bridge**. A salt bridge in the simplest cells is an inverted U-tube filled with a non-reacting electrolyte and plugged at both ends with a material like cotton or glass wool that permits ion migration but prevents the electrolyte from falling out.

The spontaneous redox reaction $Zn(s) + Cu^{2+}(aq) \rightarrow Zn^{2+}(aq) + Cu(s)$ generates a voltage in the cell above. The oxidation half-reaction

$2e^-$

$Zn(s) \rightarrow Zn^{2+}(aq) + 2e^-$ occurs at the anode. Electrons are

$Zn(s) \rightarrow Zn^{2+}(aq)$ allowed to flow through a voltmeter before they are consumed by the reduction half-reaction

$2e^-$

$Cu^{2+}(aq) + 2e^- \rightarrow Cu(s)$ at the cathode. Zinc dissolves away from $Cu^{2+}(aq) \rightarrow Cu(s)$

the anode into solution, and copper from the solution builds up onto the cathode.

To maintain electrical neutrality in both compartments, positive ions (Zn^{2+} and Na^+) migrate through the salt bridge from the anode half-cell to the cathode half-cell and negative ions (NO_3^-) migrate in the opposite direction.

An animation of the cell described above is located at http://www.mhhe.com/physsci/chemistry/essentialchemistry/flash/galvan5.swf. A summary of anode and cathode properties for both cell types is contained in the table below.

		Electrolytic cell	Electrochemical cell
Anode	Half-reaction	Oxidation	Oxidation
	Electron flow	Pulled out	Allowed out
	Electrode polarity	+	−
Cathode	Half-reaction	Reduction	Reduction
	Electron flow	Forced in	Allowed in
	Electrode polarity	−	+

The reducing and oxidizing agents in a standard electrochemical cell are depleted with time. In a **rechargeable battery** (e.g., lead storage batteries in cars) the direction of the spontaneous redox reaction is reversed and **reactants are regenerated** when electrical energy is added into the system. A **fuel cell** has the same components as a standard electrochemical cell except that **reactants are continuously supplied**.

COMPETENCY 12.0   UNDERSTAND FACTORS THAT AFFECT REACTION RATES AND METHODS FOR MEASURING REACTION RATES.

Skill 12.1   Identifying factors that affect reaction rates (e.g., concentration, temperature, pressure, catalyst)

The rate of most simple reactions **increases with temperature** because a **greater fraction of molecules have the kinetic energy** required to overcome the reaction's activation energy. The chart below shows the effect of temperature on the distribution of kinetic energies in a sample of molecules. These curves are called **Maxwell-Boltzmann distributions**. The shaded areas represent the fraction of molecules containing sufficient kinetic energy for a reaction to occur. This area is larger at a higher temperature; so more molecules are above the activation energy and more molecules react per second.

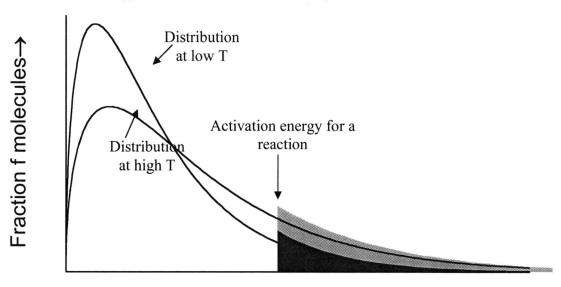

Kinetic Energy→

http://www.mhhe.com/physsci/chemistry/essentialchemistry/flash/activa2.swf provides an animated audio tutorial on energy diagrams.

Kinetic molecular theory may be applied to reaction rates in addition to physical constants like pressure. **Reaction rates increase with reactant concentration** because more reactant molecules are present and more are likely to collide with one another in a certain volume at higher concentrations. The nature of these relationships determines the rate law for the reaction. For ideal gases, the concentration of a reactant is its molar density, and this varies with pressure and temperature as discussed in.

Kinetic molecular theory also predicts that **reaction rate constants (values for k) increase with temperature** because of two reasons:
1) More reactant molecules will collide with each other per second.
2) These collisions will each occur at a higher energy that is more likely to overcome the activation energy of the reaction.

A **catalyst** is a material that increases the rate of a chemical reaction without changing itself permanently in the process. Catalysts provide an alternate reaction mechanism for the reaction to proceed in the forward and in the reverse direction. Therefore, **catalysts have no impact on the chemical equilibrium** of a reaction. They will not make a less favorable reaction more favorable.

Catalysts reduce the activation energy of a reaction. This is the amount of energy needed for the reaction to begin. Molecules with such low energies that they would have taken a long time to react will react more rapidly if a catalyst is present.

The impact of a catalyst may also be represented on an energy diagram. **A catalyst increases the rate of both the forward and reverse reactions by lowering the activation energy** for the reaction. Catalysts provide a different activated complex for the reaction at a lower energy state.

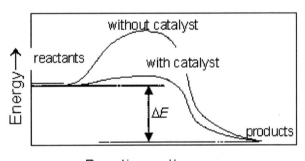

Reaction pathway→

There are two types of catalysts: **Homogeneous catalysts** are in the same physical phase as the reactants. Biological catalysts are called **enzymes**, and most are homogeneous catalysts. A typical homogenous catalytic reaction mechanism involves an initial reaction with one reactant followed by a reaction with a second reactant and release of the catalyst:

$$A + C \rightarrow AC$$

$$B + AC \rightarrow AB + C$$

Net reaction: $A + B \xrightarrow{\text{catalyst C}} AB$

Heterogeneous catalysts are present in a different physical state from the reactants. A typical heterogeneous catalytic reaction involves a solid surface onto which molecules in a fluid phase temporarily attach themselves in such a way to favor a rapid reaction. Catalytic converters in cars utilize heterogeneous catalysis to break down harmful chemicals in exhaust.

Skill 12.2 Demonstrating knowledge of reaction mechanisms for simple reactions

<u>Derive rate laws from simple reaction mechanisms</u>
A **reaction mechanism** is a series of **elementary reactions** that explain how a reaction occurs. These elementary reactions are also called elementary processes or elementary steps. **A reaction mechanism cannot be determined from reaction stoichiometry**. Stoichiometry indicates the number of molecules of reactants and products in an **overall reaction**. Elementary steps represent a **single event**. This might be a collision between two molecules or a single rearrangement of electrons within a molecule.

The simplest reaction mechanisms consist of a single elementary reaction. The number of molecules required determines the rate laws for these processes. For a **unimolecular process:**

$A \rightarrow$ products

the number of molecules of A that decompose in a given time will be proportional to the number of molecules of A present. Therefore unimolecular processes are first order:

$Rate = k\left[A\right]$.

For **bimolecular processes**, the rate law will be second order.

For $A+A \rightarrow$ products, $Rate = k\left[A\right]^2$

For $A+B \rightarrow$ products, $Rate = k\left[A\right]\left[B\right]$.

Most reaction mechanisms are multi-step processes involving **reaction intermediates**. Intermediates are chemicals that are formed during one elementary step and consumed during another, but they are not overall reactants or products. In many cases one elementary reaction in particular is the slowest and determines the overall reaction rate. This slowest reaction in the series is called the **rate limiting** (or rate determining) **step**.

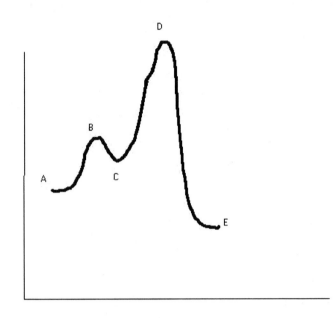

This energy diagram represents a two-step process for the reaction A→E. A is the energy of the reactants while B represents the activation energy for the reaction A→C. C is an intermediate, which when formed is immediately converted into E in the reaction C→E with an activation energy represented by D. Since the reaction C→E has a greater activation energy, it is the slow step, hence the rate determining step.

Example: The reaction $NO_2(g) + CO(g) \rightarrow NO(g) + CO_2(g)$ is composed of the following elementary reactions in the gas phase:

$$NO_2 + NO_2 \rightarrow NO + NO_3$$
$$NO_3 + CO \rightarrow NO_2 + CO_2.$$

The first elementary reaction is very slow compared to the second. Determine the rate law for the overall reaction if NO_2 and CO are both present in sufficient quantity for the reaction to occur. Also name all reaction intermediates.

Solution: The first step will be rate limiting because it is slower. In other words, almost as soon as NO_3 is available, it reacts with CO, so the rate-limiting step is the formation of NO_3. The first step is bimolecular. Therefore, the rate law for the entire reaction is: $\text{Rate} = k\left[NO_2\right]^2$.

NO_3 is formed during the first step and consumed during the second. NO_3 is the only reaction intermediate because it is neither a reactant nor a product of the overall reaction.

Skill 12.3   Determining the rate law for a chemical reaction from experimental data

Obtaining reaction rates from concentration data
The rate of any process is measured by its change per unit time. The speed of a car is measured by its change in position with time using units of miles per hour. The speed of a chemical reaction is usually measured by a change in the concentration of a reactant or product with time using units of **molarity per second** (M/s). The molarity of a chemical is represented in mathematical equations using brackets.

The **average reaction rate** is the change in concentration either reactant or product per unit time during a time interval:

$$\text{Average reaction rate} = \frac{\text{Change in concentration}}{\text{Change in time}}$$

Reaction rates are positive quantities. Product concentrations increase and reactant concentrations decrease with time, so a different formula is required depending on the identity of the component of interest:

$$\text{Average reaction rate} = \frac{\left[\text{product}\right]_{final} - \left[\text{product}\right]_{initial}}{\text{time}_{final} - \text{time}_{iniial}}$$

$$= \frac{\left[\text{reactant}\right]_{initial} - \left[\text{reactant}\right]_{final}}{\text{time}_{final} - \text{time}_{iniial}}$$

The **reaction rate** at a given time refers to the **instantaneous reaction rate**. This is found from the absolute value of the **slope of a curve of concentration vs. time**. An estimate of the reaction rate at time t may be found from the average reaction rate over a small time interval surrounding t. For those familiar with calculus notation, the following equations define reaction rate, but calculus is not needed for this skill:

$$\text{Reaction rate at time } t = \frac{d\left[\text{product}\right]}{dt} = -\frac{d\left[\text{reactant}\right]}{dt} .$$

Example: The following concentration data describes the decomposition of N_2O_5 according to the reaction $2N_2O_5 \rightarrow 4NO_2 + O_2$:

Time (sec)	$[N_2O_5]$ (M)
0	0.0200
1000	0.0120
2000	0.0074
3000	0.0046
4000	0.0029
5000	0.0018
7500	0.0006
10000	0.0002

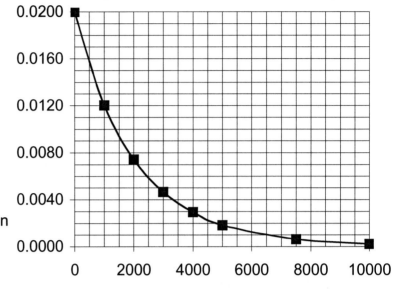

Determine the average reaction rate from 1000 to 5000 seconds and the instantaneous reaction rate at 0 and at 4000 seconds.

Solution: Average reaction rate from 0 to 7500 seconds is found from:

$$\frac{[\text{reactant}]_{\text{initial}} - [\text{reactant}]_{\text{final}}}{\text{time}_{\text{final}} - \text{time}_{\text{iniial}}} = \frac{0.0120 \text{ M} - 0.0018 \text{ M}}{5000 \text{ sec} - 1000 \text{ sec}} = 2.55 \times 10^{-6} \frac{M}{s}.$$

Instantaneous reaction rates are found by drawing lines tangent to the curve, finding the slopes of these lines, and forcing these slopes to be positive values.

At 0 seconds:

$$\text{rate=slope} = \frac{0.0200 \text{ M}}{2000 \text{ s}}$$

$$= 1.00 \times 10^{-5} \frac{M}{s}.$$

At 4000 seconds:

$$\text{rate=slope} = \frac{0.0090 \text{ M}}{6000 \text{ s}}$$

$$= 1.5 \times 10^{-6} \frac{M}{s}.$$

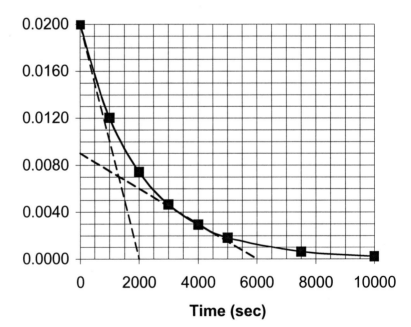

<u>Deriving rate laws from reaction rates</u>

A **rate law** is an **equation relating a reaction rate to concentration**. The rate laws for most reactions discussed in high-school level chemistry are of the form:

$$\text{Rate} = k\left[\text{reactant 1}\right]^{a}\left[\text{reactant 2}\right]^{b}\ldots$$

In the above general equation, k is called the **rate constant**. a and b are called **reaction orders**. Most reactions considered in introductory chemistry have a reaction order of zero, one, or two. The sum of all reaction orders for a reaction is called the **overall reaction order**. Rate laws cannot be predicted from the stoichiometry of a reaction. They must be determined by experiment or derived from knowledge of reaction mechanism.

If a reaction is zero order for a reactant, the concentration of that reactant has no impact on rate as long as some reactant is present. If a reaction is first order for a reactant, the reaction rate is proportional to the reactant's concentration. For a reaction that is second order with respect to a reactant, doubling that reactant's concentration increases reaction rate by a factor of four. Rate laws are determined by finding the appropriate reaction order describing **the impact of reactant concentration on reaction rate**.

Reaction rates typically have units of M/s (moles/liter-sec) and concentrations have units of M (moles/liter). For units to cancel properly in the expression above, the units found on the rate constant k must vary with overall reaction order as shown in the following table. The value of k may be determined by finding the slope of a plot charting a function of concentration against time. These functions may be memorized or computed using calculus.

Overall reaction order	Units of rate constant k	Method to determine k for rate laws with one reactant
0	M/sec	$-$(slope) of a chart of [reactant] vs. t
1	sec^{-1}	$-$(slope) of a chart of ln[reactant] vs. t
2	$M^{-1}\text{sec}^{-1}$	slope of a chart of 1/[reactant] vs. t

As an alternative to using the rate constant k, the course of **first order reactions** may be expressed in terms of a **half-life**, $t_{halflife}$. The half-life of a reaction is the time required for reactant concentration to reach half of its initial value. First order rate constants and half-lives are inversely proportional:

$$t_{halflife} = \frac{\ln 2}{k_{first\ order}} = \frac{0.693}{k_{first\ order}}$$

Example: Derive a rate law for the reaction $2N_2O_5 \rightarrow 4NO_2 + O_2$ using data from the previous example.

Solution: Three methods will be used to solve this problem.

1) In the previous example, we found the following two **instantaneous reaction rates**:

Time (sec)	[N$_2$O$_5$] (M)	Reaction rate (M/sec)
0	0.0200	1.00×10^{-5}
4000	0.0029	1.5×10^{-6}

A decrease in reactant concentration to 0.0029/0.0200=14.5% of its initial value led to a nearly proportional decrease in reaction rate to 15% of its initial value. In other words, reaction rate remains proportional to reactant concentration. The reaction is first order:

$$\text{Rate} = k\left[N_2O_5\right].$$

We may estimate a value for the rate constant by dividing reaction rates by the concentration:

$$k_{first\ order} = \frac{\text{Rate}}{\left[N_2O_5\right]}.$$

Time (sec)	[N$_2$O$_5$] (M)	Reaction rate (M/sec)	k (sec^{-1})
0	0.0200	1.00×10^{-5}	5.00×10^{-4}
4000	0.0029	1.5×10^{-6}	5.2×10^{-4}

2) We could estimate this rate constant by finding **average reaction rates** in each small time interval and assuming this rate occurs halfway between the two concentrations:

Time (sec)	[N$_2$O$_5$] (M)	Average rate (M/sec)	Halfway [N$_2$O$_5$] (M)	k (sec^{-1})
0	0.0200	8.00×10^{-6}	0.0160	5.00×10^{-4}
1000	0.0120	4.6×10^{-6}	0.0097	4.7×10^{-4}
2000	0.0074	2.8×10^{-6}	0.0060	4.7×10^{-4}
3000	0.0046	1.7×10^{-6}	0.0038	4.5×10^{-4}
4000	0.0029	1.1×10^{-6}	0.0024	4.7×10^{-4}
5000	0.0018	4.8×10^{-7}	0.0012	4.0×10^{-4}
7500	0.0006	2×10^{-7}	0.0004	4×10^{-4}
10000	0.0002			

3) If **concentration data** are given then no rate data needs to be found to determine a rate constant. For a first order reaction, chart the natural logarithm of concentration against time and find the slope.

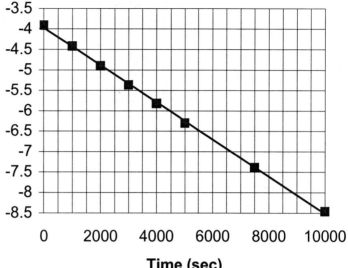

Time (sec)	$[N_2O_5]$ (M)	$\ln[N_2O_5]$
0	0.0200	-3.91
1000	0.0120	-4.41
2000	0.0074	-4.90
3000	0.0046	-5.37
4000	0.0029	-5.83
5000	0.0018	-6.30
7500	0.0006	-7.39
10000	0.0002	-8.46

The slope may be determined from a best-fit method or it may be estimated from
$$\frac{-8.46 - (-3.91)}{10000} = -5 \times 10^{-4}$$
. The rate law describing this reaction is:

Sample problem:
Given the following data for a reaction at 25°C.
$$2I^- \text{ (aq)} + S_2O_8{}^{2-} \text{ (aq)} \rightarrow I_2 \text{ (aq)} + 2\,SO_4{}^{2-} \text{ (aq)}$$

Experiment	$[I^-]$ (mol/L)	$[S_2O_8]$ (mol/L)	Initial Rate (mol/L·s)
1	0.080	0.040	12.5×10^{-6}
2	0.040	0.040	6.25×10^{-6}
3	0.080	0.020	6.25×10^{-6}
4	0.032	0.040	5.00×10^{-6}
5	0.060	0.030	7.00×10^{-6}

a. What is the rate law?
b. What is the order of the reaction with respect to I^-, S_2O_8 and overall?
c. What is the value of the rate law constant?

COMPETENCY 13.0   UNDERSTAND THE CONCEPT OF CHEMICAL EQUILIBRIUM.

Skill 13.1   Demonstrating knowledge of the key characteristics of a system at equilibrium

Several factors are important in the progress of a reaction. The most basic first step in any reaction is that the **reactants must collide with one another**. However, only a fraction of the collisions between the reactants allow the reaction to begin. This is because **the molecules must collide in the proper orientation and with sufficiently high energy**. This **activation energy** E_a is the minimum energy needed to overcome the barrier to the formation of products. That is, it is the minimum energy needed for the reaction to occur. The activation energy, E_a, is the difference between the energy of reactants and the energy of the activated complex, which is an intermediate form.   The energy change during the reaction, $\square E$, is the difference between the energy of the products and the energy of the reactants. If the energy of the products is lower than that of the reactants, the reaction will be exothermic. If reactants are lower than products, the reaction will be endothermic. Thus, **energy must be added to allow an endothermic reaction to progress towards equilibrium**. However, high activation energies can be overcome with the use of a catalyst. A **catalyst decreases E_a and so increases the rate of both the forward and reverse reactions by lowering the activation energy for the reaction**.   Note that a catalyst does not change the position of equilibrium, but merely reduces the energy requirements of a reaction.

If we return to the question of collisions between molecules, it becomes apparent that **kinetic energy** will have a bearing on the likelihood of these collisions. **Molecules that are moving around quickly will be more likely to collide and the higher number of collisions also increases the chance that the molecules will meet in the correct orientation**. Additionally, if the molecules generally have higher energy, it will be more likely for them to obtain the E_a required for the reaction to proceed. Therefore, **anything that increases the probability of these collisions and the energy of the molecules will speed the reaction's obtainment of equilibrium**. Thus it is clear that **temperature, pressure, and concentration must have an effect** on systems in equilibrium. Their effect is generalized in LeChatelier's Principle.

Skill 13.2   Solving problems involving equilibrium constants

Only a few reactions occur in which the reactants going completely to products and then the reaction is over (A + B → AB). Most reactions start with reactants going to products (A + B → AB) and then some of the products break down into reactants (A + B ← AB) while more reactants become products until equilibrium of the reaction is attained. Equilibrium occurs when the amount of reactants becoming products is equal to the amount of products becoming reactants (A + B ↔ AB).

Reaction Rates and Rate Laws

For reactions that reach equilibrium in a closed system, the K_{eq} is applicable. Given the generalized equilibrium equation: wA + xB ↔ yC + zD where the lowercase letters represent the coefficients and the capitalized letters represent the reactants (A, B) and the products (C, D), the equilibrium constant, K_{eq}, would be

$$K_{eq} = \frac{[C]^y[D]^z}{[A]^w[B]^x}$$

The square brackets indicate concentrations, usually expressed in molarity.

For the reaction: $2\,N_2(g) + 3\,H_2(g) \leftrightarrow 2\,NH_3(g)$

$$K_{eq} = \frac{[NH_3]^2}{[H_2]^3\,[N_2]^2}$$

This reaction is second degree with regard to ammonia, second degree with regard to nitrogen, and third degree with regard to hydrogen, making it seventh degree overall.

If K_{eq} is greater than one, the products are favored at equilibrium and if K_{eq} is less than one, the reactants are favored at equilibrium. K_{eq} is also called K_c, or the concentration constant, when based upon the concentrations of the reactants and products. This number is a constant for a particular reaction at a particular temperature. If the equation is a system where all the reactants and products are gases, the K_{eq} is based upon partial pressures rather than concentrations so it is a K_p.

The equilibrium constant, K_{eq}, becomes a solubility product constant, K_{sp}, for saturated solutions. It is derived from $K_{sp} = K_{eq}[A]^a[B]^b$ where A and B are reactants and a and b are their respective coefficients.

For a reaction in which all the reactants and all the products are in the same phase (known as a homogeneous reaction), the K_{eq} includes all of the products and all the reactants as shown. However, if the reaction is heterogeneous (having a combination of gases, solids, liquids, and aqueous solutions), the equilibrium expression should only contain those things that are gases, in aqueous solution, or liquids that are not H_2O.

Example problem 1: A mixture at equilibrium at 827°C contains 0.552 mol CO_2, 0.552 mol H_2, 0.448 mol CO, and 0.448 mol H_2O. What is the value of K_{eq}?
$CO_2(g) + H_2(g) \leftrightarrows CO(g) + H_2O(g)$

Solution: The equation is balanced and so all the coefficients are 1.

K_{eq} = [CO] [H_2O] / [CO_2] [H_2]
K_{eq} = (0.448)(0.448) / (0.552)(0.552)
K_{eq} = 0.2007 / 0.3047
K_{eq} = 0.659

Example problem 2: Dinitrogen tetroxide (N_2O_4), a colorless gas, and nitrogen dioxide (NO_2), a dark brown gas, exist in equilibrium with each other. A liter of a gas mixture at 100°C at equilibrium contains 0.0045 mol of dinitrogen tetroxide. Its equilibrium constant is 0.20. What is the concentration of nitrogen dioxide?

Solution: The reaction is: $N_2O_4(g) \leftrightarrows NO_2(g)$, but it has to be balanced:

$N_2O_4(g) \leftrightarrows 2 NO_2(g)$
K_{eq} = [NO_2]^2 / [N_2O_4]
Substitute what you know: 0.20 = [NO_2]^2 / (0.0045)
Solve: (0.20)(0.0045) = [NO_2]^2
9.0×10^{-4} = [NO_2]^2
Take the square root of both sides: 0.030 = [NO_2]

Skill 13.3 **Applying knowledge of Le Chatelier's principle as it applies to systems at equilibrium**

A system at equilibrium is in a state of balance because forward and reverse processes are taking place at equal rates. If equilibrium is disturbed by changing concentration, pressure, or temperature, the state of balance is upset for a period of time before the equilibrium shifts to achieve a new state of balance. **Le Chatelier's principle states that equilibrium will shift to partially offset the impact of an altered condition**.

Change in reactant and product concentrations
If a chemical reaction is at equilibrium, Le Chatelier's principle predicts that **adding a substance**—either a reactant or a product—will shift the reaction so **a new equilibrium is established by consuming some of the added substance**. Removing a substance will cause the reaction to move in the direction that forms more of that substance.

Example: The reaction $CO + 2H_2 \rightleftharpoons CH_3OH$ is used to synthesize methanol. Equilibrium is established, and then additional CO is added to the reaction vessel. Predict the impact on each reaction component after CO is added.

Solution: Le Chatelier's principle states that the reaction will shift to partially offset the impact of the added CO. Therefore, CO concentration will decrease, and the reaction will "shift to the right." H_2 concentration will also decrease and CH_3OH concentration will increase.

Change in pressure for gases
If a chemical reaction is at equilibrium in the gas phase, Le Chatelier's principle predicts that **an increase in pressure** will shift the reaction so **a new equilibrium is established by decreasing the number of gas moles present**. A decrease in the number of moles partially offsets this rise in pressure. Decreasing pressure will cause the reaction to move in the direction that forms more moles of gas. These changes in pressure might result from altering the volume of the reaction vessel at constant temperature.

Example: The reaction $N_2 + 3H_2 \rightleftharpoons 2NH_3$ is used to synthesize ammonia. Equilibrium is established. Next the reaction vessel is expanded at constant temperature. Predict the impact on each reaction component after this expansion occurs.

Solution: The expansion will result in a decrease in pressure. Le Chatelier's principle states that the reaction will shift to partially offset this decrease by increasing the number of moles present. There are 4 moles on the left side of the equation and 2 moles on the right, so the reaction will shift to the left. N_2 and H_2 concentration will increase. NH_3 concentration will decrease.

Change in temperature

Le Chatelier's principle predicts that **when heat is added** at constant pressure to a system at equilibrium, **the reaction will shift in the direction that absorbs heat** until a new equilibrium is established. For an endothermic process, the reaction will shift to the right towards product formation. For an exothermic process, the reaction will shift to the left towards reactant formation. If you understand the application of Le Chatelier's principle to concentration changes then writing "heat" on the appropriate side of the equation will help you understand its application to changes in temperature.

Example: $N_2 + 3H_2 \rightleftharpoons 2NH_3$ is an exothermic reaction. First equilibrium is established and then the temperature is decreased. Predict the impact of the lower temperature on each reaction component.

Solution: Since the reaction is exothermic, we may write it as:
$N_2 + 3H_2 \rightleftharpoons 2NH_3 + Heat.$ For the purpose of finding the impact of temperature on equilibrium processes, we may consider heat as if it were a reaction component. Le Chatelier's principle states that after a temperature decrease, the reaction will shift to partially offset the impact of a loss of heat. Therefore more heat will be produced, and the reaction will shift to the right. N_2 and H_2 concentration will decrease. NH_3 concentration will increase.

A flash animation with audio that demonstrates Le Chatelier's principle is at http://www.mhhe.com/physsci/chemistry/essentialchemistry/flash/lechv17.swf.

COMPETENCY 14.0   UNDERSTAND THE THEORIES, PRINCIPLES, AND APPLICATIONS OF ACID-BASE CHEMISTRY.

Skill 14.1   Identifying acids and bases according to different acid-base theories (e.g., Arrhenius, BrØnsted-Lowry, Lewis)

It was recognized centuries ago that many substances could be divided into the two general categories. **Acids** have a sour taste (as in lemon juice), dissolve many metals, and turn litmus paper red. **Bases** have a bitter taste (as in soaps), feel slippery, and turn litmus paper blue. The chemical reaction between an acid and a base is called **neutralization**. The products of neutralization reactions are neither acids nor bases. Litmus paper is an example of an **acid-base indicator**, a substance that changes color when added to an acid to a base.

Arrhenius definition of acids and bases
Svante **Arrhenius** proposed in the 1880s that **acids form H^+ ions and bases form OH^- ions in water**. The net ionic reaction for neutralization between an Arrhenius acid and base always produces water as shown below for nitric acid and sodium hydroxide:

$$HNO_3(aq) + NaOH(aq) \rightarrow NaNO_3(aq) + H_2O(l)$$

$$H^+(aq) + NO_3^-(aq) + Na^+(aq) + OH^-(aq) \rightarrow NO_3^-(aq) + Na^+(aq) + H_2O(l) \text{ (complete ionic)}$$

$$H^+(aq) + OH^-(aq) \rightarrow H_2O(l) \text{ (net ionic)}$$

The $H^+(aq)$ ion
In acid-base systems, **"protonated water" or "$H^+(aq)$" are shorthand for a mixture of water ions**. For example, HCl reacting in water may be represented as a dissociation:.

$$HCl(aq) \rightarrow H^+(aq) + Cl^-(aq)$$

The same reaction may be described as the transfer of a proton to water to form H_3O^+:

$$HCl(aq) + H_2O(l) \rightarrow Cl^-(aq) + H_3O^+(aq)$$

H_3O^+ is called a **hydronium ion**. Its Lewis structure is shown below to the left. In reality, the hydrogen bonds in water are so strong that H^+ ions exist in water as a mixture of species in a hydrogen bond network. Two of them are shown below at center and to the right. Hydrogen bonds are shown as dashed lines.

Brønsted-Lowry definition of acids and bases

In the 1920s, Johannes **Brønsted** and Thomas **Lowry** recognized that **acids can transfer a proton to bases** regardless of whether an OH^- ion accepts the proton. In an equilibrium reaction, the direction of proton transfer depends on whether the reaction is read left to right or right to left, so **Brønsted acids and bases exist in conjugate pairs with and without a proton.** Acids that are able to transfer more than one proton are called **polyprotic acids.**

Examples:

1) In the reaction:

$$HF(aq) + H_2O(l) \rightleftharpoons F^-(aq) + H_3O^+(aq),$$

HF transfers a proton to water. Therefore HF is the Brønsted acid and H_2O is the Brønsted base. But in the reverse direction, hydronium ions transfer a proton to fluoride ions. H_3O^+ is the conjugate acid of H_2O because it has an additional proton, and F^- is the conjugate base of HF because it lacks a proton.

2) In the reaction:

$$NH_3(aq) + H_2O(l) \rightleftharpoons NH_4^+(aq) + OH^-(aq),$$

water transfers a proton to ammonia. H_2O is the Brønsted acid and OH^- is its conjugate base. NH_3 is the Brønsted base and NH_4^+ is its conjugate acid.

3) In the reaction:

$$H_3PO_4 + HS^- \rightleftharpoons H_2PO_4^- + H_2S$$

$H_3PO_4/H_2PO_4^-$ is one conjugate acid-base pair and H_2S/HS^- is the other.

4) H_3PO_4 is a polyprotic acid. It may further dissociate to transfer more than one proton:

$$H_3PO_4 \rightleftharpoons H_2PO_4^- + H^+$$
$$H_2PO_4^- \rightleftharpoons HPO_4^{2-} + H^+$$
$$HPO_4^{2-} \rightleftharpoons PO_4^{3-} + H^+$$

Strong and weak acids and bases

Strong acids and bases are strong electrolytes, and weak acids and bases are weak electrolytes, so **strong acids and bases completely dissociate in water,** but weak acids and bases do not.

Example: $HCl(aq) + H_2O(l) \rightarrow H_3O^+(aq) + Cl^-(aq)$ goes to completion because HCl is a strong acid. The acids in the examples on the previous page were all weak.

The aqueous dissociation constants K_a and K_b quantify acid and base strength. Another way of looking at acid dissociation is that strong acids transfer protons more readily than H_3O^+ transfers protons, so they protonate water, the conjugate base of H_3O^+. In general, **if two acid/base conjugate pairs are present, the stronger acid will transfer a proton to the conjugate base of the weaker acid**.

Acid and base **strength is not related to safety**. Weak acids like HF may be extremely corrosive and dangerous.

The most **common strong acids and bases** are listed in the following table:

Strong acid		Strong base	
HCl	Hydrochloric acid	LiOH	Lithium hydroxide
HBr	Hydrobromic acid	NaOH	Sodium hydroxide
HI	Hydroiodic acid	KOH	Potassium hydroxide
HNO_3	Nitric acid	$Ca(OH)_2$	Calcium hydroxide
H_2SO_4	Sulfuric acid	$Sr(OH)_2$	Strontium hydroxide
$HClO_4$	Perchloric acid	$Ba(OH)_2$	Barium hydroxide

A flash animation tutorial demonstrating the difference between strong and weak acids is located at http://www.mhhe.com/physsci/chemistry/essentialchemistry/flash/acid13.swf.

Trends in acid and base strength
The strongest acid in a polyprotic series is always **the acid with the most protons** (e.g. H_2SO_4 is a stronger acid than HSO_4^-). The strongest acid in a series with the same central atom is always **the acid with the central atom at the highest oxidation number** (e.g. $HClO_4 > HClO_3 > HClO_2 > HClO$ in terms of acid strength). The strongest acid in a series with different central atoms at the same oxidation number is usually **the acid with the central atom at the highest electronegativity** (e.g. the K_a of $HClO > HBrO > HIO$).

Lewis definition of acids and bases
The transfer of a proton from a Brønsted acid to a Brønsted base requires that the base accept the proton. When Lewis diagrams are used to draw the proton donation of Brønsted acid-base reactions, it is always clear that the base must contain an unshared electron pair to form a bond with the proton. For example, ammonia contains an unshared electron pair in the following reaction:

$$H^+ \; + \; :\!\!\underset{\overset{|}{H}}{\overset{\overset{H}{|}}{N}}\!\!-\!\!H \; \longrightarrow \; \left[\underset{\overset{|}{H}}{\overset{\overset{H}{|}}{H\!-\!N}}\!\!-\!\!H \right]^+$$

In the 1920s, Gilbert N. **Lewis** proposed that **bases donate unshared electron pairs to acids**, regardless of whether the donation is made to a proton or to another atom. Boron trifluoride is an example of a Lewis acid that is not a Brønsted acid because it is a chemical that accepts an electron pair without involving an H^+ ion:

$$
\begin{array}{c}
F \\
\backslash \\
B{-}F \\
/ \\
F
\end{array}
\quad + \quad
\begin{array}{c}
H \\
| \\
:N{-}H \\
| \\
H
\end{array}
\quad \longrightarrow \quad
\begin{array}{c}
F \quad H \\
| \quad\;\; | \\
F{-}B{-}N{-}H \\
| \quad\;\; | \\
F \quad H
\end{array}
$$

The Lewis theory of acids and bases is more general than Brønsted-Lowry theory, but Brønsted-Lowry's definition is used more frequently. The terms "acid" and "base" most often refer to Brønsted acids and bases, and the term "Lewis acid" is usually reserved for chemicals like BF_3 that are not also Brønsted acids.

Summary of definitions

A Lewis base transfers an electron pair to a Lewis acid. A Brønsted acid transfers a proton to a Brønsted base. These exist in conjugate pairs at equilibrium. In an Arrhenius base, the proton acceptor (electron pair donor) is OH^-. All Arrhenius acids/bases are Brønsted acids/bases and all Brønsted acids/bases are Lewis acids/bases. Each definition contains a subset of the one that comes after it.

Skill 14.2   Demonstrating knowledge of the principles and applications of acid-base titrations and solving titration problems

Standard titration

In a typical acid-base **titration**, **an acid-base indicator** (such as *phenolphthalein*) or a **pH meter** is used to monitor the course of a **neutralization reaction**. The usual goal of titration is to **determine an unknown concentration** of an acid (or base) by neutralizing it with a known concentration of base (or acid).

The reagent of known concentration is usually used as the **titrant**. The titrant is poured into a **buret** (also spelled *burette*) until it is nearly full, and an initial buret reading is taken. Buret numbering is close to zero when nearly full. A known volume of the solution of unknown concentration is added to a flask and placed under the buret. The indicator is added or the pH meter probe is inserted. The initial state of a titration experiment is shown to the right above.

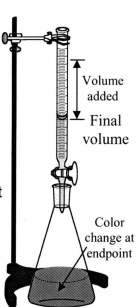

The buret stopcock is opened and titrant is slowly added until the solution permanently changes color or the pH rapidly changes. This is the titration **endpoint**, and a final buret reading is made. The final state of a titration experiment is shown to the right below. The endpoint occurs when the number of **acid and base equivalents in the flask are identical**:

$$N_{acid} = N_{base}. \text{ Therefore, } C_{acid}V_{acid} = C_{base}V_{base}.$$

The endpoint is also known as the titration **equivalence point**.

Titration data typically consist of:

$$V_{inital} \Rightarrow \text{Initial buret volume} \quad V_{final} \Rightarrow \text{Final buret volume}$$

$$C_{known} \Rightarrow \text{Concentration of known solution}$$

$$V_{unknown} \Rightarrow \text{Volume of unknown solution.}$$

To determine the unknown concentration, first find the volume of titrant at the known concentration added: $V_{known} = V_{final} - V_{initial}$.

At the equivalence point, $N_{unknown} = N_{known}$.

$$\text{Therefore, } C_{unknown} = \frac{C_{known}V_{known}}{V_{unknown}} = \frac{C_{known}\left(V_{final} - V_{initial}\right)}{V_{unknown}}.$$

Units of molarity may be used for concentration in the above expressions **unless a mole of either solution yields more than one acid or base equivalent.** In that case, concentration must be expressed using **normality**.

Example: A 20.0 mL sample of an HCl solution is titrated with 0.200 M NaOH. The initial buret volume is 1.8 mL and the final buret volume at the titration endpoint is 29.1 mL. What is the molarity of the HCl sample?

Solution: Two solution methods will be used. The first method is better for those who are good at unit manipulations and less skilled at memorizing formulas. HCl contains one acid equivalent and NaOH contains one base equivalent, so we may use molarity in all our calculations.

1) Calculate the moles of the known substance added to the flask:
$$0.200\,\frac{mol}{L} \times \frac{1\,L}{1000\,mL} \times \left(29.1\,mL - 1.8\,mL\right) = 0.00546\ mol\ NaOH.$$
At the endpoint, this base will neutralize 0.00546 mol HCl. Therefore, this amount of HCl must have been present in the sample before the titration.
$$\frac{0.00546\ mol\ HCl}{0.0200\ L} = 0.273\ M\ HCl.$$

2) Utilize the formula: $C_{unknown} = \dfrac{C_{known}\left(V_{final} - V_{initial}\right)}{V_{unknown}}$.

$$C_{HCl} = \frac{C_{NaOH}\left(V_{final} - V_{initial}\right)}{V_{HCl}} = \frac{0.200\ M\left(29.1\,mL - 1.8\,mL\right)}{20.0\,mL} = 0.273\ M\ HCl.$$

Titrating with the unknown

In a common variation of standard titration, the unknown is added to the buret as a titrant and the reagent of known concentration is placed in the flask. The chemistry involved is the same as in the standard case, and the mathematics is also identical except for the identity of the two volumes. For this variation, V_{known} will be the volume added to the flask before titration begins and $V_{unknown} = V_{final} - V_{initial}$. Therefore:

$$C_{unknown} = \frac{C_{known}V_{known}}{V_{unknown}} = \frac{C_{known}V_{known}}{V_{final} - V_{initial}}.$$

Example: 30.0 mL of a 0.150 M HNO_3 solution is titrated with $Ca(OH)_2$. The initial buret volume is 0.6 mL and the final buret volume at the equivalent point is 22.2 mL. What is the molarity of $Ca(OH)_2$ used for the titration?

Solution: The same two solution methods will be used as in the previous example. 1 mol $Ca(OH)_2$ contains 2 base equivalents because it reacts with 2 moles of H^+ via the reaction $Ca(OH)_2 + 2HNO_3 \rightarrow Ca(NO_3)_2 + 2H_2O$. Therefore, normality must be used in the formula for solution method 2.

1) First calculate the moles of the substance in the flask:

$$0.150 \frac{mol}{L} \times 0.0300\ L = 0.00450\ mol\ HNO_3.$$

This acid must be titrated with 0.00450 base equivalents for neutralization to occur at the end point. We calculate moles $Ca(OH)_2$ used in the titration from stoichiometry:

$$0.00450\ base\ equivalents \times \frac{1\ mol\ Ca(OH)_2}{2\ base\ equivalents} = 0.00225\ mol\ Ca(OH)_2.$$

The molarity of $Ca(OH)_2$ is found from the volume used in the titration:

$$\frac{0.00225\ mol\ Ca(OH)_3}{0.0222\ L - 0.0006\ L} = 0.104\ M\ Ca(OH)_3.$$

2) Utilize the formula: $C_{unknown} = \dfrac{C_{known} V_{known}}{V_{final} - V_{initial}}$ using units of normality.

For HNO_3, molarity=normality because 1 mol contains 1 acid equivalent.

$$C_{Ca(OH)_2} = \frac{C_{HNO_3} V_{HNO_3}}{V_{final} - V_{initial}} = \frac{\left(0.150\ M \times \dfrac{1\ N}{1\ M}\right)(30.0\ mL)}{22.2\ mL - 0.6\ mL} = 0.208\ N\ Ca(OH)_2.$$

This value is converted to molarity. For $Ca(OH)_2$, normality is twice molarity because 1 mol contains 2 base equivalents.

$$0.208\ N\ Ca(OH)_2 \times \frac{1\ M\ Ca(OH)_2}{2\ N\ Ca(OH)_2} = 0.104\ M\ Ca(OH)_2.$$

Interpreting titration curves

A **titration curve** is a plot of a solution's **pH charted against the volume of an added acid or base**. Titration curves are obtained if a pH meter is used to monitor the titration instead of an indicator. At the equivalence point, the titration curve is nearly vertical. This is the point where the most rapid change in pH occurs. In addition to determining the equivalence point, the **shape of titration curves** may be interpreted to determine **acid/base strength and the presence of a polyprotic acid.**

The pH at the equivalence point of a titration is the **pH of the salt solution obtained when the amount of acid is equal to amount of base**. For a strong acid and a strong base, the equivalence point occurs at the neutral pH of 7. For example, an equimolar solution of HCl and NaOH will contain NaCl(*aq*) at its equivalence point.

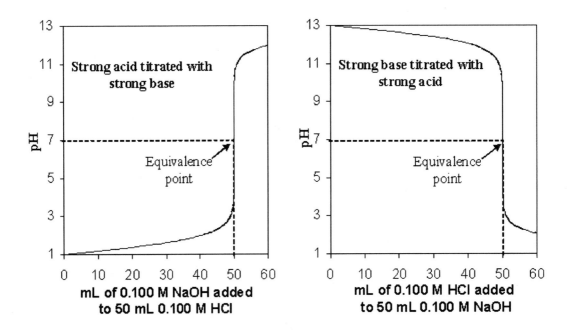

The salt solution at **the equivalence point of a titration involving a weak acid or base will not be at neutral pH**. For example, an equimolar solution of NaOH and hypochlorous acid HClO at the equivalence point of a titration will be a base because it is indistinguishable from a solution of sodium hypochlorite. A pure solution of NaClO(*aq*) will be a base because the ClO⁻ ion is the conjugate base of HClO, and it consumes H⁺(*aq*) in the reaction: $ClO^- + H^+ \rightleftharpoons HClO$.

In a similar fashion, an equimolar solution of HCl and NH₃ will be an acid because a solution of NH₄Cl(*aq*) is an acid. It generates H⁺(*aq*) in the reaction: $NH_4^+ \rightleftharpoons NH_3 + H^+$.

Contrast the following **titration curves for a weak acid or base** with those for a strong acid and strong base on the preceding page:

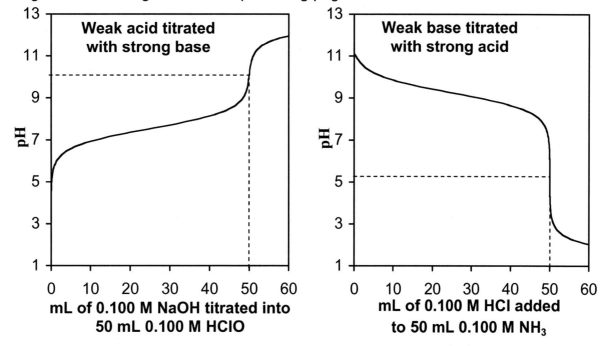

Titration of a polyprotic acid results in **multiple equivalence points** and a curve with more "bumps" as shown below for sulfurous acid and the carbonate ion.

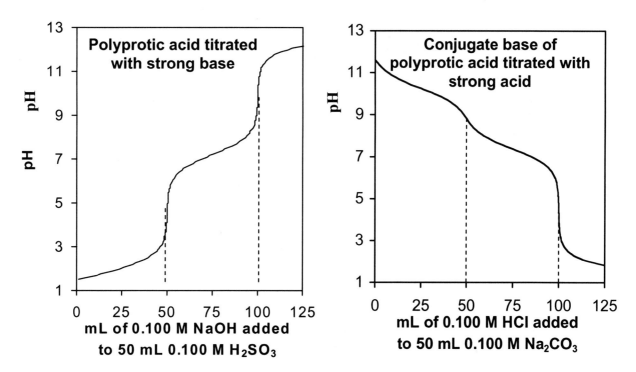

Skill 14.3   Determining the hydronium ion concentration and the pH or pOH of acid, base, and salt solutions

The concentration of $H^+(aq)$ ions is often expressed in terms of pH. **The pH of a solution is the negative base-10 logarithm of the hydrogen-ion molarity.**

$$pH = -\log\left[H^+\right] = \log\left(\frac{1}{\left[H^+\right]}\right).$$

A ten-fold increase in $[H^+]$ decreases the pH by one unit. $[H^+]$ may be found from pH using the expression:

$$\left[H^+\right] = 10^{-pH}.$$

The concentration of H^+ ions has been shown as $\left[H^+\right] = 10^{-7}$ M for pure water with $\left[H^+\right] = \left[OH^-\right]$. Thus **the pH of a neutral solution is 7**. In an **acidic solution**, $\left[H^+\right] > 10^{-7}$ M and **pH < 7**. In a basic solution, $\left[H^+\right] < 10^{-7}$ M and **pH > 7**.

Example: An aqueous solution has an H^+ ion concentration of 4.0×10^{-9}. Is the solution acidic or basic? What is the pH of the solution? What is the pOH?

Solution: The solution is basic because $\left[H^+\right] < 10^{-7}$ M.

$$pH = -\log\left[H^+\right] = -\log 4 \times 10^{-9}$$

$$= 8.4.$$

$$pH + pOH = 14. \text{ Therefore } pOH = 14 - pH = 14 - 8.4 = 5.6.$$

Skill 14.4   Recognizing factors that determine the relative strengths of acids and bases

Before we recognize factors that determine the relative strengths of acids and bases, it is important to have a clear understanding of acids and bases.

Arrhenius, a Swedish chemist, defined acids as compounds that contain hydrogen, and defined bases as compounds that dissolve in water and release OH⁻ ions. His proposals had limitations. In 1923, a Danish chemist named **Johannes Bronsted** and an Englishman named **Thomas Lowry** refined the theory of Arrhenius. According to these chemists, an acid is a substance that donates a proton (this is a hydrogen ion because hydrogen atoms have no neutrons) and bases are substances capable of splitting off or taking up hydrogen ions. Traditionally, a base contains OH⁻ ions. But according to Bronsted and Lowry, $NaHCO_3$ is also a base because it is capable of accepting hydrogen ions, which the Arrhenius theory couldn't explain.

The factors that determine the relative strengths of acids and bases:

1. pH:
Both acids and bases are related to the concentration of hydrogen ions present. As the concentration of the hydrogen ions increases, the pH value goes down and the acidity of a substance is increased.

The opposite is true for bases. As the hydrogen ion concentration decreases, the pH value goes up and the basicity of a substance is increased. Very strong acids have a pH of 1 or below. Very strong bases have pH values exceeding 12 or more. Milk is a mild acid and HCl is a strong acid.

There is an inverse relationship between the pH value and the hydrogen ion concentration. The higher the hydrogen ion concentration, lower the pH number and greater the acidity. The lower the hydrogen ion concentration, the higher the pH value and greater the strength of the base. Egg whites are weak bases and NaOH is a strong base.

2. Acid dissociation constant and basicity constant:

Acid dissociation constant, acidity constant, or the acid ionization constant, (K_a), is a specific type of equilibrium constant that indicates the extent of dissociation of ions from an acid. The acidity of a substance and its Ka value are directly proportional. A larger K_a (smaller pK_a) means a stronger acid. Using the values of K_a, the strength of acids can be determined easily.

The basicity constant, K_b, is the capability of a substance to accept hydrogens. The value of K_b and the strength of bases are directly proportional. The higher the value of K_b (pK_b), the stronger the base.

3. The relationship of K_a and pK_a:

pK_a = -log10K_a, the acidity constant is represented as the additive inverse of its common logarithm, using the same mathematical relationship as H+ is to pH. The lower the pK_a value, the higher the acidity of the substance is. In the same way, pK_b = -log10K_b. Just like pK_a, the lower the pK_b value, the higher the basicity.

Skill 14.5   Interpreting K_a and K_b values for weak acids and bases

K_a and K_b are particular types of equilibrium constants that give us an idea of the relative strengths of acids and bases, respectively. The **acid-dissociation constant, K_a, is the equilibrium constant for the ionization of a weak acid to a hydrogen ion and its conjugate base.** Likewise, **the base-dissociation constant, K_b, is the equilibrium constant for the addition of a proton to a weak base by water to form its conjugate acid and an OH⁻ ion.**

If we examine the reaction for a generic acid, HA, it is clear that these constants are derived just like other equilibrium constants:

$$HA(aq) \rightarrow H^+(aq) + A^-(aq) \qquad K_a = \frac{[H^+][A^-]}{[HA]}$$

Note that polyprotic acids have unique values for each dissociation: K_{a1}, K_{a2}, etc. K_b is simply the analogous constant in reactions involving bases.

Because K_a and K_b values vary over many orders of magnitude, it is common practice to **take the log of the value and present pK_a and pK_b values** (that is, pK_a= -log$_{10}K_a$). We can then reckon that **smaller pK_a values indicate stronger acids**, since this indicates a greater extent of dissociation. Analogously, **a larger pK_b indicates a stronger base**.

The negative base-10 log is a convenient way of representing other small numbers used in chemistry by placing the letter "p" before the symbol. Values of K_a are often represented as pK_a, with $pK_a = -\log K_a$. The concentration of OH^- (aq) ions may also be expressed in terms of pOH, with $pOH = -\log\left[OH^-\right]$.

The ion-product constant of water, $K_w = \left[H^+\right]\left[OH^-\right] = 1.0 \times 10^{-14}$ at 25 °C. The value of K_w can used to determine the relationship between pH and pOH by taking the negative log of the expression:

$$-\log K_w = -\log\left[H^+\right] - \log\left[OH^-\right] = -\log\left(10^{-14}\right).$$

Therefore: $pH + pOH = 14$.

Skill 14.6   Demonstrating knowledge of buffer solutions and indicators

A **buffer solution** is a solution that **resists a change in pH** after addition of small amounts of an acid or a base. Buffer solutions require the presence of an acid to neutralize an added base and also the presence of a base to neutralize an added acid. These two components present in the buffer also must not neutralize each other! A **conjugate acid-base pair is present in buffers** to fulfill these requirements.

Buffers are prepared by mixing together **a weak acid or base and a salt of the acid or base** that provides the conjugate.

Consider the buffer solution prepared by mixing together acetic acid—$HC_2H_3O_2$—and sodium acetate—$C_2H_3O_2^-$ containing Na^+ as a spectator ion. The equilibrium reaction for this acid/conjugate base pair is:

$$HC_2H_3O_2 \rightleftharpoons C_2H_3O_2^- + H^+$$.

If H^+ ions from a strong acid are added to this buffer solution, Le Chatelier's principle predicts that the reaction will shift to the left and much of this H^+ will be consumed to create more $HC_2H_3O_2$ from $C_2H_3O_2^-$. If a strong base that consumes H^+ is added to this buffer solution, Le Chatelier's principle predicts that the reaction will shift to the right and much of the consumed H^+ will be replaced by the dissociation of $HC_2H_3O_2$. The net effect is that **buffer solutions prevent large changes in pH that occur when an acid or base is added to pure water** or to an unbuffered solution. The amount of acid or base that a buffer solution can neutralize before dramatic pH changes begins to occur is called its **buffering capacity**. Blood and seawater both contain several conjugate acid-base pairs to buffer the solution's pH and decrease the impact of acids and bases on living things.

An excellent flash animation with audio to explain the action of buffering solutions is found at http://www.mhhe.com/physsci/chemistry/essentialchemistry/flash/buffer12.swf.

COMPETENCY 15.0   UNDERSTAND THE MOLE CONCEPT AND ITS RELATIONSHIP TO CHEMICAL FORMULAS.

Skill 15.1   Relating the mole of a substance to its molar mass and the number of particles present

The mole is the chemist's counting unit. Working with the mole should be second nature but lets review grams to mole calculations since they are very important in mass-mass stoichiometry and the balanced equations provides mole ratios not mass ratios.

Mass to moles:

1. First determine the molar mass of the substance by adding the masses for each element in the substance x number of atoms present:

Example: the molar mass of $CuSO_4$ is
Solution: 1 mole of Cu = 63.5 g + 1 mol of S = 32 g + 4 mol O = 4 x 16 or 48 g = 143.5 g/mol

2. Determine the number of moles present using the molar mass conversion: 1 mol = molar mass of substance, for example: 1 mol $CuSO_4$ = 143.5 g

Example: 315 g of $CuSO_4$ is how many moles of $CuSO_4$?

315 g x 1 mol/ 143.5 g =2.20 mol $CuSO_4$

Mole to grams conversions are just the reverse. Solving these problems is a three-step process:

1) Grams of the given compound are converted to moles.
2) Moles of the given compound are related to moles of a second compound by relating their stoichiometric coefficients from the balanced equation.
3) Moles of the second compound are converted to grams.

These steps are often combined in one series of multiplications, which may be described as **"grams to moles to moles to grams."**

Skill 15.2   Determining the mass of a substance or the volume of a gas based on the number of moles it contains at standard temperature and pressure (STP)

The **mole** concept is the key to both stoichiometry and gas laws. A mole is a definite amount of substance. Mole is a unit based on the number of identities (i.e. atoms, molecules, ions, or particles). A mole of anything has the same number of identities as the number of atoms in exactly 12 grams of carbon-12, the most abundant isotope of carbon.

The progress of reactions that produce or consume a gas may be described by measuring gas volume instead of mass. The best way to solve these problems is to use the ideal gas equation to interconvert volume and number of moles:

$$n = \frac{PV}{RT} \quad \text{and} \quad V = \frac{RT}{nP}.$$

If a volume is given, the steps are "**volume to moles to moles to grams**." If a mass is given, the steps will be "**grams to moles to moles to volume**."

Example: What volume of oxygen in liters is generated at 40 °C and 1 atm by the decomposition of 280 g of potassium chlorate in this reaction:

$$2KClO_3 \rightarrow 2KCl + 3O_2(g)?$$

Solution: We are given a mass and asked for a volume, so the steps in the solution will be "grams to moles to moles to volume."
"Grams to moles to moles...":

$$280 \text{ g KClO}_3 \times \frac{1 \text{ mol KClO}_3}{122.548 \text{ g KClO}_3} \times \frac{3 \text{ mol O}_2}{2 \text{ mol KClO}_3} = 3.427 \text{ mol O}_2.$$

"...to volume":

$$V = \frac{RT}{nP} = \frac{\left(0.08206 \frac{\text{L-atm}}{\text{mol-K}}\right)(273.15 + 40)\text{K}}{(3.427 \text{ mol O}_2)(1 \text{ atm})} = 7.50 \text{ L O}_2$$

The quantitative relationship of reactants and products is called **stoichiometry**. Stoichiometric problems require you to calculate the amounts of reactants required for certain amounts of products, or amounts of products produced from certain amounts of reactants. If, in a chemical reaction, one or more reactants or products are gases, gas laws must be considered for the calculation. Usually, the applications of the ideal gas law give results within 5% precision.

The Ideal Gas law

The volume (*V*) occupied by *n* moles of any gas has a pressure (*P*) at temperature (*T*) in Kelvin. The relationship for these variables,

$$P V = n R T,$$

where *R* is known as the gas constant (**.08205 L atm / (mol·K)**, is called the **ideal gas law** or **equation of state**.

Properties of the gaseous state predicted by the ideal gas law are within 5% for gases under ordinary conditions. In other words, given a set of conditions, we can predict or calculate the properties of a gas to be within 5% by applying the ideal gas law. Here we will review several important concepts that are helpful for solving Stoichiometry Problems Involving Gases.

Law of Partial Pressure

For gases, the partial pressure of a component is the same as if the component is by itself in the container. **The total pressure is the sum of all partial pressures of components**. This is Dalton's law of partial pressures.

In the following discussion, n_1, and P_1 represent number of moles and partial pressure of the component 1 respectively. A similar notation can be given to components 2, 3, 4, etc. When several components are present in a container, the total number of moles is the sum of number of moles of the components:

$$n_{total} = n_1 + n_2 + n_3 + \ldots + n_n$$

Since $n = (V/RT) P$, the number of moles of the first component is related to its partial pressure in the same formula,

$$n_i = (V/RT) P_i,$$

and

$$n_{total} = (V/RT) P_{total}.$$

Therefore,

$$P_{total} = P_1 + P_2 + P_3 + \ldots + P_n$$

Stoichiometry and Gas Laws

We can calculate the number of moles from certain volume, temperature and pressure of a HCl gas, for example. When n moles dissolved in V L solution, its concentration is n/V M.

Three examples are given to illustrate some calculations of stoichiometry involving gas laws. More are given in question form for you to practice.

Example 1

If 500 mL of HCl gas at 300 K and 100 kPa dissolve in 100 mL of pure water, what is the concentration? Data required: R value 8.314 kPa L / (K mol).

***Solution*:**

$$n\_HCl = \frac{0.50 \text{ L} * 100 \text{ kPa}}{(8.314 \text{ kPa L/(K mol)} * 300 \text{ K})}$$

$$= 0.02 \text{ mol}$$

Concentration of HCl, [HCl]

[HCl] = 0.02 mol / 0.1 L = 0.2 mol/L.

Discussion

Note that R = 0.08205 L atm /(K mol) will not be suitable in this case.

Example 2

If 500 mL of HCl gas at 300 K and 100 kPa dissolved in pure water requires 12.50 mL of the NaOH solution to neutralize in a titration experiment, what is the concentration of the NaOH solution?

***Solution*:**
Solution in Example 1 showed n_{HCl} = 0.02 mol. From the titration experiment, we can conclude that there were 0.02 moles of NaOH in 12.50 mL. Thus,

[NaOH] = 0.02 mol / 0.0125 L = 1.60 mol/L

***Discussion*:**
Think in terms of reaction,

HCl + NaOH = NaCl + H_2O <== Reaction
0.02 mol 0.02 mol   <== Quantities reacted

Note: that 0.02 mol of NaOH is in 0.0125 mL solution.

Example 3

A 5.0-L air sample containing H_2S at STP is treated with a catalyst to promote the reaction,

$$H_2S + O_2 = H_2O + S(solid).$$

If 3.2 g of solid S was collected, calculate the volume percentage of H_2S in the original sample.

Solution:

$$3.2 \text{ g S} \frac{1 \text{ mol } H_2S}{32 \text{ g S}} = 0.10 \text{ mol } H_2S$$

$$V\_H_2S = 0.10 \text{ mol} * 22.4 \text{ L/mol}$$
$$= 2.24 \text{ L}$$

$$\text{Volume \%} = 2.25 \text{ L} / 5.0 \text{ L}$$
$$= 0.45$$
$$= 45 \text{ \%}$$

Discussion:

Data required: Atomic mass: H, 1; O, 16; S, 32. $R = 0.08205$ L atm /(K mol) is now suitable R values or molar volume at STP (22.4 L/mol)

The volume percentage is also the mole percentage yield, but not the weight percentage.

Skill 15.3   Solving percent-composition by mass problems

The **percent composition** of a substance is the **percentage by mass of each element**. Chemical composition is used to verify the purity of a compound in the lab. An impurity will make the actual composition vary from the expected one.

To determine percent composition from a formula, do the following:
1) Write down the **number of atoms each element contributes** to the formula.
2) Multiply these values by the molecular weight of the corresponding element to determine the **grams of each element in one mole** of the formula.
3) Add the values from step 2 to obtain the **formula mass**.
4) Divide each value from step 2 by the formula weight from step 3 and multiply by 100% to obtain the **percent composition**.

The first three steps are the same as those used to determine formula mass, but we use the intermediate results to obtain the composition.

Example: What is the chemical composition of ammonium carbonate $(NH_4)_2CO_3$?

Solution:
1) One $(NH_4)_2CO_3$ contains 2 N, 8 H, 1 C, and 3 O.

2) $$\frac{2 \text{ mol N}}{\text{mol }(NH_4)CO_3} \times \frac{14.0 \text{ g N}}{\text{mol N}} = 28.0 \text{ g N/mol }(NH_4)CO_3$$

$$8(1.0) = 8.0 \text{ g H/mol }(NH_4)CO_3$$

$$1(12.0) = 12.0 \text{ g C/mol }(NH_4)CO_3$$

$$3(16.0) = 48.0 \text{ g O/mol }(NH_4)CO_3$$

Sum is $\overline{96.0 \text{ g }(NH_4)CO_3/\text{mol }(NH_4)CO_3}$

3)

4) $\%N = \dfrac{28.0 \text{ g N/mol }(NH_4)_2CO_3}{96.0 \text{ g }(NH_4)_2CO_3/\text{mol }(NH_4)_2CO_3} = 0.292 \text{ g N/g }(NH_4)_2CO_3 \times 100\% = 29.2\%$

$\%H = \dfrac{8.0}{96.0} \times 100\% = 8.3\%$ $\%C = \dfrac{12.0}{96.0} \times 100\% = 12.5\%$ $\%O = \dfrac{48.0}{96.0} \times 100\% = 50.0\%$

Skill 15.4   Determining empirical and molecular formulas from experimental data

If we know the chemical composition of a compound, we can calculate an **empirical formula** for it. An empirical formula is the **simplest formula** using the smallest set of integers to express the **ratio of atoms** present in a molecule.

To determine an empirical formula from a percent composition, do the following:
1) Change the "%" sign to grams for a basis of 100 g of the compound.
2) Determine the moles of each element in 100 g of the compound.
3) Divide the values from step 1 by the smallest value to obtain ratios.
4) Multiply by an integer if necessary to get a whole-number ratio.

Example: What is the empirical formula of a compound with a composition of 63.9% Cl, 32.5% C, and 3.6% H?

Solution:
1) We will use a basis of 100 g of the compound containing 63.9 g Cl, 32.5 g C, and 3.6 g H.

2) In 100 g, there are: $63.9 \text{ g Cl} \times \dfrac{\text{mol Cl}}{35.45 \text{ g Cl}} = 1.802 \text{ mol Cl}$

   $32.5/12.01 = 2.706 \text{ mol C}$

   $3.6/1.01 = 3.56 \text{ mol H}$

3) Dividing these values by the smallest yields:

   $\dfrac{2.706 \text{ mol C}}{1.802 \text{ mol Cl}} = 1.502 \text{ mol C/mol Cl}$

   $\dfrac{3.56 \text{ mol H}}{1.802 \text{ mol Cl}} = 1.97 \text{ mol H/mol Cl}$

   Therefore, the elements are present in a ratio of C:H:Cl=1.50:2.0:1

4) Multiply the entire ratio by 2 because you cannot have a fraction of an atom. This corresponds to a ratio of 3:4:2 for an empirical formula of $C_3H_4Cl_2$.

The **molecular formula** describing the **actual number of atoms in the molecule** might also be $C_3H_4Cl_2$ or it might be $C_6H_8Cl_4$ or some other multiple that maintains a 3:4:2 ratio.

COMPETENCY 16.0   UNDERSTAND MOLAR RELATIONSHIPS AND STOICHIOMETRY.

Skill 16.1   Solving stoichiometry problems involving moles, mass, and molarity

Example: What mass of oxygen is required to consume 95.0 g of ethane in this reaction: $2C_2H_6 + 7O_2 \rightarrow 4CO_2 + 6H_2O$?

$$\text{Solution: } 95.0 \text{ g } C_2H_6 \times \overset{\text{step 1}}{\frac{1 \text{ mol } C_2H_6}{30.1 \text{ g } C_2H_6}} \times \overset{\text{step 2}}{\frac{7 \text{ mol } O_2}{2 \text{ mol } C_2H_6}} \times \overset{\text{step 3}}{\frac{32.0 \text{ g } O_2}{1 \text{ mol } O_2}} = 359 \text{ g } O_2$$

Skill 16.2   Solving limiting-reactant and percent-yield problems

The **limiting reagent** of a reaction is the **reactant that runs out first**. This reactant **determines the amount of product formed**, and any **other reactants remain unconverted** to product and are called **excess reagents**.

Example: Consider the reaction $3H_2 + N_2 \rightarrow 2NH_3$ and suppose that 3 mol H_2 and 3 mol N_2 are available for this reaction. What is the limiting reagent?
Solution: The equation tells us that 3 mol H_2 will react with one mol N_2 to produce 2 mol NH_3. This means that 2 mol N_2 will remain and H_2 is the limiting reagent because it runs out first.

The limiting reagent may be determined by **dividing the number of moles of each reactant by its stoichiometric coefficient.** This determines the moles of reactant if each reactant were limiting. The **lowest result** will indicate the actual limiting reagent. Remember to use moles and not grams for these calculations.

Example: 50.0 g Al and 400. g Br_2 react according the the following equation:

$$2Al + 3Br_2 \rightarrow 2AlBr_3$$

until the limiting reagent is completely consumed. Find the limiting reagent, the mass of $AlBr_3$ formed, and the excess reagent remaining after the limiting reagent is consumed.

Solution: First convert both reactants to moles:

$$50.0 \text{ g Al} \times \frac{1 \text{ mol Al}}{26.982 \text{ g Al}} = 1.853 \text{ mol Al} \quad \text{and} \quad 400. \text{ g } Br_2 \times \frac{1 \text{ mol } Br_2}{159.808 \text{ g } Br_2} = 2.503 \text{ mol } Br_2.$$

The final digits in the intermediate results above are italicized because they are insignificant. Dividing by stoichiometric coefficients gives:

$$1.853 \text{ mol Al} \times \frac{\text{mol reaction}}{2 \text{ mol Al}} = 0.9265 \text{ mol reaction if Al is limiting}$$

$$2.503 \text{ mol } Br_2 \times \frac{\text{mol reaction}}{3 \text{ mol } Br_2} = 0.8343 \text{ mol reaction if } Br_2 \text{ is limiting.}$$

Br_2 is the lower value and is limiting reagent.
The reaction is expected to produce:

$$2.503 \text{ mol } Br_2 \times \frac{2 \text{ mol } AlBr_3}{3 \text{ mol } Br_2} \times \frac{266.694 \text{ g } AlBr_3}{\text{mol } AlBr_3} = 445 \text{ g } AlBr_3.$$

The reaction is expected to consume:

$$2.503 \text{ mol } Br_2 \times \frac{2 \text{ mol Al}}{3 \text{ mol } Br_2} \times \frac{26.982 \text{ g Al}}{\text{mol Al}} = 45.0 \text{ g Al.}$$

50.0 g Al – 45.0 g Al = 5.0 g Al are expected to remain.

The **percent composition** of a substance is the **percentage by mass of each element**. Chemical composition is used to verify the purity of a compound in the lab. An impurity will make the actual composition vary from the expected one.

To determine percent composition for a chemical formula, do the following:

1) Write down the **number of atoms each element contributes** to the formula.
   For example in CO_2 + NaCl, note that 2 oxygen atoms, one carbon atom and one sodium, and one chloride atom went into the equation.

2) Multiply these values by the molecular weight of the corresponding element to determine the **grams of each element in one mole** of the formula. This means you look at the periodic table to determine the molecular weight of a mole of each atom. Let's look at this equation:

$$Fe_2O_3(s) + 2Al(s) \rightarrow 2Fe(l) + Al_2O_3(s)$$

That is 2 iron and 3 oxygen and 2 aluminum moles with masses of:

Iron = 2 X 56 = 118 grams in 2 moles
Oxygen = 3 X 16 = 48 grams in 3 moles
Aluminum = 2 X 27 = 54 grams in 2 moles

This adds to a mass amount on the left side of the equation,

3) Add the values from step 2 to obtain the **formula mass**.

The total input of the equation is 220 grams of mass.

4) Divide each value from step 2 by the formula weight from step 3 and multiply by 100% to obtain the **percent composition**.

The percent yield being 100 % for the entire left side of the equation leaves a percent yield of Al_2O_3 is 54 grams plus 48 grams or 102 grams or a 46% yield of Al_2O_3.

Skill 16.3 Demonstrating knowledge of appropriate chemical notations used to represent reactions as balanced chemical equations

To write a balanced chemical equation, proceed through the following steps:

1. Determine the correct formulas for all reactants and products, using subscripts to balance ionic charges.

2. Write formulas for reactants on the left of the arrow and predict the products and write their formulas to the right of the arrow.

3. Under the reactants, list all the elements in the reactants, starting with metals, then nonmetals, listing oxygen last and hydrogen next to last. Under the products, list all the elements in the same order as those under the reactants (straight across from them).

4. Count the atoms of each element on the left side and list the numbers next to the elements. Repeat for products. Don't forget that subscripts outside a parenthesis multiply everything inside the parenthesis including subscripts inside the parenthesis.

5. For the first element in the list that has unequal numbers of atoms, use a coefficient (large numeral to the left of the compound or element) to give the correct number of atoms. NEVER change the subscripts to balance an equation.

6. Go to the next unbalanced element and balance it, moving down the list until all are balanced.

7. Start back at the beginning of the list and actually count the atoms of each element on each side of the arrow to make sure the number listed is the actual number. Re-balance and re-check as needed.

Example: $Al(OH)_3 + NaOH \rightarrow NaAlO_2 + 2\,H_2O$

$Al = 1$
$Na = 1$
$H = 3 + 1 = 4$
$O = 3 + 1 = 4$

$Al = 1$
$Na = 1$
$H = \cancel{2}\ 4$
$O = \cancel{2+1=3}\ \ 2+2=4$
Put a 2 in front of H_2O

SUBAREA IV.   **CHARACTERISTICS OF SCIENCE**

COMPETENCY 17.0   UNDERSTAND THE CHARACTERISTICS OF SCIENTIFIC KNOWLEDGE AND THE PROCESS OF SCIENTIFIC INQUIRY.

Skill 17.1   Demonstrating knowledge of the nature, purpose, and characteristics of science (e.g., reliance on verifiable evidence or scientific laws) and the limitations of science in terms of the kinds of questions that can be answered

Modern science began around the late 16th century with a new way of thinking about the world. Few scientists will disagree with Carl Sagan's assertion that "science is a way of thinking much more than it is a body of knowledge" (Broca's Brain, 1979). Thus science is a process of inquiry and investigation. It is a way of thinking and acting, not just a body of knowledge to be acquired by memorizing facts and principles. This way of thinking, the scientific method, is based on the idea that scientists begin their investigations with observations. From these observations they develop a hypothesis, which is extended in the form of a predication, and challenge the hypothesis through experimentation and thus further observations. Science has progressed in its understanding of nature through careful observation, a lively imagination, and increasing sophisticated instrumentation. Science is distinguished from other fields of study in that it provides guidelines or methods for conducting research, and the research findings must be reproducible by other scientists for those findings to be valid. It is important to recognize that scientific practice is not always this systematic. Discoveries have been made that are serendipitous and others have not started with the observation of data. Einstein's theory of relativity started not with the observation of data but with a kind of intellectual puzzle.

The Scientific method is just a logical set of steps that a scientist goes through to solve a problem. There are as many different scientific methods as there are scientists experimenting. However, there seems to be some pattern to their work.

A Law is the highest-level science can achieve. Followed by laws and theories and hypothesis. The Scientific Method is the process by which data is collected, interpreted and validated.

Law is defined as a statement of an order or relation of phenomena that so far as is known is invariable under the given conditions. Everything we observe in the universe operates according to known natural laws. If the truth of a statement is verified repeatedly in a reproducible way then it can reach the level of a natural law. Some well know and accepted natural laws of science are:

1. The First Law of Thermodynamics
2. The Second Law of Thermodynamics
3. The Law of Cause and Effect
4. The Law of Biogenesis
5. The Law of Gravity

Theory is used to explain an observation or a set of observations. It is generally accepted to be true, though no real proof exists. The important thing about a scientific law is that there are no experimental observations to prove it NOT true, and each piece of evidence that exists supports the theory as written. They are often accepted at face value, since they are often difficult to prove, and can be rewritten in order include the results of all experimental observations. An example of a theory is the big bang theory. While there is no experiment that can directly test whether or not the big bang actually occurred, there is no strong evidence indicating otherwise.

Theories provide a framework to explain the **known** information of the time, but are are subject to constant evaluation and updating. There is always the possibility that new evidence will conflict with a current theory.

Some examples of theories that have been rejected because they are now better explained by current knowledge:

Theory of Spontaneous Generation
Inheritance of Acquired Characteristics
The Blending Hypothesis

Some examples of theories that were initially rejected because they fell outside of the accepted knowledge of the time, but are well-accepted today due to increased knowledge and data include:

The sun-centered solar system
Warm-bloodedness in dinosaurs
The germ-theory of disease
Continental drift

Hypothesis is defined as a tentative assumption made in order to draw out and test its logical or empirical consequences. Many refer to a hypothesis as an educated guess about what will happen during an experiment. A hypothesis can be based on prior knowledge, prior observations. It will be proved true or false only through experimentation.

Scientific Method is defined as principles and procedures for the systematic pursuit of knowledge involving the recognition and formulation of a problem, the collection of data through observation and experiment, and the formulation and testing of hypotheses. The steps in the scientific method can be found elsewhere in this text.

Skill 17.2 Recognizing the dynamic nature of scientific knowledge through the continual testing, revision, and occasional rejection of existing theories

Probably one of the best examples of the progressive development of science would be the development of atomic theory. The ancient Greeks debated over the continuous nature of matter and two schools of thought emerged; matter is continuous or matter is not continuous. The continuous idea was promoted by Aristotle and due to his high regard among scholars that was the idea that flourished. However, there was no effort made by the Greeks to prove of disprove this idea. During the dark ages alchemists started experimenting and keeping records of their results, sending science on a pathway of experimentation and discovery. Robert Boyle and his famous J-tube experiment in 1661 gave the first experimental evidence for the existence of atoms. He even used words similar to Democritus to describe the results saying that the air consisted of atoms and a void between them. By increasing the pressure inside the J-tube, some of the void was squeezed out, decreasing the volume. Slowly, experimental evidence, including the work of Lavoisier and Prietsly, to name a few, began to mount and in 1803 John Dalton proposed the Modern Atomic Theory which contained 5 basic postulates about the nature and behavior of matter. Ben Franklin's discovery of electricity in 1746 sent scientists to work to understand this new "thing"-electricity. J.J Thomson investigated a cathode ray tube and identified the negatively charged particle in the cathode ray in 1897. His work was closely followed by Robert Millikan who gave the electron a -1 charge in his oil drop experiment.

Experiments were under way to understand how electricity and matter interact when the discoveries of x-rays and radioactivity were announced. Scientists trying to understand this new phenomena radioactivity experimented day and night. Ernest Rutherford was one of the many. He tried to understand the nature of radioactivity and classified it into three basic types. While trying to find out more about radioactivity, he conducted his gold foil experiment that ultimately provided greater insight into the subatomic nature of the atom by discovering the nucleus. He also identified the proton present in the nucleus.

Rutherford's graduate student, Neils Bohr, made slight alterations to the model of the atom proposed by Rutherford to account for his experimental results. These changes helped Rutherford's model stand up to classical physics. However, scientists looking for other patterns and information proposed more changes to the planetary model of the atom. These changes seemed to fit with spectroscopy experiments and the quantum mechanical view of the atom was formed. About the same time as this new theory was emerging, James Chadwick, a collaborator of Rutherford's, announced in 1932 the discovery of the neutron found in the nucleus. This discovery, ultimately led to the discovery of fission and the development of the nuclear bomb. The technology the came from the Manhattan project has developed the fields of medicine, computing and provided entertainment from television.

Skill 17.3   **Determining an appropriate scientific hypothesis or investigative design for addressing a given problem through scientific inquiry**

While an inquiry may start at any point in this method and may not involve all of the steps here is the pattern.

Observations
Scientific questions result from observations of events in nature or events observed in the laboratory. An **observation** is not just a look at what happens. It also includes measurements and careful records of the event. Records could include photos, drawings, or written descriptions. The observations and data collection lead to a question. In chemistry, observations almost always deal with the behavior of matter. Having arrived at a question, a scientist usually researches the scientific literature to see what is known about the question. Maybe the question has already been answered. The scientist then may want to test the answer found in the literature. Or, maybe the research will lead to a new question.

Sometimes the same observations are made over and over again and are always the same. For example, you can observe that daylight lasts longer in summer than in winter. This observation never varies. Such observations are called **laws** of nature. Probably the most important law in chemistry was discovered in the late 1700s. Chemists observed that no mass was ever lost or gained in chemical reactions. This law became known as the law of conservation of mass. Explaining this law was a major topic of chemistry in the early 19th century.

Hypothesis
If the question has not been answered, the scientist may prepare for an experiment by making a hypothesis. A **hypothesis** is a statement of a possible answer to the question. It is a tentative explanation for a set of facts and can be tested by experiments. Although hypotheses are usually based on observations, they may also be based on a sudden idea or intuition.

Experiment

An **experiment** tests the hypothesis to determine whether it may be a correct answer to the question or a solution to the problem. Some experiments may test the effect of one thing on another under controlled conditions. Such experiments have two variables. The experimenter controls one variable, callred the *independent variable*. The other variable, the *dependent variable*, is the change caused by changing the independent variable.

For example, suppose a researcher wanted to test the effect of vitamin A on the ability of rats to see in dim light. The independent variable would be the dose of Vitamin A added to the rats' diet. The dependent variable would be the intensity of light that causes the rats to react. All other factors, such as time, temperature, age, water given to the rats, the other nutrients given to the rats, and similar factors, are held constant. Chemists sometimes do short experiments "just to see what happens" or to see what products a certain reaction produces. Often, these are not formal experiments. Rather they are ways of making additional observations about the behavior of matter.

In most experiments, scientists collect quantitative data, which is data that can be measured with instruments. They also collect qualitative data, descriptive information from observations other than measurements. Interpreting data and analyzing observations are important. If data is not organized in a logical manner, wrong conclusions can be drawn. Also, other scientists may not be able to follow your work or repeat your results.

Conclusion

Finally, a scientist must draw conclusions from the experiment. A conclusion must address the hypothesis on which the experiment was based. The conclusion states whether or not the data supports the hypothesis. If it does not, the conclusion should state what the experiment *did* show. If the hypothesis is not supported, the scientist uses the observations from the experiment to make a new or revised hypothesis., Then, new experiments are planned.

Theory

When a hypothesis survives many experimental tests to determine its validity, the hypothesis may evolve into a **theory**. A theory explains a body of facts and laws that are based on the facts. A theory also reliably predicts the outcome of related events in nature. For example, the law of conservation of matter and many other experimental observations led to a theory proposed early in the 19th century. This theory explained the conservation law by proposing that all matter is made up of atoms, which are never created or destroyed in chemical reactions, only rearranged. This atomic theory also successfully predicted the behavior of matter in chemical reactions that had not been studied at the time. As a result, the atomic theory has stood for 200 years with only small modifications.

A theory also serves as a scientific **model**. A model can be a physical model made of wood or plastic, a computer program that simulates events in nature, or simply a mental picture of an idea. A model illustrates a theory and explains nature. In your chemistry course, you will develop a mental (and maybe a physical) model of the atom and its behavior. Outside of science, the word theory is often used to describe someone's unproven notion about something. In science, theory means much more. It is a thoroughly tested explanation of things and events observed in nature.

A theory can never be proven true, but it can be proven untrue. All it takes to prove a theory untrue is to show an exception to the theory. The test of the hypothesis may be observations of phenomena or a model may be built to examine its behavior under certain circumstances.

A **scientific model** is a set of ideas that describes a natural process and are developed by empirical or theoretical objects and help scientists focus of the basic fundamental processes. They may be physical representations such as a space-filling model of a molecule or a map, or they may be mathematical algorithms.

Whatever form they take, scientific models are based on what is known about the science systems or objects at the time that the models are constructed. Models usually evolve and are improved as scientific advances are made. Sometimes, a model must be discarded because new findings show it to be misleading or incorrect. How do scientists use models?

Models are developed in an effort to explain how things work in nature. Because models are not the "real thing", they can never correctly represent the system or object in all respects. The amount of detail that they contain depends upon how the model will be used as well as the sophistication and skill of the scientist doing the modeling. If a model has too many details left out, its usefulness may be limited. But too many details may make a model too complicated to be useful. So it is easy to see why models lack some features of the real system.

To overcome this difficulty, different models are often used to describe the same system or object. Scientists must then choose which model most closely fits the scientific investigation being carried out, which findings are being described, and, in some cases, which one is compatible with the sophistication of the investigation itself. For example, there are many models of atoms. The solar system model described above is adequate for some purposes, because electrons have properties of matter. They have mass and charge and they are found in motion in the space outside the nucleus. However, a highly mathematical model based on the field of quantum mechanics is necessary when describing the energy (or wave) properties of electrons in the atom.

Scientific models are based on physical observation that establish some facts about the system or object of interest. Scientists then combine these facts with appropriate laws or scientific principles and assumptions to produce a "picture" that mimics the behavior of the system or object to the greatest possible extent. It is on the basis of such models that science makes many of its most important advances, because such models provide a vehicle for making predictions about the behavior of a system or object. The predictions can then be tested as new measurements, technology or theories are applied to the subject. The new information may result in modification and refinement of the model, although certain issues may remain unresolved by the model for years. The goal, however is to continue to develop the model in such a way as to move it every closer to a true description of the natural phenomenon. In this way, models are vital to the scientific process.

Skill 17.4   Demonstrating knowledge of the principles and procedures for designing and carrying out scientific investigations (e.g., changing one variable at a time)

The design of chemical experiments must include every step to obtain the desired data. In other words, the design must be **complete** and it must include all required **controls**.

Complete design
Familiarity with individual experiments and equipment will help you evaluate if anything is missing from the design. For data requiring a difference between two values, the experiment **must determine both values**. For data utilizing the ideal gas law, the experiment **must determine three values of *P, V, n*, or *T*** in order to determine the fourth or one value and a ratio of the other two in order to determine the fourth.

Example: In a mercury manometer, the level of mercury in contact with a reaction vessel is 70.0 mm lower than the level exposed to the atmosphere. Use the following conversion factors:
760 mm Hg=1 atm=101.325 kPa.
What additional information is required to determine the pressure in the vessel in kPa?

Solution: The barometric pressure is needed to determine vessel pressure from an open-ended manometer. A manometer reading is always a **difference** between two pressures. One standard atmosphere is 760 mm mercury, but on a given day at a given location, the actual ambient pressure may vary. If the barometric pressure on the day of the experiment is 104 kPa, the pressure of the vessel is:

$$104 \text{ kPa} + 70.0 \text{ mm Hg} \times \frac{101.325 \text{ kPa}}{760 \text{ mm Hg}} = 113 \text{ kPa}.$$

<u>Controls</u>
Experimental **controls** prevent factors other than those under study from impacting the outcome of the experiment. An **experimental sample** in a controlled experiment is the unknown to be compared against one or more **control samples**. These should be nearly identical to the experimental sample except for the one aspect whose effect is being tested.

A **negative control** is a control sample that is known to lack the effect. A **positive control** is known to contain the effect. Positive controls of varying strengths are often used to generate a **calibration curve** (also called a **standard curve**).

When determining the concentration of a component in a mixture, an **internal standard** is a known concentration of a different substance that is added to the experimental sample. An **external standard** is a known concentration of the substance of interest. External standards are more commonly used. They are not added to the experimental sample; they are analyzed separately.

Replicate samples decrease the impact of random error. A mean is taken of the results from replicate samples to obtain a best value. If one replicate is obviously inconsistent with the results from other samples, it may be discarded as an **outlier** and not counted as an observation when determining the mean. Discarding an outlier is equivalent to assuming the presence of a systematic error for that particular observation. In research, this must be done with great caution because some real-world behavior generates sporadically unusual results.

Example: A pure chemical in aqueous solution is known to absorb light at 615 nm. What controls would best be used with a spectrophotometer to determine the concentration of this chemical when it is present in a mixture with other solutes in an aqueous solution?

Solution: The other solutes may also absorb light at 615 nm. The best negative control would be an identical mixture with the chemical of interest entirely absent. Known concentrations of the chemical could then be added to the negative control to create positive controls (external standards) and develop a calibration curve of the spectrophotometer absorbance reading at 615 nm as a function of concentration. Replicate samples of each standard and of the unknown should be read.

Example: Ethanol is separated from a mixture of organic compounds by gas chromatography. The concentration of each component is proportional to its peak area. However, the chromatograph detector has a variable sensitivity from one run to the next. Is an internal standard required to determine the concentration of ethanol?

Solution: Yes. The variable detector sensitivity may only be accounted for by adding a known concentration of a chemical not found in the mixture as an internal standard to the experimental sample and control samples. The variable sensitivity of the detector will be accounted for by determining the ratio of the peak area for ethanol to the peak area of the added internal standard.

Skill 17.5 Recognizing the importance of scientific ethics and strategies for avoiding bias in scientific investigations

Scientific research can be biased in the choice of what data to consider, in the reporting or recording of the data, and/or in how the data are interpreted. The scientist's emphasis may be influenced by his/her nationality, sex, ethnic origin, age, or political convictions. For example, when studying a group of animals, male scientists may focus on the social behavior of the males and typically male characteristics.

Although bias related to the investigator, the sample, the method, or the instrument may not be completely avoidable in every case, it is important to know the possible sources of bias and how bias could affect the evidence. Moreover, scientists need to be attentive to possible bias in their own work as well as that of other scientists.

Objectivity may not always be attained. However, one precaution that may be taken to guard against undetected bias is to have many different investigators or groups of investigators working on a project. By different, it is meant that the groups are made up of various nationalities, ethnic origins, ages, and political convictions and composed of both males and females. It is also important to note one's aspirations, and to make sure to be truthful to the data, even when grants, promotions, and notoriety are at risk.

Experimental bias is when a researcher favors one particular outcome over another in an experimental setup. In order to avoid bias, it is imperative to set each experiment under exactly the same conditions, including a *control* experiment, an experiment with a known negative outcome. Additionally, in order to avoid experimental bias, a researcher must not "read" particular results into data.

An example of experimental bias can be seen in the classic example of the mouse in the maze experiment. In this example, a researcher is timing mice as they move through the maze towards a piece of cheese. The experiment relies on the mouse's ability to smell the cheese as it approaches. If one mouse chases a piece of cheddar cheese, while another chases Limburger, or so called "stinky" cheese, clearly the Limburger mouse has a huge advantage over the cheddar mouse. To remove the experimental bias from this experiment, the same cheese should be used in both tests.

Skill 17.6   Recognizing that science has developed, and continues to develop, through the contributions of diverse individuals and cultures

Development of Modern Chemistry
Chemistry emerged from two ancient roots: **craft traditions** and **philosophy**. The oldest ceramic crafts (i.e., pottery) known are from roughly 10000 BC in Japan. **Metallurgical crafts** in Eurasia and Africa began to develop by trial and error around 4000-2500 BC resulting in the production of copper, bronze, iron, and steel tools. Other craft traditions in brewing, tanning, and dyeing led to many useful empirical ways to manipulate matter.

Ancient philosophers in Greece, India, China, and Japan speculated that all matter was composed of four or five elements. The Greeks thought that these were: fire, air, earth, and water. Indian philosophers and the Greek **Aristotle** also thought a fifth element—"aether" or "quintessence"—filled all of empty space. The Greek philosopher **Democritus** thought that matter was composed of indivisible and indestructible atoms. These concepts are now known as **classical elements** and **classical atomic theory**.

Before the emergence of the **scientific method**, attempts to understand matter relied on **alchemy**: a mixture of mysticism, best guesses, and supernatural explanations. Goals of alchemy were the transmutation of other metals into gold and the synthesis of an elixir to cure all diseases. Ancient Egyptian alchemists developed cement and glass. Chinese alchemists developed gunpowder in the 800s AD.

During the height of European alchemy in the 1300s, the philosopher **William of Occam** proposed the idea that when trying to explain a process or develop a theory, **the simplest explanation with the fewest variables is best**. This is known as **Occam's Razor**. European alchemy slowly developed into modern chemistry during the 1600s and 1700s. This began to occur after **Francis Bacon** and René **Descartes** described the scientific method in the early 1600s.

Robert **Boyle** was educated in alchemy in the mid-1600s, but he published a book called *The Skeptical Chemist* that attacked alchemy and advocated using the scientific method. He is sometimes called **the founder of modern chemistry** because of his emphasis on proving a theory before accepting it, but the birth of modern chemistry is usually attributed to Lavoisier. Boyle rejected the 4 classical elements and proposed the modern definition of an element. **Boyle's law** states that gas volume is proportional to the reciprocal of pressure.

Blaise **Pascal** in the mid-1600s determined the relationship between **pressure** and the height of a liquid in a **barometer**. He also helped to establish the scientific method. The SI unit of pressure is named after him.

Isaac **Newton** studied the nature of **light**, the laws of **gravity**, and the **laws of motion** around 1700. The SI unit of force is named after him.

Daniel **Bernoulli** proposed the **kinetic molecular theory** for gases in the early 1700s to explain the nature of heat and Boyle's Law. At that time, heat was thought to be related to the release of a substance called *phlogiston* from combustible materials

James **Watt** created an efficient **steam engine** in the 1760s-1780s. Later chemists and physicists would develop the theory behind this empirical engineering accomplishment. The SI unit of power is named after him.

Joseph **Priestley** studied various gases in the 1770s. He was the first to produce and drink **carbonated water**, and he was the first to isolate **oxygen** from air. Priestley thought oxygen was air with its normal phlogiston removed so it could burn more fuel and accept more phlogiston than natural air.

Antoine **Lavoisier** is called **the father of modern chemistry** because he performed **quantitative, controlled experiments**. He carefully weighed material before and after combustion to determine that burning objects gain weight. Lavoisier formulated the rule that **chemical reactions do not alter total mass** after finding that reactions in a closed container do not change weight. This disproved the plogiston theory, and he named Priestley's substance oxygen. He demonstrated that air and water were not elements. He defined an element as a substance that could not be broken down further. He published the first modern chemistry textbook, *Elementary Treatise of Chemistry*. Lavoisier was executed in the Reign of Terror at the height of the French Revolution.

Additional Gas Laws in the 1700s and 1800s
These contributions built on the foundation developed by Boyle in the 1600s.

Jacque **Charles** developed **Charles's law** in the late 1700s. This states that gas volume is proportional to absolute temperature.

William Henry developed the law stating that gas solubility in a liquid is proportional to the pressure of gas over the liquid. This is known as **Henry's Law**.

Joseph Louis **Gay-Lussac** developed the gas law stating that gas pressure is directly proportional to absolute temperature. He also determined that two volumes of hydrogen react with one of oxygen to produce water and that other reactions occurred with similar simple ratios. These observations led him to develop the **Law of Combining Volumes**.

Amedeo **Avogadro** developed the hypothesis that **equal volumes of different gases contain an equal numbers of molecules** if the gases are at the same temperature and pressure. The proportionality between volume and number of moles is called **Avagadro's Law**, and the number of molecules in a mole is called **Avagadro's Number**. Both were posthumously named in his honor.

Thomas **Graham** developed **Graham's Law** of effusion and diffusion in the 1830s. He is called the father of **colloid chemistry**.

Electricity and Magnetism in the 1700s and 1800s
Benjamin Franklin studied electricity in the mid-1700s. He developed the concept of **positive and negative electrical charges**. His most famous experiment showed that lightning is an electrical process.

Luigi **Galvani** discovered **bioelectricity**. In the late 1700s, he noticed that the legs of dead frogs twitched when they came into contact with an electrical source.

In the late 1700s, Charles Augustin **Coulomb** derived mathematical **equations for attraction and repulsion** between electrically charged objects.

Alessandro **Volta** built the first **battery** in 1800 permitting future research and applications to have a source of continuous electrical current available. The SI unit of electric potential difference is named after him.

André-Marie **Ampère** created a mathematical theory in the 1820s for magnetic fields and electric currents. The SI unit of electrical current is named after him.

Michael **Faraday** is best known for work in the 1820s and 1830s establishing that a moving magnetic field induces an electric potential. He built the first **dynamo** for electricity generation. He also discovered benzene, invented oxidation numbers, and popularized the terms *electrode*, *anode*, and *cathode*. The SI unit of electrical capacitance is named in his honor.

James Clerk **Maxwell** derived the **Maxwell Equations** in 1864. These expressions completely describe **electric and magnetic fields** and their interaction with matter. Also see Ludwig Boltzmann below for Maxwell's contribution to thermodynamics.

Nineteenth Century Chemistry: Caloric Theory and Thermodynamics
Lavoisier proposed in the late 18th century that the heat generated by combustion was due to a weightless material substance called **caloric** that flowed from one place to another and was never destroyed.

In 1798, **Benjamin Thomson**, also known as **Count Rumford** measured the heat produced when cannon were bored underwater and concluded that caloric was not a conserved substance because heat could continue to be generated indefinitely by this process.

Sadi **Carnot** in the 1820s used caloric theory in developing theories for the **heat engine** to explain the engine already developed by Watt. Heat engines perform mechanical work by expanding and contracting a piston at two different temperatures.

In the 1820s, Robert **Brown** observed dust particles and particles in pollen grains moving in a random motion. This was later called **Brownian motion**.

Germain Henri **Hess** developed **Hess's Law** in 1840 after studying the heat required or emitted from reactions composed of several steps.

James Prescott **Joule** determined the equivalence of heat energy to mechanical work in the 1840s by carefully measuring the heat produced by friction. Joule attacked the caloric theory and played a major role in the acceptance of **kinetic molecular theory**. The SI unit of energy is named after him.

William Thomson, 1st Baron of Kelvin also called **Lord Kelvin** recognized the existence of **absolute temperature** in the 1840s and proposed the temperature scale named after him. He failed in an attempt to reconcile caloric theory with Joule's discovery and caloric theory began to fall out of favor.

Hermann von **Helmholtz** in the 1840s proposed that **energy is conserved** during physical and chemical processes, not heat as proposed in caloric theory

Rudolf **Clausius** in the 1860s introduced the concept of **entropy**.

In the 1870s, Ludwig **Boltzmann** generalized earlier work by Maxwell solving the **velocity or energy distribution among gas molecules**. Maxwell-Boltzmann distribution for kinetic energy is useful when graphing at two temperatures. Maxwell's contribution to electromagnetism is described above.

CHEMISTRY   189

Johannes **van der Waals** in the 1870s was the first to consider **intermolecular attractive forces** in modeling the behavior of liquids and non-ideal gases.

Francois Marie **Raoult** studied colligative properties in the 1870s. He developed **Raoult's Law** relating solute and solvent mole fraction to vapor pressure lowering.

Jacobus **van't Hoff** was the first to fully describe **stereoisomerism** in the 1870s. He later studied **colligative properties** and the impact of temperature on equilibria

Josiah Willard **Gibbs** studied thermodynamics and statistical mechanics in the 1870s. He formulated the concept now called **Gibbs free energy** that will determine whether or not a chemical process at constant pressure will spontaneously occur.

Henri Louis **Le Chatelier** described chemical **equilibrium** in the 1880s using **Le Chatelier's Principle**.

In the 1880s, Svante **Arrhenius** developed the idea of **activation energy**. He also described the dissociation of salts—including **acids and bases**—into ions. Before then, salts in solution were thought to exist as intact molecules and ions were mostly thought to exist as electrolysis products. Arrhenius also predicted that CO_2 emissions would lead to global warming.

In 1905, **Albert Einstein** created a **mathematical model of Brownian motion** based on the impact of water molecules on suspended particles. Kinetic molecular theory could now be observed under the microscope. Einstein's more famous later work in physics on **relativity** may be applied to chemistry by correlating the energy change of a chemical reaction with extremely small changes in the total mass of reactants and products.

Nineteenth and Twentieth Century: Atomic Theory

The contributions to atomic theory of John **Dalton**, **J. J. Thomson**, Max **Planck**, Ernest **Rutherford**, Niels **Bohr**, Louis **de Broglie**, Werner **Heisenberg, and** Erwin **Schrödinger** are discussed later in this book.

Wolfgang **Pauli** helped to develop quantum mechanics in the 1920s by forming the concept of spin and the **exclusion principle**.

Friedrich **Hund** determined a set of **rules to determine the ground state** of a multi-electron atom in the 1920s. One particular rule is called **Hund's Rule** in introductory chemistry courses.

Discovery and Synthesis: Nineteenth Century:

Humphry **Davy** used Volta's battery in the early 1800s for **electrolysis of salt solutions**. He synthesized several pure elements using electrolysis to generate non-spontaneous reactions.

Jöns Jakob **Berzelius** isolated several elements, but he is best known for inventing modern **chemical notation** by using one or two letters to represent elements in the early 1800s.

Friedrich **Wöhler** isolated several elements, but he is best known for the chemical **synthesis of an organic compound** in 1828 using the carbon in silver cyanide. Before Wöhler, many had believed that a transcendent "life-force" was needed to make the molecules of life.

Justus **von Liebig** studied the chemicals involved in agriculture in the 1840s. He has been called the **father of agricultural chemistry**.

Louis **Pasteur** studied **chirality** in the 1840s by separating a mixture of two chiral molecules. His greater contribution was in biology for discovering the germ theory of disease.

Henry **Bessemer** in the 1850s developed the **Bessemer Process** for mass producing steel by blowing air through molten iron to oxidize impurities.

Friedrich August **Kekulé** von Stradonitz studied the chemistry of carbon in the 1850s and 1860s. He proposed the **ring structure of benzene** and that carbon was tetravalent.

Anders Jonas **Ångström** was one of the founders of the science of spectroscopy. In the 1860s, he found hydrogen and other **elements in the spectrum of the sun**. A non-SI unit of length equal to 0.1 nm is named for him.

Alfred **Nobel** invented the explosive **dynamite** in the 1860s and continued to develop other explosives. In his will he used his fortune to establish the **Nobel Prizes**.

Dmitri **Mendeleev** developed the first modern **periodic table** in 1869.

Discovery and Synthesis: Turn of the 20th Century

William **Ramsay** and Lord **Rayleigh (**John William Strutt) isolated the **noble gases**.

Wilhelm Konrad **Röntgen** discovered **X-rays**.

Antoine Henri **Becquerel discovered radioactivity** using uranium salts.

Marie **Curie** named the property radioactivity and determined that it was **a property of atoms** that did not depend on which molecule contained the element.

Pierre and Marie **Curie** utilized the properties of radioactivity to **isolate radium** and other radioactive elements. Marie Curie was the first woman to receive a Nobel Prize and the first person to receive two. Her story continues to inspire. See http://nobelprize.org/physics/articles/curie/index.html for her biography.

Frederick **Soddy** and William **Ramsay** discovered that **radioactive decay can produce helium** (alpha particles).

Fritz **Haber** developed the **Haber Process** for synthesizing ammonia from hydrogen and nitrogen using an iron **catalyst**. Ammonia is still produced by this method to make fertilizers, textiles, and other products.

Robert Andrew **Millikan** determined the **charge of an electron** using an oil-drop experiment.

Discovery and Synthesis: 20th Century

Gilbert Newton **Lewis** described **covalent bonds** as sharing electrons in the 1910s and the **electron pair donor/acceptor theory of acids and bases** in the 1920s. Lewis dot structures and Lewis acids are named after him.

Johannes Nicolaus **Brønsted** and Thomas Martin **Lowry** simultaneously developed the **proton donor/acceptor theory of acids and bases** in the 1920s.

Irving **Langmuir** in the 1920s developed the science of **surface chemistry** to describe interactions at the interface of two phases. This field is important to heterogeneous catalysis.

Fritz **London** studied the electrical nature of chemical bonding in the 1920s. The weak intermolecular **London dispersion forces** are named after him.

Hans Wilhelm **Geiger** developed the **Geiger counter** for measuring ionizing radiation in the 1930s.

Wallace **Carothers** and his team first synthesized **organic polymers** (including neoprene, polyester and nylon) in the 1930s.

In the 1930s, Linus **Pauling** published his results on **the nature of the covalent bond.** Pauling electronegativity is named after him. In the 1950s, Pauling determined the □-helical structure of proteins.

Lise **Meitner** and Otto **Hahn** discovered **nuclear fission** in the 1930s.

Glenn Theodore **Seaborg** created and isolated several **elements larger than uranium** in the 1940s. Seaborg reorganized the periodic table to its current form.

James **Watson** and Francis **Crick** determined the double helix structure of DNA in the 1950s.

Neil **Bartlett** produced **compounds containing noble gases** in the 1960s, proving that they are not completely chemically inert.

Harold Kroto, Richard Smalley, and Robert Curl discovered the **buckyball C_{60}** in the 1980s.

COMPETENCY 18.0 UNDERSTAND SCIENTIFIC TOOLS, INSTRUMENTS, MATERIALS, AND SAFETY PRACTICES.

Skill 18.1 Recognizing procedures for the safe and proper use of scientific tools, instruments, chemicals, and other materials in investigations

The descriptions and diagrams in this skill are included to help you **identify** the techniques. They are **not meant as a guide to perform the techniques** in the lab.

Handling liquids
A **beaker** (below left) is a cylindrical cup with a notch at the top. They are often used for making solutions. An **Erlenmeyer** flask (below center) is a conical flask. A liquid in an Erlenmeyer flask will evaporate more slowly than when it is in a beaker and it is easier to swirl about. A **round-bottom flask** (below-right) is also called a Florence flask. It is designed for uniform heating, but it requires a stand to keep it upright.

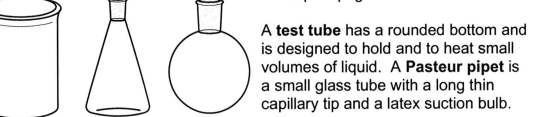

A **test tube** has a rounded bottom and is designed to hold and to heat small volumes of liquid. A **Pasteur pipet** is a small glass tube with a long thin capillary tip and a latex suction bulb.

A **crucible** is a cup-shaped container made of porcelain or metal for holding chemical compounds when heating them to very high temperatures. A **watch glass** is a concave circular piece of glass that is usually used as surface to evaporate a liquid and observe precipitates or crystallization. A **Dewar flask** is a double walled vacuum flask with a metallic coating to provide good thermal insulation and short term storage of liquid nitrogen.

Fitting and cleaning glassware
If a thermometer or funnel must be threaded through a stopper or a piece of tubing and it won't fit, either **make the hole larger or use a smaller piece of glass**. Use soapy water or glycerol to **lubricate** the glass before inserting it. Hold the glass piece as close as possible to the stopper during insertion. It's also good practice to wrap a towel around the glass and the stopper during this time. **Never apply undue pressure**.

Glassware sometimes contains **tapered ground-glass joints** to allow direct glass-to-glass connections. A thin layer of joint **grease** must be applied when assembling an apparatus with ground-glass joints. Too much grease will contaminate the experiment, and too little will permit the components to be permanently locked together. Disassemble the glassware with a **twisting** motion immediately after the experiment is over.

Cleaning glassware becomes more difficult with time, so it should be cleaned soon after the experiment is completed. Wipe off any lubricant with paper towel moistened in a solvent like hexane before washing the glassware. Use a brush with lab soap and water. Acetone may be used to dissolve most organic residues. Spent solvents should be transferred to a waste container for proper disposal.

Heating
A **hot plate** (shown below) is used to heat Erlenmeyer flasks, beakers and other 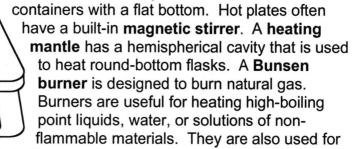 containers with a flat bottom. Hot plates often have a built-in **magnetic stirrer**. A **heating mantle** has a hemispherical cavity that is used to heat round-bottom flasks. A **Bunsen burner** is designed to burn natural gas. Burners are useful for heating high-boiling point liquids, water, or solutions of non-flammable materials. They are also used for bending glass tubing. Smooth boiling is achieved by adding **boiling stones** to a liquid.

Boiling and melting point determination
Boiling point is determined by heating the liquid along with a boiling stone in a clamped test tube with a clamped thermometer positioned just above the liquid surface and away from the tube walls. The constant highest-value temperature reading after boiling is achieved is the boiling point.

Melting point is determined by placing pulverized solid in a capillary tube and using a rubber band to fasten the capillary to a thermometer so the sample is at the level of the thermometer bulb. The thermometer and sample are inserted into a **Thiele tube** filled with mineral or silicon oil. The Thiele tube has a sidearm that is heated with a Bunsen burner to create a flow of hot oil. This flow maintains an even temperature during heating. The melting point is read when the sample turns into a liquid. Many **electric melting point devices** are also available that heat the sample more slowly to give more accurate results. These are also safer to use than a Thiele tube with a Bunsen burner.

Centrifugation
A **centrifuge** separates two immiscible phases by spinning the mixture (placed in a **centrifuge tube**) at high speeds. A **microfuge** or microcentrifuge is a small centrifuge. The weight of material placed in a centrifuge must be **balanced**, so if one sample is placed in a centrifuge, a tube with roughly an equal mass of water should be placed opposite the sample.

Filtration

The goal of **gravity filtration** is to remove solids from a liquid and obtain a liquid without solid particulates. Filter paper is folded, placed in a funnel on top of a flask, and wetted with the solvent to seal it to the funnel. Next the mixture is poured through, and the solid-free liquid is collected from the flask.

The goal of **vacuum filtration** is usually to remove liquids from a solid to obtain a solid that is dry. An **aspirator** or a **vacuum pump** is used to provide suction though a rubber tube to a **filter trap**. The trap is attached to a **filter flask** (show to the right) by a second rubber tube. The filter flask is an Erlenmeyer flask with a thick wall and a hose barb for the vacuum tube. Filter flasks are used to filter material using a **Büchner funnel** (shown to the right) or a smaller **Hirsch funnel**. These porcelain or plastic funnels hold a circular piece of filter paper. A single-hole rubber stopper supports the funnel in the flask while maintaining suction.

Mixing

Heterogeneous reaction mixtures in flasks are often mixed by **swirling**. To use a magnetic stirrer, a bar magnet coated with Teflon called a flea or a **stir bar** is slid into the container, and the container is placed on the stirrer. The container should be moved and the stir speed adjusted for smooth mixing. Mechanical stirring paddles, agitators, vortexers, or rockers are also used for mixing.

Decanting

When a course solid has settled at the bottom of a flask of liquid, **decanting** the solution simply means pouring out the liquid and leaving the solid behind.

Extraction

Compounds in solution are often separated based on their **solubility differences**. During **liquid-liquid extraction** (also called **solvent extraction**), a second solvent immiscible to the first is added to the solution in a **separatory funnel** (shown at right). Usually one solvent is nonpolar and the other is a polar solvent like water. The two solvents are immiscible and separate from each other after the mixture is shaken to allow solute exchange. One layer contains the compound of interest, and the other contains impurities to be discarded. The solutions in the two layers are separated from each other by draining liquid through the stopcock.

Distillation

Liquids in solution are often separated based on their **boiling point differences**. During simple **distillation**, the solution is placed in a round-bottom flask called the **distillation flask** or **still pot**, and boiling stones are added. The apparatus shown below is assembled (note that clamps and stands are not show), and the still pot is heated using a heating mantle. Hot vapor during boiling escapes through the **distillation head**, enters the **condenser**, and is cooled and condensed back to a liquid. The vapor loses its heat to water flowing through the outside of the condenser. The condensate or **distillate** falls into the **receiving flask**. The apparatus is open to the atmosphere through a vent above the receiving flask. The distillate will contain a higher concentration of material with the lower boiling point. The less volatile component will achieve a high concentration in the still pot. Head temperature is monitored during the process. Distillation may also be used to remove a solid from a pure liquid by boiling and condensing the liquid.

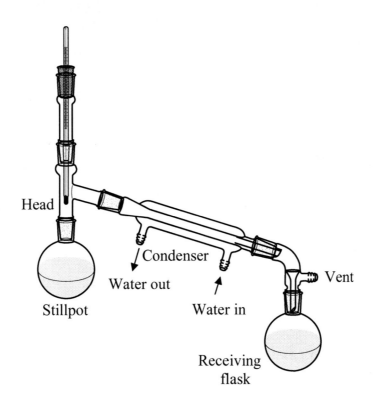

Head

Condenser

Water out

Vent

Stillpot

Water in

Receiving
flask

Skill 18.2 Identifying appropriate tools and units for measuring objects or substances in chemistry

The tools and units used for measuring in chemistry can be divided in to two types:

1. Specific to chemistry
2. General

1. Specific to chemistry:

i) Moles and molar masses:
These are unique to chemistry. Mole is defined as atomic mass expressed in grams. For example, the atomic mass of hydrogen is 1.008 amu (atomic mass units). One atomic mass unit is equivalent to 1/12th of the mass of a carbon atom. Here in comes Avogadro's constant, which is 6.02×10^{23}. A mole of any element or compound has 6.02×10^{23} atoms or particles. Whether it is hydrogen, sodium, or uranium, the number of atoms in one mole is constant, which is Avogadro's constant.

ii) Burettes and pipettes:
These two tools are used for measuring in titrations. At other times, pipettes are used to measure specific amounts of liquids.

II. Common tools and units for measurement:

The system of measurement in science, including chemistry, is Systema Internaciole or Standard International measurements (SI units of measurement). These are used throughout the world and are based on the Metric system.

i) Length:
Length is measured in millimeters (mm), centimeters (cm), meters (m) and kilometers (km).

ii) Mass:
The units for measuring mass are milligrams (mg), grams (g), kilograms (kg) and metric tons. Mass is measured using an electronic balance and care must be taken to use the balance properly.

iii) Temperature:
Is measured in degrees Celsius using a thermometer.

iv) Volume:
Is measured in milliliters (mL) and liters (L). Graduated cylinders and beakers are used for this purpose. While measuring the volume, care must be taken to minimize parallax error.

Skill 18.3   Identifying potential safety hazards associated with scientific equipment, materials, procedures, and settings

The necessity of safety in a laboratory is obvious. The information below is meant as an aid to you. It is not an exhaustive list. It is your responsibility to obtain all pertinent safety regulations and information from your institution, state, and federal authorities where applicable.

A chemical hygiene plan (CHP) is a written report or manual that summarizes all of the science department's safety regulations, proper laboratory procedures for handling hazardous chemicals, and training procedures. The goal in developing these rules and procedures should be to minimize the exposure of employees and students to hazardous chemicals. The CHP should include:

- General laboratory rules and procedures
- Personal protection equipment requirements
- Spill and accident procedures
- Chemical storage rules and procedures
- Safety equipment requirements and inspection procedures
- Employee safety training requirements
- Exposure and medical evaluation processes
- Emergency evacuation plan

Here is some information that will help with a chemical hygiene plan.

Chemical purchase, use, and disposal
- Inventory all chemicals on hand at least annually. Keep the list up-to-date as chemicals are consumed and replacement chemicals are received.
- If possible, limit the purchase of chemicals to quantities that will be consumed within one year and that are packaged in small containers suitable for direct use in the lab without transfer to other containers.
- Label all chemicals to be stored with date of receipt or preparation and have labels initialed by the person responsible.
- Generally, bottles of chemicals should not remain:
  - Unused on shelves in the lab for more than one week. Move these chemicals to the storeroom or main stockroom.
  - In the storeroom near the lab unused for more than one month. Move these chemicals to the main stockroom.
  - Check shelf life of chemicals. Properly dispose of any out dated chemicals.
- Ensure that the disposal procedures for waste chemicals conform to environmental protection requirements.
- Do not purchase or store large quantities of flammable liquids. Fire department officials can recommend the maximum quantities that may be kept on hand.
- Never open a chemical container until you understand the label and the relevant portions of the MSDS.

CHEMISTRY   199

Chemical Storage Plan for Laboratories

- Chemicals should be stored according to hazard class (ex. flammables, oxidizers, health hazards/toxins, corrosives, etc.).

- Store chemicals away from direct sunlight or localized heat.

- All chemical containers should be properly labeled, dated upon receipt, and dated upon opening.

- Store hazardous chemicals below shoulder height of the shortest person working in the lab.

- Shelves should be painted or covered with chemical-resistant paint or chemical-resistant coating.

- Shelves should be secure and strong enough to hold chemicals being stored on them. Do not overload shelves.

- Personnel should be aware of the hazards associated with all hazardous materials.

- Separate solids from liquids.

Below are examples of chemical groups that can be used to categorize storage. Use these groups as examples when separating chemicals for compatibility. Please note: reactive chemicals must be more closely analyzed since they have a greater potential for violent reactions.

Acids

- Make sure that all acids are stored by compatibility (ex. separate inorganics from organics).
- Store concentrated acids on lower shelves in chemical-resistant trays or in a corrosives cabinet. This will temporarily contain spills or leaks and protect shelving from residue.
- Separate acids from incompatible materials such as bases, active metals (ex. sodium, magnesium, potassium) and from chemicals which can generate toxic gases when combined (ex. sodium cyanide and iron sulfide).

Bases

- Store bases away from acids.
- Store concentrated bases on lower shelves in chemical-resistant trays or in a corrosives cabinet. This will temporarily contain spills or leaks and protect shelving from residue.

Flammables

- Approved flammable storage cabinets should be used for flammable liquid storage.
- You may store 20 gallons of flammable liquids per 100 sq.ft.in a properly fire separated lab. The maximum allowable quantity for flammable liquid storage in any size lab is not to exceed 120 gallons.
- You may store up to 10 gallons of flammable liquids outside of approved flammable storage cabinets.
- An additional 25 gallons may be stored outside of an approved storage cabinet if it is stored in approved safety cans not to exceed 2 gallons in size.
- Use only explosion-proof or intrinsically safe refrigerators and freezers for storing flammable liquids.

Peroxide-Forming Chemicals

- Peroxide-forming chemicals should be stored in airtight containers in a dark, cool, and dry place.
- Unstable chemicals such as peroxide-formers must always be labeled with date received, date opened, and disposal/expiration date.
- Peroxide-forming chemicals should be properly disposed of before the date of expected peroxide formation (typically 6-12 months after opening).
- Suspicion of peroxide contamination should be immediately investigated. Contact Laboratory Safety for procedures.

Water-Reactive Chemicals

- Water reactive chemicals should be stored in a cool, dry place.
- Do not store water reactive chemicals under sinks or near water baths.
- Class D fire extinguishers for the specific water reactive chemical being stored should be made available.

Oxidizers

- Make sure that all oxidizers are stored by compatibility.
- Store oxidizers away from flammables, combustibles, and reducing agents.

Toxins

- Toxic compounds should be stored according to the nature of the chemical, with appropriate security employed when necessary.
- A "Poison Control Network" telephone number should be posted in the laboratory where toxins are stored. Color coded labeling systems that may be found in your lab:

Hazard	**Color Code**
Flammables	Red
Health Hazards/Toxins	Blue
Reactives/Oxidizers	Yellow
Contact Hazards	White
General Storage	Gray, Green, Orange

Please Note: Chemicals with labels that are colored and striped may react with other chemicals in the same hazard class. See MSDS for more information. Chemical containers which are not color coded should have hazard information on the label. Read the label carefully and store accordingly.

Schools are regulated by the Environmental Protection Agency, as well as state and local agencies when it comes to disposing of chemical waste. Check with your state science supervisor, local college or university environmental health and safety specialists and the Laboratory Safety Workshop for advice in the disposal of chemical waste. The American Chemical Society publishes an excellent guidebook, *Laboratory Waste Management, A Guidebook* (1994).

The following are merely guidelines for disposing of chemical waste.

You may dispose of hazardous waste as outlined below. It is the responsibility of the generator to ensure hazardous waste does not end up in ground water, soil or the atmosphere through improper disposal.

1. **Sanitary Sewer** - Some chemicals (acids or bases) may be neutralized and disposed to the sanitary sewer. This disposal option must be approved by the local waste water treatment authority prior to disposal. This may not be an option for some small communities that do not have sufficient treatment capacity at the waste water treatment plant for these types of wastes. Hazardous waste may NOT be disposed of in this manner. This includes heavy metals.

2. **Household Hazardous Waste Facility** - Waste chemicals may be disposed through a county household hazardous waste facility (HHW) or through a county contracted household hazardous waste disposal company. Not all counties have a program to accept waste from schools. Verify with your county HHW facility that they can handle your waste prior to making arrangements.

3. **Disposal Through a Contractor** - A contractor may be used for the disposal of the waste chemicals. Remember that you must keep documentation of your hazardous waste disposal for at least three years. This information must include a waste manifest, reclamation agreement or any written record which describes the waste and how much was disposed, where it was disposed and when it was disposed. Waste analysis records must also be kept when making a determination is necessary. **Any unknown chemicals should be considered hazardous!**

Safety

Disclaimer: The information presented below is intended as a starting point for identification purposes only and should not be regarded as a comprehensive guide for safety procedures in the laboratory. It is the responsibility of the readers of this book to consult with professional advisers about safety procedures in their laboratory.

The following list is a summary of the requirements for chemical laboratories contained in the above documents:

1) Dousing shower and eye-wash with a floor drain are required where students handle potentially dangerous materials.
2) Accessible fully-charged fire extinguishers of the appropriate type and fire blankets must be present if a fire hazard exists.
3) There must be a master control valve or switch accessible to and within 15 feet of the instructor's station for emergency cut-off of all gas cocks, compressed air valves, water, or electrical services accessible to students. Valves must completely shut-off with a one-quarter turn. This master control is in addition to the regular main gas supply cut-off, and the main supply cut-off must be shut down upon activation of the fire alarm system.
4) A high capacity emergency exhaust system with a source of positive ventilation must be installed, and signs providing instructions must be permanently installed at the emergency exhaust system fan switch.
5) Fume hoods must contain supply fans that automatically shut down when the emergency exhaust fan is turned on.
6) Rooms and/or cabinets for chemical storage must have limited student access and ventilation to the exterior of the building separate from the air-conditioning system. The rooms should be kept at moderate temperature, be well-illuminated, and contain doors lockable from the outside and operable at all times from the inside. Cabinet shelves must have a half-inch lip on the front and be constructed of non-corrosive material.
7) Appropriate caution signs must be placed at hazardous work and storage areas.

Therefore, all chemistry laboratories should be equipped with the following safety equipment. Both teachers and students should be familiar with the operation of this equipment.

<u>**Fire extinguisher**</u>: Fire extinguishers are rated for the type of fire it will extinguish. Chemical laboratories should have a combination ABC extinguisher along with a type D fire extinguisher. If a type D extinguisher is not available, a bucket of dry sand will do. Make sure you are trained to use the type of extinguisher available in your setting.

- **Class A** fires are ordinary materials like burning paper, lumber, cardboard, plastics etc.

- **Class B** fires involve <u>flammable</u> or <u>combustible</u> liquids such as gasoline, kerosene, and common <u>organic</u> <u>solvents</u> used in the laboratory.

- **Class C** fires involve energized electrical equipment, such as appliances, switches, panel boxes, power tools, <u>hot plates</u> and stirrers. Water is usually a dangerous extinguishing medium for class C fires because of the risk of electrical shock unless a specialized water mist extinguisher is used.

- **Class D** fires involve combustible metals, such as magnesium, titanium, <u>potassium and sodium</u> as well as <u>pyrophoric organometallic</u> reagents such as alkyllithiums, Grignards and diethylzinc. These materials burn at high temperatures and will react violently with water, air, and/or other chemicals. Handle with care!!

- **Class K** fires are kitchen fires. This class was added to the NFPA portable extinguishers Standard 10 in 1998. <u>Kitchen extinguishers</u> installed before June 30, 1998 are "grandfathered" into the standard.

Some fires may be a combination of these! Your fire extinguishers should have ABC ratings on them. These ratings are determined under <u>ANSI</u>/UL Standard 711 and look something like "3-A:40-B:C". Higher numbers mean more firefighting power. In this example, the extinguisher has a good firefighting capacity for Class A, B and C fires. NFPA has <u>a brief description of UL 711</u> if you want to know more.

Eyewash:

In the event of an eye injury or chemical splash, use the eyewash immediately.

Help the injured person by holding their eyelids open while rinsing.

Rinse copiously and have the eyes checked by a physician afterwards.

Fire Blanket:

A fire blanket can be used to smother a fire. However, use caution when using a fire blanket on a clothing fire. Some fabrics are polymers that melt onto the skin. Stop, Drop and Roll is the best method for extinguishing clothing on fire.

Safety Shower:

Use a safety shower in the event of a chemical spill. Pull the overhead handle and remove clothing that may be contaminated with chemicals, to allow the skin to be rinsed.

Eye protection:

Everyone present must wear eye protection when anyone in the laboratory is performing any of the following activities:
1) Handling hazardous chemicals
2) Handling laboratory glassware
3) Using an open flame.

Safety glasses do not offer protection from splashing liquids. Safety glasses appear similar to ordinary glasses and may be used in an environment that only requires protection from **flying fragments**. Safety glasses with side-shields offer additional protection from **flying fragments approaching from the side**.

Safety goggles offer protection from both flying fragments and splashing liquids. **Only safety goggles** are suitable for eye protection where **hazardous chemicals** are used and handled. Safety goggles with no ventilation (type G) or with indirect ventilation (type H) are both acceptable. Goggles should be marked "Z87" to show they meet federal standards.

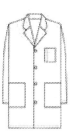

Skin protection:

Wear gloves made of a material known to resist penetration by the chemical being handled. Check gloves for holes and the absence of interior contamination. Wash hands and arms and clean under fingernails after working in a laboratory.

Wear a lab coat or apron. Wear footwear that completely covers the feet.

Ventillation:

Using a Fume Hood

A fume hood carries away vapors from reagents or reactions you may be working with. Using a fume hood correctly will reduce your personal exposure to potentially harmful fumes or vapors. When using a fume hood, keep the following in mind.

• Place equipment or reactions as far back in the hood as is practical. This will improve the efficiency of fume collection and removal.

• Turn on the light inside the hood using the switch on the outside panel, near the electrical outlets.

• The glass sash of the hood is a safety shield. The sash will fall automatically to the appropriate height for efficient operation and should not be raised above this level, except to move equipment in and out of the hood. Keep the sash between your body and the inside of the hood. If the height of the automatic stop is too high to protect your face and body, lower the sash below this point. Do not stick your head inside a hood or climb inside a hood.

• Wipe up all spills immediately. Clean the glass of your hood, if a splash occurs.

• When you are finished using a hood, lower the sash to the level marked by the sticker on the side.

Work habits

- Never work alone in a laboratory or storage area.
- Never eat, drink, smoke, apply cosmetics, chew gum or tobacco, or store food or beverages in a laboratory environment or storage area.
- Keep containers closed when they are not in use.
- Never pipet by mouth.
- Restrain loose clothing and long hair and remove dangling jewelry.
- Tape all Dewar flasks with fabric-based tape.
- Check all glassware before use. Discard if chips or star cracks are present.
- Never leave heat sources unattended.
- Do not store chemicals and/or apparatus on the lab bench or on the floor or aisles of the lab or storage room.
- Keep lab shelves organized.
- Never place a chemical, not even water, near the edges of a lab bench.
- Use a fume hood that is known to be in operating condition when working with toxic, flammable, and/or volatile substances.
- Never put your head inside a fume hood.
- Never store anything in a fume hood.
- Obtain, read, and be sure you understand the MSDS (see below) for each chemical that is to be used before allowing students to begin an experiment.
- Analyze new lab procedures and student-designed lab procedures in advance to identify any hazardous aspects. Minimize and/or eliminate these components before proceeding. Ask yourself these questions:
  o What are the hazards?
  o What are the worst possible things that could go wrong?
  o How will I deal with them?
  o What are the prudent practices, protective facilities and equipment necessary to minimize the risk of exposure to the hazards?
- Analyze close calls and accidents to eliminate their causes and prevent them from occurring again.
- Identify which chemicals may be disposed of in the drain by consulting the MSDS or the supplier. Clear one chemical down the drain by flushing with water before introducing the next chemical.
- Preplan for emergencies.
  o Keep the fire department informed of your chemical inventory and its location.
  o Consult with a local physician about toxins used in the lab and ensure that your area is prepared in advance to treat victims of toxic exposure.
  o Identify devices that should be shut off if possible in an emergency.
  o Inform your students of the designated escape route and alternate route.

Substitutions
- When feasible, substitute less hazardous chemicals for chemicals with greater hazards in experiments.
- Dilute substances when possible instead of using concentrated solutions.
- Use lesser quantities instead of greater quantities in experiments when possible.
- Use films, videotapes, computer displays, and other methods rather than experiments involving hazardous substances.

Label information

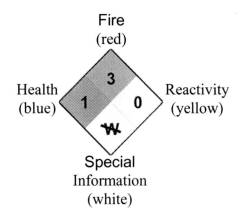

Fire (red)
Health (blue)
Reactivity (yellow)
Special Information (white)

Chemical labels contain safety information in four parts:
1) There will be a signal word. From most to least potentially dangerous, this word will be "Danger!" "Warning!" or "Caution."
2) Statements of hazard (e.g., "Flammable", "May Cause Irritation") follow the signal word. Target organs may be specified.
3) Precautionary measures are listed such as "Keep away from ignition sources" or "Use only with adequate ventilation."
4) First aid information is usually included such as whether to induce vomiting and how to induce vomiting if the chemical is ingested.

Chemical hazard pictorial
Several different pictorials are used on labels to indicate the level of a chemical hazard. The most common is the **"fire diamond" NFPA (National Fire Prevention Association) pictorial** shown at left. A zero indicates a minimal hazard and a four indicates a severe risk. Special information includes if the chemical reacts with water, **OX** for an oxidizer, **COR ACID** for a corrosive acid, and **COR ALK** for a corrosive base. The "Health" hazard level is for **acute toxicity only**.

Pictorials are designed for **quick reference in emergency situations**, but they are also useful as minimal summaries of safety information for a chemical. They are not required on chemicals you purchase, so it's a good idea to add a label pictorial to every chemical you receive if one is not already present. **The entrance to areas where chemicals are stored should carry a fire diamond label** to represent the materials present.

Procedures for flammable materials: minimize fire risk

The vapors of a flammable liquid **or solid** may travel across the room to an ignition source and cause a fire or explosion.

- Store in an approved safety cabinet for flammable liquids. Store in safety cans if possible.
- Minimize volumes and concentrations used in an experiment with flammables.
- Minimize the time containers are open.
- Minimize ignition sources in the laboratory.
- Ensure that there is good air movement in the laboratory before the experiment.
- Check the fire extinguishers and be certain that you know how to use them.
- Tell the students that the "Stop, Drop, and Roll" technique is best for a clothing fire outside the lab, but in the lab they should walk calmly to the safety shower and use it. Practice this procedure with students in drills.
- A fire blanket should not be used for clothing fires because clothes often contain polymers that melt onto the skin. Pressing these fabrics into the skin with a blanket increases burn damage.
- If a demonstration of an exploding gas or vapor is performed, it should be done behind a safety shield using glass vessels taped with fabric tape.

Procedures for corrosive materials: minimize risk of contact

Corrosive materials **destroy or permanently change living tissue** through chemical action. **Irritants** cause inflammation due to an immune response but not through chemical action. The effect is usually reversible but can be severe and long lasting. **Sensitizers** are irritants that cause no symptoms after the first exposure but may cause irritation during a later exposure.

- Always store corrosives below eye level.
- Only diluted corrosives should be used in pre-high school laboratories and their use at full-strength in high school should be limited.
- Dilute corrosive materials by **adding them to water**. Adding water to a concentrated acid or base can cause rapid boiling and splashing.
- Wear goggles and face shield when handling hazardous corrosives. The face, ears, and neck should be protected.
- Wear gloves known to be impervious to the chemical. Wear sleeve gauntlets and a lab apron made of impervious material if splashing is likely.
- Always wash your hands after handling corrosives.
- Splashes on skin should be flushed with flowing water for 15 minutes while a doctor is called.

- If someone splashes a corrosive material on their clothing:
  - First use the safety shower with clothing on.
  - Have them remove all clothing while under the safety shower including shoes and socks. This is no time for modesty.
  - They should stay under the shower for 15 minutes while a doctor is called.
- Splashes in eyes should be dealt with as follows:
  - Take the victim to the eyewash fountain within 30 seconds.
  - Have them hold their eyelids open with thumb and forefinger and use the eyewash.
  - They must continuously move their eyeballs during 15 minutes of rinsing to cleanse the optic nerve at the back of the eye. A doctor should be called.

Procedures for toxic materials: minimize exposure

Toxic effects are either **chronic** or **acute**. Chronic effects are seen after repeated exposures or after one long exposure. Acute effects occur within a few hours at most.

- Use the smallest amount needed at the lowest concentration for the shortest period of time possible. Weigh the risks against the educational benefits.
- Be aware of the five different routes of exposure
  1) Inhalation-the ability to smell a toxin is not a proper indication of unsafe exposure. Work in the fume hood when using toxins. Minimize dusts and mists by cleaning often, cleaning spills rapidly, and maintaining good ventilation in the lab.
  2) Absorption through intact skin-always wear impervious gloves if the MSDS indicates this route of exposure.
  3) Ingestion
  4) Absorption through other body orifices such as ear canal and eye socket.
  5) Injection by a cut from broken contaminated glassware or other sharp equipment.
- Be aware of the first symptoms of overexposure described by the MSDS. Often these are headache, nausea, and dizziness. Get to fresh air and do not return until the symptoms have passed. If the symptom returns when you come back into the lab, contact a physician and have the space tested.
- Be aware of whether vomiting should be induced in case of ingestion
- Be aware of the recommended procedure in case of unconsciousness.

Procedures for reactive materials: minimize incompatibility

Many chemicals are **self-reactive**. For example, they explode when dried out or when disturbed under certain conditions or they react with components of air. These materials generally **should not be allowed into the high school**. Other precautions must be taken to minimize reactions between **incompatible pairs**.

- Store fuels and oxidizers separately.
- Store reducing agents and oxidizing agents separately.
- Store acids and bases separately.
- Store chemicals that react with fire-fighting materials (i.e., water or carbon dioxide) under conditions that minimize the possibility of a reaction if a fire is being fought in the storage area.
- MSDSs list other incompatible pairs.
- Never store chemicals in alphabetical order by name.
- When incompatible pairs must be supplied to students, do so under direct supervision with very dilute solutions and/or small quantities.

Material Safety Data Sheet (MSDS) information

Many chemicals have a mixture of toxic, corrosive, flammability, and reactivity risks. The **Material Safety Data Sheet** or **MSDS** for a chemical contains detailed safety information that is not presented on the label. This includes acute and chronic health effects, first aid and firefighting measures, what to do in case of a spill, and ecological and disposal considerations.

The MSDS will state whether the chemical is a known or suspected carcinogen, mutagen, or teratogen. A **carcinogen** is a compound that causes cancer (malignant tumors). A **mutagen** alters DNA with the potential effects of causing cancer or birth defects in unconceived children. A **teratogen** produces birth defects and is detrimental during fetal development

There are many parts of an MSDS that are not written for the layperson. Their level of detail and technical content intimidate many people outside the fields of toxicology and industrial safety. According to the American Chemical Society (http://membership.acs.org/c/ccs/pubs/chemical_safety_manual.pdf), an MSDS places "an over-emphasis on the toxic characteristics of the subject chemical."

In a high school chemistry lab, the value of an MSDS is in the words and not in the numerical data it contains, but some knowledge of the numbers is useful for comparing the dangers of one chemical to another. Numerical results of animal toxicity studies are often presented in the form of **LD$_{50}$ values**. These represent the **dose required to kill 50% of animals** tested.

Exposure limits may be presented in three ways:

1) PEL (Permissible Exposure Limit) or TLV-TWA (Threshold Limit Value-Time Weighted Average). This is the maximum permitted concentration of the airborne chemical in volume parts per million (ppm) for a **worker exposed 8 hours daily**.
2) TLV-STEL (Threshold Limit Value-Short Term Exposure Limit). This is the maximum concentration permitted for a 15-minute exposure period.
3) TLV-C (Threshold Limit Value-Ceiling). This is the concentration that should never be exceeded at any moment.

http://hazard.com/msds/index.php contains a large database of MSDSs. http://www.ilpi.com/msds/ref/demystify.html contains a useful "MSDS demystifier." Cut and paste an MSDS into the web page, and hypertext links will appear to a glossary of terms.

Facilities and equipment
- Use separate labeled containers for general trash, broken glass, for each type of hazardous chemical waste—ignitable, corrosive, reactive, and toxic.
- Keep the floor area around safety showers, eyewash fountains, and fire extinguishers clear of all obstructions.
- Never block escape routes.
- Never prop open a fire door.
- Provide safety guards for all moving belts and pulleys.
- Instruct everyone in the lab on the proper use of the safety shower and eyewash fountain (see Corrosive materials above). Most portable eyewash devices cannot maintain the required flow for 15 minutes. A permanent eyewash fountain is preferred.
- If contamination is suspected in the breathing air, arrange for sampling to take place.
- Regularly inspect fire blankets, if present, for rips and holes. Maintain a record of inspection.
- Regularly check safety showers and eyewash fountains for proper rate of flow. Maintain a record of inspection.
- Keep up-to-date emergency phone numbers posted next to the telephone.
- Place fire extinguishers near an escape route.
- Regularly maintain fire extinguishers and maintain a record of inspection. Arrange with the local fire department for training of teachers and administrators in the proper use of extinguishers.
- Regularly check fume hoods for proper airflow. Ensure that fume hood exhaust is not drawn back into the intake for general building ventilation.
- Secure compressed gas cylinders at all times and transport them only while secured on a hand truck.
- Restrict the use and handling of compressed gas to those who have received formal training.

- Install chemical storage shelves with lips. Never use stacked boxes for storage instead of shelves.
- Only use an explosion-proof refrigerator for chemical storage.
- Have appropriate equipment and materials available in advance for spill control and cleanup. Consult the MSDS for each chemical to determine what is required. Replace these materials when they become outdated.
- Provide an appropriate supply of first aid equipment and instruction on its proper use.

Additional comments: Teach safety to students

- Weigh the risks and benefits inherent in lab work, inform students of the hazards and precautions involved in their assignment, and involve students in discussions about safety before every assignment.
- If an incident happens, it can be used to improve lab safety via student participation. Ask the student involved. The student's own words about what occurred should be included in the report.
- Safety information supplied by the manufacturer on a chemical container should be seen by students who actually use the chemical. If you distribute chemicals into smaller containers to be used by students, copy the hazard and precautionary information from the original label onto the labels for the students' containers. Students interested in graphic design may be able to help you perform this task. Labels for many common chemicals may be found here: http://beta.ehs.cornell.edu/labels/cgi-bin/label_selection.pl
- Organize a student safety committee whose task is to conduct one safety inspection and present a report. A different committee may be organized each month or every other month.

Additional comments: General

- Every chemical is hazardous. The way it is used determines the probability of harm.
- Every person is individually and personally responsible for the safe use of chemicals.
- If an accident might happen, it will eventually happen. Proper precautions will ensure the consequences are minimized when it does occur.
- Every accident is predicted by one or more **close calls** where nobody is injured and no property is damaged but something out of the ordinary occurred. Examples might be a student briefly touching a hot surface and saying "Ouch!" with no injury, two students engaged in horseplay, or a student briefly removing safety goggles to read a meniscus level. **Eliminate the cause of a close call and you have stopped a future accident.**

Also see: http://www.labsafety.org/40steps.htm, http://www.flinnsci.com/Sections/Safety/safety.asp, and the American Chemical Society safety publications listed under References.

Skill 18.4   Recognizing appropriate protocols for maintaining safety and for responding to emergencies during laboratory activities

All science labs should contain the following items of **safety equipment**. Those marked with an asterisk are requirements by state laws.

* fire blanket which is visible and accessible
*Ground Fault Circuit Interrupters (GCFI) within two feet of water supplies
*signs designating room exits
*emergency shower capable of providing a continuous flow of water
*emergency eye wash station which can be activated by the foot or forearm
*eye protection for every student and a means of sanitizing equipment
*emergency exhaust fans providing ventilation to the outside of the building
*master cut-off switches for gas, electric and compressed air. Switches must have permanently attached handles. Cut-off switches must be clearly labeled.
*an ABC fire extinguisher
*storage cabinets for flammable materials
-chemical spill control kit
-fume hood with a motor which is spark proof
-protective laboratory aprons made of flame retardant material
-signs which will alert potential hazardous conditions
-containers for broken glassware, flammables, corrosives, and waste.
-containers should be labeled.

Students should wear safety goggles when performing dissections, heating, or while using acids and bases. Hair should always be tied back and objects should never be placed in the mouth. Food should not be consumed while in the laboratory. Hands should always be washed before and after laboratory experiments. In case of an accident, eye washes and showers should be used for eye contamination or a chemical spill that covers the student's body. Small chemical spills should only be contained and cleaned by the teacher. Kitty litter or a chemical spill kit should be used to clean spill. For large spills, the school administration and the local fire department should be notified. Biological spills should also be handled only by the teacher. Contamination with biological waste can be cleaned by using bleach when appropriate.

Accidents and injuries should always be reported to the school administration and local health facilities. The severity of the accident or injury will determine the course of action to pursue.

It is the responsibility of the teacher to provide a safe environment for their students. Proper supervision greatly reduces the risk of injury and a teacher should never leave a class for any reason without providing alternate supervision. After an accident, two factors are considered; **foreseeability** and **negligence**. Foreseeability is the anticipation that an event may occur under certain circumstances. Negligence is the failure to exercise ordinary or reasonable care. Safety procedures should be a part of the science curriculum and a well managed classroom is important to avoid potential lawsuits.

All laboratory solutions should be prepared as directed in the lab manual. Care should be taken to avoid contamination. All glassware should be rinsed thoroughly with distilled water before using and cleaned well after use. All solutions should be made with distilled water as tap water contains dissolved particles that may affect the results of an experiment. Unused solutions should be disposed of according to local disposal procedures.

Material safety data sheets are available for every chemical and biological substance. These are available directly from the company of acquisition or the internet. The manuals for equipment used in the lab should be read and understood before using them.

COMPETENCY 19.0   UNDERSTAND THE SKILLS AND PROCEDURES FOR
                   ANALYZING AND COMMUNICATING SCIENTIFIC
                   DATA.

Skill 19.1   Applying the concepts of precision, accuracy, and error
              analysis in evaluating experimental data

A measurement is **precise** when individual measurements of the same quantity **agree with one another**. A measurement is **accurate** when they **agree with the true value** of the quantity being measured. An **accurate** measurement is **valid**. We get the right answer. A **precise** measurement is **reproducible**. We get a similar answer each time. These terms are related to **sources of error** in a measurement. Precise measurements are near the **arithmetic mean** of the values. The arithmetic mean is the sum of the measurements divided by the number of measurements. The **mean** is commonly called the **average**. It is the **best estimate** of the quantity.

Random error results from **limitations in equipment or techniques**. A larger **random error decreases precision**. Remember that all measurements reported to proper number of significant digits contain an imprecise final digit to reflect random error.

Systematic error results from **imperfect equipment or technique**. A larger **systematic error decreases accuracy**. Instead of a random error with random fluctuations, there is a result that is too large or small.

Example: An environmental engineering company creates a solution of 5.00 ng/L of a toxin and distributes it to four toxicology labs to test their protocols. Each lab tests the material 5 times. Their results are charted as points on the number lines below. Interpret this data in terms of precision, accuracy, and type of error.

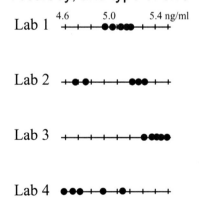

Solution: Results from lab 1 are both accurate and precise when compared to results from the other labs. Results from lab 2 are less precise than those from lab 1. Lab 2 seems to use a protocol that contains a greater random error. However, the mean result from lab 2 is still close to the known value. Lab 3 returned results that were about as precise as lab 1 but inaccurate compared to labs 1 and 2. Lab 3 most likely uses a protocol that yields a systematic error. The data from lab 4 is both imprecise and inaccurate. Systematic and random errors are larger than in lab 1.

Skill 19.2 **Applying appropriate mathematical concepts and computational skills to analyze data (e.g., using ratios; determining mean, median, and mode)**

Mean is the mathematical average of all the items. To calculate the mean, all the items must be added up and divided by the number of items. This is also called the arithmetic mean or more commonly as the "**average**".

The **median** depends on whether the number of items is odd or even. If the number is odd, then the median is the value of the item in the middle. This is the value that denotes that the number of items having higher or equal value to that is same as the number of items having equal or lesser value than that. If the number of the items is even, the median is the average of the two items in the middle, such that the number of items having values higher or equal to it is same as the number of items having values equal or less than that.

Mode is the value o the item that occurs the most often, if there are not many items. Bimodal is a situation where there are two items with equal frequency.

Range is the difference between the maximum and minimum values. The range is the difference between two extreme points on the **distribution curve**.

Skill 19.3 **Using appropriate presentation methods (e.g., tables, graphs) and criteria for organizing and analyzing data (e.g., detecting patterns)**

Data collected is initially organized into tables. Trends or patterns in data can be difficult to identify using tables of numbers. For example, here is a table of carbon dioxide concentrations taken over many years atop Mauna Loa Observatory in Hawaii.

Atmospheric CO_2 concentrations at Mauna Loa

Year	Jan.	Feb.	March	April	May	June	July	Aug.	Sept.	Oct.	Nov.	Dec.	Annual
1958	-99.99	-99.99	315.71	317.45	317.5	-99.99	315.86	314.93	313.19	-99.99	313.34	314.67	-99.99
1959	315.58	316.47	316.65	317.71	318.29	318.16	316.55	314.8	313.84	313.34	314.81	315.59	315.98
1960	316.43	316.97	317.58	319.03	320.03	319.59	318.18	315.91	314.16	313.83	315	316.19	316.91
1961	316.89	317.7	318.54	319.48	320.58	319.78	318.58	316.79	314.99	315.31	316.1	317.01	317.65
1962	317.94	318.56	319.69	320.58	321.01	320.61	319.61	317.4	316.26	315.42	316.69	317.69	318.45
1963	318.74	319.08	319.86	321.39	322.24	321.47	319.74	317.77	316.21	315.99	317.07	318.36	318.99
1964	319.57	-99.99	-99.99	-99.99	322.23	321.89	320.44	318.7	316.7	316.87	317.68	318.71	-99.99
1965	319.44	320.44	320.89	322.13	322.16	321.87	321.21	318.87	317.81	317.3	318.87	319.42	320.03
1966	320.62	321.59	322.39	323.7	324.07	323.75	322.4	320.37	318.64	318.1	319.79	321.03	321.37
1967	322.33	322.5	323.04	324.42	325	324.09	322.55	320.92	319.26	319.39	320.72	321.96	322.18
1968	322.57	323.15	323.89	325.02	325.57	325.36	324.14	322.11	320.33	320.25	321.32	322.9	323.05
1969	324	324.42	325.64	326.66	327.38	326.7	325.89	323.67	322.38	321.78	322.85	324.12	324.62

1970	325.06	325.98	326.93	328.13	328.07	327.66	326.35	324.69	323.1	323.07	324.01	325.13	325.68
1971	326.17	326.68	327.18	327.78	328.92	328.57	327.37	325.43	323.36	323.56	324.8	326.01	326.32
1972	326.77	327.63	327.75	329.72	330.07	329.09	328.05	326.32	324.84	325.2	326.5	327.55	327.46
1973	328.54	329.56	330.3	331.5	332.48	332.07	330.87	329.31	327.51	327.18	328.16	328.64	329.68
1974	329.35	330.71	331.48	332.65	333.09	332.25	331.18	329.4	327.44	327.37	328.46	329.58	330.25
1975	330.4	331.41	332.04	333.31	333.96	333.59	331.91	330.06	328.56	328.34	329.49	330.76	331.15
1976	331.74	332.56	333.5	334.58	334.87	334.34	333.05	330.94	329.3	328.94	330.31	331.68	332.15
1977	332.92	333.42	334.7	336.07	336.74	336.27	334.93	332.75	331.58	331.16	332.4	333.85	333.9
1978	334.97	335.39	336.64	337.76	338.01	337.89	336.54	334.68	332.76	332.54	333.92	334.95	335.5
1979	336.23	336.76	337.96	338.89	339.47	339.29	337.73	336.09	333.91	333.86	335.29	336.73	336.85
1980	338.01	338.36	340.08	340.77	341.46	341.17	339.56	337.6	335.88	336.01	337.1	338.21	338.69
1981	339.23	340.47	341.38	342.51	342.91	342.25	340.49	338.43	336.69	336.85	338.36	339.61	339.93
1982	340.75	341.61	342.7	343.56	344.13	343.35	342.06	339.82	337.97	337.86	339.26	340.49	341.13
1983	341.37	342.52	343.1	344.94	345.75	345.32	343.99	342.39	339.86	339.99	341.16	342.99	342.78
1984	343.7	344.51	345.28	347.08	347.43	346.79	345.4	343.28	341.07	341.35	342.98	344.22	344.42
1985	344.97	346	347.43	348.35	348.93	348.25	346.56	344.69	343.09	342.8	344.24	345.56	345.9
1986	346.29	346.96	347.86	349.55	350.21	349.54	347.94	345.91	344.86	344.17	345.66	346.9	347.15
1987	348.02	348.47	349.42	350.99	351.84	351.25	349.52	348.1	346.44	346.36	347.81	348.96	348.93
1988	350.43	351.72	352.22	353.59	354.22	353.79	352.39	350.44	348.72	348.88	350.07	351.34	351.48
1989	352.76	353.07	353.68	355.42	355.67	355.13	353.9	351.67	349.8	349.99	351.3	352.53	352.91
1990	353.66	354.7	355.39	356.2	357.16	356.22	354.82	352.91	350.96	351.18	352.83	354.21	354.19
1991	354.72	355.75	357.16	358.6	359.34	358.24	356.17	354.03	352.16	352.21	353.75	354.99	355.59
1992	355.98	356.72	357.81	359.15	359.66	359.25	357.03	355	353.01	353.31	354.16	355.4	356.37
1993	356.7	357.16	358.38	359.46	360.28	359.6	357.57	355.52	353.7	353.98	355.33	356.8	357.04
1994	358.36	358.91	359.97	361.26	361.68	360.95	359.55	357.49	355.84	355.99	357.58	359.04	358.88
1995	359.96	361	361.64	363.45	363.79	363.26	361.9	359.46	358.06	357.75	359.56	360.7	360.88
1996	362.05	363.25	364.03	364.72	365.41	364.97	363.65	361.49	359.46	359.6	360.76	362.33	362.64
1997	363.18	364	364.57	366.35	366.79	365.62	364.47	362.51	360.19	360.77	362.43	364.28	363.76
1998	365.32	366.15	367.31	368.61	369.3	368.87	367.64	365.77	363.9	364.23	365.46	366.97	366.63
1999	368.15	368.86	369.58	371.12	370.97	370.33	369.25	366.91	364.6	365.09	366.63	367.96	368.29
2000	369.08	369.4	370.45	371.59	371.75	371.62	370.04	368.04	366.54	366.63	368.2	369.43	369.4
2001	370.17	371.39	372	372.75	373.88	373.17	371.48	369.42	367.83	367.96	369.55	371.1	370.89
2002	372.29	372.94	373.38	374.71	375.4	375.26	373.87	371.35	370.57	370.1	371.93	373.63	372.95

(Carbon Dioxide Information Analysis Center (CDIAC))

However, more often than not, the data is compiled into graphs. Graphs help scientists visualize and interpret the variation in data. Depending on the nature of the data, there are many types of graphs. Bar graphs, pie charts and line graphs are just a few methods used to pictorially represent numerical data.

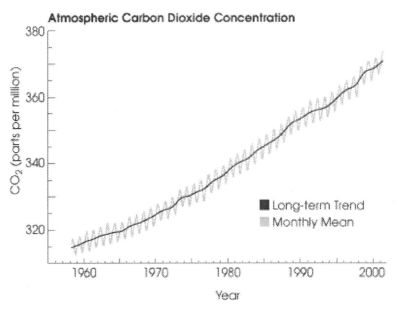

Atmospheric CO_2 measured at Mauna Loa. This is a famous graph called the Keeling Curve (courtesy NASA).

Interpretation of graphical data shows that on the x-axis is the variable of time in units of years and the y-axis represents the variable of CO_2 concentration in units of parts per million (ppm). The best fit line (solid dark line) shows the trend in CO_2 concentrations during the time period. The steady upward-sloping line indicates a trend of increasing CO_2 concentrations during the time period. However, the light blue line which indicates monthly mean CO_2 levels shows a periodic trend in CO_2 levels during the year. This periodic trend is accounted for by the changes in the seasons. In the spring and summer, deciduous trees and plants undergo increased increased photosynthesis and remove more CO_2 from the atmosphere in the Northern Hemisphere.

The interpretation of data and construction and interpretation of graphs are central practices in science. Graphs are effective visual tools, which relay information quickly and reveal trends easily. While there are several different types of graphical displays, extracting information from them can be described in three basic steps.

1. Describe the graph: What does the title say? What is displayed on the x- and y-axis, including the units.
   - Determine the set-up of the graph.
   - Make sure the units used are understood.
     For example, g·cm^3 means g/cm^3
   - Notice symbols used and check for legend or explanation.

2. Describe the data: Identify the range of data. Are patterns reflected in the data?

3. Interpret the data: How do patterns seen in the graph relate to other things? What conclusions can be drawn from the patterns?

There are seven basic types of graphs.

Column Graphs

Column graphs, consist of patterned rectangles displayed along a baseline called the x-category or the horizontal axis. The height of the rectangle represents the amount of data. Column graphs best show:
• changes in data over time (short time series)
• comparisons of several items (relationship between two series)

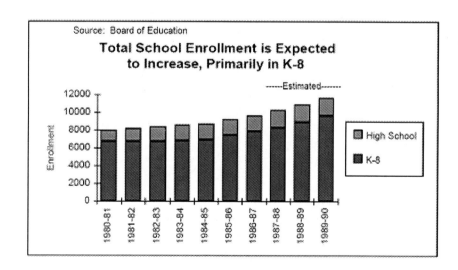

Bar Graphs
Column graphs in which the rectangles are arranged horizontally. The length of each rectangle represents its value. Bar graphs are sometimes referred to as histograms. Bar graphs best show data series with no natural order.

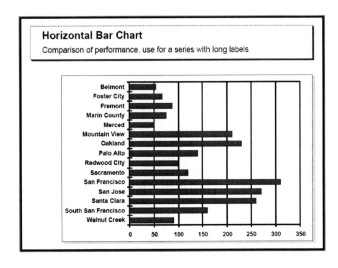

Bar graphs are good for looking at differences amongst similar things. If the data are a time series, a carefully chosen column graph is generally more appropriate but bar graphs can be used to vary a presentation when many column graphs of time series are used. One advantage of bar graphs is that there is greater horizontal space for variable descriptors because the vertical axis is the category axis.

Line Graphs
Line graphs show data points connected by lines; different series are given different line markings (for example, dashed or dotted) or different tick marks. Line graphs are useful when the data points are more important than the transitions between them. They best show:
>   • the comparison of long series
>   • a general trend is the message.

Line graphs are good for showing trends or changes over time.

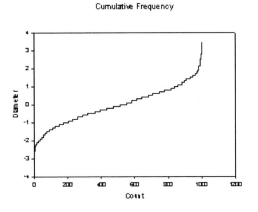

Pie Charts
A pie chart is a circle with radii connecting the center to the edge. The area between two radii is called a slice. Data values are proportionate to the angle between the radii.
Pie charts best show:
>   • parts of a whole

Be careful of too many slices since they result in a cluttered graph. Six slices are as many as can be handled on one pie.

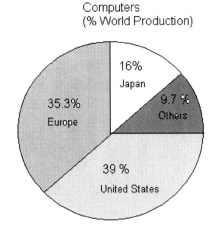

Area Graphs

Area charts show the relative contributions over time that each data series makes to a whole picture and are "stacked line graphs" in the sense that values are added to the variables below. Unlike line graphs, the space between lines is filled with shadings.

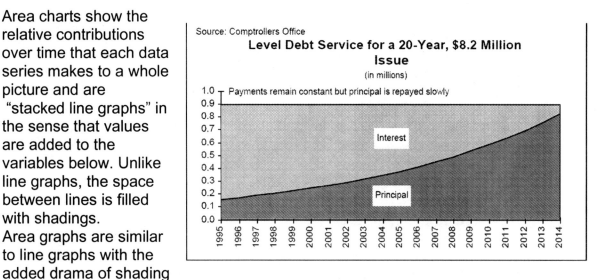

Area graphs are similar to line graphs with the added drama of shading between lines to emphasize variation between whatever the lines represent. They differ from line graphs in that the shaded areas are "added" one on top of the next. Thus, the scale provides accurate measurements only for the lowest part of the graph. This can cause misinterpretation if not fully understood. If reasonable, consider putting the "flattest" graph on the bottom.

Scatter Graphs

A scatter plot is the simplest type of graph. It simply plots the data points against their values, without adding an connecting lines, bars or other stuff. The first variable is measured along the x-axis and the second along the y-axis. Because of this, scatter graphs do not have descriptors in the same sense as other graphs. Scatter graphs best show

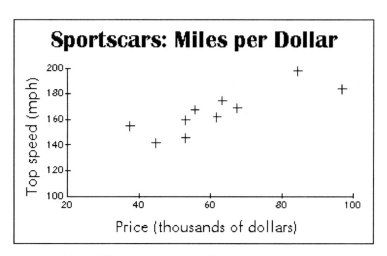

possible relationships between two variables. The purpose of the graph is to try to decide if some partial or indirect relationship—a correlation—exists.

Skill 19.4 Using data to support or challenge scientific arguments and claims

Conclusions must be communicated by clearly describing the information using accurate data, visual presentation and other appropriate media such as a power point presentation. Examples of visual presentations are graphs (bar/line/pie), tables/charts, diagrams, and artwork. Modern technology must be used whenever necessary. The method of communication must be suitable to the audience. Written communication is as important as oral communication. The scientist's strongest ally is a solid set of reproducible data.

Skill 19.5 Identifying appropriate methods for communicating the outcomes of scientific investigations (e.g., publication in peer-reviewed journals)

When the results of repeated experiments are consistent and patterns become apparent, the next stage of the process is reporting the results, often by publishing a scientific paper. Hundreds of scientific societies throughout the world publish journals containing articles that report research. The published work is then permanently available to the scientific community. Other scientists are then free to examine the results, repeat the experiments, or take the research further by designing new experiments. Some may critique the oriiginal research, pointing out possible errors or alternative interpretations of the data.

A scientist may also present research to other scientists at meetings sponsoored by one of many scientific societies. In the United States, the American Chemical Society hosts many gatherings of research chemists. It is through presentations like these that the researcher has an opportunity to interact directly with others in the field.

As a result of publication and presentation of research, science is a group activity, providing many opportunities for correcting errors.

Skill 19.6   Demonstrating knowledge of criteria for determining the reliability of resources for gaining scientific information

Because people often attempt to use scientific evidence in support of political or personal agendas, the ability to evaluate the credibility of scientific claims is a necessary skill in today's society. In evaluating scientific claims made in the media, public debates, and advertising, one should follow several guidelines.

First, scientific, peer-reviewed journals are the most accepted source for information on scientific experiments and studies. One should carefully scrutinize any claim that does not reference peer-reviewed literature.

Second, the media and those with an agenda to advance (advertisers, debaters, etc.) often overemphasize the certainty and importance of experimental results. One should question any scientific claim that sounds fantastical or overly certain.

Finally, knowledge of experimental design and the scientific method is important in evaluating the credibility of studies. For example, one should look for the inclusion of control groups and the presence of data to support the given conclusions.

COMPETENCY 20.0 UNDERSTAND THE UNIFYING CONCEPTS OF SCIENCE AND TECHNOLOGY.

Skill 20.1 Demonstrating knowledge of the unifying concepts (e.g., system, model, change, scale) of science and technology

The following are the concepts and processes generally recognized as common to all scientific disciplines:

- Systems, order, and organization

- Evidence, models, and explanation

- Constancy, change, and measurement

- Evolution and equilibrium

- Form and function

Because the natural world is so complex, the study of science involves the **organization** of items into smaller groups based on interaction or interdependence. These groups are called **systems**. Examples of organization are the periodic table of elements and the five-kingdom classification scheme for living organisms. Examples of systems are the solar system, cardiovascular system, Newton's laws of force and motion, and the laws of conservation.

Order refers to the behavior and measurability of organisms and events in nature. The arrangement of planets in the solar system and the life cycle of bacterial cells are examples of order.

Scientists use **evidence** and **models** to form **explanations** of natural events. Models are miniaturized representations of a larger event or system. Evidence is anything that furnishes proof.

Constancy and **change** describe the observable properties of natural organisms and events. Scientists use different systems of **measurement** to observe change and constancy. For example, the freezing and melting points of given substances and the speed of sound are constant under constant conditions. Growth, decay, and erosion are all examples of natural change.

Evolution is the process of change over a long period of time. While biological evolution is the most common example, one can also classify technological advancement, changes in the universe, and changes in the environment as evolution.

Equilibrium is the state of balance between opposing forces of change. Homeostasis and ecological balance are examples of equilibrium.

Form and **function** are properties of organisms and systems that are closely related. The function of an object usually dictates its form and the form of an object usually facilitates its function. For example, the form of the heart (e.g. muscle, valves) allows it to perform its function of circulating blood through the body.

Skill 20.2   Recognizing the characteristics of systems, how the components of a system interact (e.g., negative and positive feedback), and how different systems interact

Because the natural world is so complex, the study of science involves the **organization** of items into smaller groups based on interaction or interdependence. These groups are called **systems**. Examples of organization are the periodic table of elements and the five-kingdom classification scheme for living organisms. Examples of systems are the solar system, cardiovascular system, Newton's laws of force and motion, and the laws of conservation.

In human systems, feedback loops serve to regulate bodily functions in relation to environmental conditions. Positive feedback loops enhance the body's response to external stimuli and promote processes that involve rapid deviation from the initial state. For example, positive feedback loops function in stress response and the regulation of growth and development. Negative feedback loops help maintain stability in spite of environmental changes and function in homeostasis. For example, negative feedback loops function in the regulation of blood glucose levels and the maintenance of body temperature.

Feedback loops regulate the secretion of classical vertebrate hormones in humans. The pituitary gland and hypothalamus respond to varying levels of hormones by increasing or decreasing production and secretion. High levels of a hormone cause down-regulation of the production and secretion pathways, while low levels of a hormone cause up-regulation of the production and secretion pathways.

Skill 20.3   Identifying types and characteristics of models used in science and technology and the advantages and limitations of models

The model is a basic element of the scientific method. Many things in science are studied with models. A model is any simplification or substitute for what we are actually studying, understanding or predicting. A model is a substitute, but it is similar to what it represents. We encounter models at every step of our daily living. The Periodic Table of the elements is a model that chemists use for predicting the properties of the elements. Physicists use Newton's laws to predict how objects will interact. In geology, the continental drift model predicts the past positions of continents. At every step of scientific study, models are extensively used. The primary activity of the hundreds of thousands of US scientists is to produce new models, resulting in tens of thousands of scientific papers published per year.

Types of models:

* Scale models: some models are basically downsized or enlarged copies of their target systems like the models of protein, DNA etc.
* Idealized models: An idealization is a deliberate simplification of something complicated with the objective of making it easier to understand. Some examples are frictionless planes, point masses, and isolated systems.
* Analogical models: These models draw parallels between new phenomenon and the behavior of familiar systems. Examples of analogical models are the billiard model of a gas, the computer model of the mind, or the liquid drop model of the nucleus.
*Phenomenological models: These models simply predict the occurrence of certain events in response to others, but do not specifically explain why or how. They are usually defined as models that are independent of theories.
*Theory models: Unlike phenomenological modes, these models are actually derived from theories about how one event or condition influences another.

Uses of models:
1. Models are crucial for understanding the structure and function of processes in science.
2. Models help us to visualize the organs/systems they represent.
3. Models are very useful to predict how similar systems might behave and foresee future events.

Limitations:
1. Models can never predict every aspect of a system and so cannot replace the performance of an actual experiment.
3. Caution must be exercised before presenting the models to the class, as they may not be accurate.
4. It is the responsibility of the educator to analyze the model critically for the proportions, content value, and other important data.
5. One must be careful about the representation style. This style differs from person to person.

Sample Test

Directions: Read each item and select the best response.

1. A piston compresses a gas at constant temperature. Which gas properties increase?

   I. Average speed of molecules
   II. Pressure
   III. Molecular collisions with container walls per second

   A. I and II
   B. I and III
   C. II and III
   D. I, II, and III

2. The temperature of a liquid is raised at atmospheric pressure. Which liquid property increases?

   A. critical pressure
   B. vapor pressure
   C. surface tension
   D. viscosity

3. Potassium crystallizes with two atoms contained in each unit cell. What is the mass of potassium found in a lattice 1.00×10^6 unit cells wide, 2.00×10^6 unit cells high, and 5.00×10^5 unit cells deep?

   A. 85.0 ng
   B. 32.5 μg
   C. 64.9 μg
   D. 130. μg

4. A gas is heated in a sealed container. Which of the following occur?

   A. gas pressure rises
   B. gas density decreases
   C. the average distance between molecules increases
   D. all of the above

5. How many molecules are in 2.20 pg of a protein with a molecular weight of 150. kDa?

   A. 8.83×10^9
   B. 1.82×10^9
   C. 8.83×10^6
   D. 1.82×10^6

6. At STP, 20. μL of O_2 contain 5.4×10^{16} molecules. According to Avogadro's hypothesis, how many molecules are in 20. μL of Ne?

   A. 5.4×10^{15}
   B. 1.0×10^{16}
   C. 2.7×10^{16}
   D. 5.4×10^{16}

7. An ideal gas at 50.0 °C and 3.00 atm is in a 300. cm^3 cylinder. The cylinder volume changes by moving a piston until the gas is at 50.0 °C and 1.00 atm. What is the final volume?

   A. 100. cm^3
   B. 450. cm^3
   C. 900. cm^3
   D. 1.20 dm^3

8. Which gas law may be used to solve the previous question?

   A. Charles's law
   B. Boyle's law
   C. Graham's law
   D. Avogadro's law

9. A blimp is filled with 5000. m^3 of helium at 28.0 °C and 99.7 kPa. What is the mass of helium used?

   $$R = 8.3144 \frac{J}{mol\text{-}K}$$

   A. 797 kg
   B. 810. kg
   C. 879 kg
   D. 8.57×10^3 kg

10. Which of the following are able to flow from one place to another?

    I. Gases
    II. Liquids
    III. Solids
    IV. Supercritical fluids

    A. I and II
    B. II only
    C. I, II, and IV
    D. I, II, III, and IV

11. One mole of an ideal gas at STP occupies 22.4 L. At what temperature will one mole of an ideal gas at one atm occupy 31.0 L?

    A. 34.6 °C
    B. 105 °C
    C. 378 °C
    D. 442 °C

12. Why does CaCl$_2$ have a higher normal melting point than NH$_3$?

    A. Covalent bonds are stronger than London dispersion forces.
    B. Covalent bonds are stronger than hydrogen bonds.
    C. Ionic bonds are stronger than London dispersion forces.
    D. Ionic bonds are stronger than hydrogen bonds.

13. Which intermolecular attraction explains the following trend in straight-chain alkanes?

Condensed structural formula	Boiling point (°C)
CH_4	-161.5
CH_3CH_3	-88.6
$CH_3CH_2CH_3$	-42.1
$CH_3CH_2CH_2CH_3$	-0.5
$CH_3CH_2CH_2CH_2CH_3$	36.0
$CH_3CH_2CH_2CH_2CH_2CH_3$	68.7

   A. London dispersion forces
   B. Dipole-dipole interactions
   C. Hydrogen bonding
   D. Ion-induced dipole interactions

14. List the substances NH_3, PH_3, $MgCl_2$, Ne, and N_2 in order of increasing melting point.

   A. $N_2 < Ne < PH_3 < NH_3 < MgCl_2$
   B. $N_2 < NH_3 < Ne < MgCl_2 < PH_3$
   C. $Ne < N_2 < NH_3 < PH_3 < MgCl_2$
   D. $Ne < N_2 < PH_3 < NH_3 < MgCl_2$

15. 1-butanol, ethanol, methanol, and 1-propanol are all liquids at room temperature. Rank them in order of increasing viscosity.

   A. 1-butanol < 1-propanol < ethanol < methanol
   B. methanol < ethanol < 1-propanol < 1-butanol
   C. methanol < ethanol < 1-butanol < 1-propanol
   D. 1-propanol < 1-butanol < ethanol < methanol

16. Which gas has a diffusion rate of 25% the rate for hydrogen?

   A. helium
   B. methane
   C. nitrogen
   D. oxygen

17. 2.00 L of an unknown gas at 1500. mm Hg and a temperature of 25.0 °C weighs 7.52 g. Assuming the ideal gas equation, what is the molecular mass of the gas?

760 mm Hg=1 atm
R=0.08206 L-atm/(mol-K)

   A. 21.6 u
   B. 23.3 u
   C. 46.6 u
   D. 93.2 u

18. Which substance is most likely to be a gas at room temperature?

   A. SeO_2
   B. F_2
   C. $CaCl_2$
   D. I_2

19. What pressure is exerted by a mixture of 2.7 g of H_2 and 59 g of Xe at STP on a 50. L container?

   A. 0.69 atm
   B. 0.76 atm
   C. 0.80 atm
   D. 0.97 atm

20. A few minutes after opening a bottle of perfume, the scent is detected on the other side of the room. What law relates to this phenomenon?

A. Graham's law
B. Dalton's law
C. Boyle's law
D. Avogadro's law

21. Which of the following are true?

A. Solids have no vapor pressure.
B. Dissolving a solute in a liquid increases its vapor pressure.
C. The vapor pressure of a pure substance is characteristic of that substance and its temperature.
D. All of the above

22. Find the partial pressure of N_2 in a container at 150. kPa holding H_2O and N_2 at 50 °C. The vapor pressure of H_2O at 50 °C is 12 kPa.

A. 12 kPa
B. 138 kPa
C. 162 kPa
D. The value cannot be determined.

23. The normal boiling point of water on the Kelvin scale is closest to:

A. 112 K
B. 212 K
C. 273 K
D. 373 K
E.

24. Which phase may be present at the triple point of a substance?

I. Gas
II. Liquid
III. Solid
IV. Supercritical fluid

A. I, II, and III
B. I, II, and IV
C. II, III, and IV
D. I, II, III, and IV

25. In the following phase diagram, _____ occurs as P is decreased from A to B at constant T and _____ occurs as T is increased from C to D at constant P.

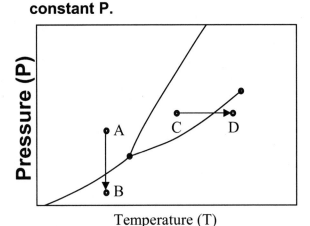

A. deposition, melting
B. sublimation, melting
C. deposition, vaporization
D. sublimation, vaporization

26. Heat is added to a pure solid at its melting point until it all becomes liquid at its freezing point. Which of the following occur?

   A. Intermolecular attractions are weakened.
   B. The kinetic energy of the molecules does not change.
   C. The freedom of the molecules to move about increases.
   D. All of the above.

27. Which of the following occur when NaCl dissolves in water?

   A. Heat is required to break bonds in the NaCl crystal lattice.
   B. Heat is released when hydrogen bonds in water are broken.
   C. Heat is required to form bonds of hydration.
   D. The oxygen end of the water molecule is attracted to the Cl⁻ ion.

28. The solubility of $CoCl_2$ is 54 g per 100 g of ethanol. Three flasks each contain 100 g of ethanol. Flask #1 also contains 40 g $CoCl_2$ in solution. Flask #2 contains 56 g $CoCl_2$ in solution. Flask #3 contains 5 g of solid $CoCl_2$ in equilibrium with 54 g $CoCl_2$ in solution. Which of the following describe the solutions present in the liquid phase of the flasks?

   A. #1-saturated, #2-supersaturated, #3-unsaturated.
   B. #1-unsaturated, #2-miscible, #3-saturated.
   C. #1-unsaturated, #2-supersaturated, #3-saturated.
   D. #1-unsaturated, #2-not at equilibrium, #3-miscible.

29. The solubility at 1.0 atm of pure CO_2 in water at 25 °C is 0.034 M. According to Henry's law, what is the solubility at 4.0 atm of pure CO_2 in water at 25 °C? Assume no chemical reaction occurs between CO_2 and H_2O.

   A. 0.0085 M
   B. 0.034 M
   C. 0.14 M
   D. 0.25 M

30. Carbonated water is bottled at 25 °C under pure CO_2 at 4.0 atm. Later the bottle is opened at 4 °C under air at 1.0 atm that has a partial pressure of 3×10^{-4} atm CO_2. Why do CO_2 bubbles form when the bottle is opened?

   A. CO_2 falls out of solution due to a drop in solubility at the lower total pressure.
   B. CO_2 falls out of solution due to a drop in solubility at the lower CO_2 pressure.
   C. CO_2 falls out of solution due to a drop in solubility at the lower temperature.
   D. CO_2 is formed by the decomposition of carbonic acid.

31. When KNO_3 dissolves in water, the water grows slightly colder. An increase in temperature will _____ the solubility of KNO_3.

   A. increase
   B. decrease
   C. have no effect on
   D. have an unknown effect with the information given on

32. An experiment requires 100. mL of a 0.500 M solution of $MgBr_2$. How many grams of $MgBr_2$ will be present in this solution?

   A. 9.21 g
   B. 11.7 g
   C. 12.4 g
   D. 15.6 g

33. 500. mg of RbOH are added to 500. g of ethanol (C_2H_6O) resulting in 395 mL of solution. Determine the molarity and molality of RbOH.

   A. 0.0124 M, 0.00488 m
   B. 0.0124 M, 0.00976 m
   C. 0.0223 M, 0.00488 m
   D. 0.0223 M, 0. 00976 m

34. 20.0 g H_3PO_4 in 1.5 L of solution are intended to react with KOH according to the following reaction:
   $$H_3PO_4 + 3\,KOH \rightarrow K_3PO_4 + 3\,H_2O$$
   What is the molarity and normality of the H_3PO_4 solution?

   A. 0.41 M, 1.22 N
   B. 0.41 M, 0.20 N
   C. 0.14 M, 0.045 N
   D. 0.14 M, 0. 41 N

35. Aluminum sulfate is a strong electrolyte. What is the concentration of all species in a 0.2 M solution of aluminum sulfate?

   A. 0.2 M Al^{3+}, 0.2 M SO_4^{2-}
   B. 0.4 M Al^{3+}, 0.6 M SO_4^{2-}
   C. 0.6 M Al^{3+}, 0.4 M SO_4^{2-}
   D. 0.2 M $Al_2(SO_4)_3$

36. 15 g of formaldehyde (CH_2O) are dissolved in 100. g of water. Calculate the weight percentage and mole fraction of formaldehyde in the solution.

    A. 13%, 0.090
    B. 15%, 0.090
    C. 13%, 0.083
    D. 15%, 0.083

37. Which of the following would make the best solvent for Br_2?

    A. H_2O
    B. CS_2
    C. NH_3
    D. molten NaCl

38. Which of the following is most likely to dissolve in water?

    A. H_2
    B. CCl_4
    C. SF_6
    D. CH_3OH

39. Which of the following is not a colligative property?

    A. Viscosity lowering
    B. Freezing point lowering
    C. Boiling point elevation
    D. Vapor pressure lowering

40. $$BaCl_2(aq) + Na_2SO_4(aq) \rightarrow$$
    $$BaSO_4(s) + 2NaCl(aq)$$
    is an example of a _____ reaction.

    A. acid-base
    B. precipitation
    C. redox
    D. nuclear

41. List the following aqueous solutions in order of increasing boiling point.

    I.   0.050 m $AlCl_3$
    II. 0.080 m $Ba(NO_3)_2$
    III. 0.090 m NaCl
    IV. 0.12 m ethylene glycol ($C_2H_6O_2$)

    A. I < II < III < IV
    B. I < III < IV < II
    C. IV < III < I < II
    D. IV < III < II < I

42. Osmotic pressure is the pressure required to prevent _____ flowing from low to high _____ concentration across a semipermeable membrane.

    A. solute, solute
    B. solute, solvent
    C. solvent, solute
    D. solvent, solvent

43. A solution of NaCl in water is heated on a mountain in an open container until it boils at 100. °C. The air pressure on the mountain is 0.92 atm. According to Raoult's law, what mole fraction of Na^+ and Cl^- are present in the solution?

    A. 0.04 Na^+, 0.04 Cl^-
    B. 0.08 Na^+, 0.08 Cl^-
    C. 0.46 Na^+, 0.46 Cl^-
    D. 0.92 Na^+, 0.92 Cl^-

44. Write a balanced nuclear equation for the emission of an alpha particle by polonium-209.

    A. $^{209}_{84}Po \rightarrow\ ^{205}_{81}Pb +\ ^4_2He$
    B. $^{209}_{84}Po \rightarrow\ ^{205}_{82}Bi +\ ^4_2He$
    C. $^{209}_{84}Po \rightarrow\ ^{209}_{85}At +\ ^0_{-1}e$
    D. $^{209}_{84}Po \rightarrow\ ^{205}_{82}Pb +\ ^4_2He$

45. Write a balanced nuclear equation for the decay of calcium-45 to scandium-45.

    A. $^{45}_{20}Ca \rightarrow\ ^{41}_{18}Sc +\ ^4_2He$
    B. $^{45}_{20}Ca +\ ^0_1e \rightarrow\ ^{45}_{21}Sc$
    C. $^{45}_{20}Ca \rightarrow\ ^{45}_{21}Sc +\ ^0_{-1}e$
    D. $^{45}_{20}Ca +\ ^0_1p \rightarrow\ ^{45}_{21}Sc$

46. ^3_1H decays with a half-life of 12 years. 3.0 g of pure ^3_1H were placed in a sealed container 24 years ago. How many grams of ^3_1H remain?

    A. 0.38 g
    B. 0.75 g
    C. 1.5 g
    D. 3.0 g

47. Oxygen-15 has a half-life of 122 seconds. What percentage of a sample of oxygen-15 has decayed after 300. seconds?

    A. 18.2%
    B. 21.3%
    C. 78.7%
    D. 81.8%

48. Which of the following isotopes is commonly used for medical imaging in the diagnose of diseases?

    A. cobalt-60
    B. technetium-99m
    C. tin-117m
    D. plutonium-238

49. Carbon-14 dating would be useful in obtaining the age of which object?

    A. a 20th century Picasso painting
    B. a mummy from ancient Egypt
    C. a dinosaur fossil
    D. all of the above

50. Which of the following isotopes can create a chain reaction of nuclear fission?

    A. uranium-235
    B. uranium-238
    C. plutonium-238
    D. all of the above

51. List the following scientists in chronological order from earliest to most recent with respect to their most significant contribution to atomic theory:

    I. John Dalton
    II. Niels Bohr
    III. J. J. Thomson
    IV. Ernest Rutherford

    A. I, III, II, IV
    B. I, III, IV, II
    C. I, IV, III, II
    D. III, I, II, IV

52. Match the theory with the scientist who first proposed it:

    I. Electrons, atoms, and all objects with momentum also exist as waves.
    II. Electron density may be accurately described by a single mathematical equation.
    III. There is an inherent indeterminacy in the position and momentum of particles.
    IV. Radiant energy is transferred between particles in exact multiples of a discrete unit.

    A. I-de Broglie, II-Planck, III-Schrödinger, IV-Thomson
    B. I-Dalton, II-Bohr, III-Planck, IV-de Broglie
    C. I-Henry, II-Bohr, III-Heisenberg, IV-Schrödinger
    D. I-de Broglie, II-Schrödinger, III-Heisenberg, IV-Planck

53. How many neutrons are in $^{60}_{27}\text{Co}$?

    A. 27
    B. 33
    C. 60
    D. 87

54. The terrestrial composition of an element is: 50.7% as an isotope with an atomic mass of 78.9 u and 49.3% as an isotope with an atomic mass of 80.9 u. Both isotopes are stable. Calculate the atomic mass of the element.
   A. 79.0 u
   B. 79.8 u
   C. 79.9 u
   D. 80.8 u

55. Which of the following is a correct electron arrangement for oxygen?

   A.
      1s   2s   2p

   B. $1s^2 1p^2 2s^2 2p^2$
   C. 2, 2, 4
   D. none of the above

56. Which of the following statements about radiant energy is not true?

   A. The energy change of an electron transition is directly proportional to the wavelength of the emitted or absorbed photon.
   B. The energy of an electron in a hydrogen atom depends only on the principle quantum number.
   C. The frequency of photons striking a metal determines whether the photoelectric effect will occur.
   D. The frequency of a wave of electromagnetic radiation is inversely proportional to its wavelength

57. Match the orbital diagram for the ground state of carbon with the rule/principle it violates:

I.
   1s   2s   2p

II.
   1s   2s   2p

III.
   1s   2s   2p

IV.
   1s   2s   2p

   A. I-Pauli exclusion, II-Aufbau, III-no violation, IV-Hund's
   B. I-Aufbau, II-Pauli exclusion, III-no violation, IV-Hund's
   C. I-Hund's, II-no violation, III-Pauli exclusion, IV-Aufbau
   D. I-Hund's, II-no violation, III-Aufbau, IV-Pauli exclusion

58. Select the list of atoms that are arranged in order of increasing size.

   A. Mg, Na, Si, Cl
   B. Si, Cl, Mg, Na
   C. Cl, Si, Mg, Na
   D. Na, Mg, Si, Cl

59. Based on trends in the periodic
table, which of the following
properties would you expect to
be greater for Rb than for K?

   I. Density
   II. Melting point
   III. Ionization energy
   IV. Oxidation number in a
      compound with chlorine

   A. I only
   B. I, II, and III
   C. II and III
   D. I, II, III, and IV

60. Which oxide forms the
strongest acid in water?

   A. Al_2O_3
   B. Cl_2O_7
   C. As_2O_5
   D. CO_2

61. Rank the following bonds from
least to most polar:

        C-H, C-Cl, H-H, C-F

   A. C-H < H-H < C-F < C-Cl
   B. H-H < C-H < C-F < C-Cl
   C. C-F < C-Cl < C-H < H-H
   D. H-H < C-H < C-Cl < C-F

62. At room temperature, $CaBr_2$ is
expected to be:

   A. a ductile solid
   B. a brittle solid
   C. a soft solid
   D. a gas

63. Which of the following is a
proper Lewis dot structure of
CHClO?

A.

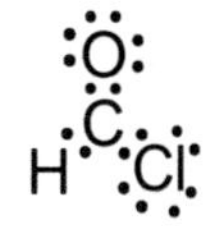

B.

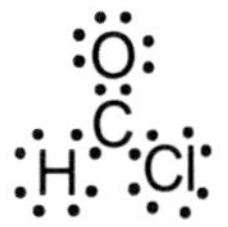

C.

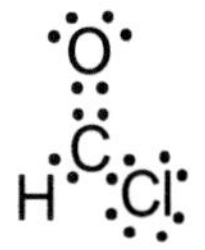

D.

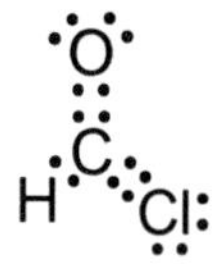

64. In C_2H_2, each carbon atom
contains the following valence
orbitals:

   A. p only
   B. p and sp hybrids
   C. p and sp^2 hybrids
   D. sp^3 hybrids only

65. Which statement about molecular structures is false?

A. 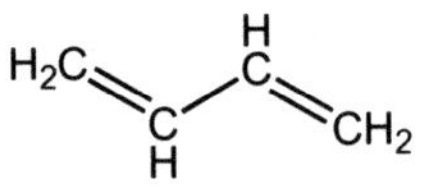 is a conjugated molecule

B. A bonding σ orbital connects two atoms by the straight line between them.

C. A bonding π orbital connects two atoms in a separate region from the straight line between them.

D. The anion with resonance forms

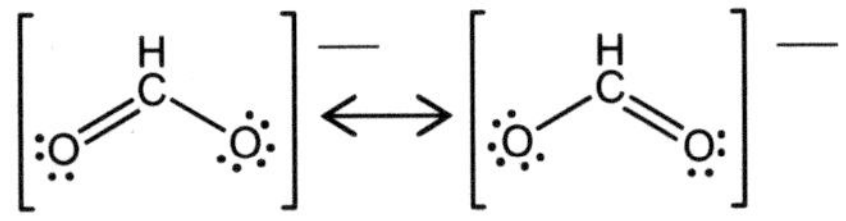

will always exist in one form or the other.

66. What is the shape of the PH_3 molecule? Use the VSEPR model.

A. Trigonal pyramidal
B. Trigonal bipyramidal
C. Trigonal planar
D. Tetrahedral

67. What is the chemical composition of magnesium nitrate?

A. 11.1% Mg, 22.2% N, 66.7% O
B. 16.4% Mg, 18.9% N, 64.7% O
C. 20.9% Mg, 24.1% N, 55.0% O
D. 28.2% Mg, 16.2% N, 55.7% O

68. The IUPAC name for Cu_2SO_3 is:

A. Dicopper sulfur trioxide
B. Copper (II) sulfate
C. Copper (I) sulfite
D. Copper (II) sulfite

69. Which name or formula is not represented properly?

A. Cl_4S
B. $KClO_3$
C. Calcium dihydrogen phosphate
D. Sulfurous acid

70. Household "chlorine bleach" is sodium hypochlorite. Which of the following best represent the production of sodium hypochlorite, sodium chloride, and water by bubbling chlorine gas through aqueous sodium hydroxide?

A. $4Cl(g) + 4NaOH(aq) \rightarrow$
$NaClO_2(aq) + 3NaCl(aq) + 2H_2O(l)$

B. $2Cl_2(g) + 4NaOH(aq) \rightarrow$
$NaClO_2(aq) + 3NaCl(aq) + 2H_2O(l)$

C. $2Cl(g) + 2NaOH(aq) \rightarrow$
$NaClO(aq) + NaCl(aq) + H_2O(l)$

D. $Cl_2(g) + 2NaOH(aq) \rightarrow$
$NaClO(aq) + NaCl(aq) + H_2O(l)$

71. Balance the equation for the neutralization reaction between phosphoric acid and calcium hydroxide by filling in the blank stoichiometric coefficients.

$\underline{}H_3PO_4 + \underline{}Ca(OH)_2 \rightarrow$

$\underline{}Ca_3(PO_4)_2 + \underline{}H_2O$

A. 4, 3, 1, 4
B. 2, 3, 1, 8
C. 2, 3, 1, 6
D. 2, 1, 1, 2

72. Write an equation showing the reaction between calcium nitrate and lithium sulfate in aqueous solution. Include all products.

A. $CaNO_3(aq) + Li_2SO_4(aq) \rightarrow$
$CaSO_4(s) + Li_2NO_3(aq)$

B. $Ca(NO_3)_2(aq) + Li_2SO_4(aq) \rightarrow$
$CaSO_4(s) + 2LiNO_3(aq)$

C. $Ca(NO_3)_2(aq) + Li_2SO_4(aq) \rightarrow$
$2LiNO_3(s) + CaSO_4(aq)$

D. $Ca(NO_3)_2(aq) + Li_2SO_4(aq) + 2H_2O(l) \rightarrow$
$2LiNO_3(aq) + Ca(OH)_2(aq) + H_2SO_4(aq)$

73. Find the mass of CO_2 produced by the combustion of 15 kg of isopropyl alcohol in the reaction:

$2C_3H_7OH + 9O_2 \rightarrow 6CO_2 + 8H_2O$

A. 33 kg
B. 44 kg
C. 50 kg
D. 60 kg

74. What is the density of nitrogen gas at STP? Assume an ideal gas and a value of 0.08206 L•atm/(mol•K) for the gas constant.

A. 0.62 g/L
B. 1.14 g/L
C. 1.25 g/L
D. 2.03 g/L

75. Find the volume of methane that will produce 12 m^3 of hydrogen in the reaction:

$CH_4(g) + H_2O(g) \rightarrow CO(g) + 3H_2(g)$

Assume temperature and pressure remain constant.

A. 4.0 m^3
B. 32 m^3
C. 36 m^3
D. 64 m^3

76. A 100. L vessel of pure O_2 at 500. kPa and 20. °C is used for the combustion of butane:

$$2C_4H_{10} + 13O_2 \rightarrow 8CO_2 + 10H_2O$$

Find the mass of butane to consume all the O_2 in the vessel. Assume O_2 is an ideal gas and use a value of $R =$ 8.314 J/(mol•K).

A. 183 g
B. 467 g
C. 1.83 kg
D. 7.75 kg

77. Consider the reaction between iron and hydrogen chloride gas:

$$Fe(s) + 2HCl(g) \rightarrow FeCl_2(s) + H_2(g)$$

7 moles of iron and 10 moles of HCl react until the limiting reagent is consumed. Which statements are true?

I. HCl is the excess reagent
II. HCl is the limiting reagent
III. 7 moles of H_2 are produced
IV. 2 moles of the excess reagent remain

A. I and III
B. I and IV
C. II and III
D. II and IV

78. 32.0 g of hydrogen and 32.0 grams of oxygen react to form water until the limiting reagent is consumed. What is present in the vessel after the reaction is complete?

A. 16.0 g O_2 and 48.0 g H_2O
B. 24.0 g H_2 and 40.0 g H_2O
C. 28.0 g H_2 and 36.0 g H_2O
D. 28.0 g H_2 and 34.0 g H_2O

79. Three experiments were performed at the same initial temperature and pressure to determine the rate of the reaction

$$2ClO_2(g) + F_2(g) \rightarrow 2ClO_2F(g)$$

Results are shown in the table below. Concentrations are given in millimoles per liter (mM).

Exp.	Initial $[ClO_2]$ (mM)	Initial $[F_2]$ (mM)	Initial rate of $[ClO_2F]$ increase (mM/sec)
1	5.0	5.0	0.63
2	5.0	20	2.5
3	10	10	2.5

What is the rate law for this reaction?

A. $\text{Rate} = k\left[F_2\right]$

B. $\text{Rate} = k\left[ClO_2\right]\left[F_2\right]$

C. $\text{Rate} = k\left[ClO_2\right]^2\left[F_2\right]$

D. $\text{Rate} = k\left[ClO_2\right]\left[F_2\right]^2$

80. The reaction

$$(CH_3)_3CBr(aq) + OH^-(aq) \rightarrow$$

$$(CH_3)_3COH(aq) + Br^-(aq)$$

occurs in three elementary steps:

$(CH_3)_3CBr \rightarrow (CH_3)_3C^+ + Br^-$ is slow

$(CH_3)_3C^+ + H_2O \rightarrow (CH_3)_3COH_2^+$ is fast

$(CH_3)_3COH_2^+ + OH^- \rightarrow$
$(CH_3)_3COH + H_2O$ is fast

What is the rate law for this reaction?

A. Rate $= k\left[(CH_3)_3CBr\right]$

B. Rate $= k\left[OH^-\right]$

C. Rate $= k\left[(CH_3)_3CBr\right]\left[OH^-\right]$

D. Rate $= k\left[(CH_3)_3CBr\right]^2$

81. Which statement about equilibrium is <u>not</u> true?

A. Equilibrium shifts to minimize the impact of changes.
B. Forward and reverse reactions have equal rates at equilibrium.
C. A closed container of air and water is at a vapor-liquid equilibrium if the humidity is constant.
D. The equilibrium between solid and dissolved forms is maintained when salt is added to an unsaturated solution.

82. Which statements about reaction rates are true?

I. Catalysts shift an equilibrium to favor product formation.
II. Catalysts increase the rate of forward and reverse reactions.
III. A greater temperature increases the chance that a molecular collision will overcome a reaction's activation energy.
IV. A catalytic converter contains a homogeneous catalyst.

A. I and II
B. II and III
C. II, III, and IV
D. I, III, and IV

83. Write the equilibrium expression K_{eq} for the reaction

$$CO_2(g) + H_2(g) \rightleftharpoons CO(g) + H_2O(l)$$

A. $\dfrac{\left[CO\right]\left[H_2O\right]}{\left[CO_2\right]\left[H_2\right]^2}$

B. $\dfrac{\left[CO_2\right]\left[H_2\right]}{\left[CO\right]\left[H_2O\right]}$

C. $\dfrac{\left[CO\right]\left[H_2O\right]}{\left[CO_2\right]\left[H_2\right]}$

D. $\dfrac{\left[CO\right]}{\left[CO_2\right]\left[H_2\right]}$

84. What could cause this change in the energy diagram of a reaction?

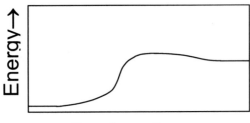

Reaction pathway→

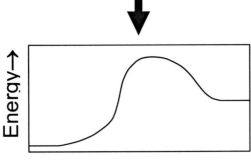

Reaction pathway→

A. Adding catalyst to an endothermic reaction
B. Removing catalyst from an endothermic reaction
C. Adding catalyst to an exothermic reaction
D. Removing catalyst from an exothermic reaction

85. $BaSO_4$ ($K_{sp} = 1X10^{-10}$) is added to pure H_2O. How much is dissolved in 1 L of saturated solution?

A. 2 mg
B. 10 μg
C. 2 μg
D. 100 pg

86. The exothermic reaction $2NO(g) + Br_2(g) \rightleftharpoons 2NOBr(g)$ is at equilibrium. According to LeChatelier's principle:

A. Adding Br_2 will increase [NO].
B. An increase in container volume (with T constant) will increase [NOBr].
C. An increase in pressure (with T constant) will increase [NOBr].
D. An increase in temperature (with P constant) will increase [NOBr].

87. At a certain temperature, T, the equilibrium constant for the reaction $2NO(g) \rightleftharpoons N_2(g) + O_2(g)$ is $K_{eq} = 2X10^3$. If a 1.0 L container at this temperature contains 90 mM N_2, 20 mM O_2, and 5 mM NO, what will occur?

A. The reaction will make more N_2 and O_2.
B. The reaction is at equilibrium.
C. The reaction will make more NO.
D. The temperature, T, is required to solve this problem.

88. Which statement about acids and bases is <u>not</u> true?

A. All strong acids ionize in water.
B. All Lewis acids accept an electron pair.
C. All Brønsted bases use OH^- as a proton acceptor
D. All Arrhenius acids form H^+ ions in water.

89. Which of the following are listed from weakest to strongest acid?

    A. H_2SO_3, H_2SeO_3, H_2TeO_3
    B. HBrO, $HBrO_2$, $HBrO_3$, $HBrO_4$
    C. HI, HBr, HCl, HF
    D. H_3PO_4, $H_2PO_4^-$, HPO_4^{2-}

90. NH_4F is dissolved in water. Which of the following are conjugate acid/base pairs present in the solution?

    I. NH_4^+/NH_4OH
    II. HF/F^-
    III. H_3O^+/H_2O
    IV. H_2O/OH^-

    A. I, II, and III
    B. I, III, and IV
    C. II and IV
    D. II, III, and IV

91. What are the pH and the pOH of 0.010 M $HNO_3(aq)$?

    A. pH = 1.0, pOH = 9.0
    B. pH = 2.0, pOH = 12.0
    C. pH = 2.0, pOH = 8.0
    D. pH = 8.0, pOH = 6.0

92. What is the pH of a buffer made of 0.128 M sodium formate (HCOONa) and 0.072 M formic acid (HCOOH)? The pK_a of formic acid is 3.75.

    A. 2.0
    B. 3.0
    C. 4.0
    D. 5.0

93. A sample of 50.0 ml KOH is titrated with 0.100 M $HClO_4$. The initial buret reading is 1.6 ml and the reading at the endpoint is 22.4 ml. What is [KOH]?

    A. 0.0416 M
    B. 0.0481 M
    C. 0.0832 M
    D. 0.0962 mM

94. Rank the following from lowest to highest pH. Assume a small volume for the component given in moles:

    I.   0.01 mol HCl added to 1 L H_2O
    II. 0.01 mol HI added to 1 L of an acetic acid/sodium acetate solution at pH 4.0
    III. 0.01 mol NH_3 added to 1 L H_2O
    IV. 0.1 mol HNO_3 added to 1 L of a 0.1 M $Ca(OH)_2$ solution

    A. I < II < III < IV
    B. I < II < IV < III
    C. II < I < III < IV
    D. II < I < IV < III

95. The curve below resulted from the titration of a _____ _____ with a _____ _____ titrant.

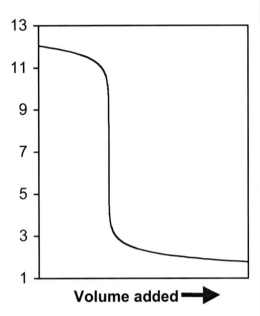

Volume added ➡

A. weak acid, strong base
B. weak base, strong acid
C. strong acid, strong base
D. strong base, strong acid

96. Which statement about thermochemistry is true?

A. Particles in a system move about less freely at high entropy
B. Water at 100 °C has the same internal energy as water vapor at 100°C
C. A decrease in the order of a system corresponds to an increase in entropy.
D. At its sublimation temperature, dry ice has a higher entropy than gaseous CO_2

97. What is the heat change of 36.0 g H_2O at atmospheric pressure when its temperature is reduced from 125 °C to 40. °C? Use the following data:

Values for water

Heat capacity of solid	37.6 J/mol•°C
Heat capacity of liquid	75.3 J/mol•°C
Heat capacity of gas	33.1 J/mol•°C
Heat of fusion	6.02 kJ/mol
Heat of vaporization	40.67 kJ/mol

A. −92.0 kJ
B. −10.8 kJ
C. 10.8 kJ
D. 92.0 kJ

98. What is the standard heat of combustion of $CH_4(g)$? Use the following data:

Standard heats of formation

$CH_4(g)$	−74.8 kJ/mol
$CO_2(g)$	−393.5 kJ/mol
$H_2O(l)$	−285.8 kJ/mol

A. −890.3 kJ/mol
B. −604.6 kJ/mol
C. −252.9 kJ/mol
D. −182.5 kJ/mol

99. Which reaction creates products at a lower total entropy than the reactants?

A. Dissolution of table salt:
$NaCl(s) \rightarrow Na^+(aq) + Cl^{\check{s}}(aq)$

B. Oxidation of iron:
$4Fe(s) + 3O_2(g) \rightarrow 2Fe_2O_3(s)$

C. Dissociation of ozone:
$O_3(g) \rightarrow O_2(g) + O(g)$

D. Vaporization of butane:
$C_4H_{10}(l) \rightarrow C_4H_{10}(g)$

100. Which statement about reactions is true?

A. All spontaneous reactions are both exothermic and cause an increase in entropy.
B. An endothermic reaction that increases the order of the system cannot be spontaneous.
C. A reaction can be non-spontaneous in one direction and also non-spontaneous in the opposite direction.
D. Melting snow is an exothermic process.

101. 10. kJ of heat are added to one kilogram of Iron at 10. °C. What is its final temperature? The specific heat of iron is 0.45 J/g•°C.

A. 22 °C
B. 27 °C
C. 32 °C
D. 37 °C

102. Which reaction is not a redox process?

A. Combustion of octane:
$2C_8H_{18} + 25O_2 \rightarrow 16CO_2 + 18H_2O$

B. Depletion of a lithium battery:
$Li + MnO_2 \rightarrow LiMnO_2$

C. Corrosion of aluminum by acid:
$2Al + 6HCl \rightarrow 2AlCl_3 + 3H_2$

D. Taking an antacid for heartburn:
$CaCO_3 + 2HCl \rightarrow CaCl_2 + H_2CO_3$
$\rightarrow CaCl_2 + CO_2 + H_2O$

103. Given the following heats of reaction:
$\Delta H = -0.3$ kJ / mol for
$Fe(s) + CO_2(g) \rightarrow FeO(s) + CO(g)$
$\Delta H = 5.7$ kJ / mol for
$2Fe(s) + 3CO_2(g) \rightarrow Fe_2O_3(s) + 3CO(g)$
and $\Delta H = 4.5$ kJ / mol for
$3FeO(s) + CO_2(g) \rightarrow Fe_3O_4(s) + CO(g)$

use Hess's Law to determine the heat of reaction for:

$3Fe_2O_3(s) + CO(g) \rightarrow 2Fe_3O_4(s) + CO_2(g)$

A. −10.8 kJ/mol
B. −9.9 kJ/mol
C. −9.0 kJ/mol
D. −8.1 kJ/mol

104. What is the oxidant in the reaction:

$$2H_2S + SO_2 \rightarrow 3S + 2H_2O \ ?$$

A. H_2S
B. SO_2
C. S
D. H_2O

105. Molten NaCl is subjected to electrolysis. What reaction takes place at the cathode?

A. $2Cl^-(l) \rightarrow Cl_2(g) + 2e^-$
B. $Cl_2(g) + 2e^- \rightarrow 2Cl^-(l)$
C. $Na^+(l) + e^- \rightarrow Na(l)$
D. $Na^+(l) \rightarrow Na(l) + e^-$

106. What is the purpose of the salt bridge in an electrochemical cell?

A. To receive electrons from the oxidation half-reaction
B. To relieve the buildup of positive charge in the anode half-cell
C. To conduct electron flow
D. To permit positive ions to flow from the cathode half-cell to the anode half-cell

107. Given:
$E° = -2.37V$ for $Mg^{2+}(aq) + 2e^- \rightarrow Mg(s)$
and
$E° = 0.80$ V for $Ag^+(aq) + e^- \rightarrow Ag(s)$,
what is the standard potential of a voltaic cell composed of a piece of magnesium dipped in a 1 M Ag^+ solution and a piece of silver dipped in 1 M Mg^{2+}?

A. 0.77 V
B. 1.57 V
C. 3.17 V
D. 3.97 V

108.

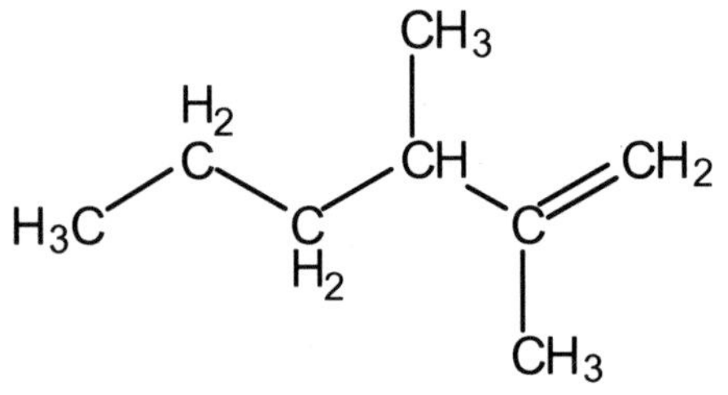

A proper name for this hydrocarbon is:

A. 4,5-dimethyl-6-hexene
B. 2,3-dimethyl-1-hexene
C. 4,5-dimethyl-6-hexyne
D. 2-methyl-3-propyl-1-butene

CHEMISTRY 248

109. An IUPAC approved name for this molecule is:

A. butanal
B. propanal
C. butanoic acid
D. propanoic acid

110. Which molecule has a systematic name of methyl ethanoate?

A.

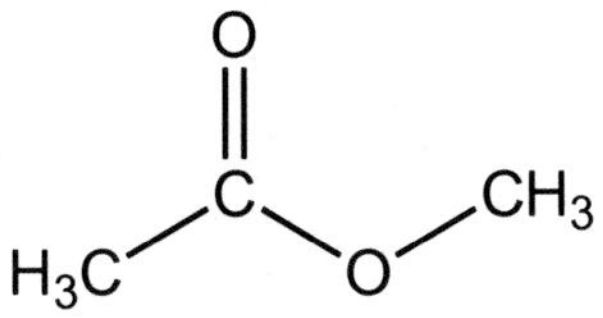

B.

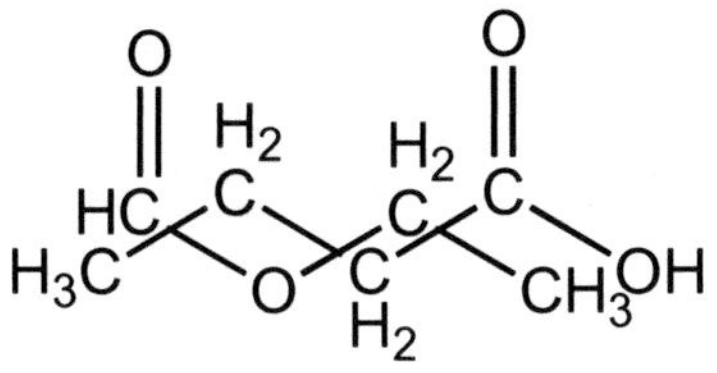

C.

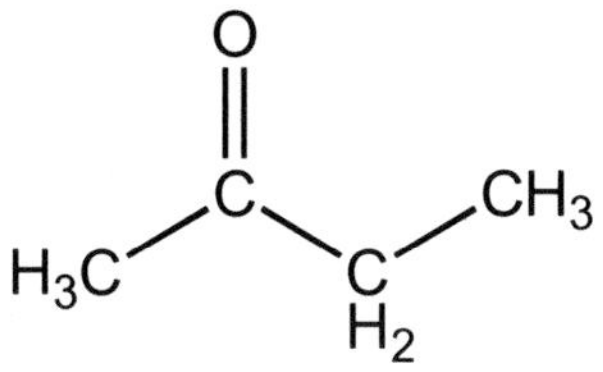

D.

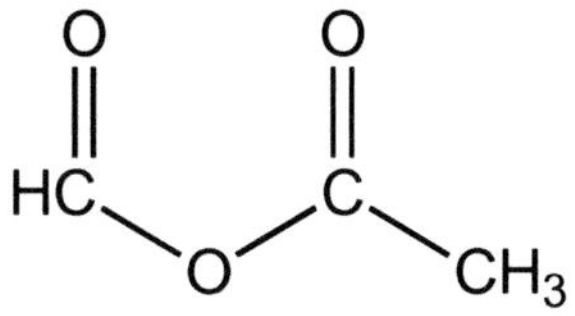

111. This compound

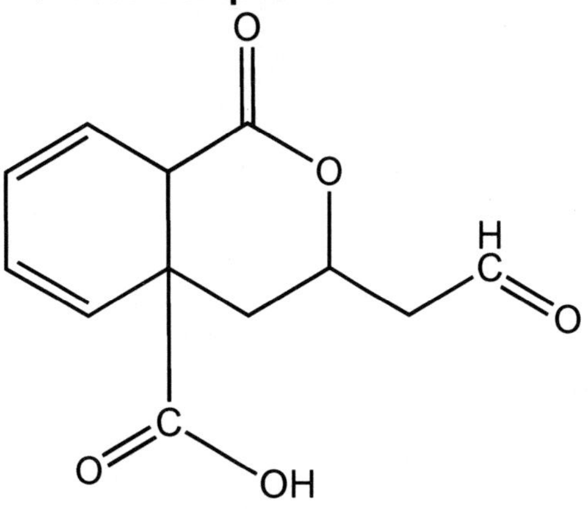

contains an:

A. alkene, carboxylic acid, ester, and ketone
B. aldehyde, alkyne, ester, and ketone
C. aldehyde, alkene, carboxylic acid, and ester
D. acid anhydride, aldehyde, alkene, and amine

112. Which group of scientists made contributions in the same area of chemistry?

A. Volta, Kekulé, Faraday, London
B. Hess, Joule, Kelvin, Gibbs
C. Boyle, Charles, Arrhenius, Pauli
D. Davy, Mendeleev, Ramsay, Galvani

113. **Which of the following pairs are isomers?**

I.

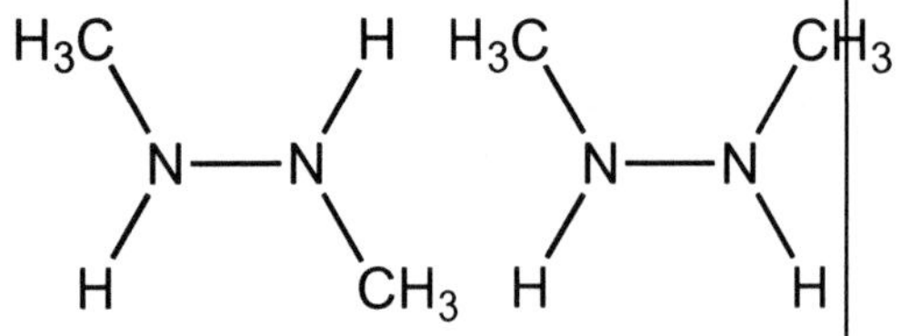

II. pentanal 2-pentanone

III.

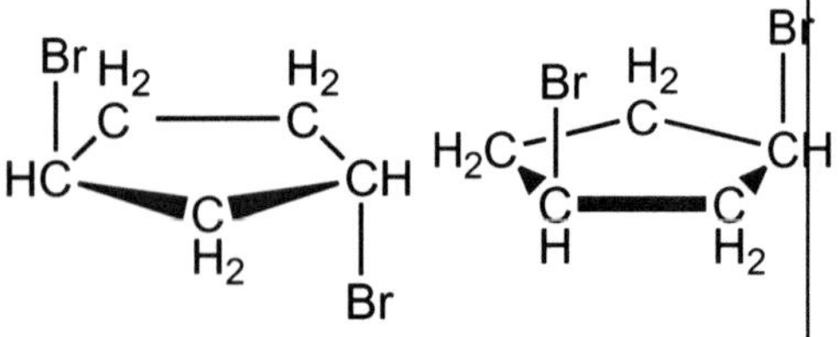

IV.

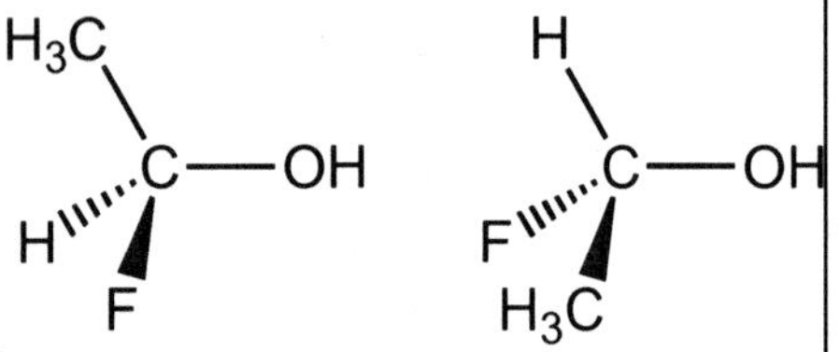

A. I and IV
B. II and III
C. I, II, and III
D. I, II, III, and IV

114. **Which instrument would be most useful for separating two different proteins from a mixture?**

A. UV/Vis spectrophotometer
B. Mass spectrometer
C. Gas chromatograph
D. Liquid chromatograph

115. **Classify these biochemicals.**

I.

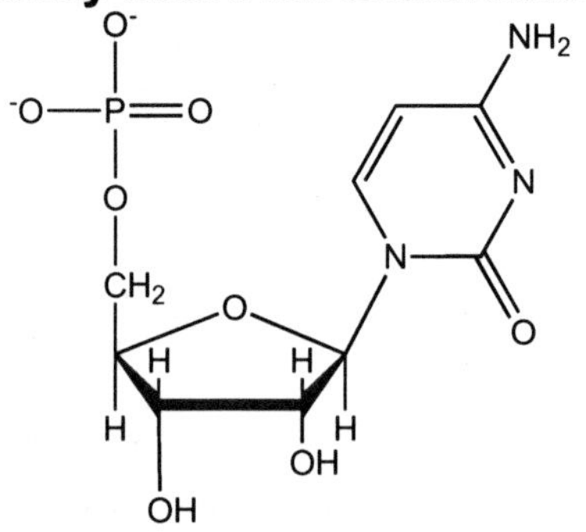

II.

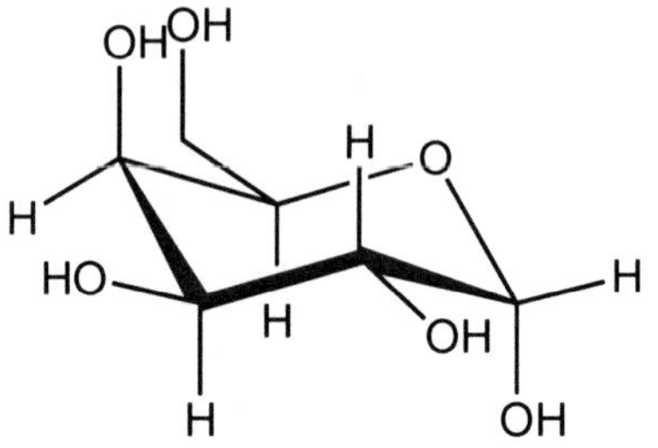

III.

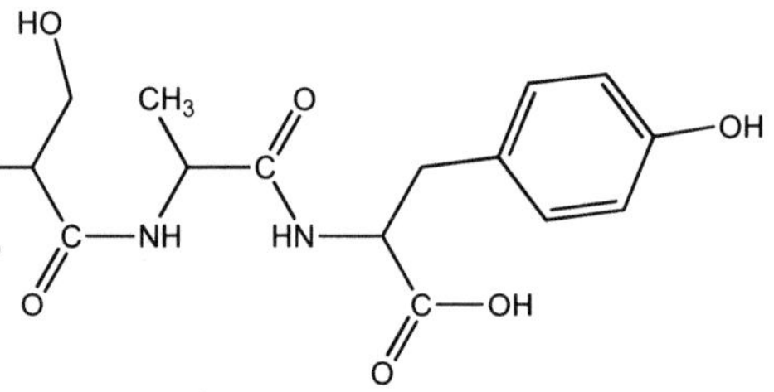

IV.

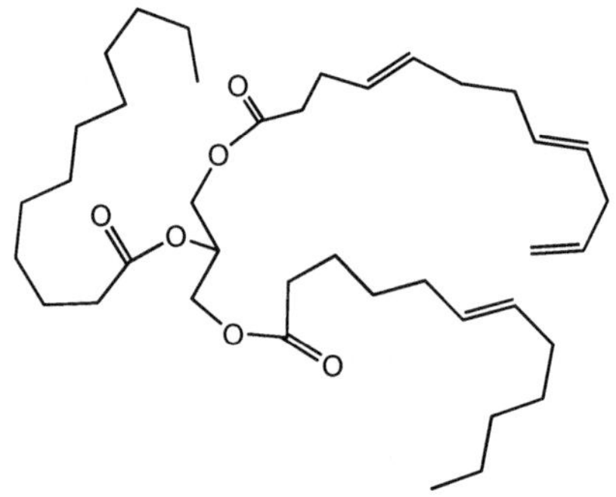

A. I-nucleotide, II-sugar, III-peptide, IV-fat
B. I-disaccharide, II-sugar, III-fatty acid, IV-polypeptide
C. I-disaccharide, II-amino acid, III-fatty acid, IV-polysaccharide
D. I I-nucleotide, II-sugar, III-triacylglyceride, and IV-DNA

116. You create a solution of 2.00 μg/ml of a pigment and divide the solution into 12 samples. You give four samples each to three teams of students. They use a spectrophotometer to determine the pigment concentration. Here is their data:

Team	Concentration (μg/ml)			
	sample 1	sample 2	sample 3	sample 4
1	1.98	1.93	1.92	1.88
2	1.70	1.72	1.69	1.70
3	1.78	1.99	2.87	2.20

Which of the following are true?

A. Team 1 has the most precise data
B. Team 3 has the most accurate data in spite of it having low precision
C. The data from team 2 is characteristic of a systematic error
D. The data from team 1 is more characteristic of random error than the data from team 3.

117. Which pair of measurements have an identical meaning?

A. 32 micrograms and 0.032 g
B. 26 nm and 2.60×10^{-8} m
C. 3.01×10^{-5} m^3 and 30.1 ml
D. 0.0020 L and 20 cm^3

118. Match the instrument with the quantity it measures

II. eudiometer
III. calorimeter
IV. manometer
V. hygrometer

A. I-volume, II-mass, III-radioactivity, IV-humidity
B. I-volume, II-heat, III-pressure, IV-humidity
C. I-viscosity, II-mass, III-pressure, IV-surface tension
D. I-viscosity, II-heat, III-radioactivity, IV-surface tension

119. Four nearly identical gems from the same mineral are weighed using different balances. Their masses are:

3.4533 g, 3.459 g, 3.4656 g, 3.464 g

The four gems are then collected and added to a volumetric cylinder containing 10.00 ml of liquid, and a new volume of 14.97 ml is read. What is the average mass of the four stones and what is the density of the mineral?

A. 3.460 g, and 2.78 g/ml
B. 3.460 g and 2.79 g/ml
C. 3.4605 g and 2.78 g/ml
D. 3.461 g and 2.79 g/ml

120. Which list includes equipment that would <u>not</u> be used in vacuum filtration.

A. Rubber tubing, Florence flask, Büchner funnel
B. Vacuum pump, Hirsch funnel, rubber stopper with a single hole
C. Aspirator, filter paper, filter flask
D. Lab stand, clamp, filter trap

121. Which of the following statements about lab safety is <u>not</u> true?

A. Corrosive chemicals should be stored below eye level.
B. A chemical splash on the eye or skin should be rinsed for 15 minutes in cold water.
C. MSDS means "Material Safety Data Sheet."
D. A student should "stop, drop, and roll" if their clothing catches fire in the lab.

122. Which of the following lists consists entirely of chemicals that are considered safe enough to be in a high school lab?

A. hydrochloric acid, lauric acid, potassium permanganate, calcium hydroxide
B. ethyl ether, nitric acid, sodium benzoate, methanol
C. cobalt (II) sulfide, ethylene glycol, benzoyl peroxide, ammonium chloride
D. picric acid, hydrofluoric acid, cadmium chloride, carbon disulfide.

123. The following procedure was developed to find the specific heat capacity of metals:

1. **Place pieces of the metals in an ice-water bath so their initial temperature is 0 °C.**
2. **Weigh a styrofoam cup.**
3. **Add water at room temperature to the cup and weigh it again**
4. **Add a cold metal from the bath to the cup and weigh the cup a third time.**
5. **Monitor the temperature drop of the water until a final temperature at thermal equilibrium is found.**

_____ is also required as additional information in order to obtain heat capacities for the metals. The best control would be to follow the same protocol except to use _____ in step 4 instead of a cold metal.

A. The heat capacity of water / a metal at 100 °C
B. The heat of formation of water / ice from the 0 °C bath
C. The heat of capacity of ice / glass at 0 °C
D. The heat capacity of water / water from the 0 °C bath

124. Which statement about the impact of chemistry on society is <u>not</u> true?

    A. Partial hydrogenation creates *trans* fat.
    B. The Haber Process incorporates nitrogen from the air into molecules for agricultural use.
    C. The CO_2 concentration in the atmosphere has decreased in the last ten years.
    D. The concentration of ozone-destroying chemicals in the stratosphere has decreased in the last ten years.

125. Which statement about everyday applications of chemistry is <u>true</u>?

    A. Rainwater found near sources of air pollution will most likely be basic.
    B. Batteries run down more quickly at low temperatures because chemical reactions are proceeding more slowly.
    C. Benzyl alcohol is a detergent used in shampoo.
    D. Adding salt decreases the time required for water to boil.

Answer Key

1. C	26. D	51. B	76. A	101. C
2. B	27. A	52. D	77. D	102. D
3. D	28. C	53. B	78. C	103. B
4. A	29. C	54. C	79. B	104. B
5. C	30. B	55. D	80. A	105. C
6. D	31. A	56. A	81. D	106. D
7. C	32. A	57. C	82. B	107. C
8. B	33. B	58. C	83. D	108. B
9. A	34. D	59. A	84. B	109. C
10. C	35. B	60. B	85. A	110. A
11. B	36. C	61. D	86. C	111. C
12. D	37. B	62. B	87. A	112. B
13. A	38. D	63. C	88. C	113. B
14. D	39. A	64. B	89. B	114. D
15. B	40. B	65. D	90. D	115. A
16. D	41. C	66. A	91. B	116. C
17. C	42. C	67. B	92. C	117. C
18. B	43. A	68. C	93. A	118. B
19. C	44. D	69. A	94. A	119. B
20. A	45. C	70. D	95. D	120. A
21. C	46. B	71. C	96. C	121. D
22. B	47. D	72. B	97. A	122. A
23. D	48. B	73. A	98. A	123. D
24. A	49. B	74. C	99. B	124. C
25. D	50. A	75. A	100. B	125. B

Rationales with Sample Questions

Note: The first insignificant digit should be carried through intermediate calculations. This digit is shown using *italics* in the solutions below.

1. **A piston compresses a gas at constant temperature. Which gas properties increase?**

   II. **Average speed of molecules**
   III. **Pressure**
   IV. **Molecular collisions with container walls per second**

   A. I and II
   B. I and III
   C. II and III
   D. I, II, and III

C. A decrease in volume (V) occurs at constant temperature (T). Average molecular speed is determined only by temperature and will be constant. V and P are inversely related, so pressure will increase. With less wall area and at higher pressure, more collisions occur per second.

2. **The temperature of a liquid is raised at atmospheric pressure. Which liquid property increases?**

   A. critical pressure
   B. vapor pressure
   C. surface tension
   D. viscosity

B. The critical pressure of a liquid is its vapor pressure at the critical temperature and is always a constant value. A rising temperature increases the kinetic energy of molecules and decreases the importance of intermolecular attraction. More molecules will be free to escape to the vapor phase (vapor pressure increases), but the effect of attractions at the liquid-gas interface will fall (surface tension decreases) and molecules will flow against each other more easily (viscosity decreases).

3. **Potassium crystallizes with two atoms contained in each unit cell. What is the mass of potassium found in a lattice 1.00×10^6 unit cells wide, 2.00×10^6 unit cells high, and 5.00×10^5 unit cells deep?**

    A. 85.0 ng
    B. 32.5 µg
    C. 64.9 µg
    D. 130. µg

D. First we find the number of unit cells in the lattice by multiplying the number in each row, stack, and column:

1.00×10^6 unit cell lengths $\times\ 2.00 \times 10^6$ unit cell lengths $\times\ 5.00 \times 10^5$ unit cell lengths

$= 1.00 \times 10^{18}$ unit cells

Avogadro's number and the molecular weight of potassium (K) are used in the solution:

$$1.00 \times 10^{18} \text{ unit cells} \times \frac{2 \text{ atoms of K}}{\text{unit cell}} \times \frac{1 \text{ mole of K}}{6.02 \times 10^{23} \text{ atoms of K}} \times \frac{39.098 \text{ g K}}{1 \text{ mole of K}}$$

$$= 1.30 \times 10^{-4} \text{ g}$$

$$= 130. \text{ µg}$$

4. **A gas is heated in a sealed container. Which of the following occur?**

    A. gas pressure rises
    B. gas density decreases
    C. the average distance between molecules increases
    D. all of the above

A. The same material is kept in a constant volume, so neither density nor the distance between molecules will change. Pressure will rise because of increasing molecular kinetic energy impacting container walls.

5. **How many molecules are in 2.20 pg of a protein with a molecular weight of 150. kDa?**

   A. 8.83×10^9
   B. 1.82×10^9
   C. 8.83×10^6
   D. 1.82×10^6

C. The prefix "p" for "pico-" indicates 10^{-12}. A kilodalton is 1000 atomic mass units.

$$2.20 \text{ pg protein} \times \frac{10^{-12} \text{ g}}{1 \text{ pg}} \times \frac{1 \text{ mole protein}}{150 \times 10^3 \text{ g protein}} \times \frac{6.02 \times 10^{23} \text{ molecules protein}}{1 \text{ mole protein}} =$$
$$= 8.83 \times 10^6 \text{ molecules}$$

6. **At STP, 20. μL of O_2 contain 5.4×10^{16} molecules. According to Avogadro's hypothesis, how many molecules are in 20. μL of Ne at STP?**

   A. 5.4×10^{15}
   B. 1.0×10^{16}
   C. 2.7×10^{16}
   D. 5.4×10^{16}

D. Avogadro's hypothesis states that equal volumes of different gases at the same temperature and pressure contain equal numbers of molecules.

7. **An ideal gas at 50.0 °C and 3.00 atm is in a 300. cm³ cylinder. The cylinder volume changes by moving a piston until the gas is at 50.0 °C and 1.00 atm. What is the final volume?**

   A. 100. cm³
   B. 450. cm³
   C. 900. cm³
   D. 1.20 dm³

C. A three-fold decrease in pressure of a constant quantity of gas at constant temperature will cause a three-fold increase in gas volume.

8. **Which gas law may be used to solve the previous question?**

    A. Charles's law
    B. Boyle's law
    C. Graham's law
    D. Avogadro's law

B. The inverse relationship between volume and pressure is Boyle's law.

9. **A blimp is filled with 5000. m³ of helium at 28.0 °C and 99.7 kPa. What is the mass of helium used?**

$$R = 8.3144 \frac{J}{mol\text{-}K}$$

    A. 797 kg
    B. 810. kg
    C. 1.99×10^3 kg
    D. 8.57×10^3 kg

A. First the ideal gas law is manipulated to solve for moles.

$$PV = nRT \implies n = \frac{PV}{RT}$$

Temperature must be expressed in Kelvin: $T = (28.0 + 273.15)\,K = 301.15\,K$.

The ideal gas law is then used with the knowledge that joules are equivalent to Pa-m³:

$$n = \frac{PV}{RT} = \frac{(99.7 \times 10^3\ Pa)(5000.\ m^3)}{\left(8.3144 \frac{m^3\text{-}Pa}{mol\text{-}K}\right)(301.15\ K)} = 1.991 \times 10^3\ mol\ He\,.$$

Moles are then converted to grams using the molecular weight of helium:

$$1.991 \times 10^3\ mol\ He \times \frac{4.0026\ g\ He}{1\ mol\ He} = 797 \times 10^3\ g\ He = 797\ kg\ He\,.$$

10. **Which of the following are able to flow from one place to another?**

    I. Gases
    II. Liquids
    III. Solids
    IV. Supercritical fluids

    A. I and II
    B. II only
    C. I, II, and IV
    D. I, II, III, and IV

C. Gases and liquids both flow. Supercritical fluids have some traits in common with gases and some in common with liquids, and so they flow also. Solids have a fixed volume and shape.

11. **One mole of an ideal gas at STP occupies 22.4 L. At what temperature will one mole of an ideal gas at one atm occupy 31.0 L?**

    A. 34.6 °C
    B. 105 °C
    C. 378 °C
    D. 442 °C

B. Either Charles's law, the combined gas law, or the ideal gas law may be used with temperature in Kelvin.

Charles's law or the combined gas law with $P_1 = P_2$ may be manipulated to equate a ratio between temperature and volume when P and n are constant.

$$V \propto T \text{ or } \frac{P_1 V_1}{T_1} = \frac{P_2 V_2}{T_2} \Rightarrow \frac{T_1}{V_1} = \frac{T_2}{V_2} \Rightarrow T_2 = V_2 \frac{T_1}{V_1}$$

$$T_2 = 31.0 \text{ L} \frac{273.15 \text{ K}}{22.4 \text{ L}} = 378 \text{ K} = 105 \text{ °C}.$$

The ideal gas law may also be used with the appropriate gas constant:

$$PV = nRT \Rightarrow T = \frac{PV}{nR}$$

$$T = \frac{(1 \text{ atm})(31.0 \text{ L})}{(1 \text{ mol})\left(0.08206 \frac{\text{L-atm}}{\text{mol-K}}\right)} = 378 \text{ K} = 105 \text{ °C}.$$

12. **Why does CaCl$_2$ have a higher normal melting point than NH$_3$?**

    A. London dispersion forces in CaCl$_2$ are stronger than covalent bonds in NH$_3$.
    B. Covalent bonds in NH$_3$ are stronger than dipole-dipole bonds in CaCl$_2$.
    C. Ionic bonds in CaCl$_2$ are stronger than London dispersion forces in NH$_3$.
    D. Ionic bonds in CaCl$_2$ are stronger than hydrogen bonds in NH$_3$.

D. London dispersion forces are weaker than covalent bonds, eliminating choice A. A higher melting point will result from stronger intermolecular bonds, eliminating choice B. CaCl$_2$ is an ionic solid resulting from a cation on the left and an anion on the right of the periodic table. The dominant attractive forces between NH$_3$ molecules are hydrogen bonds.

13. **Which intermolecular attraction explains the following trend in straight-chain alkanes?**

Condensed structural formula	Boiling point (°C)
CH$_4$	-161.5
CH$_3$CH$_3$	-88.6
CH$_3$CH$_2$CH$_3$	-42.1
CH$_3$CH$_2$CH$_2$CH$_3$	-0.5
CH$_3$CH$_2$CH$_2$CH$_2$CH$_3$	36.0
CH$_3$CH$_2$CH$_2$CH$_2$CH$_2$CH$_3$	68.7

    A. London dispersion forces
    B. Dipole-dipole interactions
    C. Hydrogen bonding
    D. Ion-induced dipole interactions

A. Alkanes are composed entirely of non-polar C-C and C-H bonds, resulting in no dipole interactions or hydrogen bonding. London dispersion forces increase with the size of the molecule, resulting in a higher temperature requirement to break these bonds and a higher boiling point.

14. List NH_3, PH_3, $MgCl_2$, Ne, and N_2 in order of increasing melting point.

    A. $N_2 <$ Ne $< PH_3 < NH_3 < MgCl_2$
    B. $N_2 < NH_3 <$ Ne $< MgCl_2 < PH_3$
    C. Ne $< N_2 < NH_3 < PH_3 < MgCl_2$
    D. Ne $< N_2 < PH_3 < NH_3 < MgCl_2$

D. Higher melting points result from stronger intermolecular forces. $MgCl_2$ is the only material listed with ionic bonds and will have the highest melting point. Dipole-dipole interactions are present in NH_3 and PH_3 but not in Ne and N_2. Ne and N_2 are also small molecules expected to have very weak London dispersion forces and so will have lower melting points than NH_3 and PH_3. NH_3 will have stronger intermolecular attractions and a higher melting point than PH_3 because hydrogen bonding occurs in NH_3. Ne has a molecular weight of 20 and a spherical shape and N_2 has a molecular weight of 28 and is not spherical. Both of these factors predict stronger London dispersion forces and a higher melting point for N_2. Actual melting points are: Ne (25 K) $< N_2$ (63 K) $< PH_3$ (140 K) $< NH_3$ (195 K) $< MgCl_2$ (987 K).

15. 1-butanol, ethanol, methanol, and 1-propanol are all liquids at room temperature. Rank them in order of increasing viscosity.

    A. 1-butanol $<$ 1-propanol $<$ ethanol $<$ methanol
    B. methanol $<$ ethanol $<$ 1-propanol $<$ 1-butanol
    C. methanol $<$ ethanol $<$ 1-butanol $<$ 1-propanol
    D. 1-propanol $<$ 1-butanol $<$ ethanol $<$ methanol

B. Higher viscosities result from stronger intermolecular attractive forces. The molecules listed are all alcohols with the -OH functional group attached to the end of a straight-chain alkane. In other words, they all have the formula $CH_3(CH_2)_{n-1}OH$. The only difference between the molecules is the length of the alkane corresponding to the value of n. With all else identical, larger molecules have greater intermolecular attractive forces due to a greater molecular surface for the attractions. Therefore the viscosities are ranked: methanol (CH_3OH) $<$ ethanol (CH_3CH_2OH) $<$ 1-propanol ($CH_3CH_2CH_2OH$) $<$ 1-butanol ($CH_3CH_2CH_2CH_2OH$).

16. Which gas has a diffusion rate of 25% the rate for hydrogen?

   A. helium
   B. methane
   C. nitrogen
   D. oxygen

D. Graham's law of diffusion states:

$$\frac{r_1}{r_2} = \sqrt{\frac{M_2}{M_1}} \; .$$

Hydrogen (H_2) has molecular weight of 2.0158 u. Using the unknown for material #1 and hydrogen for material #2 in the equation for Graham's law, the ratio of rates is:

$$\frac{r_{unknown}}{r_{hydrogen}} = \sqrt{\frac{2.0158 \text{ u}}{M_{unknown}}} = 0.25. \quad \text{Squaring both sides yields} \quad \frac{2.0158 \text{ u}}{M_{unknown}} = 0.0625 \, .$$

Solving for $M_{unknown}$ gives:

$$M_{unknown} = \frac{2.0158 \text{ u}}{0.0625} = 32 \text{ u} \, .$$

The given possibilities are: He (4.0 u), CH_4 (16 u), N_2 (28 u), and O_2 (32 u).

17. 2.00 L of an unknown gas at 1500. mm Hg and a temperature of 25.0 °C weighs 7.52 g. Assuming the ideal gas equation, what is the molecular weight of the gas?

$$760 \text{ mm Hg} = 1 \text{ atm}$$
$$R = 0.08206 \text{ L-atm/(mol-K)}$$

A. 21.6 u
B. 23.3 u
C. 46.6 u
D. 93.2 u

C. Pressure and temperature must be expressed in the proper units. Next the ideal gas law is used to find the number of moles of gas.

$$P = 1500 \text{ mm Hg} \times \frac{1 \text{ atm}}{760 \text{ mm Hg}} = 1.974 \text{ atm and } T = 25.0 + 273.15 = 298.15 \text{ K}$$

$$PV = nRT \implies n = \frac{PV}{RT}$$

$$n = \frac{(1.974 \text{ atm})(2.00 \text{ L})}{\left(0.08206 \frac{\text{L-atm}}{\text{mol-K}}\right)(298.15 \text{ K})} = 0.1613 \text{ mol.}$$

The molecular mass may be found from the mass of one mole.

$$\frac{7.52 \text{ g}}{0.1613 \text{ mol}} = 46.6 \frac{\text{g}}{\text{mol}} \implies 46.6 \text{ u}$$

18. Which substance is most likely to be a gas at STP?

A. SeO_2
B. F_2
C. $CaCl_2$
D. I_2

B. A gas at STP has a normal boiling point under 0 °C. The substance with the lowest boiling point will have the weakest intermolecular attractive forces and will be the most likely gas at STP. F_2 has the lowest molecular weight, is not a salt, metal, or covalent network solid, and is non-polar, indicating the weakest intermolecular attractive forces of the four choices. F_2 actually is a gas at STP, and the other three are solids.

19. What pressure is exerted by a mixture of 2.7 g of H2 and 59 g of Xe at 0 °C on a 50. L container?

A. 0.69 atm
B. 0.76 atm
C. 0.80 atm
D. 0.97 atm

C. Grams of gas are first converted to moles:

$$2.7 \text{ g H}_2 \times \frac{1 \text{ mol H}_2}{2 \times 1.0079 \text{ g H}_2} = 1.33 \text{ mol H}_2 \quad \text{and} \quad 59 \text{ g Xe} \times \frac{1 \text{ mol H}_2}{131.29 \text{ g H}_2} = 0.449 \text{ mol Xe}$$

.

Dalton's law of partial pressures for an ideal gas is used to find the pressure of the mixture:

$$P_{total}V = \left(n_{H_2} + n_{Xe}\right)RT \Rightarrow P_{total} = \frac{\left(n_{H_2} + n_{Xe}\right)RT}{V}$$

$$P_{total} = \frac{\left(1.33 \text{ mol} + 0.449 \text{ mol}\right)\left(0.08206 \frac{\text{L-atm}}{\text{mol-K}}\right)\left(273.15 \text{ K}\right)}{50. \text{ L}} = 0.80 \text{ atm.}$$

20. A few minutes after opening a bottle of perfume, the scent is detected on the other side of the room. What law relates to this phenomenon?

A. Graham's law
B. Dalton's law
C. Boyle's law
D. Avogadro's law

A. Graham's law describes the rate of diffusion (or effusion) of a gas, in this instance, the rate of diffusion of molecules in perfume vapor.

21. **Which of the following statements are true of vapor pressure at equilibrium?**

    A. Solids have no vapor pressure.
    B. Dissolving a solute in a liquid increases its vapor pressure.
    C. The vapor pressure of a pure substance is characteristic of that substance and its temperature.
    D. All of the above

C. Only temperature and the identity of the substance determine vapor pressure. Solids have a vapor pressure, and solutes decrease vapor pressure.

22. **Find the partial pressure of N_2 in a container holding H_2O and N_2 at 150. kPa and 50 °C. The vapor pressure of H_2O at 50 °C is 12 kPa.**

    A. 12 kPa
    B. 138 kPa
    C. 162 kPa
    D. The value cannot be determined.

B. The partial pressure of H_2O vapor in the container is its vapor pressure. The partial pressure of N_2 may be found by manipulating Dalton's law:
$$P_{total} = P_{H_2O} + P_{N_2} \Rightarrow P_{N_2} = P_{total} - P_{H_2O}$$
$$P_{N_2} = P_{total} - P_{H_2O} = 150. \text{ kPa} - 12 \text{ kPa} = 138 \text{ kPa}$$

23. **The normal boiling point of water on the Kelvin scale is closest to:**

    A. 112 K
    B. 212 K
    C. 273 K
    D. 373 K

D. Temperature in Kelvin are equal to Celsius temperatures plus 273.15. Since the normal boiling point of water is 100 °C, it will boil at 373.15 K, corresponding to answer D.

24. Which phase may be present at the triple point of a substance?

    I. Gas
    II. Liquid
    III. Solid
    IV. Supercritical fluid

    A. I, II, and III
    B. I, II, and IV
    C. II, III, and IV
    D. I, II, III, and IV

A. Gas, liquid and solid may exist together at the triple point.

25. In the following phase diagram, _____ occurs as P is decreased from A to B at constant T and _____ occurs as T is increased from C to D at constant P.

    A. deposition, melting
    B. sublimation, melting
    C. deposition, vaporization
    D. sublimation, vaporization

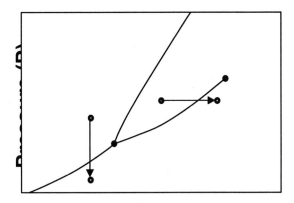

Temperature (T)

D. Point A is located in the solid phase, point C is located in the liquid phase. Points B and D are located in the gas phase. The transition from solid to gas is sublimation and the transition from liquid to gas is vaporization.

26. Heat is added to a pure solid at its melting point until it all becomes liquid at its freezing point. Which of the following occur?

    A. Intermolecular attractions are weakened.
    B. The kinetic energy of the molecules does not change.
    C. The freedom of the molecules to move about increases.
    D. All of the above

D. Intermolecular attractions are lessened during melting. This permits molecules to move about more freely, but there is no change in the kinetic energy of the molecules because the temperature has remained the same.

27. Which of the following occur when NaCl dissolves in water?

    A. Heat is required to break bonds in the NaCl crystal lattice.
    B. Heat is released when hydrogen bonds in water are broken.
    C. Heat is required to form bonds of hydration.
    D. The oxygen end of the water molecule is attracted to the Cl^- ion.

A. The lattice does break apart, H-bonds in water are broken, and bonds of hydration are formed, but the first and second process require heat while the third process releases heat. The oxygen end of the water molecule has a partial negative charge and is attracted to the Na^+ ion.

28. The solubility of $CoCl_2$ is 54 g per 100 g of ethanol. Three flasks each contain 100 g of ethanol. Flask #1 also contains 40 g $CoCl_2$ in solution. Flask #2 contains 56 g $CoCl_2$ in solution. Flask #3 contains 5 g of solid $CoCl_2$ in equilibrium with 54 g $CoCl_2$ in solution. Which of the following describe the solutions present in the liquid phase of the flasks?

    A. #1-saturated, #2-supersaturated, #3-unsaturated.
    B. #1-unsaturated, #2-miscible, #3-saturated.
    C. #1-unsaturated, #2-supersaturated, #3-saturated.
    D. #1-unsaturated, #2-not at equilibrium, #3-miscible.

C. Flask #1 contains less solute than the solubility limit, and is unsaturated. Flask #2 contains more solute than the solubility limit, and is supersaturated and also not at equilibrium. Flask #3 contains the solubility limit and is a saturated solution. The term "miscible" applies only to liquids that mix together in all proportions.

29. The solubility at 1.0 atm of pure CO_2 in water at 25 °C is 0.034 M. According to Henry's law, what is the solubility at 4.0 atm of pure CO_2 in water at 25 °C? Assume no chemical reaction occurs between CO_2 and H_2O.

    A. 0.0085 M
    B. 0.034 M
    C. 0.14 M
    D. 0.25 M

C. Henry's law states that CO_2 solubility in M (mol/L) will be proportional to the partial pressure of the gas. A four-fold increase in pressure from 1.0 atm to 4.0 atm will increase solubility four-fold from 0.034 M to 0.14 M.

30. Carbonated water is bottled at 25 °C under pure CO_2 at 4.0 atm. Later the bottle is opened at 4 °C under air at 1.0 atm that has a partial pressure of 3×10^{-4} atm CO_2. Why do CO_2 bubbles form when the bottle is opened?

    A. CO_2 leaves the solution due to a drop in solubility at the lower total pressure.
    B. CO_2 leaves the solution due to a drop in solubility at the lower CO_2 pressure.
    C. CO_2 leaves the solution due to a drop in solubility at the lower temperature.
    D. CO_2 is formed by the decomposition of carbonic acid.

B. A is incorrect because if the water were bottled under a different gas at a high pressure, it would not be carbonated. CO_2 partial pressure is the important factor in solubility. C is incorrect because a decrease in temperature will increase solubility, and the chance from 298 K to 277 K is relatively small. D may occur, but this represents a small fraction of the gas released.

31. When KNO_3 dissolves in water, the water grows slightly colder. An increase in temperature will _____ the solubility of KNO_3.

    A. increase
    B. decrease
    C. have no effect on
    D. have an unknown effect with the information given on

A. The decline in water temperature indicates that the net solution process is endothermic (requiring heat). A temperature increase supplying more heat will favor the solution and increase solubility according to Le Chatelier's principle.

32. An experiment requires 100. mL of a 0.500 M solution of $MgBr_2$. How many grams of $MgBr_2$ will be present in this solution?

    A. 9.21 g
    B. 11.7 g
    C. 12.4 g
    D. 15.6 g

A.

$$0.100 \text{ L solution} \times \frac{0.500 \text{ mol MgBr}_2}{\text{L}} \times \frac{(24.305 + 2 \times 79.904) \text{ g MgBr}_2}{\text{mol MgBr}_2} = 9.21 \text{ g MgBr}_2$$

33. **500. mg of RbOH are added to 500. g of ethanol (C_2H_6O) resulting in 395 mL of solution. Determine the molarity and molality of RbOH.**

A. 0.0124 M, 0.00488 m
B. 0.0124 M, 0.00976 m
C. 0.0223 M, 0.00488 m
D. 0.0223 M, 0. 00976 m

B. First we determine the moles of solute present:

$$0.500 \text{ g RbOH} \times \frac{1 \text{ mol RbOH}}{\left(85.468 + 15.999 + 1.0079\right) \text{ g RbOH}} = 0.004879 \text{ mol RbOH}.$$

This value is used to calculate molarity and molality:

$$\frac{0.04879 \text{ mol RbOH}}{0.395 \text{ L solution}} = 0.0124 \text{ M RbOH}$$

and

$$\frac{0.04879 \text{ mol RbOH}}{0.500 \text{ kg ethanol}} = 0.00976 \text{ } m \text{ RbOH}.$$

34. **20.0 g H_3PO_4 in 1.5 L of solution are intended to react with KOH according to the following reaction: $H_3PO_4 + 3\,KOH \rightarrow K_3PO_4 + 3\,H_2O$. What is the molarity and normality of the H_3PO_4 solution?**

A. 0.41 M, 1.22 N
B. 0.41 M, 0.20 N
C. 0.14 M, 0.045 N
D. 0.14 M, 0. 41 N

D. We use two methods to solve this problem. In the first method, we determine the moles of solute present and use it to calculate molarity and normality:

$$20.0 \text{ g } H_3PO_4 \times \frac{1 \text{ mol } H_3PO_4}{\left(3 \times 1.0079 + 30.974 + 4 \times 15.999\right) \text{ g } H_3PO_4} = 0.204 \text{ mol } H_3PO_4.$$

$$\frac{0.204 \text{ mol } H_3PO_4}{1.5 \text{ L solution}} = 0.136 \frac{\text{mol } H_3PO_4}{L} = 0.14 \text{ M } H_3PO_4$$

and

$$\frac{0.204 \text{ mol } H_3PO_4}{1.5 \text{ L solution}} \times \frac{3 \text{ reaction equivalents}}{1 \text{ mol } H_3PO_4} = 0.408 \frac{\text{reaction equivalents}}{L} = 0.41 \text{ N } H_3PO_4.$$

Alternatively, molarity may be found in one step and normality may be determined from the molarity:

$$\frac{20.0 \text{ g } H_3PO_4}{1.5 \text{ L}} \times \frac{1 \text{ mol } H_3PO_4}{\left(3 \times 1.0079 + 30.974 + 4 \times 15.999\right) \text{ g } H_3PO_4} = 0.136 \frac{\text{mol } H_3PO_4}{L} = 0.14 \text{ M } H_3PO_4$$

and

$$0.136 \frac{\text{mol } H_3PO_4}{L} \times \frac{3 \text{ reaction equivalents}}{1 \text{ mol } H_3PO_4} = 0.408 \frac{\text{reaction equivalents}}{L} = 0.41 \text{ N.}$$

35. Aluminum sulfate is a strong electrolyte. What is the concentration of all species in a 0.2 M solution of aluminum sulfate?

   A. 0.2 M Al^{3+}, 0.2 M SO_4^{2-}
   B. 0.4 M Al^{3+}, 0.6 M SO_4^{2-}
   C. 0.6 M Al^{3+}, 0.4 M SO_4^{2-}
   D. 0.2 M $Al_2(SO_4)_3$

B. A strong electrolyte will completely ionize into its cation and anion. Aluminum sulfate is $Al_2(SO_4)_3$. Each mole of aluminum sulfate ionizes into 2 moles of Al^{3+} and 3 moles of SO_4^{2-}:

$$0.2\,\frac{mol\ Al_2(SO_4)_3}{L} \times \frac{2\ mol\ Al^{3+}}{mol\ Al_2(SO_4)_3} = 0.4\,\frac{mol\ Al^{3+}}{L}\ and$$

$$0.2\,\frac{mol\ Al_2(SO_4)_3}{L} \times \frac{3\ mol\ SO_4^{2-}}{mol\ Al_2(SO_4)_3} = 0.6\,\frac{mol\ SO_4^{2-}}{L}.$$

36. 15 g of formaldehyde (CH_2O) are dissolved in 100. g of water. Calculate the weight percentage and mole fraction of formaldehyde in the solution.

   A. 13%, 0.090
   B. 15%, 0.090
   C. 13%, 0.083
   D. 15%, 0.083

C. Remember to use the total amounts in the denominator.

$$\text{For weight percentage: } \frac{15\ g\ CH_2O}{(15+100)\ g\ total} = 0.13 = 13\%.$$

For mole fraction, first convert grams of each substance to moles:

$$15\ g\ CH_2O \times \frac{mol\ CH_2O}{(12.011+2\times1.0079+15.999)\ g\ CH_2O} = 0.4996\ mol\ CH_2O$$

$$100\ g\ H_2O \times \frac{mol\ H_2O}{(2\times1.0079+15.999)\ g\ H_2O} = 5.551\ mol\ H_2O.$$

Again use the total amount in the denominator $\dfrac{0.4996\ mol\ CH_2O}{(0.4996+5.551)\ mol\ total} = 0.083.$

37. Which of the following would make the best solvent for Br$_2$?

 A. H$_2$O
 B. CS$_2$
 C. NH$_3$
 D. molten NaCl

B. The best solvents for a solute have intermolecular bonds of similar strength to the solute ("like dissolves like"). Bromine is a non-polar molecule with intermolecular attractions due to weak London dispersion forces. The relatively strong hydrogen bonding in H$_2$O and NH$_3$ and the very strong electrostatic attractions in molten NaCl would make each of them a poor solvent for Br$_2$ because these molecules would prefer to remain attracted to one another. CS$_2$ is a fairly small non-polar molecule.

38. Which of the following is most likely to dissolve in water?

 A. H$_2$
 B. CCl$_4$
 C. (SiO$_2$)$_n$
 D. CH$_3$OH

D. The best solutes for a solvent have intermolecular bonds of similar strength to the solvent. H$_2$O molecules are connected by fairly strong hydrogen bonds. H$_2$ and CCl$_4$ are molecules with intermolecular attractions due to weak London dispersion forces. (SiO$_2$)$_n$ is a covalent network solid and is essentially one large molecule with bonds that much stronger than hydrogen bonds. CH$_3$OH (methanol) is miscible with water because it contains hydrogen bonds between molecules.

39. Which of the following is not a colligative property?

 A. Viscosity lowering
 B. Freezing point lowering
 C. Boiling point elevation
 D. Vapor pressure lowering

A. Vapor pressure lowering, boiling point elevation, and freezing point lowering may all be visualized as a result of solute particles interfering with the interface between phases in a consistent way. This is not the case for viscosity.

40. $BaCl_2(aq) + Na_2SO_4(aq) \rightarrow BaSO_4(s) + 2NaCl(aq)$ is an example of a _____ reaction.

    A. acid-base
    B. precipitation
    C. redox
    D. nuclear

B. $BaSO_4$ falls out of the solution as a precipitate, but the charges on Ba^{2+} and SO_4^{2-} remain unchanged, so this is not a redox reaction. Neither $BaCl_2$ nor Na_2SO_4 are acids or bases, and the nuclei involved also remain unaltered

41. **List the following aqueous solutions in order of increasing boiling point.**

    I.   0.050 *m* $AlCl_3$
    II. 0.080 *m* $Ba(NO_3)_2$
    III. 0.090 *m* NaCl
    IV. 0.12 *m* ethylene glycol ($C_2H_6O_2$)

    A. I < II < III < IV
    B. I < III < IV < II
    C. IV < III < I < II
    D. IV < III < II < I

C. <u>Particles</u> in solution determine colligative properties. The first three materials are strong electrolyte salts, and $C_2H_6O_2$ is a non-electrolyte.

$AlCl_3(aq)$ is Al^{3+} +3 Cl^-. So $0.050 \dfrac{\text{mol } AlCl_3}{\text{kg } H_2O} \times \dfrac{4 \text{ mol particles}}{\text{mol } AlCl_3} = 0.200$ *m* particles

$Ba(NO_3)_2(aq)$ is Ba^{2+} +2 NO_3^-. So $0.080 \dfrac{\text{mol } Ba(NO_3)_2}{\text{kg } H_2O} \times \dfrac{3 \text{ mol particles}}{\text{mol } Ba(NO_3)_2} = 0.240$ *m* particles

$NaCl(aq)$ is Na^+ +Cl^-. So $0.090 \dfrac{\text{mol } NaCl}{\text{kg } H_2O} \times \dfrac{2 \text{ mol particles}}{\text{mol } NaCl} = 0.180$ *m* particles

$C_2H_6O_2(aq)$ is not an electrolyte. So $0.12 \dfrac{\text{mol } C_2H_6O_2}{\text{kg } H_2O} \times \dfrac{1 \text{ mol particles}}{\text{mol } C_2H_6O_2} = 0.12$ *m* particles

The greater the number of dissolved particles, the greater the boiling point elevation.

42. Osmotic pressure is the pressure required to prevent _____ flowing from low to high _____ concentration across a semipermeable membrane.

    A. solute, solute
    B. solute, solvent
    C. solvent, solute
    D. solvent, solvent

C. Osmotic pressure is the pressure required to prevent osmosis, which is the flow of solvent across the membrane from low to high solute concentration. This is also the direction from high to low solvent concentration.

43. A solution of NaCl in water is heated on a mountain in an open container until it boils at 100. °C. The air pressure on the mountain is 0.92 atm. According to Raoult's law, what mole fraction of Na^+ and Cl^- are present in the solution?

    A. 0.04 Na^+, 0.04 Cl^-
    B. 0.08 Na^+, 0.08 Cl^-
    C. 0.46 Na^+, 0.46 Cl^-
    D. 0.92 Na^+, 0.92 Cl^-

A. The vapor pressure of H_2O at 100. °C is exactly 1 atm. Boiling point decreases with external pressure, so the boiling point of pure H_2O at 0.9 atm will be less than 100. °C. Adding salt raises the boiling point at 0.92 atm to 100. °C by decreasing vapor pressure to 0.92 atm. According to Raoult's law:

$$P^{vapor}_{solution} = P^{vapor}_{pure\ solvent}\left(mole\ fraction\right)_{solvent} \Rightarrow \left(mole\ fraction\right)_{solvent} = \frac{P^{vapor}_{solution}}{P^{vapor}_{pure\ solvent}}.$$

$$\text{Therefore, } \left(mole\ fraction\right)_{H_2O} = \frac{0.92\ atm\ at\ 100.\ °C}{1.0\ atm\ at\ 100.\ °C} = 0.92\ \frac{mol\ H_2O}{mol\ total}.$$

The remaining 0.08 mole fraction of solute is evenly divided between the two ions:

$$\left(mole\ fraction\right)_{solute} = 1 - \left(mole\ fraction\right)_{H_2O} = 1 - 0.92 = 0.08\ \frac{mol\ solute\ particles}{mol\ total}$$

$$\left(mole\ fraction\right)_{Na^+} = 0.08\ \frac{mol\ solute\ particles}{mol\ total} \times \frac{1\ mol\ Na^+}{2\ mol\ solute\ particles} = 0.04\ \frac{mol\ Na^+}{mol\ total}$$

$$\left(mole\ fraction\right)_{Cl^-} = 0.08\ \frac{mol\ solute\ particles}{mol\ total} \times \frac{1\ mol\ Cl^-}{2\ mol\ solute\ particles} = 0.04\ \frac{mol\ Cl^-}{mol\ total}.$$

44. Write a balanced nuclear equation for the emission of an alpha particle by polonium-209.

A. $^{209}_{84}Po \rightarrow\ ^{205}_{81}Pb +\ ^{4}_{2}He$

B. $^{209}_{84}Po \rightarrow\ ^{205}_{82}Bi +\ ^{4}_{2}He$

C. $^{209}_{84}Po \rightarrow\ ^{209}_{85}At +\ ^{0}_{-1}e$

D. $^{209}_{84}Po \rightarrow\ ^{205}_{82}Pb +\ ^{4}_{2}He$

D. The periodic table before skill 1.1 shows that polonium has an atomic number of 84. The emission of an alpha particle, $^{4}_{2}He$ (eliminating choice C), will leave an atom with an atomic number of 82 and a mass number of 205 (eliminating choice A). The periodic table identifies this element as lead, $^{205}_{82}Pb$, not bismuth (eliminating choice B).

45. Write a balanced nuclear equation for the decay of calcium-45 to scandium-45.

A. $^{45}_{20}Ca \rightarrow\ ^{41}_{18}Sc +\ ^{4}_{2}He$

B. $^{45}_{20}Ca +\ ^{0}_{1}e \rightarrow\ ^{45}_{21}Sc$

C. $^{45}_{20}Ca \rightarrow\ ^{45}_{21}Sc +\ ^{0}_{-1}e$

D. $^{45}_{20}Ca +\ ^{0}_{1}p \rightarrow\ ^{45}_{21}Sc$

C. All four choices are balanced mathematically. "A" leaves scandium-41 as a decay product, not scandium-45. "B" and "D" require the addition of particles not normally present in the atom. If these reactions do occur, they are not decay reactions because they are not spontaneous. "C" involves the common decay mechanism of beta emission.

46. $^{3}_{1}H$ decays with a half-life of 12 years. 3.0 g of pure $^{3}_{1}H$ were placed in a sealed container 24 years ago. How many grams of $^{3}_{1}H$ remain?

A. 0.38 g
B. 0.75 g
C. 1.5 g
D. 3.0 g

B. Every 12 years, the amount remaining is cut in half. After 12 years, 1.5 g will remain. After another 12 years, 0.75 g will remain.

47. Oxygen-15 has a half-life of 122 seconds. What percentage of a sample of oxygen-15 has decayed after 300. seconds?

    A. 18.2%
    B. 21.3%
    C. 78.7%
    D. 81.8%

D. We may assume a convenient number (like 100.0 g) for a sample size. The amount remaining may be found from:

$$A_{remaining} = A_{initially} \left(\frac{1}{2}\right)^{\frac{t}{t_{halflife}}}$$

$$= 100.0 \text{ g }^{15}O \left(\frac{1}{2}\right)^{\frac{300.\text{ seconds}}{122\text{ seconds}}} = 18.2 \text{ g }^{15}O$$

We are asked to determine the percentage that has decayed. This will be 100.0 g − 18.2 g = 81.8 g or 81.8% of the initial sample.

48. Which of the following isotopes is commonly used for medical imaging in the diagnose of diseases?

    A. cobalt-60
    B. technetium-99m
    C. tin-117m
    D. plutonium-238

B. The other three isotopes have limited medical applications (tin-117m has been used for the relief of bone cancer pain), but only Tc-99m is used routinely for imaging.

49. Carbon-14 dating would be useful in obtaining the age of which object?

    A. a 20th century Picasso painting
    B. a mummy from ancient Egypt
    C. a dinosaur fossil
    D. all of the above

B. C-14 is used in archeology because its half-life is 5730 years. Too little C-14 would have decayed from the painting and nearly all of the C-14 would have decayed from the fossil. In both cases, an estimate of age would be impossible with this isotope.

50. **Which of the following isotopes can create a chain reaction of nuclear fission?**

    A. uranium-235
    B. uranium-238
    C. plutonium-238
    D. all of the above

A. Uranium-235 and plutonium-239 are the two fissile isotopes used for nuclear power. ^{238}U is the most common uranium isotope. ^{238}Pu is used as a heat source for energy in space probes and some pacemakers.

51. **List the following scientists in chronological order from earliest to most recent with respect to their most significant contribution to atomic theory:**

    I.   **John Dalton**
    II. **Niels Bohr**
    III. **J. J. Thomson**
    IV. **Ernest Rutherford**

    A. I, III, II, IV
    B. I, III, IV, II
    C. I, IV, III, II
    D. III, I, II, IV

B. Dalton founded modern atomic theory. J.J. Thomson determined that the electron is a subatomic particle but he placed it in the center of the atom. Rutherford discovered that electrons surround a small dense nucleus. Bohr determined that electrons may only occupy discrete positions around the nucleus.

52. Match the theory with the scientist who first proposed it:

I. Electrons, atoms, and all objects with momentum also exist as waves.
II. Electron density may be accurately described by a single mathematical equation.
III. There is an inherent indeterminacy in the position and momentum of particles.
IV. Radiant energy is transferred between particles in exact multiples of a discrete unit.

A. I-de Broglie, II-Planck, III-Schrödinger, IV-Thomson
B. I-Dalton, II-Bohr, III-Planck, IV-de Broglie
C. I-Henry, II-Bohr, III-Heisenberg, IV-Schrödinger
D. I-de Broglie, II-Schrödinger, III-Heisenberg, IV-Planck

D. Henry's law relates gas partial pressure to liquid solubility.

53. How many neutrons are in $_{27}^{60}\text{Co}$?

A. 27
B. 33
C. 60
D. 87

B. The number of neutrons is found by subtracting the atomic number (27) from the mass number (60).

54. The terrestrial composition of an element is: 50.7% as an isotope with an atomic mass of 78.9 u and 49.3% as an isotope with an atomic mass of 80.9 u. Both isotopes are stable. Calculate the atomic mass of the element.

A. 79.0 u
B. 79.8 u
C. 79.9 u
D. 80.8 u

C.

Atomic mass of element = (Fraction as 1st isotope) (Atomic mass of 1st isotope)

+

(Fraction as 2nd isotope) (Atomic mass of 2nd isotope)

$$= (0.507)\,(78.9\text{ u}) + (0.493)\,(80.9\text{ u}) = 79.89\text{ u} = 79.9\text{ u}$$

55. Which of the following is a correct electron arrangement for oxygen?

A.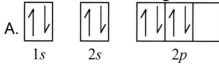

   $1s$ $\quad$ $2s$ $\qquad$ $2p$

B. $1s^21p^22s^22p^2$

C. 2, 2, 4

D. none of the above

D. Choice A violates Hund's rule. The two electrons on the far right should occupy the final two orbitals. B should be $1s^22s^22p^4$. There is no $1p$ subshell. C should be 2, 6. Number lists indicate electrons in shells.

56. Which of the following statements about radiant energy is <u>not</u> true?

   A. The energy change of an electron transition is directly proportional to the wavelength of the emitted or absorbed photon.
   B. The energy of an electron in a hydrogen atom depends only on the principle quantum number.
   C. The frequency of photons striking a metal determines whether the photoelectric effect will occur.
   D. The frequency of a wave of electromagnetic radiation is inversely proportional to its wavelength.

A. The energy change (ΔE) is <u>inversely</u> proportional to the wavelength (λ) of the photon according the equations:

$$\Delta E = \frac{hc}{\lambda}.$$

where h is Planck's constant and c is the speed of light.

Choice B is true for hydrogen. Atoms with more than one electron are more complex. The frequency of individual photons, not the number of photons determines whether the photoelectric effect occurs, so choice C is true. Choice D is true. The proportionality constant is the speed of light according to the equation:

$$\nu = \frac{c}{\lambda}.$$

57. **Match the orbital diagram for the ground state of carbon with the rule/principle it violates:**

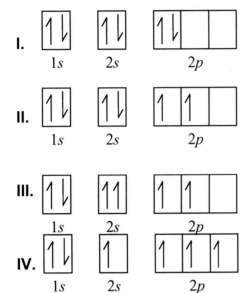

A. I-Pauli exclusion, II-Aufbau, III-no violation, IV-Hund's
B. I-Aufbau, II-Pauli exclusion, III-no violation, IV-Hund's
C. I-Hund's, II-no violation, III-Pauli exclusion, IV-Aufbau
D. I-Hund's, II-no violation, III-Aufbau, IV-Pauli exclusion

C. Diagram I violates Hund's rule because a second electron is added to a degenerate orbital before all orbitals in the subshell have one electron. Diagram III violates the Pauli exclusion principle because both electrons in the 2s orbital have the same spin. They would have the same 4 quantum numbers. Diagram IV violates the Aufbau principle because an electron occupies the higher energy 2p orbital before 2s orbital has been filled; this configuration is not at the ground state.

58. **Select the list of atoms that are arranged in order of increasing size.**

A. Mg, Na, Si, Cl
B. Si, Cl, Mg, Na
C. Cl, Si, Mg, Na
D. Na, Mg, Si, Cl

C. These atoms are all in the same row of the periodic table. Size increases further to the left for atoms in the same row.

59. Based on trends in the periodic table, which of the following properties would you expect to be greater for Rb than for K?

   I.   Density
   II. Melting point
   III. Ionization energy
   IV. Oxidation number in a compound with chlorine

   A. I only
   B. I, II, and III
   C. II and III
   D. I, II, III, and IV

A. Rb is underneath K in the alkali metal column (group 1) of the periodic table. There is a general trend for density to increase lower on the table for elements in the same row, so we select choice I. Rb and K experience metallic bonds for intermolecular forces and the strength of metallic bonds decreases for larger atoms further down the periodic table resulting in a lower melting point for Rb, so we do not choose II. Ionization energy decreases for larger atoms further down the periodic table, so we do not choose III. Both Rb and K would be expected to have a charge of +1 and therefore an oxidation number of +1 in a compound with chlorine, so we do not choose IV.

60. Which oxide forms the strongest acid in water?

   A. Al_2O_3
   B. Cl_2O_7
   C. As_2O_5
   D. CO_2

B. The strength of acids formed from oxides increases with electronegativity and with oxidation state. We know Cl has a greater electronegativity than Al, As, and C because it is closer to the top right of the periodic table. The oxidation numbers of our choices are +3 for Al, +7 for Cl, +5 for As, and +4 for C. Both its electronegativity and its oxidation state indicate Cl_2O_7 will form the strongest acid.

61. Rank the following bonds from least to most polar:

C-H, C-Cl, H-H, C-F

 A. C-H < H-H < C-F < C-Cl
 B. H-H < C-H < C-F < C-Cl
 C. C-F < C-Cl < C-H < H-H
 D. H-H < C-H < C-Cl < C-F

D. Bonds between atoms of the same element are completely non-polar, so H-H is the least polar bond in the list, eliminating choices A and C. The C-H bond is considered to be non-polar even though the electrons of the bond are slightly unequally shared. C-Cl and C-F are both polar covalent bonds, but C-F is more strongly polar because F has a greater electronegativity.

62. At room temperature, $CaBr_2$ is expected to be:

 A. a ductile solid
 B. a brittle solid
 C. a soft solid
 D. a gas

B. Ca is a metal because it is on the left of the periodic table, and Br is a non-metal because it is on the right. The compound they form together will be an ionic salt, and ionic salts are brittle solids (choice B) at room temperature. NaCl is another example.

63. Which of the following is a proper Lewis dot structure of CHClO?

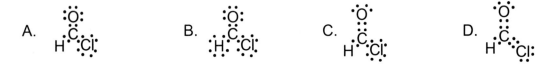

C. C has 4 valence shell electrons, H has 1, Cl has 7, and O has 6. The molecule has a total of 18 valence shell electrons. This eliminates choice B which has 24. Choice B is also incorrect because has an octet around a hydrogen atom instead of 2 electrons and because there are only six electrons surrounding the central carbon. A single bond connecting all atoms would give choice A. This is incorrect because there are only 6 electrons surrounding the central carbon. A double bond between C and O gives the correct answer, C. A double bond between C and O and also between C and Cl would give choice D. This is incorrect because there are 10 electrons surrounding the central carbon.

64. In C_2H_2, each carbon atom contains the following valence orbitals:

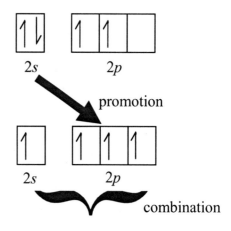

    A. *p* only
    B. *p* and *sp* hybrids
    C. *p* and *sp²* hybrids
    D. *sp³* hybrids only

B. An isolated C has the valence electron configuration $2s^2 2p^2$. Before bonding, one *s* electron is promoted to an empty *p* orbital. In C_2H_2, each C atom bonds to 2 other atoms. Bonding to two other atoms is achieved by combination into two *p* orbitals and two *sp* hybrids.

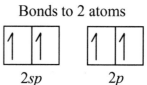

65. Which statement about molecular structures is false?

    A.   is a conjugated molecule.

    B. A bonding σ orbital connects two atoms by the straight line between them.
    C. A bonding π orbital connects two atoms in a separate region from the straight line between them.
    D. The anion with resonance forms will always exist in one form or the other.

D. A conjugated molecule is a molecule with double bonds on adjacent atoms such as the molecule shown in A. Choice B and C give the definition of sigma and pi molecular orbitals. D is false because a resonance form is one of multiple equivalent Lewis structures, but these structures do not describe the actual state of the molecule. The anion will exist in a state between the two forms.

66. What is the shape of the PH$_3$ molecule? Use the VSEPR model.

   A. Trigonal pyramidal
   B. Trigonal bipyramidal
   C. Trigonal planar
   D. Tetrahedral

A. The Lewis structure for PH$_3$ is given to the right. This structure contains 4 electron pairs around the central atom, so the geometral arrangement is tetrahedral. However, the shape of a molecule is given by its atom locations, and there are only three atoms so choice D is not correct. Four electrons pairs with one unshared pair (3 bonds and one lone pair) give a trigonal pyramidal shape as shown to the left.

67. **What is the chemical composition of magnesium nitrate?**

    A. 11.1% Mg, 22.2% N, 66.7% O
    B. 16.4% Mg, 18.9% N, 64.7% O
    C. 20.9% Mg, 24.1% N, 55.0% O
    D. 28.2% Mg, 16.2% N, 55.7% O

B. First find the formula for magnesium nitrate. Mg is an alkali earth metal (**Skill 3.1**) and will always have a 2+ charge. The nitrate ion is NO_3^- (**Skill 5.2**). Two nitrate ions are required for each Mg^{2+} ion. Therefore the formula is $Mg(NO_3)_2$

    Skill 5.1 describes determination chemical composition.
        1) Determine the number of atoms for elements in $Mg(NO_3)_2$: 1 Mg, 2 N, 6 O.
        2) Multiply by the molecular weight of the elements to determine the grams of each in one mole of the formula.

$$\frac{1 \text{ mol Mg}}{\text{mol Mg(NO}_3)_2} \times \frac{24.3 \text{ g Mg}}{\text{mol Mg}} = 24.3 \text{ g Mg/mol Mg(NO}_3)_2$$

$$2(14.0) = 28.0 \text{ g N/mol Mg(NO}_3)_2$$

$$6(16.0) = 96.0 \text{ g O/mol Mg(NO}_3)_2$$

        3) Determine formula mass $148.3 \text{ g Mg(NO}_3)_2/\text{mol Mg(NO}_3)_2$
        4) Divide to determine % composition

$$\%Mg = \frac{24.3 \text{ g Mg/mol Mg(NO}_3)_2}{148.3 \text{ g Mg(NO}_3)_2/\text{mol Mg(NO}_3)_2} = 0.164 \text{ g Mg/g Mg(NO}_3)_2 \times 100\% = 16.4\%$$

$$\%N = \frac{28.0}{148.3} \times 100\% = 18.9\% \qquad \%O = \frac{96.0}{148.3} \times 100\% = 64.7\%$$

Answer A is the fractional representation of the presence of each atom in the formula. Composition is based on mass percentage. Answer C is the chemical composition of $Mg(NO_2)_2$, magnesium nitrite. Answer D is the chemical composition of "MgNO₃", a formula that results from not balancing charges.

68. The IUPAC name for Cu$_2$SO$_3$ is:

A. Dicopper sulfur trioxide
B. Copper (II) sulfate
C. Copper (I) sulfite
D. Copper (II) sulfite

C. Cu$_2$SO$_3$ is an ionic compound containing copper cation and the SO$_3$ anion. Choice A is wrong because it uses the naming system for molecular compounds. The SO$_3$ anion is 2– and is named sulfite. It takes two copper cations in to neutralize this charge, so Cu has a charge of 1+, and the name is copper (I) sulfite.

69. Which name or formula is not represented properly?

A. Cl$_4$S
B. KClO$_3$
C. Calcium dihydrogen phosphate
D. Sulfurous acid

A A is the answer because the atoms in the sulfur tetrachloride molecule are placed in order of increasing electronegativity. This formla is properly written as SCl$_4$. B is a proper formula for potassium chlorate. Calcium dihydrogen phosphate is Ca(H$_2$PO$_4$)$_2$. It derives its name from the Ca^{2+} cation in combination with an anion composed of a phosphate anion (PO$_4^{3-}$) that is doubly protonated to give a H$_2$PO$_4^-$ ion. Sulfurous acid is H$_2$SO$_3$(aq).

70. Household "chlorine bleach" is sodium hypochlorite. Which of the following best represent the production of sodium hypochlorite, sodium chloride, and water by bubbling chlorine gas through aqueous sodium hydroxide?

A. $4Cl(g) + 4NaOH(aq) \rightarrow NaClO_2(aq) + 3NaCl(aq) + 2H_2O(l)$
B. $2Cl_2(g) + 4NaOH(aq) \rightarrow NaClO_2(aq) + 3NaCl(aq) + 2H_2O(l)$
C. $2Cl(g) + 2NaOH(aq) \rightarrow NaClO(aq) + NaCl(aq) + H_2O(l)$
D. $Cl_2(g) + 2NaOH(aq) \rightarrow NaClO(aq) + NaCl(aq) + H_2O(l)$

D. Chlorine gas is a diatomic molecule, eliminating choices A and C. The hypochlorite ion is ClO$^-$ eliminating choices A and B. All of the equations are properly balanced.

71. **Balance the equation for the neutralization reaction between phosphoric acid and calcium hydroxide by filling in the blank stoichiometric coefficients.**

$$\_\_H_3PO_4 + \_\_Ca(OH)_2 \rightarrow \_\_Ca_3(PO_4)_2 + \_\_H_2O$$

A. 4, 3, 1, 4
B. 2, 3, 1, 8
C. 2, 3, 1, 6
D. 2, 1, 1, 2

C. We are given the unbalanced equation (**step 1**).

Next we determine the number of atoms on each side (**step 2**). For reactants (left of the arrow): 5H, 1P, 6O, and 1Ca. For products: 2H, 2P, 9O, and 3Ca.

We assume that the molecule with the most atoms—i.e. $Ca_3(PO_4)_2$—has a coefficient of one, and find the other coefficients required to have the same number of atoms on each side of the equation (**step 3**). Assuming $Ca_3(PO_4)_2$ has a coefficient of one means that there will be 3 Ca and 2 P on the right because H_2O has no Ca or P. A balanced equation would also have 3 Ca and 2 P on the left. This is achieved with a coefficient of 2 for H_3PO_4 and 3 for $Ca(OH)_2$. Now we have:

$$2H_3PO_4 + 3Ca(OH)_2 \rightarrow Ca_3(PO_4)_2 + ?H_2O$$

The coefficient for H_2O is found by a balance on H or on O. Whichever one is chosen, the other atom should be checked to confirm that a balance actually occurs. For H, there are 6 H from $2H_3PO_4$ and 6 from $3Ca(OH)_2$ for a total of 12 H on the left. There must be 12 H on the right for balance. None are accounted for by $Ca_3(PO_4)_2$, so all 12 H must occur on H_2O. It has a coefficient of 6.

$$2H_3PO_4 + 3Ca(OH)_2 \rightarrow Ca_3(PO_4)_2 + 6H_2O$$

This is choice C, but if time is available, it is best to check that the remaining atom is balanced. There are 8 O from $2H_3PO_4$ and 6 from $3Ca(OH)_2$ for a total of 14 on the left, and 8 O from $Ca_3(PO_4)_2$ and 6 from $6H_2O$ for a total of 14 on the right. The equation is balanced.

Mulitplication by a whole number (**step 4**) is not required because the stoichiometric coefficients from step 3 already are whole numbers.

An alternative method would be to try the coefficients given for answer A, answer B, etc. until we recognize a properly balanced equation.

72. Write an equation showing the reaction between calcium nitrate and lithium sulfate in aqueous solution. Include all products.

A. $CaNO_3(aq) + Li_2SO_4(aq) \rightarrow CaSO_4(s) + Li_2NO_3(aq)$

B. $Ca(NO_3)_2(aq) + Li_2SO_4(aq) \rightarrow CaSO_4(s) + 2LiNO_3(aq)$

C. $Ca(NO_3)_2(aq) + Li_2SO_4(aq) \rightarrow 2LiNO_3(s) + CaSO_4(aq)$

D. $Ca(NO_3)_2(aq) + Li_2SO_4(aq) + 2H_2O(l) \rightarrow 2LiNO_3(aq) + Ca(OH)_2(aq) + H_2SO_4(aq)$

B. When two ionic compounds are in solution, a precipitation reaction should be considered. We can determine from their names that the two reactants are the ionic compounds $Ca(NO_3)_2$ and Li_2SO_4. The compounds are present in aqueous solution as their four component ions Ca^{2+}, NO_3^-, Li^+, and SO_4^{2-}. Solubility rules indicate that nitrates are always soluble but sulfate will form a solid precipitate with Ca^{2+} forming $CaSO_4(s)$. Choice A results from assuming that the nitrate anion has a 2– charge instead of its 1– charge. B is correct. C assumes lithium nitrate is the precipitate. Choice D includes the reverse of a neutralization reaction. Water would not decompose due to the addition of these salts.

73. Find the mass of CO_2 produced by the combustion of 15 kg of isopropyl alcohol in the reaction:

$$2C_3H_7OH + 9O_2 \rightarrow 6CO_2 + 8H_2O$$

A. 33 kg
B. 44 kg
C. 50 kg
D. 60 kg

A. Remember "grams to moles to moles to grams." Step 1 converts mass to moles for the known value. In this case, kg and kmol are used. Step 2 relates moles of the known value to moles of the unknown value by their stoichiometry coefficients. Step 3 converts moles off the unknown value to a mass.

$$15 \times 10^3 \text{ g } C_4H_8O \times \underbrace{\frac{1 \text{ mol } C_4H_8O}{60 \text{ g } C_4H_8O}}_{\text{step 1}} \times \underbrace{\frac{6 \text{ mol } CO_2}{2 \text{ mol } C_4H_8O}}_{\text{step 2}} \times \underbrace{\frac{44 \text{ g } CO_2}{1 \text{ mol } CO_2}}_{\text{step 3}} = 33 \times 10^3 \text{ g } CO_2$$

$$= 33 \text{ kg } CO_2$$

74. **What is the density of nitrogen gas at STP? Assume an ideal gas and a value of 0.08206 L-atm/(mol-K) for the gas constant.**

   A. 0.62 g/L
   B. 1.14 g/L
   C. 1.25 g/L
   D. 2.03 g/L

C The molecular mass M of N_2 is 28.0 g/mol.

$$d = \frac{nM}{V} = \frac{PM}{RT} = \frac{(1\text{ atm})\left(28.0\frac{g}{mol}\right)}{\left(0.08206\frac{L\bullet atm}{mol\bullet K}\right)(273.15\text{ K})} = 1.25\frac{g}{L}$$

Choice A results from forgetting that nitrogen is a diatomic gas. Choice B results from using a value of 25 °C for standard temperature. This is the thermodynamic standard temperature, but not STP.

A faster method is to recall that one mole of an ideal gas at STP occupies 22.4 L.

$$d \text{ (in }\frac{g}{L}) = \frac{M \text{ (in }\frac{g}{mol})}{22.4\frac{L}{mol}} = \frac{28.0\frac{g}{mol}}{22.4\frac{L}{mol}} = 1.25\frac{g}{L} .$$

75. **Find the volume of methane that will produce 12 m^3 of hydrogen in the reaction: $CH_4(g) + H_2O(g) \rightarrow CO(g) + 3H_2(g)$. Assume temperature and pressure remain constant.**

   A. 4.0 m^3
   B. 32 m^3
   C. 36 m^3
   D. 64 m^3

A Stoichiometric coefficients may be used directly for ideal gas volumes at constant T and P because of Avogadro's Law.

$$12 \text{ m}^3 \text{ H}_2 \times \frac{1 \text{ m}^3 \text{ CH}_4}{3 \text{ m}^3 \text{ H}_2} = 4.0 \text{ m}^3 \text{ CH}_4$$

12 g of H_2 will be produced from 32 g of CH_4 (incorrect choice B).

76. A 100. L vessel of pure O_2 at 500. kPa and 20. °C is used for the combustion of butane:

$$2C_4H_{10} + 13O_2 \rightarrow 8CO_2 + 10H_2O.$$

Find the mass of butane to consume all the O_2 in the vessel. Assume O_2 is an ideal gas and use a value of $R = 8.314$ J/(mol•K).

   A. 183 g
   B. 467 g
   C. 1.83 kg
   D. 7.75 kg

A We are given a volume and asked for a mass. The steps will be "volume to moles to moles to mass."

"Volume to moles…" requires the ideal gas law, but first several units must be altered.

    Units of joules are identical to m^3•Pa.
    500 kPa is 500×10^3 Pa.
    100 L is 0.100 m^3.
    20 °C is 293.15 K.
$PV = nRT$ is rearranged to give:

$$n = \frac{PV}{RT} = \frac{\left(500 \times 10^3 \text{ Pa}\right)\left(0.100 \text{ m}^3 \text{ O}_2\right)}{\left(8.314 \frac{\text{m}^3 \cdot \text{Pa}}{\text{mol} \cdot \text{K}}\right)(293.15 \text{ K})} = 20.51 \text{ mol O}_2$$

"…to moles to mass" utilizes stoichiometry. The molecular weight of butane is 58.1 u.

$$20.51 \text{ mol O}_2 \times \frac{2 \text{ mol C}_4\text{H}_{10}}{13 \text{ mol O}_2} \times \frac{58.1 \text{ g C}_4\text{H}_{10}}{1 \text{ mol C}_4\text{H}_{10}} = 183 \text{ g C}_4\text{H}_{10}$$

77. Consider the reaction between iron and hydrogen chloride gas:
$$Fe(s) + 2HCl(g) \rightarrow FeCl_2(s) + H_2(g) .$$

7 moles of iron and 10 moles of HCl react until the limiting reagent is consumed. Which statements are true?

I.   HCl is the excess reagent
II. HCl is the limiting reagent
III. 7 moles of H_2 are produced
IV. 2 moles of the excess reagent remain

A. I and III
B. I and IV
C. II and III
D. II and IV

D   The limiting reagent is found by dividing the number of moles of each reactant by its stoichiometric coefficient. The lowest result is the limiting reagent.

$$7 \text{ mol Fe} \times \frac{1 \text{ mol reaction}}{1 \text{ mol Fe}} = 7 \text{ mol reaction if Fe is limiting}$$

$$10 \text{ mol HCl} \times \frac{1 \text{ mol reaction}}{2 \text{ mol HCl}} = 5 \text{ mol reaction if HCl is limiting.}$$

Therefore, HCl is the limiting reagent (II is true) and Fe is the excess reagent.

5 moles of the reaction take place, so 5 moles of H_2 are produced, and of the 7 moles of Fe supplied, 5 are consumed, leaving 2 moles of the excess reagent (IV is true).

78. **32.0 g of hydrogen and 32.0 grams of oxygen react to form water until the limiting reagent is consumed. What is present in the vessel after the reaction is complete?**

    A. 16.0 g O_2 and 48.0 g H_2O
    B. 24.0 g H_2 and 40.0 g H_2O
    C. 28.0 g H_2 and 36.0 g H_2O
    D. 28.0 g H_2 and 34.0 g H_2O

C First the equation must be constructed:

$$2H_2 + O_2 \rightarrow 2H_2O$$

A fast and intuitive solution would be to recognize that:
1) One mole of H_2 is about 2.0 g, so about 16 moles of H_2 are present.
2) One mole of O_2 is 32.0 g, so one mole of is O_2 is present
3) Imagine the 16 moles of H_2 reacting with one mole of O_2. 2 moles of H_2 will be consumed before the one mole of O_2 is gone. O_2 is limiting. (Eliminate choice A.)
4) 16 moles less 2 leaves 14 moles of H_2 or about 28 g. (Eliminate choice B.)
5) The reaction began with 64.0 g total. Conservation of mass for chemical reactions forces the total final mass to be 64.0 g also. (Eliminate choice D.)

A more standard solution is presented next. First, mass is converted to moles:

$$32.0 \text{ g } H_2 \times \frac{1 \text{ mol } H_2}{2.016 \text{ g } H_2} = 15.87 \text{ mol } H_2 \quad \text{and} \quad 32.0 \text{ g } O_2 \times \frac{1 \text{ mol } O_2}{32.00 \text{ g } O_2} = 1.000 \text{ mol } O_2$$

Dividing by stoichiometric coefficients give

$$15.87 \text{ mol } H_2 \times \frac{1 \text{ mol reaction}}{2 \text{ mol } H_2} = 7.935 \text{ mol reaction if } H_2 \text{ is limiting}$$

$$1.000 \text{ mol } O_2 \times \frac{1 \text{ mol reaction}}{1 \text{ mol } O_2} = 1.000 \text{ mol reaction if } O_2 \text{ is limiting.}$$

O_2 is the limiting reagent, so no O_2 will remain in the vessel.

$$1.000 \text{ mol } O_2 \text{ consumed} \times \frac{2 \text{ mol } H_2O \text{ produced}}{1 \text{ mol } O_2} \times \frac{18.016 \text{ g } H_2O}{1 \text{ mol } H_2O} = 36.0 \text{ g } H_2O \text{ produced}$$

Rem

$$1.000 \text{ mol } O_2 \text{ consumed} \times \frac{2 \text{ mol } H_2 \text{ consumed}}{1 \text{ mol } O_2} \times \frac{2.016 \text{ g } H_2}{1 \text{ mol } H_2} = 4.03 \text{ g } H_2 \text{ consumed}$$

aining H_2 is found from:
32.0 g H_2 initially − 4.03 g H_2 consumed =28.0 g H_2 remain.

79. Three experiments were performed at the same initial temperature and pressure to determine the rate of the reaction

$$2ClO_2(g) + F_2(g) \rightarrow 2ClO_2F(g).$$

Results are shown in the table below. Concentrations are given in millimoles per liter (mM).

Exp.	Initial $[ClO_2]$ (mM)	Initial $[F_2]$ (mM)	Initial rate of $[ClO_2F]$ increase (mM/sec)
1	5.0	5.0	0.63
2	5.0	20	2.5
3	10	10	2.5

What is the rate law for this reaction?

A. $Rate = k[F_2]$

B. $Rate = k[ClO_2][F_2]$

C. $Rate = k[ClO_2]^2[F_2]$

D. $Rate = k[ClO_2][F_2]^2$

B A four-fold increase in $[F_2]$ at constant $[ClO_2]$ between experiment one and two caused a four-fold increase in rate. Rate is therefore proportional to $[F_2]$ at constant $[ClO_2]$, eliminating choice D (Choice D predicts rate to increase by a factor of 16).

Between experiment 1 and 3, $[F_2]$ and $[ClO_2]$ both double in value. Once again, there is a four-fold increase in rate. If rate were only dependent on $[F_2]$ (choice A), there would be a two-fold increase. The correct answer, B, attributes a two-fold increase in rate to the doubling of $[F_2]$ and a two-fold increase to the doubling of $[ClO_2]$, resulting in a net four-fold increase. Choice C predicts a rate increase by a factor of 8.

If this were an elementary reaction describing a collision event between three molecules, choice C would be expected, but stoichiometry cannot be used to predict a rate law.

80. The reaction
$$(CH_3)_3CBr(aq) + OH^-(aq) \rightarrow (CH_3)_3COH(aq) + Br^-(aq)$$
occurs in three elementary steps:
$$(CH_3)_3CBr \rightarrow (CH_3)_3C^+ + Br^- \text{ is slow}$$
$$(CH_3)_3C^+ + H_2O \rightarrow (CH_3)_3COH_2^+ \text{ is fast}$$
$$(CH_3)_3COH_2^+ + OH^- \rightarrow (CH_3)_3COH + H_2O \text{ is fast}$$
What is the rate law for this reaction?

A. $\text{Rate} = k\left[(CH_3)_3CBr\right]$

B. $\text{Rate} = k\left[OH^-\right]$

C. $\text{Rate} = k\left[(CH_3)_3CBr\right]\left[OH^-\right]$

D. $\text{Rate} = k\left[(CH_3)_3CBr\right]^2$

A The first step will be rate-limiting. It will determine the rate for the entire reaction because it is slower than the other steps. This step is a unimolecular process with the rate given by answer A. Choice C would be correct if the reaction as a whole were one elementary step instead of three, but the stoichiometry of a reaction composed of multiple elementary steps cannot be used to predict a rate law.

81. Which statement about equilibrium is <u>not</u> true?

A. Equilibrium shifts to minimize the impact of changes.
B. Forward and reverse reactions have equal rates at equilibrium.
C. A closed container of air and water is at a vapor-liquid equilibrium if the humidity is constant.
D. The equilibrium between solid and dissolved forms is maintained when salt is added to an unsaturated solution.

D Choice A is a restatement of Le Chatelier's Principle. B is a definition of equilibrium. A constant humidity (Choice C) occurs if the rate of vaporization and condensation are equal, indicating equilibrium. No solid is present in an **un**saturated solution. If solid is added, all of it dissolves indicating a lack of equilibrium. D would be true for a saturated soution.

82. Which statements about reaction rates are true?

I. A catalyst will shift an equilibrium to favor product formation.
II. Catalysts increase the rate of forward and reverse reactions.
III. A greater temperature increases the chance that a molecular collision will overcome a reaction's activation energy.
IV. A catalytic converter contains a homogeneous catalyst.

A. I and II
B. II and III
C. II, III and IV
D. I, III, and IV

B Catalysts provide an alternate mechanism in both directions, but do not alter equilibrium (I is false, II is true). The kinetic energy of molecules increases with temperature, so the energy of their collisions increases also (III is true). Catalytic converters contain a heterogeneous catalyst (IV is false).

83. Write the equilibrium expression K_{eq} for the reaction
$CO_2(g) + H_2(g) \rightleftharpoons CO(g) + H_2O(l)$

A. $\dfrac{[CO][H_2O]}{[CO_2][H_2]^2}$

B. $\dfrac{[CO_2][H_2]}{[CO][H_2O]}$

C. $\dfrac{[CO][H_2O]}{[CO_2][H_2]}$

D. $\dfrac{[CO]}{[CO_2][H_2]}$

D Product concentrations are multiplied together in the numerator and reactant concentrations in the denominator, eliminating choice B. The stoichiometric coefficient of H_2 is one, eliminating choice A. For heterogeneous reactions, concentrations of pure liquids or solids are absent from the expression because they are constant, eliminating choice C. D is correct.

84. What could cause this change in the energy diagram of a reaction?

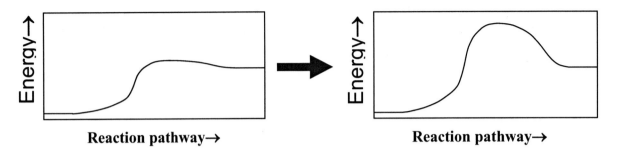

A. Adding catalyst to an endothermic reaction
B. Removing catalyst from an endothermic reaction
C. Adding catalyst to an exothermic reaction
D. Removing catalyst from an exothermic reaction

B   The products at the end of the reaction pathway are at a greater energy than the reactants, so the reaction is endothermic (narrowing down the answer to A or B). The maximum height on the diagram corresponds to activation energy. An increase in activation energy could be caused by removing a heterogeneous catalyst.

85. $BaSO_4$ (K_{sp} = 1X10^{-10}) is added to pure H_2O. How much is dissolved in 1 L of saturated solution?

A. 2 mg
B. 10 μg
C. 2 μg
D. 100 pg

A $BaSO_4(s) \rightleftharpoons Ba^{2+}(aq) + SO_4^{2-}(aq)$, therefore: $K_{sp} = \left[Ba^{2+}\right]\left[SO_4^{2-}\right]$.

In a saturated solution: $\left[Ba^{2+}\right] = \left[SO_4^{2-}\right] = \sqrt{1\times10^{-10}} = 1\times10^{-5}$ M.

The mass in one liter is found from the molarity:

$$1\times10^{-5} \frac{\text{mol } Ba^{2+} \text{ or } SO_4^{2-}}{L} \times \frac{1 \text{ mol dissolved } BaSO_4}{1 \text{ mol } Ba^{2+} \text{ or } SO_4^{2-}} \times \frac{(137+32+4\times16)g \ BaSO_4}{1 \text{ mol } BaSO_4}$$

$$= 0.002 \frac{g}{L} \ BaSO_4 \times 1 \text{ L solution} \times \frac{1000 \text{ mg}}{g} = 2 \text{ mg } BaSO_4$$

86. The exothermic reaction $2NO(g) + Br_2(g) \rightleftharpoons 2NOBr(g)$ is at equilibrium. According to LeChatelier's principle:

    A. Adding Br_2 will increase [NO].
    B. An increase in container volume (with T constant) will increase [NOBr].
    C. An increase in pressure (with T constant) will increase [NOBr].
    D. An increase in temperature (with P constant) will increase [NOBr].

C LeChatelier's principle predicts that equilibrium will shift to partially offset any change. Adding Br_2 will be partially offset by reducing [Br_2] and [NO] via a shift to the right (not choice A). For the remaining possibilities, we may write the reaction as: 3 moles $\rightleftharpoons$ 2 moles + heat. An increase in container volume will decrease pressure. This change will be partially offset by increasing the number of moles present, shifting the reaction to the left (not choice B). An increase in pressure will be offset by a decrease the number of moles present, shifting the reaction to the right (choice C, correct). Raising the temperature by adding heat will shift the reaction to the left (not choice D).

87. At a certain temperature, T, the equilibrium constant for the reaction $2NO(g) \rightleftharpoons N_2(g) + O_2(g)$ is $K_{eq} = 2 \times 10^3$. If a 1.0 L container at this temperature contains 90 mM N_2, 20 mM O_2, and 5 mM NO, what will occur?

    A. The reaction will make more N_2 and O_2.
    B. The reaction is at equilibrium.
    C. The reaction will make more NO.
    D. The temperature, T, is required to solve this problem.

A Calculate the reaction quotient at the actual conditions:

$$Q = \frac{[N_2][O_2]}{[NO]^2} = \frac{(0.090\ M)(0.020\ M)}{(0.005\ M)^2} = 72$$

This value is less than K_{eq}: $72 < 2 \times 10^3$, therefore $Q < K_{eq}$. To achieve equilibrium, the numerator of Q must be larger relative to the denominator. This occurs when products turn into reactants. Therefore NO will react to make more N_2 and O_2.

88. Which statement about acids and bases is <u>not</u> true?

    A. All strong acids ionize in water.
    B. All Lewis acids accept an electron pair.
    C. All Brønsted bases use OH^- as a proton acceptor.
    D. All Arrhenius acids form H^+ ions in water.

C   Choice A is the definition of a strong acid, choice B is the definition of a Lewis acid, and choice D is the definition of an Arrhenius acid. By definition, all Arrhenius bases form OH^- ions in water, and all Brønsted bases are proton acceptors. But not all Brønsted bases use OH^- as a proton acceptor. NH_3 is a Brønsted base for example.

89. Which of the following are listed from weakest to strongest acid?

    A. H_2SO_3, H_2SeO_3, H_2TeO_3
    B. $HBrO$, $HBrO_2$, $HBrO_3$, $HBrO_4$
    C. HI, HBr, HCl, HF
    D. H_3PO_4, $H_2PO_4^-$, HPO_4^{2-}

B   The electronegativity of the central atom decreases from S to Se to Te as period number increases in the same periodic table group. The acidity of the oxide also decreases. Choice B is correct because acid strength increases with the oxidation state of the central atom. C is wrong because HI, HBr, and HCl are all strong acids but HF is a weak acid. D is wrong because acid strength is greater for polyprotic acids.

90. NH₄F is dissolved in water. Which of the following are conjugate acid/base pairs present in the solution?

  I. NH_4^+/NH_4OH
  II. HF/F^-
  III. H_3O^+/H_2O
  IV. H_2O/OH^-

  A. I, II, and III
  B. I, III, and IV
  C. II and IV
  D. II, III, and IV

D NH₄F is soluble in water and completely dissociates to NH_4^+ and F^-. F^- is a weak base with HF as its conjugate acid (**II**). NH_4^+ is a weak acid with NH₃ as its conjugate base. A conjugate acid/base pair must have the form HX/X (where X is one lower charge than HX). NH_4^+/NH_4OH (**I**) is <u>not</u> a conjugate acid/base pair, eliminating choice A and B. H_3O^+/H_2O and H_2O/OH^- (**III and IV**) are always present in water and in all aqueous solutions as conjugate acid/base pairs. All of the following equilibrium reactions occur in NH₄F(*aq*):

$$NH_4^+(aq) + OH^-(aq) \rightleftharpoons NH_3(aq) + H_2O(l)$$
$$F^-(aq) + H_3O^+(aq) \rightleftharpoons HF(aq) + H_2O(l)$$
$$2H_2O(l) \rightleftharpoons H_3O^+(aq) + OH^-(aq)$$

91. What are the pH and the pOH of 0.010 M HNO₃(*aq*)?

  A. pH = 1.0, pOH = 9.0
  B. pH = 2.0, pOH = 12.0
  C. pH = 2.0, pOH = 8.0
  D. pH = 8.0, pOH = 6.0

B HNO₃ is a strong acid, so it completely dissociates:

$$\left[H^+ \right] = 0.010 \text{ M} = 1.0 \times 10^{-2} \text{ M.}$$
$$pH = -\log_{10}\left[H^+ \right] = -\log_{10}\left(1.0 \times 10^{-2} \right) = 2.0 \text{ (choices B or C).}$$
$$\text{From } pH + pOH = 14: \ pOH = 12.0 \text{ (choice B).}$$

92. What is the pH of a buffer made of 0.128 M sodium formate (HCOONa) and 0.072 M formic acid (HCOOH)? The pK_a of formic acid is 3.75.

  A. 2.0
  B. 3.0
  C. 4.0
  D. 5.0

C From the pK_a, we may find the K_a of formic acid:
$$K_a = 10^{-pK_a} = 10^{-3.75} = 1.78 \times 10^{-4}$$
This is the equilibrium constant:
$$K_a = \frac{[H^+][HCOO^-]}{[HCOOH]} = 1.78 \times 10^{-4} \text{ for the dissociation:}$$
$$HCOOH \rightleftharpoons H^+ + HCOO^-.$$
The pH is found by solving for the H^+ concentration:
$$[H^+] = K_a \frac{[HCOOH]}{[HCOO^-]} = (1.78 \times 10^{-4})\frac{0.072}{0.128} = 1.0 \times 10^{-4} \text{ M}$$
$$pH = -\log_{10}[H^+] = -\log_{10}(1.0 \times 10^{-4}) = 4.0 \text{ (choice C)}$$

93. A sample of 50.0 ml KOH is titrated with 0.100 M $HClO_4$. The initial buret reading is 1.6 ml and the reading at the endpoint is 22.4 ml. What is [KOH]?

  A. 0.0416 M
  B. 0.0481 M
  C. 0.0832 M
  D. 0.0962 M

A $HClO_4$ and KOH are both strong electrolytes. If you are good at memorizing formulas, solve the problem this way:
$$C_{unknown} = \frac{C_{known}(V_{final} - V_{initial})}{V_{unknown}} = \frac{0.100 \text{ M}(22.4 \text{ ml} - 1.6 \text{ ml})}{50.0 \text{ ml}} = 0.0416 \text{ M}.$$
The problem may also be solved by finding the moles of known substance:
$$0.100 \frac{mol}{L} \times \frac{1 L}{1000 \text{ mL}} \times (22.4 \text{ mL} - 1.6 \text{ mL}) = 0.00208 \text{ mol } HClO_4$$
This will neutralize 0.00208 mol KOH, and $\frac{0.00208 \text{ mol}}{0.0500 \text{ L}} = 0.0416$ M

94. Rank the following from lowest to highest pH. Assume a small volume for the added component:

I. 0.01 mol HCl added to 1 L H_2O
II. 0.01 mol HI added to 1 L of an acetic acid/sodium acetate solution at pH 4.0
III. 0.01 mol NH_3 added to 1 L H_2O
IV. 0.1 mol HNO_3 added to 1 L of a 0.1 M $Ca(OH)_2$ solution

A. I < II < III < IV
B. I < II < IV < III
C. II < I < III < IV
D. II < I < IV < III

A HCl is a strong acid. Therefore solution I has a <u>pH of 2</u> because
$$pH = -\log_{10}\left[H^+\right] = -\log_{10}(0.01) = 2.$$

HI is also a strong acid and would have a pH of 2 at this concentration in water, but the buffer will prevent pH from dropping this low. Solution II will have a pH <u>above 2</u> and below 4, eliminating choices C and D.

If a strong base were in solution III, its pOH would be 2. Using the equation pH + pOH = 14, its pH would be 12. Because NH_3 is a weak base, the pH of solution III will be greater than 7 and <u>less than 12</u>.

A neutralization reaction occurs in solution IV between 0.1 mol of H^+ from the strong acid HNO_3 and <u>0.2 mol of OH^-</u> from the strong base $Ca(OH)_2$. Each mole of $Ca(OH)_2$ contributes two base equivalents for the neutralization reaction. The base is the excess reagent, and 0.1 mol of OH^- remain after the reaction. This resulting solution will have a pOH of 1 and a <u>pH of 13</u>.

A is correct because: 2 < between 2 and 4 < between 7 and 12 < 13

95. The curve below resulted from the titration of a _____ _____ with a _____ _____ titrant.

A. weak acid, strong base
B. weak base, strong acid
C. strong acid, strong base
D. strong base, strong acid

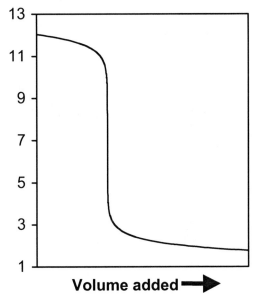

D The pH is above 7 initially and decreases, so an acid titrant is neutralizing a base. This eliminates A and C. The maximum slope (equivalence point) at the neutral pH of 7 indicates a strong base titrated with a strong acid, D.

96. Which statement about thermochemistry is true?

A. Particles in a system move about less freely at high entropy
B. Water at 100 °C has the same internal energy as water vapor at 100°C
C. A decrease in the order of a system corresponds to an increase in entropy.
D. At its sublimation temperature, dry ice has a higher entropy than gaseous CO_2

C At high entropy, particles have a large freedom of molecular motion (A is false). Water and water vapor at 100 °C contain the same translational kinetic energy, but water vapor has additional internal energy in the form of resisting the intermolecular attractions between molecules (B is false). We also know water vapor has a higher internal energy because heat must be added to boil water. Entropy may be thought of as the disorder in a system (C is correct). Sublimation is the phase change from solid to gas, and there is less freedom of motion for particles in solids than in gases. Solid CO_2 (dry ice) has a lower entropy than gaseous CO_2 because entropy decreases during a phase change that prevents molecular motion (D is false).

97. What is the heat change of 36.0 g H_2O at atmospheric pressure when its temperature is reduced from 125 °C to 40. °C? Use the following data:

A. −92.0 kJ
B. −10.8 kJ
C. 10.8 kJ
D. 92.0 kJ

Values for water	
Heat capacity of solid	37.6 J/mol•°C
Heat capacity of liquid	75.3 J/mol•°C
Heat capacity of gas	33.1 J/mol•°C
Heat of fusion	6.02 kJ/mol
Heat of vaporization	40.67 kJ/mol

A Heat is evolved from the substance as it cools, so the heat change will be negative, eliminating choices C and D. Data in the table are given using moles, so the first step is to convert the mass of water to moles:

$$36.0 \text{ g } H_2O \times \frac{1 \text{ mol } H_2O}{18.02 \text{ g } H_2O} = 2.00 \text{ mol } H_2O$$

There are three contributions to the heat evolved. First, the heat evolved when cooling the vapor from 125 °C to 100 °C is found from the heat capacity of the gas:

$$q_1 = n \times C \times \Delta T = 2.00 \text{ mol } H_2O(g) \times 33.1 \frac{J}{mol \text{ °C}} \times (100 \text{ °C} - 125 \text{ °C})$$
$$= -1655 \text{ J to cool vapor}$$

Next, the heat evolved during condensation is found from the heat of vaporization:

$$q_2 = n \times (-\Delta H_{vaporization}) = 2.00 \text{ mol } H_2O \times (-40.67 \frac{kJ}{mol})$$
$$= -81.34 \text{ kJ to condense vapor}$$

Incorrect answer B results from using a heat of vaporization of 40.67 J/mol instead of kJ/mol.

Finally, the heat evolved when cooling the liquid from 100 °C to 40 °C is found from the heat capacity of the liquid:

$$q_3 = n \times C \times \Delta T = 2.00 \text{ mol } H_2O(g) \times 75.3 \frac{J}{mol \text{ °C}} \times (40 \text{ °C} - 100 \text{ °C})$$
$$= -9036 \text{ J to cool liquid}$$

The total heat change is the sum of these contributions:

$$q = q_1 + q_2 + q_3 = -1.655 \text{ kJ} + (-81.34 \text{ kJ}) + (-9.036 \text{ kJ}) = -92.03 \text{ kJ}$$
$$= -92.0 \text{ kJ (Choice A)}$$

98. What is the standard heat of combustion of $CH_4(g)$? Use the following
data:

A. −890.3 kJ/mol
B. −604.5 kJ/mol
C. −252.9 kJ/mol
D. −182.5 kJ/mol

Standard heats of formation	
$CH_4(g)$	−74.8 kJ/mol
$CO_2(g)$	−393.5 kJ/mol
$H_2O(l)$	−285.8 kJ/mol

A   First we must write a balanced equation for the combustion of CH_4. The
balanced equation is:

$$CH_4(g) + 2O_2(g) \rightarrow CO_2(g) + 2H_2O(l).$$

The heat of combustion may be found from the sum of the productions minus
the sum of the reactants of the heats of formation:

$$\Delta H_{rxn} = H_{product\ 1} + H_{product\ 2} + \ldots - \left(H_{reactant\ 1} + H_{reactant\ 2} + \ldots\right)$$

$$= \Delta H_f^\circ(CO_2) + 2\Delta H_f^\circ(H_2O) - \left(\Delta H_f^\circ(CH_4) + 2\Delta H_f^\circ(O_2)\right)$$

The heat of formation of an element in its most stable form is zero by

definition, so $\Delta H_f^\circ(O_2(g)) = 0 \ \dfrac{kJ}{mol}$, and the remaining values are found from

the table:

$$\Delta H_{rxn} = -393.5 \ \frac{kJ}{mol} + 2(-285.8 \ \frac{kJ}{mol}) - \left(-74.8 \ \frac{kJ}{mol} + 2(0)\right) = -890.3 \ \frac{kJ}{mol} \ \text{(choice A)}$$

99. Which reaction creates products at a lower total entropy than the
reactants?

A. Dissolution of table salt: $NaCl(s) \rightarrow Na^+(aq) + Cl^-(aq)$
B. Oxidation of iron: $4Fe(s) + 3O_2(g) \rightarrow 2Fe_2O_3(s)$
C. Dissociation of ozone: $O_3(g) \rightarrow O_2(g) + O(g)$
D. Vaporization of butane: $C_4H_{10}(l) \rightarrow C_4H_{10}(g)$

B   Choice A is incorrect because two particles are at a greater entropy than one
and because ions in solution have more freedom of motion than a solid. For
B (the correct answer), the products are at a lower entropy than the reactants
because there are fewer product molecules and they are all in the solid form
but one of the reactants is a gas. Reaction B is still spontaneous because it
is highly exothermic. For C, there are more product molecules than
reactants, and for D, the gas phase is always at a higher entropy than the
liquid.

100. **Which statement about reactions is true?**

    A. All spontaneous reactions are both exothermic and cause an increase in entropy.

    B. An endothermic reaction that increases the order of the system cannot be spontaneous.

    C. A reaction can be non-spontaneous in one direction and also non-spontaneous in the opposite direction.

    D. Melting snow is an exothermic process

B All reactions that are both exothermic and cause an increase in entropy will be spontaneous, but the converse (choice A) is not true. Some spontaneous reactions are exothermic but decrease entropy and some are endothermic and increase entropy. Choice B is correct. The reverse reaction of a non-spontaneous reaction (choice C) will be spontaneous. Melting snow (choice D) requires heat. Therefore it is an endothermic process

101. **10. kJ of heat are added to one kilogram of Iron at 10. °C. What is its final temperature? The specific heat of iron is 0.45 J/g•°C.**

    A. 22 °C

    B. 27 °C

    C. 32 °C

    D. 37 °C

C The expression for heat as a function of temperature change:

$$q = n \times C \times \Delta T$$

may be rearranged to solve for the temperature change:

$$\Delta T = \frac{q}{n \times C}.$$

In this case, n is a mass and C is the specific heat of iron:

$$\Delta T = \frac{10000 \text{ J}}{1000 \text{ g} \times 0.45 \dfrac{\text{J}}{\text{g °C}}} = 22 \text{ °C}.$$

This is not the final temperature (choice A is incorrect). It is the temperature difference between the initial and final temperature.

$$\Delta T = T_{final} - T_{initial} = 22 \text{ °C}$$

Solving for the final temperature gives us:

$$T_{final} = \Delta T + T_{initial} = 22 \text{ °C} + 10 \text{ °C} = 32 \text{ °C (Choice C)}$$

102. Which reaction is <u>not</u> a redox process?

A. Combustion of octane: $2C_8H_{18} + 25O_2 \rightarrow 16CO_2 + 18H_2O$

B. Depletion of a lithium battery: $Li + MnO_2 \rightarrow LiMnO_2$

C. Corrosion of aluminum by acid: $2Al + 6HCl \rightarrow 2AlCl_3 + 3H_2$

D. Taking an antacid for heartburn:
$CaCO_3 + 2HCl \rightarrow CaCl_2 + H_2CO_3 \rightarrow CaCl_2 + CO_2 + H_2O$

D The oxidation state of atoms is altered in a redox process. During combustion (choice A), the carbon atoms are oxidized from an oxidation number of –4 to +4. Oxygen atoms are reduced from an oxidation number of 0 to –2. All batteries (choice B) generate electricity by forcing electrons from a redox process through a circuit. Li is oxidized from 0 in the metal to +1 in the $LiMnO_2$ salt. Mn is reduced from +4 in manganese(IV) oxide to +3 in lithium manganese(III) oxide salt. Corrosion (choice C) is due to oxidation. Al is oxidized from 0 to +3. H is reduced from +1 to 0. Acid-base neutralization (choice D) transfers a proton (an H atom with an oxidation state of +1) from an acid to a base. The oxidation state of all atoms remains unchanged (Ca at +2, C at +4, O at –2, H at +1, and Cl at –1), so D is correct. Note that choices C and D both involve an acid. The availability of electrons in aluminum metal favors electron transfer but the availability of CO_3^{2-} as a proton acceptor favors proton transfer.

103. Given the following heats of reaction:

$\Delta H = -0.3$ kJ / mol for $\qquad Fe(s) + CO_2(g) \rightarrow FeO(s) + CO(g)$

$\Delta H = 5.7$ kJ / mol for $\qquad 2Fe(s) + 3CO_2(g) \rightarrow Fe_2O_3(s) + 3CO(g)$

and $\Delta H = 4.5$ kJ / mol for $\quad 3FeO(s) + CO_2(g) \rightarrow Fe_3O_4(s) + CO(g)$

use Hess's Law to determine the heat of reaction for:

$$3Fe_2O_3(s) + CO(g) \rightarrow 2Fe_3O_4(s) + CO_2(g)?$$

A. −10.8 kJ/mol
B. −9.9 kJ/mol
C. −9.0 kJ/mol
D. −8.1 kJ/mol

B We are interested in $3Fe_2O_3$ as a reactant. Only the second reaction contains this molecule, so we will take three times the opposite of the second reaction. We are interested in $2Fe_3O_4$ as a product, so we will take two times the third reaction. An intermediate result is:

$3Fe_2O_3(s) + 9CO(g) \rightarrow 6Fe(s) + 9CO_2(g) \qquad \Delta H = -3 \times 5.7$ kJ/mol $= -17.1$ kJ/mol

$6FeO(s) + 2CO_2(g) \rightarrow 2Fe_3O_4(s) + 2CO(g) \qquad \Delta H = 2 \times 4.5$ kJ/mol $= 9.0$ kJ/mol

$3Fe_2O_3(s) + 6FeO(s) + 7CO(g) \rightarrow$
$\qquad 2Fe_3O_4(s) + 6Fe(s) + 7CO_2(g)$

$\Delta H = (-17.1 + 9.0)$ kJ/mol $= -8.1$ kJ/mol

However, D is not the correct answer because it is not ΔH for the reaction of the problem statement. We may use six times the first reaction to eliminate both FeO and Fe from the intermediate result and obtain the reaction of interest:

$3Fe_2O_3(s) + 6FeO(s) + 7CO(g) \rightarrow$
$\qquad 2Fe_3O_4(s) + 6Fe(s) + 7CO_2(g)$

$\Delta H = -8.1$ kJ/mol

$6Fe(s) + 6CO_2(g) \rightarrow 6FeO(s) + 6CO(g) \qquad \Delta H = 6 \times (-0.3$ kJ/mol$) = -1.8$ kJ/mol

$3Fe_2O_3(s) + CO(g) \rightarrow 2Fe_3O_4(s) + CO(g)$

$\Delta H = (-8.1 + -1.8)$ kJ/mol
$= -9.9$ kJ/mol (choice B)

104. What is the oxidant in the reaction: $2H_2S + SO_2 \rightarrow 3S + 2H_2O$?

    A. H_2S
    B. SO_2
    C. S
    D. H_2O

B The S atom in H_2S has an oxidation number of –2 and is oxidized by SO_2 (the oxidant, choice B) to elemental sulfer (oxidation number = 0). The S atom in SO_2 has an oxidation number of +4 and is reduced. The two half-reactions are:

$$SO_2 + 4e^- + 4H^+ \xrightarrow{\text{reduction}} S + 2H_2O$$

$$2H_2S \xrightarrow{\text{oxidation}} 2S + 4e^- + 4H^+$$

105. Molten NaCl is subjected to electrolysis. What reaction takes place at the cathode?

    A. $2Cl^-(l) \rightarrow Cl_2(g) + 2e^-$
    B. $Cl_2(g) + 2e^- \rightarrow 2Cl^-(l)$
    C. $Na^+(l) + e^- \rightarrow Na(l)$
    D. $Na^+(l) \rightarrow Na(l) + e^-$

C Reduction (choices B and C) always occurs at the cathode. Molten NaCl is composed of ions in liquid form before electrolysis (answer C). A and D are oxidation reactions, and D is also not properly balanced because a +1 charge is on the left and a –1 charge is on the right. The two half-reactions are:

$$Na^+(l) + e^- \xrightarrow{\text{reduction at cathode}} Na(l)$$

$$2Cl^-(l) \xrightarrow{\text{oxidation at anode}} Cl_2(g) + 2e^-$$

The net reaction is:

$$2NaCl(l) \rightarrow 2Na(l) + Cl_2(g)$$

106. What is the purpose of the salt bridge in a voltaic cell?

    A. To receive electrons from the oxidation half-reaction
    B. To relieve the buildup of positive charge in the anode half-cell
    C. To conduct electron flow
    D. To permit positive ions to flow from the cathode half-cell to the anode half-cell

D   The anode receives electrons from the oxidation half-reaction (choice A) and the circuit conducts electron flow (choice C) to the cathode which supplies electrons for the reduction half-reaction. This flow of electrons from the anode to the cathode is relieved by a flow of ions through the salt bridge from the cathode to the anode (answer D). The salt bridge relieves the buildup of positive charge in the cathode half-cell (choice B is incorrect).

107. Given $E°=-2.37$ V for $Mg^{2+}(aq)+2e^-\rightarrow Mg(s)$ and $E°=0.80$ V for $Ag^+(aq)+e^- \rightarrow Ag(s)$, what is the standard potential of a voltaic cell composed of a piece of magnesium dipped in a 1 M Ag^+ solution and a piece of silver dipped in 1 M Mg^{2+}?

    A. 0.77 V
    B. 1.57 V
    C. 3.17 V
    D. 3.97 V

C $Ag^+(aq)+e^-\rightarrow Ag(s)$ has a larger value for $E°$ (reduction potential) than $Mg^{2+}(aq)+2e^-\rightarrow Mg(s)$. Therefore, in the cell described, reduction will occur at the Ag electrode and it will be the cathode. Using the equation:

$$E^o_{cell} = E^o(\text{cathode}) - E^o(\text{anode}), \text{ we obtain:}$$

$$E^o_{cell} = 0.80 \text{ V} - (-2.37 \text{ V}) = 3.17 \text{ V (Answer C)}.$$

Choice D results from the incorrect assumption that electrode potentials depend on the amount of material present. The balanced net reaction for the cell is:

$$Mg(s) \rightarrow Mg^{2+}(aq) + 2e^- \qquad\qquad E^o_{ox} = 2.37 \text{ V}$$

$$\underline{2Ag^+(aq) + 2e^- \rightarrow 2Ag(s) \qquad\qquad E^o_{red} = 0.80 \text{ V (\textbf{not} 1.60 V)}}$$

$$Mg(s) + 2Ag^+(aq) \rightarrow 2Ag(s) + Mg^{2+}(aq) \quad E^o_{cell} = 3.17 \text{ V (\textbf{not} 3.97 V)}$$

108. A proper name for this hydrocarbon is:

A. 4,5-dimethyl-6-hexene
B. 2,3-dimethyl-1-hexene
C. 4,5-dimethyl-6-hexyne
D. 2-methyl-3-propyl-1-butene

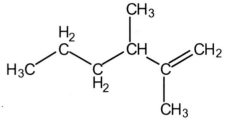

B The hydrocarbon contains a double bond and no triple bonds, so it is an alkene. Choice C describes an alkyne. The longest carbon chain is six carbons long, corresponding to a parent molecule of 1-hexene (circled to the left). Choice D is an improper name because it names the molecule as a substituted butane, using a shorter chain as the parent molecule.

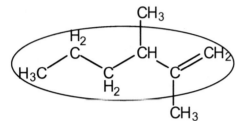

Finally, the lowest possible set of locant numbers must be used. Choice A is an improper name because the larger possible set of locant numbers is chosen.

109. An IUPAC approved name for this molecule is:

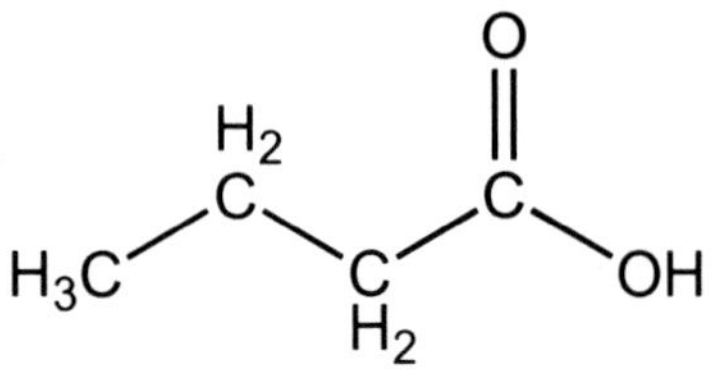

A. butanal
B. propanal
C. butanoic acid
D. propanoic acid

C The COOH group means that the molecule is a carboxylic acid and its name will use the suffix –oic acid. The presence of 4 carbon atoms means the prefix butan- will be used. An alternate name for the molecule is butyric acid. Choices A and B would be used for aldehydes (CHO group). Choices B and D would be used for 3 carbon atoms:

butanal (also called butyraldehyde):

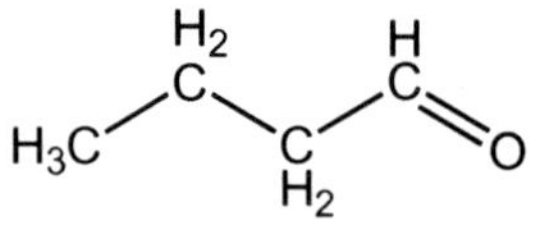

propanal (also called propionaldehyde):

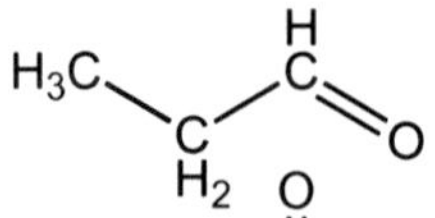

propanoic acid (also called propionic acid):

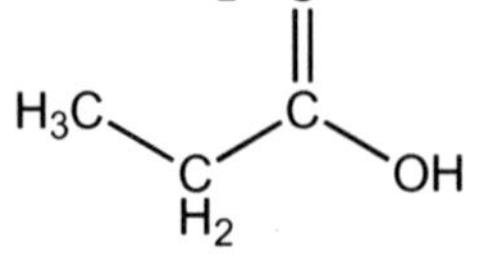

110. Which molecule has a systematic name of methyl ethanoate?

A.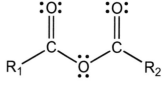

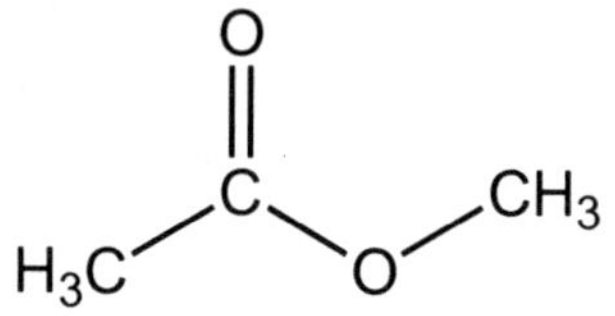

B.

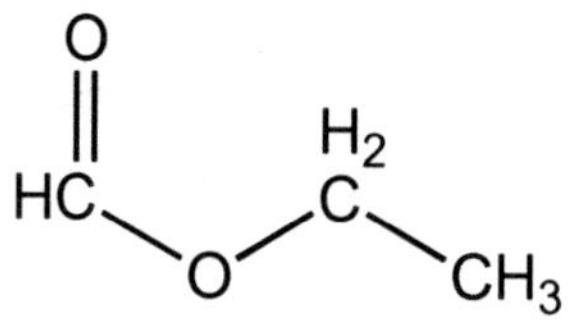

C.

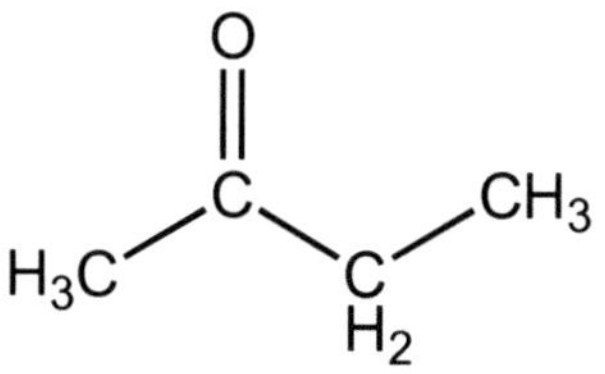

D.

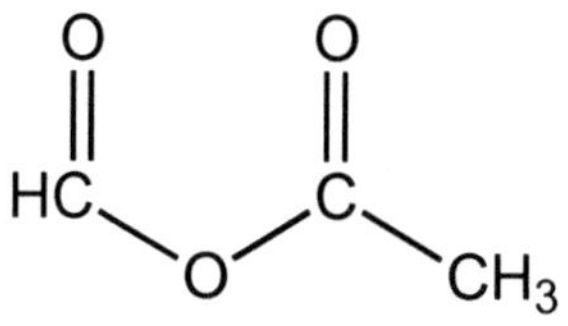

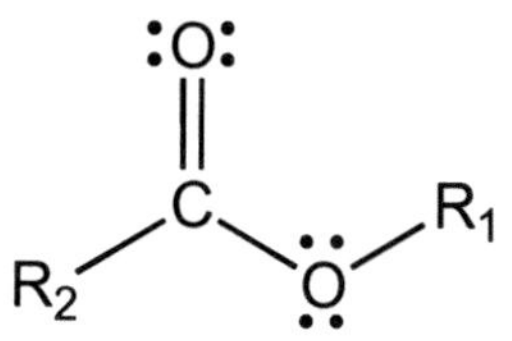

A The suffix –*oate* is used for esters. The ester group is shown to the right. Choice C is a ketone (ethyl methyl ketone or 2-butanone). The ketone group is shown to the left. Choice D is an acid anhydride (ethanoic methanoic anhydride). The acid anhydride group is shown below to the right. A and B are both esters. The hydrocarbon R_2 with the carbonyl group receives the –*oate* suffix and the hydrocarbon R_1 with the -*yl* suffix is attached to the other oxygen. Choice B is ethyl methanoate and A is correct.

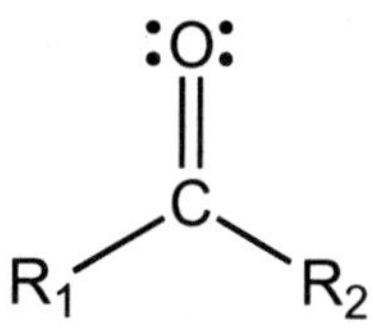

111. This compound contains an:

A. alkene, carboxylic acid, ester, and ketone
B. aldehyde, alkyne, ester, and ketone
C. aldehyde, alkene, carboxylic acid, and ester
D. acid anhydride, aldehyde, alkene, and amine

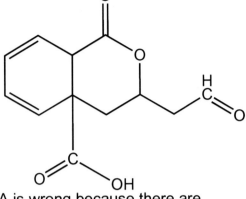

C The derivatives are circled below:

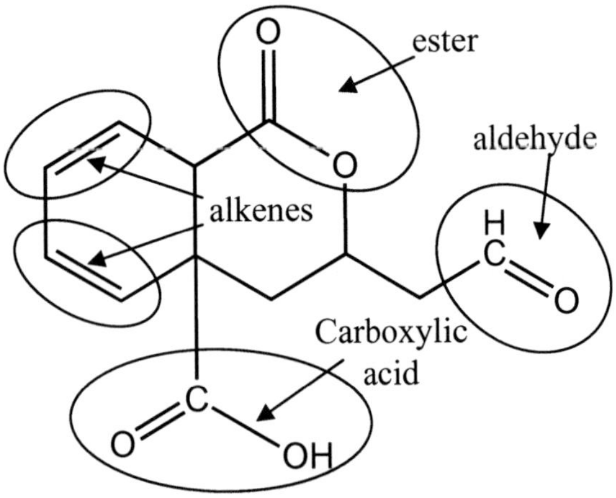

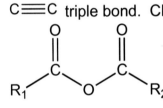

Choice A is wrong because there are no ketones in the molecule. A ketone has a carbonyl group linked to two hydrocarbons as shown to the right. All the carbonyls in the molecule are linked to at least one oxygen atom. Choice B is wrong because there are no ketones and no alkynes in the molecule. An alkyne contains a

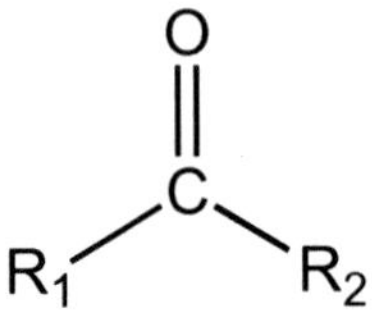

C≡C triple bond. Choice D is wrong because there are no acid anhydrides (shown to the left) and no amines (shown to the right). Amines require at least one N-C bond and there are no nitrogen atoms in the molecule.

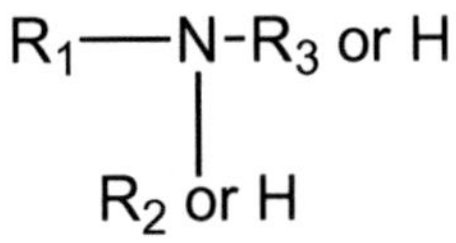

112. Which group of scientists made contributions in the same area of chemistry?

A. Volta, Kekulé, Faraday, London
B. Hess, Joule, Kelvin, Gibbs
C. Boyle, Charles, Arrhenius, Pauli
D. Davy, Mendeleev, Ramsay, Galvani

B Hess, Joule, Kelvin, and Gibbs all contributed to thermochemistry and have thermodynamic entities named after them. Volta, Faraday, and Galvani (choice D) contributed to electrochemistry, Kekulé to organic chemistry, London to chemical bonding, Boyle and Charles to gas laws, Arrhenius to acid/base chemistry and thermochemstry, Pauli to quantum theory, Davy and Ramsay to element isolation, and Mendeleev to the periodic table.

113. Which of the following pairs are isomers?

I.

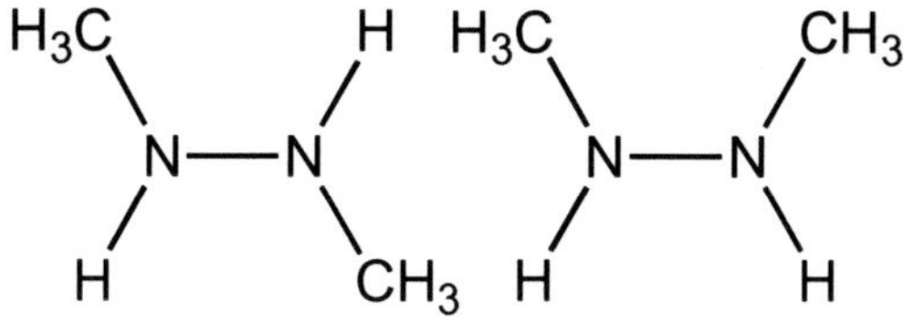

II. pentanal 2-pentanone

III.

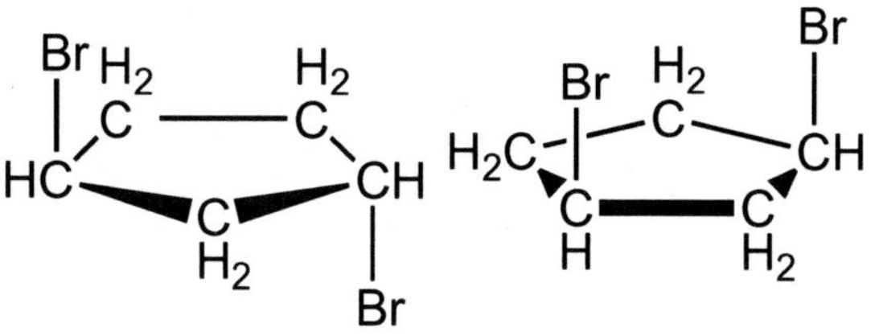

IV.

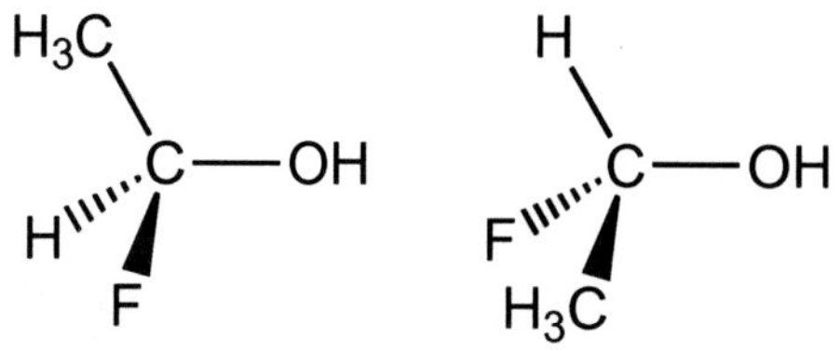

A. I and IV
B. II and III
C. I, II, and III
D. I, II, III, and IV

B In pair I, the N—N bond may freely rotate in the molecule because it is not a double bond. The identical molecule is represented twice.

For pair II, pentanal is

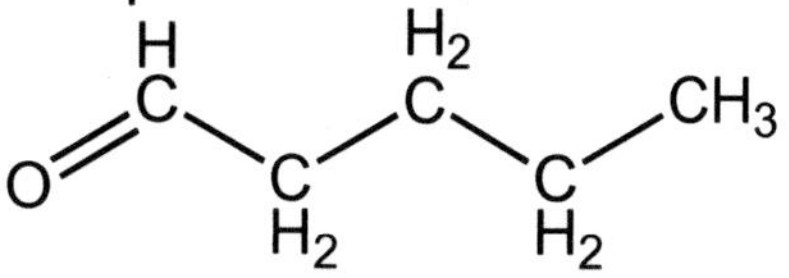

and 2-pentanone is:

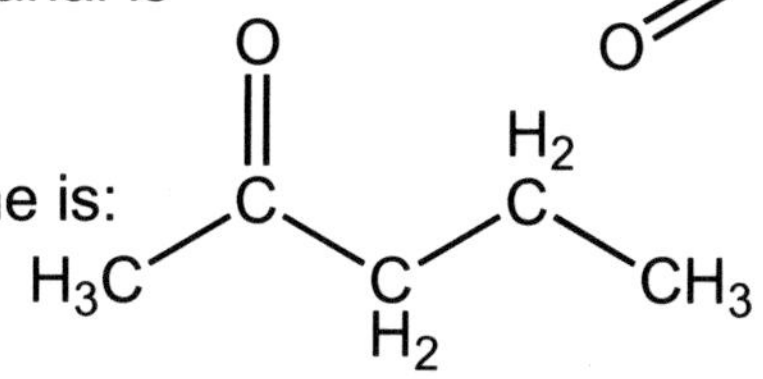

Both molecules are $C_5H_{10}O$, and they are isomers because they have the same formula with a different arrangement of atoms.

In pair III, both molecules are 1,3-dibromocyclopentane, $C_5H_8Br_2$. In the first molecule, the bromines are in a *trans* configuration, and in the second molecule, they are *cis*. The two molecules are also viewed from different perspectives. Unlike pair I, no bond rotation may occur because the intervening atoms are locked into place by the ring, so they are different arrangements and are isomers.

In pair IV (1-fluoroethanol), there is a chiral center, so stereoisomers are possible, but as in pair I, the same molecule is represented twice. Rotating the C-O bond indicates that the two structures are superimposable. This molecule: to the right is a stereoisomer to the molecule represented in IV. The answer is B (pairs II and III).

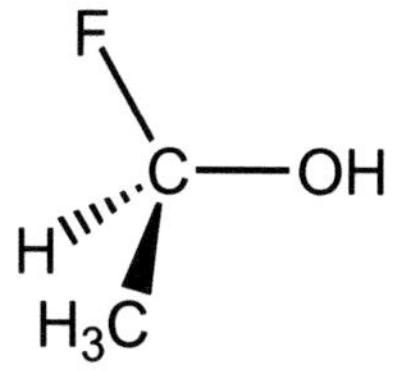

114. **Which instrument would be most useful for separating two different proteins from a mixture?**

    A. UV/Vis spectrophotometer
    B. Mass spectrometer
    C. Gas chromatograph
    D. Liquid chromatograph

D UV/Vis spectrophotometry measures the light at ultraviolet and visible wavelengths that can pass through the mixture, and mass spectrometry determines molecular weights. Both might be used to find the concentration of each protein, but neither is a separation technique. Gas chromatography is used for small molecules in the gas phase. Proteins are too large to exist in the gas phase. Liquid chromatography (answer D) is used to separate large molecules.

115. **Classify these biochemicals.**

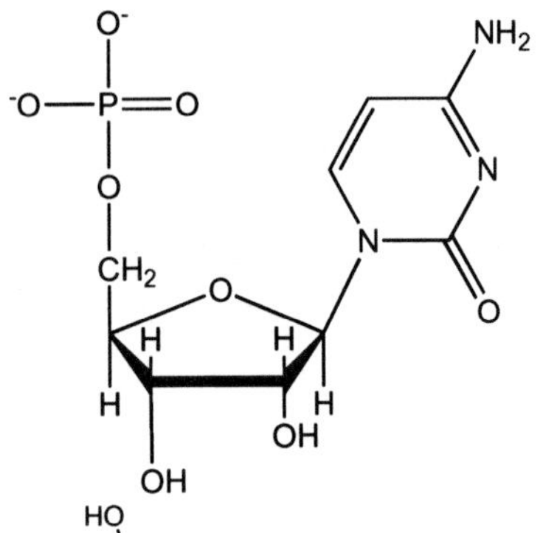

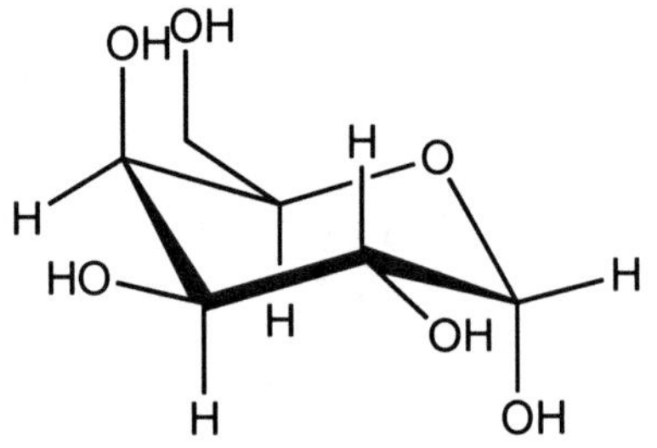

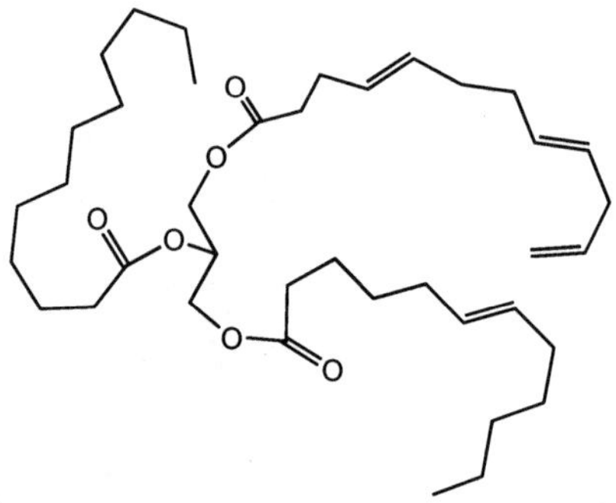

    A. I-nucleotide, II-sugar, III-peptide, IV-fat
    B. I-disaccharide, II-sugar, III-fatty acid, IV-polypeptide
    C. I-disaccharide, II-amino acid, III-fatty acid, IV- polysaccharide
    D. I-nucleotide, II-sugar, III-triacylglyceride, and IV-DNA

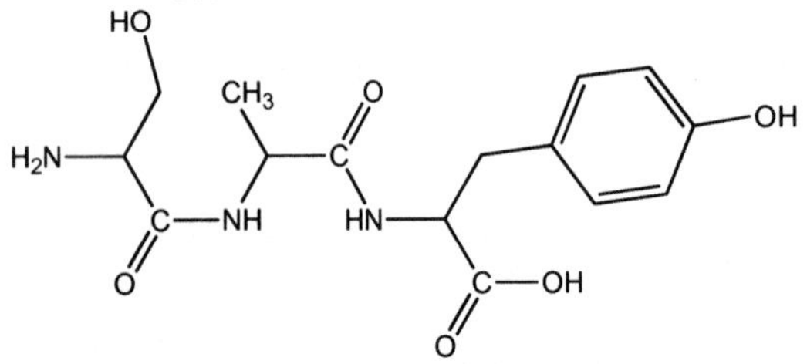

A I is a phosphate (PO_4) linked to a sugar and an amine: a nucleotide. II has the formula $C_nH_{2n}O_n$, indicative of a sugar. III contains three amino acids linked with peptide bonds. It is a tripeptide. IV is a triacylglyceride, a fat molecule.

116. You create a solution of 2.00 µg/ml of a pigment and divide the solution into 12 samples. You give four samples each to three teams of students. They use a spectrophotometer to determine the pigment concentration. Here is their data:

Team	Concentration (µg/ml)			
	sample 1	sample 2	sample 3	sample 4
1	1.98	1.93	1.92	1.88
2	1.70	1.72	1.69	1.70
3	1.78	1.99	2.87	2.20

Which of the following are true?

A. Team 1 has the most precise data
B. Team 3 has the most accurate data in spite of it having low precision
C. The data from team 2 is characteristic of a systematic error
D. The data from team 1 is more characteristic of random error than the data from team 3.

C For choice A, the data from team 2 are closer to the mean for team 2 than the data from team 1 are to its mean. Therefore, team 1's data does not have the most precision.

For choice B, the mean from team 1 is near 1.9 µg/ml (we don't need to calculate exact values). It differs from the actual value by 0.1 µg/ml. The mean from team 2 is near 1.7 µg/ml and is inaccurate by 0.3 µg/ml. The mean from team 3 is not obvious, but it may be calculated as 2.21 µg/ml, differing from the actual value by about 0.2 µg/ml. Team 3's data is less accurate than the data from team 1.

The data from team 2 is clustered close to a central value but this value is wrong. Low accuracy with high precision is indicative of a systematic error. (C is correct).

For choice D, a lack of precision is indicative of random error, and the data from team 1 is more precise than the data from team 3.

117. Which pair of measurements have an identical meaning?

    A. 32 micrometers and 0.032 g
    B. 26 nm and 2.60×10^{-8} m
    C. 3.01×10^{-5} m^3 and 30.1 ml
    D. 0.0020 L and 20 cm^3

C For A, the prefix *micro—* indicates 10^{-6}. 32 micrograms is 0.000032 g. For B, the two measurements do not have the same meaning because they differ in the number of significant figures. 26 nm is 2.6×10^{-8} m. The symbol "n" for *nano—* indicates 10^{-9}. For C and D, unit conversions between cubic meters and liters are required.

$$\text{For C: } 3.01 \times 10^{-5} \text{ m}^3 \times \frac{1000 \text{ L}}{1 \text{ m}^3} \times \frac{1000 \text{ ml}}{1 \text{ L}} = 30.1 \text{ ml (C is correct).}$$

$$\text{For D: } 0.0020 \text{ L} \times \frac{1 \text{ m}^3}{1000 \text{ L}} \times \frac{(100)^3 \text{ cm}^3}{1 \text{ m}^3} = 2.0 \text{ cm}^3 \text{ (D is incorrect).}$$

118. Match the instrument with the quantity it measures

    I.   eudiometer
    II. calorimeter
    III. manometer
    IV. hygrometer

    A. I-volume, II-mass, III-radioactivity, IV-humidity
    B. I-volume, II-heat, III-pressure, IV-humidity
    C. I-viscosity, II-mass, III-pressure, IV-surface tension
    D. I-viscosity, II-heat, III-radioactivity, IV-surface tension

B A eudiometer is a straight tube used to measure gas volume by liquid exclusion. A calorimeter is a device used to measure changes in heat. A manometer is a U-shaped tube used to measure pressure. A hygrometer measures humidity (Answer B). Mass is measured with a balance, radioactivity is measured with a Geiger counter or scintillation counter. Viscosity is measured with a viscometer, surface tension is measured by several different techniques.

119. Four nearly identical gems from the same mineral are weighed using different balances. Their masses are:

3.4533 g, 3.459 g, 3.4656 g, 3.464 g.

The four gems are then collected and added to a volumetric cylinder containing 10.00 ml of liquid, and a new volume of 14.97 ml is read. What is the average mass of the four stones and what is the density of the mineral?

A. 3.460 g, and 2.78 g/ml
B. 3.460 g and 2.79 g/ml
C. 3.4605 g and 2.78 g/ml
D. 3.461 g and 2.79 g/ml

B The average mass is the sum of the four readings divided by four:

(3.4533 g + 3.459 g + 3.4656 g + 3.464 g)/4 = 3.460475 g (caculator value)

This value must be rounded off to three significant digits <u>after the decimal point</u> because this is the lowest precision of the added values. The four is an exact number. This means rounding downwards to 3.460 g, eliminating choices C and D. The volume of the collected stones is found from the increase in the level read off the cylinder:

14.97 ml − 10.00 ml = 4.97 ml

The density is found by dividing the sum of the masses by this volume:

$$\frac{3.4533 \text{ g} + 3.459 \text{ g} + 3.4656 \text{ g} + 3.464 \text{ g}}{4.97 \text{ ml}} = \frac{13.8419 \text{ g}}{4.97 \text{ ml}} = 2.7850905 \text{ g/ml (caculator value)}$$

This value must be rounded off to three <u>total</u> significant digits because this is the lower precision of the numerator and the denominator. The first insignificant digit is a 5. In this case there are additional non-zero digits after the 5, so rounding occurs upwards to 2.79 g/ml (answer B).

120. Which list includes equipment that would **not** be used in vacuum filtration.

    A. Rubber tubing, Florence flask, Büchner funnel
    B. Vacuum pump, Hirsch funnel, rubber stopper with a single hole
    C. Aspirator, filter paper, filter flask
    D. Lab stand, clamp, filter trap

A Florence flasks are round-bottomed and are used for uniform heating. They do not have the hose barb or the thick wall needed to serve as a filter flask during vacuum filtration. Only a designated filter flask should be used during vacuum filtration. Every other piece of equipment could be used in filtration. A spatula is often used to scrape dried product off of filter paper.

121. Which of the following statements about lab safety is **not** true?

    A. Corrosive chemicals should be stored below eye level.
    B. A chemical splash on the eye or skin should be rinsed for 15 minutes in cold water.
    C. MSDS means "Material Safety Data Sheet."
    D. A student should "stop, drop, and roll" if their clothing catches fire in the lab.

D In the lab, the safety shower should be used.

122. Which of the following lists consists entirely of chemicals that are considered safe enough to be in a high school lab?

    A. hydrochloric acid, lauric acid, potassium permanganate, calcium hydroxide
    B. ethyl ether, nitric acid, sodium benzoate, methanol
    C. cobalt (II) sulfide, ethylene glycol, benzoyl peroxide, ammonium chloride
    D. picric acid, hydrofluoric acid, cadmium chloride, carbon disulfide.

A Hydrochloric acid (HCl) is a common acid reagent in high school chemistry. Lauric acid is the fatty acid $CH_3(CH_2)_{10}COOH$ also known as dodecanoic acid. Potassium permanganate ($KMnO_4$) is a strong oxidizer. Calcium hydroxide ($Ca(OH)_2$) is a strong base. These chemicals in their pure state are hazardous, but they are considered safe enough to be in high schools. Ethyl ether (Choice B) should not be in high schools because it may form highly explosive organic peroxides over time. Benzoyl peroxide (choice C) at low concentrations in gel form is an acne medication, but the pure compound is highly explosive. Choice D consists entirely of chemicals that are too dangerous for high schools. Picric acid is highly explosive, hydrofluoric acid is very corrosive and very toxic, all cadmium compounds are highly toxic, and carbon disulfide is explosive and toxic.

123. The following procedure was developed to find the specific heat capacity of metals:

1. Place pieces of the metals in an ice-water bath so their initial temperature is 0 °C.
2. Weigh a styrofoam cup.
3. Add water at room temperature to the cup and weigh it again
4. Add a cold metal from the bath to the cup and weigh the cup a third time.
5. Monitor the temperature drop of the water until a final temperature at thermal equilibrium is found.

_____ is also required as additional information in order to obtain heat capacities for the metals. The best control would be to follow the same protocol except to use _____ in step 4 instead of a cold metal.

A. The heat capacity of water / a metal at 100 °C
B. The heat of formation of water / ice from the 0 °C bath
C. The heat of capacity of ice / glass at 0 °C
D. The heat capacity of water / water from the 0 °C bath

D The equation:

$$q = n \times C \times \Delta T$$

is used to determine what additional information is needed. The specific heat, C, of the metals may be found from the heat added, the amount of material, and the temperature change. The amount of metal is found from the difference in weight between steps 3 and 4, and the temperature change is found from the difference between the final temperature and 0 °C. The additional value required is the heat added, q. This may be found from the heat removed from the water if the amount of water, the heat capacity of water, and the temperature change of water are known. The amount of water is found from the difference in weight between step 2 and 3, and the temperature change is found from the difference between the final temperature and room temperature. The only additional information required is the heat capacity of water, eliminating choices B and C. Heat of formation (choice B) is only used for chemical reactions.

A good control simplifies only the one aspect under study without adding anything new. Metal at 100 °C (choice A) would alter the temperature of the experiment and glass (choice C) would add an additional material to the study. Ice (choice B) would require consideration of the heat of fusion. Choice D is an ideal control because the impact of water at 0 °C on room temperature water is simpler than the impact of metals at 0 °C on room temperature water, and nothing new is added.

124. Which statement about the impact of chemistry on society is <u>not</u> true?

A. Partial hydrogenation creates *trans* fat.
B. The Haber Process incorporates nitrogen from the air into molecules for agricultural use.
C. The CO_2 concentration in the atmosphere has decreased in the last ten years.
D. The concentration of ozone-destroying chemicals in the stratosphere has decreased in the last ten years.

C CO_2 concentrations in the atmosphere continue to increase (answer C), but the concentration of ozone destroying chemicals has fallen (answer D) due to international agreements.

125. Which statement about everyday applications of chemistry is <u>true</u>?

A. Rainwater found near sources of air pollution will most likely be basic.
B. Batteries run down more quickly at low temperatures because chemical reactions are proceeding more slowly.
C. Benzyl alcohol is a detergent used in shampoo.
D. Adding salt decreases the time required for water to boil.

B Sources of air pollution (choice A) will most likely cause acid rain.

Low temperatures decrease reaction rates, and this is also true of electrochemical reactions in batteries. At low temperature, less current is supplied and the effect will be a short life for applications that demand current. (Answer B is correct).

Benzyl alcohol (choice C) has the formula shown to the right. Like detergents, this molecule has a non-polar region (the benzene ring) and a polar region (the hydroxyl group). But, unlike detergents, the non-polar region for benzyl alcohol is small and short. Detergents have long, "tail-like" non-polar regions that can surround oils and grease. Benzyl alcohol is sometimes included in shampoo to prevent itching and bacterial growth.

Adding salt (choice D) increases the boiling point of water, thus increasing the time required for water to boil. It decreases the time required to cook food once boiling occurs.

XAMonline, INC. 21 Orient Ave. Melrose, MA 02176

Toll Free number 800-509-4128

TO ORDER Fax 781-662-9268 OR www.XAMonline.com

GEORGIA ASSESSMENTS FOR THE CERTIFICATION OF EDUCATORS -GACE - 2007

PO#   Store/School:

Address 1:

Address 2 (Ship to other):

City, State Zip

Credit card number_____-_____-_____-_____   expiration_____

EMAIL _____

PHONE   **FAX**

13# ISBN 2007	TITLE	Qty	Retail	Total
978-1-58197-533-8	Basic Skills 200, 201, 202			
978-1-58197-528-4	Biology 026, 027			
978-1-58197-529-1	Science 024, 025			
978-1-58197-532-1	Physics Sample Test 030, 031			
978-1-58197-531-4	Art Education Sample Test 109, 110			
978-1-58197-574-1	English 020, 021			
978-1-58197-545-1	History 034, 035			
978-1-58197-527-7	Health and Physical Education 115, 116			
978-1-58197-540-6	Chemistry 028, 029			
978-1-58197-534-5	Reading 117, 118			
978-1-58197-547-5	Media Specialist 101, 102			
978-1-58197-573-4	Middle Grades Language Arts 011			
978-1-58197-535-2	Middle Grades Reading 012			
978-1-58197-539-0	Middle Grades Science 014			
978-1-58197-543-7	Middle Grades Mathematics 013			
978-1-58197-546-8	Middle Grades Social Science 015			
978-1-58197-536-9	Mathematics 022, 023			
978-1-58197-549-9	Political Science 032, 033			
978-1-58197-544-4	Paraprofessional Assessment 177			
978-1-58197-542-0	Professional Pedagogy Assessment 171, 172			
978-1-58197-537-6	Early Childhood Education 001, 002			
978-1-58197-548-2	School Counseling 103, 104			
978-1-58197-541-3	Spanish 141, 142			
978-1-58197-538-3	Special Education General Curriculum 081, 082			
978-1-58197-530-7	French Sample Test 143, 144			

	SUBTOTAL	
FOR PRODUCT PRICES GO TO WWW.XAMONLINE.COM	**Ship**	$8.25
	TOTAL	

CPSIA information can be obtained at www.ICGtesting.com
Printed in the USA
237711LV00001B/45/A

9 781581 975406